MICROS

LAN
MANAGER

MICROSOFT®

LAN MANAGER

A Programmer's Guide

VERSION 2

RALPH RYAN

Microsoft
PRESS
®

PUBLISHED BY
Microsoft Press
A Division of Microsoft Corporation
One Microsoft Way
Redmond, Washington 98052-6399

Library of Congress Cataloging-in-Publication Data

Ryan, Ralph, 1948–
    The Microsoft LAN manager : a programmer's guide / Ralph Ryan.
       p.   cm.
    ISBN 1-55615-166-7 : $29.95
    1. OS/2 (Computer operating system)   2. Microsoft LAN manager
(Computer program) I. Title.
    QA76.76.063R93   1990
    650'.028'55369--dc20
                                  90-5418
                                  CIP

Printed and bound in the United States of America.

2 3 4 5 6 7 8 9 FGFG 4 3 2 1 0

Distributed to the book trade in Canada by General Publishing Company, Ltd.

Distributed to the book trade outside the United States and Canada by Penguin Books Ltd.

Penguin Books Ltd., Harmondsworth, Middlesex, England
Penguin Books Australia Ltd., Ringwood, Victoria, Australia
Penguin Books N.Z. Ltd., 182-190 Wairau Road, Auckland 10, New Zealand

British Cataloging in Publication Data available

Project Editor: Megan E. Sheppard
Technical Editor: Michael Halvorson
Acquisitions Editor: Dean Holmes

For Barbara,
for Being

CONTENTS

SECTION THREE: Programming Technique

Acknowledgments

Many people at Microsoft helped review this book and put it in its final form. Special thanks to Liz Chalmers, Ben Goetter, Peter Heymann, Pierre Laurent, Pradyumna Misra, Greg Moeller, John Murray, Larry Osterman, Eric Peterson, Ken Reneris, Henry Sanders, Kevin Schofield, Barat Shah, Ron Simons, Brian Valentine, Steve White, and Hans Witt. Extra-special hyper-thanks to Megan Sheppard and Mike Halvorson.

Ralph Ryan
May 1990

THE FUNDAMENTALS

INTRODUCTION

This book is about Microsoft LAN Manager, which allows the power of OS/2, DOS, and UNIX to be extended onto a local area network (LAN). LAN Manager is a platform for *distributed applications:* applications in which cooperating programs run on more than one computer at a time. This book teaches you core LAN Manager version 2.0 technology and describes LAN Manager variations that you might encounter.

Is This the Book for You?

As the name "programmer's guide" suggests, this book is written primarily for programmers—particularly those programmers who write distributed applications (based on OS/2, DOS, or UNIX) that use the features of LAN Manager. But this book is also for programmers who write administration programs for LAN Manager. (LAN Manager has an open architecture, which permits the addition of administrative features.) In addition, network administrators can use this book both to learn more about how the system works and to broaden their basic administrative skills.

What You'll Need

In order to fully use this book, you need software that's appropriate both to your hardware and to the type of operating system you intend to write programs for:

- If you plan to write programs for OS/2 servers or workstations, you need the following software installed on your hard disk:

    □ OS/2 1.1 or later (OS/2 1.21 recommended). The level of support for the LAN Manager API varies with different versions of OS/2. See the *Microsoft LAN Manager Programmer's Reference* for details.

    □ The Microsoft LAN Manager Programmer's Toolkit or the Microsoft Network Development Kit. (The latter includes Microsoft LAN Manager 2.0, the Microsoft LAN Manager Programmer's Toolkit, Microsoft OS/2 1.21, and the Microsoft OS/2 Programmer's Toolkit.)

    □ The Microsoft C Compiler, version 5.1 or later.

- If you plan to write programs for DOS workstations, you have two options: You can use the OS/2 installation above to create "bound" programs with the Microsoft C Compiler, or you can install the following software on a computer dedicated to DOS development:

    □ DOS version 3.1 or later

    □ The Microsoft LAN Manager Programmer's Toolkit

□ The Microsoft C Compiler, version 5.1 or later

■ If you plan to write programs for UNIX servers, you need the following:

□ A version of UNIX that supports Microsoft LAN Manager

□ A LAN Manager for UNIX Software Development Kit compatible with your version of UNIX

□ A UNIX C compiler

LAN Manager for UNIX currently runs under SCO UNIX System V/386 Release 3.2, AT&T UNIX, and Hewlett-Packard's version of UNIX, HP-UX.

How Is This Book Organized?

This book is organized into three sections followed by two appendixes. Section 1 introduces LAN Manager and networking concepts:

■ Chapter 1 contains a history of LAN Manager development at Microsoft.

■ Chapter 2 introduces some programming fundamentals that OS/2 programmers should know.

■ Chapter 3 examines the architecture and concepts of the LAN Manager workstation and server.

Section 2 describes the LAN Manager Applications Programming Interface (API). This section is the heart of the book, and it examines the LAN Manager programming interface in detail. Sample programs in this section illustrate real-world uses of the APIs.

■ Chapter 4 presents the architecture of the APIs.

■ Chapters 5 through 12 describe all categories of APIs.

Section 3 describes how to write applications that make use of LAN Manager features:

■ Chapter 13 describes how to write distributed applications.

■ Chapter 14 provides general tips and hints for writing and debugging LAN Manager programs.

■ Chapter 15 examines the similarities and differences among core LAN Manager, LAN Manager for DOS, LAN Manager for UNIX, and the IBM LAN Server.

The two appendixes provide reference material you can use as you read this book and write LAN Manager programs:

- Appendix A lists each LAN Manager API name, a one-sentence description, and the page number it is first described on.

- Appendix B lists each of the LAN Manager error codes.

A Brief History of LAN Manager

In 1983 and 1984, Microsoft and IBM were designing DOS version 3.0 to support the soon-to-be-announced IBM PC/AT personal computer. It was decided that, in addition to supporting the AT's new 20-MB hard disk, 1.2-MB floppy disk, and CMOS clock, the new operating system should support local area networking. Accordingly, IBM began work on the IBM PC Network Adapter and released specifications for essential network support using the NetBIOS and the Network Control Block (NCB) data structures for machine-to-machine communication. IBM also released specifications for a higher-level (more abstract) protocol known as the Server Message Block (SMB) for client-to-server communication.

DOS version 3.0, released in April 1984 with the IBM PC/AT, contained some of the basic elements for networking personal computers. DOS version 3.1, released in July 1984, supplied the remaining pieces. DOS 3.1 contained support for a *redirector,* a piece of operating-system software that allowed remote-file access. The redirector used SMB protocols and the NetBIOS to make remote files appear as if they were on a logical disk drive on the local computer.

The Advent of PC-LAN and MS-NET

IBM took the redirector and added some workstation and server software that made files and printers available across the network. The result was a product called the *Personal Computer Local Area Network Program* (PC-LAN). Microsoft then released its own version, known as *Microsoft Networks* (MS-NET), which supported third-party personal computers and network cards. The two products were similar and interoperable: MS-NET workstations could use resources shared by PC-LAN servers and vice versa. They differed in that PC-LAN supported interstation messages (not supported by MS-NET) and nondedicated servers; that is, a computer operating as a PC-LAN server could also be an ordinary workstation. The MS-NET server was dedicated: It could not be used simultaneously as a workstation.

Following the release of DOS version 3.1, Microsoft began—on its own—to develop a multitasking, protected-mode operating system for the Intel 80286 microprocessor. (The protected mode of the 80286 microprocessor provided hardware protection that prevented programs from interfering with each other or with the operating system. This was in contrast to the real mode of the 80286, which ran like a fast 8086 microprocessor and allowed programs full access to all memory, including the memory containing the operating system. The protected mode also allowed access to 16 MB of memory; real mode limited access to 640 KB.) When this project began to grow in scope, it was split into two projects.

The DOS 4 project

DOS 4 (not to be confused with the 1988 product of the same name) was a real-mode, multitasking operating system. IBM chose not to license DOS 4. Although it decided not to release DOS 4 as a retail product, Microsoft did make deliveries to several of its large customers for special applications under development.

Part of the DOS 4 operating system was a network upgrade known as MS-NET 2.0, which provided support for interstation messaging and a non-dedicated server. This upgrade made MS-NET 2.0 and PC-LAN functionally the same.

The DOS 5 project

The second project, called DOS 5, eventually became the OS/2 operating system. It was a full multitasking protected-mode operating system. OS/2 was jointly developed by Microsoft and IBM. Part of the OS/2 development at Microsoft involved the creation of an OS/2 redirector. Development of both the OS/2 redirector and LAN Manager were well under way before IBM decided to license this additional technology and incorporate it into its OS/2 Extended Edition.

In September 1988, the first version of LAN Manager was shipped to 3Com, which had helped Microsoft design and develop LAN Manager. The resulting 3Com product, *3+Open*, incorporated the core LAN Manager and included DOS LAN Manager, an upgrade to MS-NET that allowed DOS workstations to use the power of LAN Manager servers.

In October 1988, IBM released the first version of its OS/2 Extended Edition, which contained the OS/2 redirector (or "requester," as IBM called it). The IBM LAN Server was a companion product built from the LAN Manager server technology.

In January 1990, Microsoft announced the LAN Manager for UNIX product, a portable version of LAN Manager, developed jointly by Hewlett-Packard and Microsoft. The LAN Manager for UNIX interfaces were adopted by X/OPEN (a consortium of UNIX manufacturers) as the portable networking interface for UNIX.

Figure 1-1 provides a visual history of LAN Manager and shows the relationships among the different versions of DOS, OS/2, and LAN Manager.

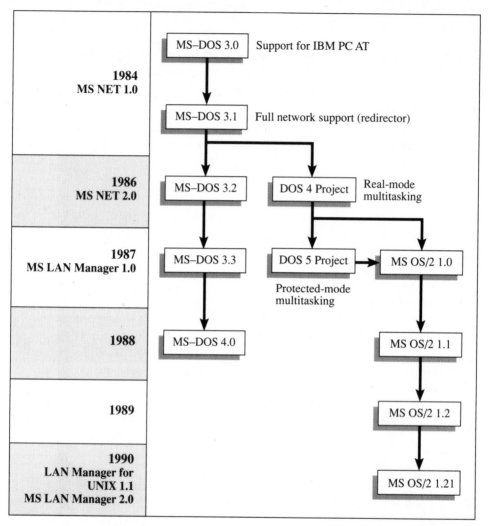

Figure 1-1.
The history of MS LAN Manager.

The LAN Manager Project

Every year, for the last ten or so years, pundits have declared the long-awaited arrival of "The Year of the LAN." This is in recognition that—eventually—most personal computers in office environments will be on local area networks. LAN Manager is designed to provide support for this "Year of the LAN"—whenever it actually occurs.

Goals of the LAN Manager Project

Several goals were on the minds of developers as they set out to design LAN Manager—the product that was intended to be the basis for personal computer networks of the future:

- **Interoperability.** PC-LAN and MS-NET systems were expected to be around for years to come, and LAN Manager workstations and servers had to be able to work with them transparently.

- **Increased performance.** PC-LAN and MS-NET systems were seen by many people as having performance characteristics inferior to those of their major competitors. Therefore, enhanced performance was a major goal.

- **Full-featured administrative support.** The skills of network administrators vary widely, but a good LAN product would make it easy for all administrators to do their jobs well. Of particular importance was the ability to remotely administer servers.

- **Distributed-applications platform.** The proliferation of personal computers on LANs required a change in how applications work. Applications would have to be spread out into cooperating programs on more than one computer, and the LAN software would have to make it easy for developers to create these applications.

- **A rich applications programming interface.** Programmers needed to be able to create applications that added value to the core product.

Microsoft LAN Manager: A Programmer's Guide

In essence, this book is a consolidation and distillation of knowledge from many different people who developed LAN Manager—a product that continues to develop even as you read this. Although this book focuses on the second version of LAN Manager, LAN Manager 2.0, the general principles you learn here will still be true for later versions—even those with new features and capabilities.

INSIDE LAN MANAGER

This chapter describes the internal structure of LAN Manager and introduces some important LAN Manager concepts. Although you'll use little of this information directly when you create LAN Manager programs, you'll benefit by understanding exactly what LAN Manager is and what it does.

LAN Manager Architecture

Figure 2-1 shows the three levels of LAN Manager architecture: the *systems level,* the *API (Applications Programming Interface) level,* and the *applications level.*

- The utilities and user-interface programs use the APIs to gain access to systems-level services and data structures.

- The workstation and server services use the APIs and can also access LAN Manager data structures directly.

- OS/2 provides file-system services through OS/2 APIs.

- The redirector packages system calls, sends them to another computer for execution, and unpackages the returned results.

- The NetBIOS software provides computer-to-computer communication and controls use of the network hardware.

The following sections discuss the parts of these levels in greater detail.

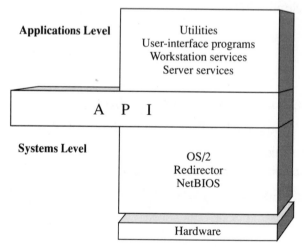

Figure 2-1.
LAN Manager: An architectural overview.

The NetBIOS: Independence and Control

Under DOS, all hardware-specific software is grouped into a set of interfaces known as the *BIOS* (Basic Input/Output System). So when DOS is ported to different hardware, the BIOS is the only part that requires change.

As shown in Figure 2-2, the NetBIOS provides a regular interface and independence from network hardware—just as the BIOS does for computer hardware—and at the same time, it provides a set of commands for establishing and controlling network communications between computers. LAN Manager uses the NetBIOS as a device driver to handle all low-level details of network communications.

> **NOTE:** *This section presents an overview of the NetBIOS. For details on writing programs using the NetBIOS interface, see Chapter 12.*

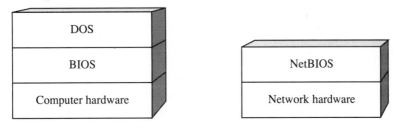

Figure 2-2.
Similar purposes: The BIOS and the NetBIOS.

What Does the NetBIOS Do?

The NetBIOS has three main functions: It registers unique names on the local area network, it establishes virtual circuits, and it supports datagram communication.

Unique-name registration

Each computer on the network has a unique name built into the network hardware. This is the *permanent node name,* a 48-bit number provided by the manufacturer. But because 48-bit numbers don't lend themselves to easy memorization, the NetBIOS lets you register one or more unique names for each machine on the network and then use the name(s) when you establish communications:

- The first name registered is the *computer name,* a synonym for the permanent node name.

- The second name is the *username,* which distinguishes the person using the computer from the computer name.

- Additional names (called *alias names*) can be added through the Net-BIOS, as you'll see in the discussion of the LAN Manager Messenger service.

The NetBIOS also accepts a special kind of name shared by multiple workstations. Such *group names* allow all workstations with the same group name to receive data at the same time.

Virtual-circuit maintenance

Another main function of the NetBIOS is the establishment and maintenance of a *virtual circuit* between two names. A virtual circuit is a point-to-point reliable duplex connection; that is, once a virtual circuit is established, it handles all routing problems between the two ends and handles any necessary retransmissions to ensure successful data transmission. Although the two names will usually be on different computers on the network, you can create a virtual circuit between two names on the same computer, or even from one name back to itself (a *loopback*).

Datagram-communication support

In addition to virtual-circuit communication, the NetBIOS also supports *datagram communication*. A datagram is a one-way message; that is, its arrival is not confirmed. A good analogy is that datagrams are like letters sent through regular postal channels: Delivery is not ensured. Virtual circuits are like letters mailed with "return receipt requested": Delivery is always confirmed. Datagram communication is faster than virtual circuits, but it is less reliable.

How Is the NetBIOS Used?

As described earlier, the main functions of the NetBIOS are to establish a virtual circuit and to allow data to be transferred reliably between two computers. The basic data structure in the NetBIOS interface is an *NCB* (Network Control Block). NCBs are submitted to the NetBIOS using the NetBios APIs (described in Chapter 12). The following discussion examines some of these NCB types (ADDNAME, LISTEN, CALL, RECEIVE, and SEND) and describes their role in establishing computer-to-computer communication.

The role of the NCB

After unique names are associated with each computer (ADDNAME NCB), the server indicates its willingness to establish a virtual circuit (LISTEN NCB). Then a workstation can initiate communication with a server by requesting a virtual circuit to a specific name (CALL NCB). Each computer's NetBIOS drivers exchange the necessary messages to set up the virtual circuit. The server indicates its willingness to receive data on a specific virtual circuit (RECEIVE NCB). The workstation then issues a SEND NCB that the NetBIOS matches up with the corresponding RECEIVE at the server. Figure 2-3 documents this process.

Note that you can send a message on a virtual circuit only after the server submits a RECEIVE NCB. The contents of a SEND/RECEIVE are arbitrary: They simply allow a block of data to get from here to there. Higher-level protocols are used to structure the contents of the SEND/RECEIVE data. (These protocols are discussed in the section on the Client-Server model.)

NOTE: *A NetBIOS can use one of several internal protocols to communicate to another NetBIOS: NETBEUI, XNS, TCP/IP, or OSI. But no matter which protocols are used inside the NetBIOS, the interface remains the same: NCBs are passed to the NetBIOS driver through the NetBIOS APIs.*

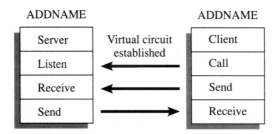

Figure 2-3.
The process of establishing a virtual circuit.

What Are Communications Protocols?

Communications protocols let you structure the functions required by network communications so that higher-level functions needn't be concerned with the details of lower-level functions. This use of levels of abstractions is the same principle you would use in good software design where an API provides services to system functions: The applications need know only the interface specifications and the functional description; the details of implementation are left to the lower layers.

NOTE: *Chapter 12 examines in detail the protocol layers that lie below the NetBIOS interface and introduces the Protocol Manager, a part of the LAN Manager that allows different network protocols to be used by the same NetBIOS.*

The Client-Server Model

Notice that in the model of NetBIOS communications, one side is always passive, waiting for a virtual circuit with a LISTEN NCB and then waiting for data with a RECEIVE. The other side is active, initiating the virtual circuit with a CALL NCB or initiating a transaction with a SEND NCB. The passive side is called a *server,* and the active side is called a *client.* This model is used throughout the LAN Manager architecture: Applications, API calls, and systems services all have client and server sides. The concept is generalized so that some computers, called *servers,* mainly handle the server side of these different LAN Manager functions. Other computers, called *workstations,* mainly handle the client side of LAN Manager functions.

A server, which is usually more powerful than a workstation, contains resources—such as disks, printers, or serial-communications devices—that can be used by the clients.

The Peer-to-Peer Model

An alternative to the Client-Server model is the Peer-to-Peer model, in which any computer can initiate transactions with any other computer.

Sharing Resources

In the Client-Server model, the server resources must be "shared" by the server before they can be used by clients. A share associates a specific resource with a publicly known name; clients then use this name to access the resource. An administrator is usually responsible for creating a share.

Using Resources

To use a shared resource, you associate a local device name (a drive name such as X: or a device name such as LPT7 or COM4) with the public "share" name. For example, at a server named "toolbox," an administrator might issue a command such as

```
net share tools=c:\progs\tools
```

A clarification

Client and server are logical concepts: They can exist on the same physical computer. A LAN Manager server can also be a client, either of itself or of another server. Synonyms for client are workstation, re-director, requester, and consumer. Throughout this book, the term *workstation* represents the client computer.

This shares the specified directory under the public name "tools." At a workstation a user can then issue the following command:

```
net use x: \\toolbox\tools
```

This associates virtual drive X: on the workstation with the shared resource *tools* on the *toolbox* server.

Advantages of the Client-Server model

- Providing access to shared resources requires additional memory and processing power (as well as the resources themselves), so the Client-Server model allows a large number of less powerful machines to work with a small number of more powerful ones.

- The Client-Server model allows security to be centralized at the servers. In a Peer-to-Peer model, security processing must be distributed across all machines.

As the average workstation becomes more powerful, LAN Manager will evolve in the direction of the Peer-to-Peer model and will support a model of distributed security.

Names

Whenever you talk about networking, you'll talk about names. Table 2-1 summarizes—from least to most abstract—the names that LAN Manager uses:

Name	Description
computer name	The unique name identifying a workstation on the network.
username	The unique name identifying the person currently using the workstation.
alias name	A unique name that is a synonym or an alias for the person currently using the workstation.
domain name	A name shared by multiple workstations, identifying a logical grouping of workstations and servers.
share name	The public name by which a resource is made available to workstations for use.

Table 2-1.   *(continued)*
Names used by LAN Manager.

Table 2-1. *continued*

Name	Description
net name	The computer name plus the public name for a resource. This unambiguously identifies the resource for the rest of the network.
redirected device name	A device name associated with a net name.
fully qualified pathname	A name that unambiguously identifies a file or directory.
relative pathname	A file or directory name that is relative to a location in the file system.
Uniform Naming Convention (UNC) name	An unambiguous, fully qualified pathname (including server name) identifying a shared resource. Lets a workstation use a server resource directly without explicitly connecting first.

Sessions and Connections

In learning about the NetBIOS, you learned about a virtual circuit, a reliable computer-to-computer communications link. After a workstation and a server set up a virtual circuit between themselves, they need to exchange information about their memory buffer sizes, software versions, and valid usernames:

- Memory buffer information allows data transfers to be done as efficiently as possible.

- The version information allows both ends to take advantage of performance improvements and functional additions if both ends support them.

- The username and password from the workstation allow the server to control who has access to what resources on the server.

A successful exchange of this information establishes a *session* between the workstation and server. Once a session is established, this information exchange needn't reoccur.

When a workstation executes a net use command to map a redirected device name onto a server share name, it establishes a *connection* between the workstation and the server. More than one connection can be active during the session between the workstation and the server. If a workstation references a resource by its UNC name, the connection is established implicitly by the LAN Manager software.

Explicit connections are established by the *NetUseAdd* API (described in Chapter 5). Because a session is established with the first attempted connection to a resource on a server, the workstation never needs to explicitly establish a session.

Server Message Blocks

The NetBIOS cares nothing about the data area of a SEND NCB; it simply acts as a transfer agent, sending the data to the receiving computer. Under LAN Manager (and MS-NET before it) such data is structured as an *SMB* (Server Message Block)—a system call (or response) packaged for shipment to a remote system. The SMB is then transported inside an NCB. An important part of LAN Manager is interoperability with PC-LAN and MS-NET workstations and servers. The SMBs defined for these two original LAN products are called the *core SMBs*. LAN Manager has extended the kinds of SMBs (a "new dialect"), providing new features and enhancing the performance of the network. When a workstation and a server try to create a session, they "negotiate" to find an SMB dialect they both understand.

Session vs. connection

Definitions for the terms *session* and *connection* vary, depending on your source of information. For example, some books use the term session as a synonym for virtual circuit. In this book, the terms are always used in the following manner:

- A *session* is a logical extension of a virtual circuit between a workstation and a server. A session validates the user's permission to access the server, and it establishes what performance and functional features the two ends can use.

- A *connection* is a logical linking of a workstation to a server resource within the context of a session.

LANMAN.INI

Configuration information for LAN Manager exists in the LANMAN.INI text file, where it is organized into sections called *components*. Each component contains a set of parameters. Component names are marked with square brackets, and parameters are of the following form:

```
keyword = value
```

Figure 2-4 shows some of the components and parameters from a sample LANMAN.INI file.

```
[server]
     alertnames = Ralph,Barbara
     auditing = yes
     autodisconnect = 120
     maxusers = 32
     security = user
     srvcomment = Programmer's Guide Test Server
[messenger]
     logfile = messages.log
     sizemessbuf = 4096
```

Figure 2-4.
Entries from a LANMAN.INI file.

Chapter 5 presents the APIs used to read and update the LANMAN.INI configuration file.

LAN Manager Services

Most programs included with LAN Manager are *services*—programs written to specific guidelines so that they can be started, stopped, paused, or continued through LAN Manager commands. Chapter 6 describes the guidelines for writing this type of service program and extending the power and functionality of LAN Manager.

Logging On

One of the most important features of LAN Manager is the security system at the server. This feature allows an administrator to determine who has permission to do what with any resource. Whenever a workstation tries to access a server resource, the username is checked against a list of permissions for that resource. For this to work properly, the server needs to verify that users are who they say they are. When a workstation attempts to establish a session to a server, a username and password accompany the session request. These must match a corresponding username and password in an accounts database at the server. If there is no match, the session cannot be established and no access to the server resources is allowed. The process of checking this username and password is called *logging on to the server*. A user does not need to explicitly log on to a server. This is done automatically by the server whenever the first connection is attempted to a share at each server.

Before a workstation can log on to any servers, the username and password must first be checked to see whether the user is allowed to use the network at all. This process is called *logging on to the network* and must be done explicitly by the user before any other network activity. It can be accomplished using the net logon command or as part of the full-screen user interface.

Whenever a user tries to log on to the network, the username, password, and computer name are sent to one of the servers for validation. The user does not need to know the name of the server that will do the checking. The LAN Manager will automatically find it and send the validation request there.

The server checks to see whether the username and password correspond to entries in its own database. It actually uses the same checking mechanism that server logon uses, but then it adds a number of features of its own. Network logon can restrict a user's logons to certain hours of the day, can restrict which workstations a user can log on from, and can provide scripts that will be run automatically at the workstation if the logon is successful. The details of network logon are described in more detail later in this chapter, in the section about the netlogon service at the server.

After network logon, the username and password are saved at the workstation. Whenever a password is required for a network operation (such as server logon), unless the user explicitly provides one, the default will be the password used at network logon.

The Workstation

At a LAN Manager workstation, programs at the applications level use the API interfaces to communicate with the programs at the systems level. Figure 2-5 shows the basic architecture of a LAN Manager workstation, and the following paragraphs describe the elements of the architecture.

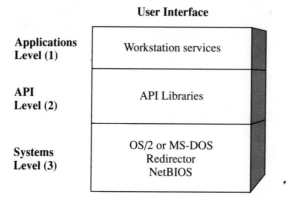

User Interface

Applications Level (1)	Workstation services
API Level (2)	API Libraries
Systems Level (3)	OS/2 or MS-DOS Redirector NetBIOS

Figure 2-5.
Basic architecture of a LAN Manager workstation.

The Systems Level

In addition to the operating system itself, the following items are significant at the systems level:

The NetBIOS

At a workstation, the NetBIOS is a device driver loaded at system boot. The redirector uses the NetBIOS to communicate with the server software.

The redirector

The redirector and the operating system work closely together. The redirector packages and passes system calls from the operating system to a specified remote resource. The server software at the remote resource then issues the proper operating-system API call in its own local environment, packages the results, and returns them to the redirector.

The redirector is also the site of many of LAN Manager's performance optimizations.

The *Microsoft LAN Manager Administrator's Guide* describes how to configure your network for best performance.

The API Level

The API level acts as an intermediary: It lets programs at the applications level communicate with and use the services of the systems level. Applications needn't be aware of the operating system, the redirector, or NetBIOS; they need only understand the API. Section 2 introduces the LAN Manager APIs and provides sample programs that use them.

NOTE: *For a more in-depth discussion of OS/2 and the OS/2 APIs, refer to the following books:*

- Inside OS/2, *Gordon Letwin. Microsoft Press, 1988.*

- Advanced OS/2 Programming, *Ray Duncan. Microsoft Press, 1989.*

- Programming the OS/2 Presentation Manager, *Charles Petzold. Microsoft Press, 1989.*

The Applications Level: WKSTA.EXE

When you start LAN Manager with a net start command, the WKSTA.EXE program begins running in the background and is present until a net stop command is issued. (Under OS/2, WKSTA.EXE is a multithread program that runs as long as the computer is operating as a workstation; under MS-DOS, WKSTA.EXE is a terminate-and-stay-resident program that runs in the background until the computer is rebooted.)

After initializing a number of LAN Manager internal data structures, the WKSTA.EXE program controls browsing, second-class mailslots, and error logging.

Browsing Browsing workstations receive periodic announcements about server status. On a computer running server software, the browser is augmented with a companion piece, the *announcer*, which periodically issues a broadcast message containing information about the server. The broadcast is sent to all workstations and servers sharing a NetBIOS group name. This logical grouping of workstations and servers is called a *domain*. The LAN-MAN.INI file at each computer is configured with a domain parameter. Each workstation issues a NetBIOS RECEIVE DATAGRAM on its own domain name, and all workstations with the same domain name receive the same server announcements. This allows workstations to be kept current with a list of active servers in their own domain. You can also configure a workstation so that it receives browser announcements from other domains. Chapter 7 describes the *NetServerEnum* API, which allows a program to obtain a list of these active servers.

Mailslots As the name suggests, a mailslot is like a post-office box that one process can send information to and another process can take information from. Mailslots are of two types:

- First-class mailslots have guaranteed delivery and, if remote, must exist on a LAN Manager server.

- Second-class mailslots use datagrams and don't guarantee reliable delivery. However, second-class mailslots can exist on a workstation.

(Second-class mailslots are one of the few parts of LAN Manager that do not use the Client-Server model.)

Because part of WKSTA.EXE is dedicated to second-class mail, the client workstation can receive as well as send second-class mail. This also allows a limited broadcast facility. For example, data written to a mailslot named *\MAILSLOT\WHO goes to all workstations in the domain with a mailslot named WHO. Mailslots are discussed in more detail in Chapter 10.

Error Logging   Under OS/2, a third part of WKSTA.EXE is dedicated to error logging. Chapter 8 describes the error-logging APIs, which allow error information to be recorded in a file for later use. Software error conditions that cannot be directly reported to the user are noted in the error log.

However, if the redirector encounters a reportable error condition, it cannot use the error-log APIs: These APIs require information to be written to a file, and as a system-level program, the redirector does not have access to OS/2's file-system APIs. The redirector error information is therefore kept in a memory buffer, and the WKSTA.EXE thread (an application-level program with access to the OS/2 file system APIs) can periodically execute the appropriate error-log API calls. The WKSTA program is a LAN Manager service and thus can be started, stopped, paused, and continued.

Interstation Messages

Most workstations also run two services that provide interstation messages: the Messenger service and its companion, the Netpopup service.

The Messenger service

Chapter 5 describes the Message APIs, which allow programs to send messages and to log received messages to a file. Messages are always sent to a name: It might be a username, or it might be an alias name. There are Message APIs for adding or deleting additional names by which messages might be received.

The Messenger service also provides message forwarding. This feature allows messages for a particular name to be received at another workstation.

The Netpopup service

Whenever a message arrives at the workstation, the Netpopup service is notified by the Messenger service. Netpopup then uses the *VioPopup* APIs to write to the screen that a message has arrived. It also displays part of the message text on the screen.

A few distinctions

In talking about the Messenger service, it is useful to make a distinction between two similar-sounding features: *messaging* and *electronic mail.*

- Messaging is a method of sending text from either a file or the keyboard to another workstation. Successful messaging requires that the destination be running the Messenger service and that it register the receiving username or aliasname. If either of these conditions is not met, the message is not sent.

- Electronic mail, or "e-mail," lets you send data between workstations. Electronic mail is always delivered: If the destination name isn't present, the message is stored on the network until it can be reliably delivered. Although e-mail isn't currently a part of core LAN Manager, some vendors have added their own e-mail service to LAN Manager.

Note also that messaging differs from mailslots: Mailslots are a LAN Manager API for interprocess communication; messaging is an interworkstation service for sending text messages.

The User Interface

To most users, the user interface *is* LAN Manager: It is all they see and care about. To a programmer, the user interface is simply a part of the greater LAN Manager architecture. The user-interface programs are C applications; they have no secret knowledge of the underlying system, and they use the same APIs discussed throughout this book. In fact, by using the LAN Manager APIs, programmers can create their own user interface that retains all functions of the original. In addition, some examples later in the book show how to extend the functions of the user interface.

The Server

LAN Manager servers run under OS/2 or UNIX. Figure 2-6 shows the basic architecture of a LAN Manager server. Note that a server is also a workstation under LAN Manager.

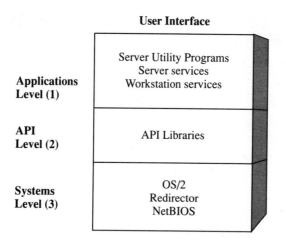

User Interface

Applications Level (1)	Server Utility Programs Server services Workstation services
API Level (2)	API Libraries
Systems Level (3)	OS/2 Redirector NetBIOS

Figure 2-6.
The basic architecture of a LAN Manager server.

The server is conceptually straightforward and is, at the same time, the cornerstone of the Client-Server model: It provides a platform for shared resources and distributed services. This section describes many important server features.

Basic Server Features

In its most visible role, the server shares resources: directory trees from the file system; printer queues; serial devices; and named pipes. But equally important is the server's role as the heart of a multiuser operating system. This job entails responsibility for three important tasks: *security, administration,* and *auditing.* The following sections discuss each of these tasks in turn.

Security: Who can do what?

The server must be configured to start up in one of two security modes: *share mode* or *user mode.*

Share-Mode Security   Share-mode security requires that users provide a valid password and permission level before they can connect to a share. (Both MS-NET and PC-LAN servers use share-mode security.)

Share-mode permissions apply to all resources covered by the share. For example, suppose a directory on the *toolsvr* server were shared with the following command:

```
net share public=c:\bin qwerty /perm:R
```

Any user knowing the "qwerty" password could connect to the resource with a command of the following form:

```
net use x: \\toolsvr\public qwerty
```

The user would have read-only access to all files and subdirectories in the directory tree underneath *c:\bin*.

The share-mode security system lets administrators operate in the same way as they did with MS-NET or PC-LAN, but it doesn't make use of the advanced features of user-mode security.

User-Mode Security User-mode security lets you grant access permissions down to the file level; that is, any file, directory, print queue, serial device, or named pipe can be associated with a list of users and permission levels. For example, under user-mode security, a file can be read-only by one user and read/write by another.

User-mode security is part of the server subsystem known as the *User Accounts System* (UAS). Let's take a more detailed look at the UAS and its two databases: *user accounts* and *access control*.

The user-accounts database

The user-accounts database contains records with usernames and their passwords. Users can establish a session with the server only if they have a valid account. The user accounts database also contains records that describe *groups*. A group is a collection of usernames that can be referred to collectively by a single name. A username can belong to any number of groups. For example, Barbara might be a member of the groups named "writers," "systems," and "partyanimals" but not a member of groups named "editors" or "marketing."

The access-control database

The access-control database is a set of records that names a resource (such as a file, a directory, a named pipe, and so on) and a list of usernames or groups. Each username record declares exactly what permissions that user or group has for that particular resource.

Chapter 9 examines the APIs for working with users, groups, and access rights.

User Accounts and Groups

There are three types of accounts:

- Admin-type accounts have no restrictions: They are intended for administrators who need access to all server resources and services. All admin accounts are automatically members of a special group named ADMINS.

- User-type accounts are intended for ordinary users, who must be given permission to use server resources. User-type accounts are automatically members of a group named USERS. This makes it easy to assign permissions to all user-type accounts at once.

- Guest-type accounts can never be included in the USERS group, but outside of that difference, they are just like user-type accounts. They, too, must be given permission to use server resources. Guest-type accounts are automatically members of a group named GUESTS.

NOTE: *Information in the user database is encoded with a one-way encoding algorithm so that even if users were to acquire an accounts file, they could not decipher the passwords. Passwords sent across the network are always encoded.*

And now, our special guest....

You can also create a special guest-type account in the [server] component of the LANMAN.INI file:

```
guestacc = A_GUEST_NAME
```

A user can log on using this name and the password that the administrator supplies for the account.

This account handles a common administrative problem: It allows any user to log on as a guest—even if his or her username is not in the user database—provided the user's password matches the guest account password. When the user establishes a connection, he or she must always include the password, as in

```
net use x: \\toolsvr\public guestpass
```

Notice that there is no need to log on with a special username.

Access Control Lists

An *Access Control List* (ACL) names a resource and contains a list of users or groups along with their associated permissions. Table 2-2 lists the available permissions along with the OS/2 APIs they affect.

Permission	Affected OS/2 APIs
X (execute)	DosOpen (for execute), DosQFileInfo, DosQFileMode, DosFindFirst
R (read)	DosOpen (for read or execute), DosQFileInfo, DosQFileMode, DosFindFirst
W (write)	DosOpen (for write), DosQFileInfo, DosQFileMode, DosFindFirst
C (create)	DosMkDir, DosOpen (for create); see text for special cases
D (delete)	DosDelete, DosRmdir, DosQFileInfo, DosQFileMode, DosFindFirst
A (attribute)	DosSetFileInfo, DosSetFileMode, DosQFileInfo, DosQFileMode, DosFindFirst
P (permission)	Access API calls to change permissions

Table 2-2.
ACL permissions.

- Execute permission (X) allows a file to be opened for execution. This can be set only at an OS/2 workstation because MS-DOS does not support this open mode.

- Read permission (R) allows an existing file to be opened for reading or for executing.

- Write permission (W) allows an existing file to be opened for writing.

- Create permission (C) is necessary when *DosOpen* is called with the create bit set, whether or not the file already exists. Other read or write operations on the file require an R or a W permission, with one exception: C permission is sufficient to read or write to the file while it is open from the create. Once closed, the file requires R or W permission to read or write. This also means that a user with C permission on a directory can put new files there but cannot read, write to, or list the files without further permissions.

- Delete permission (D) is required to delete a file or to remove a directory. Note that the *DosMove* API needs D permission at the source and C permission at the destination. Copying a file requires R permission at the source and C permission at the destination.

- Attribute permission (A) allows manipulation of the OS/2 file attributes.

- Permission permission (P) allows a user to manipulate the access control list for the resource. This is a convenient way of allowing users to do the administration of their own files, granting permissions to other users without the administrator having to get involved.

How Access Rights Are Determined

When a workstation uses the *DosOpen* API on a remote file, spooled print queue, character device, or named pipe, the redirector passes the call to the server. The server must determine whether the user logged on to the workstation has permission to do the requested operation. To make this determination, the server uses the algorithm shown in Figure 2-7. This algorithm contains two new concepts: a *parent entry* and a *drive-level entry*.

- For a file or directory, the parent entry is the directory that contains it. For named pipes, print queues, or character devices, the parent entry is a name that *looks* like a directory name. Although no directories exist for pipes and so on, the ACLs allow this construct to be used. For example, *pipe**dirname* is a "parent" of *pipe**dirname**nmpipe*.

- For files and directories, a drive-level entry contains permissions for the entire disk drive. For print queues, serial devices, and named pipes, the drive-level entry is an artificial ACL record built into LAN Manager (\PRINT, \COMM, \PIPE).

```
If there is an access control list for the resource
    If there is a record for this user
        Return these permissions
    Else if the user is in any groups that have
            entries in the ACL
        Accumulate permissions from all groups
                in the ACL that contain this user
        Return these permissions
    Else
        Fail
Else if there is a parent entry for the resource
    If there is a record for this user
        Return these permissions
    Else if the user is in any groups that have
            entries in the ACL
        Accumulate permissions from all groups
                in the ACL that contain this user
        Return these permissions
    Else
        Fail
```

Figure 2-7.
An algorithm to determine access rights.

(continued)

Figure 2-7. *continued*

```
Else if there is a drive-level entry for the resource
    If there is a record for this user
        Return these permissions
    Else if the user is in any groups that have
            entries in the ACL
        Accumulate permissions from all groups
                in the ACL that contain this user
        Return these permissions
    Else
        Fail
Else
    Fail
```

The algorithm moves from specific to general permissions and stops after establishing a set of permissions for the user or after failing.

Access rights: An example

The server in this example has the following access control lists:

Resource	Access Control List
C:\BIN\M.DAT	BARBARA:RW RALPH:R
C:\BIN	WRITERS(group):R SYSTEMS(group):W
C:	GUEST:X
C:BIN\X.CMD	(None)

Suppose Barbara tries to open the M.DAT file for reading with *DosOpen*:

- Because the ACL record for the file grants Barbara RW privilege, permission is granted.

Suppose Ralph attempts RW access on the M.DAT file:

- Because the M.DAT ACL record grants Ralph only R access, permission is denied.

Suppose Russ (who belongs to both the WRITERS and the SYSTEMS groups) attempts RW access on X.CMD:

- Because no ACL record exists for X.CMD, the second step of the algorithm looks for a parent record (in this case, the record for BIN). Russ has no entry to BIN, but his R access from WRITERS and W access from SYSTEMS give Russ RW permission on X.CMD.

Note that someone logged on as GUEST would have execute privilege on X.CMD because of the disk-level ACL entry.

Even those requests granted by server security are subject to the local server's OS/2 file-system checks. For example, suppose a user is granted RW access to a file by the server. If the file's OS/2 attributes are read-only, or if another process has the file open in deny-write share mode, the *DosOpen* call fails.

A resource's access permissions are independent of its share status. Although users cannot access a resource unless it is shared, administrators can add, delete, and change the access permissions of a resource whether it is shared or not.

Local Security with HPFS386

To prevent unauthorized users or distributed applications running at the server from directly accessing the OS/2 file system, LAN Manager 2.0 provides a replacement file system for the OS/2 server called HPFS386. HPFS386 is an advanced version of the OS/2 1.2 High-Performance File System for 386-based computers. It enforces local security on the server by protecting the HPFS386 partition from physical and remote access at all times, whether LAN Manager is running or not. File-system access is allowed only if the local user or remote program has been granted permission by the system administrator. For information about installing HPFS386 and for tips on enforcing local security, consult the *Microsoft LAN Manager Administrator's Guide*.

If the HPFS386 file system is not being used, you can enforce local security in a couple of ways:

- You can use the LAN Manager loopback driver, which allows a server to create connections to itself without invoking the overhead of the whole network for file access. A distributed application could create shares and uses for all of the local server resources it would need. This would then be subject to server security checks and would allow an administrator to control access to the rest of the server's resources.

- The UAS also supports a "local logon"—a username and password registered by the server software. Server application programs can be written to require that this logon name be in the accounts database and have administrative privilege. See Chapter 8.

Administration: The Power to Do Anything

Many LAN Manager features require that the user have administrative privilege. This privilege is granted in two ways, depending on the mode of the server.

- If the server is running user-mode security, a user can have administrative privilege simply by having a server account that is declared to be an administrative account.

- If the server is running share-mode security, a user can have administrative privilege by having a valid connection to a share named ADMIN$. This share is not created automatically in a share-mode server. An administrator must create it with a command of the following form:

```
net share admin$ password
```

The potential administrator could establish the connection with a command of the following form:

```
net use \\servername\admin$ password
```

This command is usually unnecessary. The user-interface programs try to create this connection by using the default password at the workstation.

> **NOTE:** *If the ADMIN$ share is created without a password, anyone can become an administrator at that server. Share-mode security is intended for the convenience of administrators who want to use MS-NET-like security while learning the rest of LAN Manager. Future versions of LAN Manager will not support share-mode security.*

You must have administrative privilege to accomplish most of the administrative functions at the server, including remote execution of most of the server APIs.

Operators

If you want to grant users some—but not all—administrative rights, you can assign operator privileges to user accounts. Four kinds of operator privilege are available:

- Accounts privilege lets users change the accounts database.

- Print privilege lets users configure spooled print queues.

- Comm privilege lets users change the configuration of the character-device queues.

- Server privilege lets users make general changes to the server environment, such as adding and deleting shares.

Auditing: Who Did What, with What, and to Whom?

In the multiuser environment of the server, tracking who has used what resources and—perhaps more important—who has tried to use resources for which they had no permission is an important task. The server does some of this tracking for you by generating *audit records* under the circumstances noted in Table 2-3.

Record Type	Occurs When...
Server status change	The server starts, stops, pauses, or continues.
Session logon	The username and password are valid in establishing a session.
Session logoff	The end of a session occurs.
Password error	A failed attempt to log on (no active account, or bad password) occurs.
Connection start	A user connects to a server share.
Connection stop	A user disconnects from a server share.
Connection rejection	A connection is rejected.
Access granted	*DosOpen* of a file, device, queue, or pipe is granted access by the security system.
Access rejected	*DosOpen* fails access validation.
Close resource	*DosClose* on a file, device, queue, or pipe occurs.
ACL modification	The Access Control List database is modified.
UAS modification	The User Accounts System database is modified.
Network logon	A user logs on to the network through a domain controller.
Network logoff	A user logs off the network.
Account limit exceeded	A user remains logged on past the time he or she was configured for.

Table 2-3.
Audit records and their causes.

To supplement the resource security system, you can configure the ACL record to generate an audit record every time a *DosOpen* or *DosClose* call is used on a particular resource or whenever access to the resource is denied.

Except for the audit records shown in Table 2-3, audit records are an open format: Applications can develop their own. Chapter 8 examines the APIs used to read and write audit records and describes the server audit records in more detail.

Interprocess Communication: The Heart of Distributed Applications

From a programmer's perspective, one of the most powerful features of OS/2 is multitasking. This allows applications to be split into more than one process and do portions of the application in parallel. Communication between these cooperating processes is done through interprocess communication (IPC). OS/2 provides a rich set of IPC mechanisms, but the most important ones for LAN Manager are those that allow communication between processes running on different computers. This intercomputer IPC allows the creation of distributed applications.

MS-DOS is a single-tasking operating system, but under LAN Manager a process on a DOS workstation can communicate with one or more simultaneous processes running on OS/2 servers.

This section describes three IPC mechanisms that are important for LAN Manager distributed applications: named pipes, mailslots, and the *NetAlertRaise* API.

Named Pipes

A *named pipe* is a bidirectional communications mechanism that any two processes can use to communicate with each other. One process (the *server* side of the application) creates the pipe, and the other (the *client* side) opens it by name with *DosOpen*. Either process can use *DosRead* and *DosWrite* on the handle. What one writes, the other can read, and vice versa.

Using a named pipe in a distributed environment is easy. The server side of the application creates a local named pipe. The client side can use *DosOpen* to open the named pipe, using its UNC name, which has the following form:

servername\pipe*pipename*

where *servername* is the server on which the process creating the named pipe runs, and *pipename* is the local named-pipe name.

> **NOTE:** *Named pipes are subject to the access validation of the server security system. The ACL for a named pipe determines which users can open the pipe with the* DosOpen *function.*

Mailslots

A *mailslot* is a mechanism for reading and writing blocks of data called *messages*. Once a mailslot is created, another process can access it by name and write messages to it. The process that creates the mailslot can read messages from it.

The *NetAlertRaise* API

The LAN Manager *NetAlertRaise* API also accommodates IPC: It notifies a process that a particular *event* has occurred. (An event is a text string plus a buffer of data.) Multiple processes can register interest in the event; all are notified if the event occurs. LAN Manager uses five events:

Event Name	Condition
MESSAGE	The Messenger service at the workstation has received a message.
PRINTING	The print spooler has completed printing a job, or a problem requires human intervention.
ADMIN	The server has detected a condition that an administrator might be interested in (disk full, excessive I/O errors, excessive password validation failures, and so on).
USER	The server has detected a condition that the user might be interested in, such as a timed-out session.
ERROR LOG	A new entry has been made into the system error log.

Alerts are limited to the local environment: They cannot be used remotely.

For more information on the IPC APIs, see Chapter 10.

Other LAN Manager Server Services

The LAN Manager server has several additional service programs that can optionally be run to extend the power of the server:

Service	Function
Alerter	Exports the Alert events over the network
Netlogon	Processes user requests to log on to the network
Netrun	Allows applications programs to be executed at the server

The remainder of this chapter discusses these services.

The Alerter: Help for the Administrator

The Alerter is a server-based LAN Manager service that exports server alerts and makes them available remotely. The Alerter registers interest in *printing, admin,* and *user* events. Whenever such events occur, the Alerter is notified. It packages the alert information and uses interstation messaging APIs to announce the event:

- *printing* and *user* events are announced to the user for whom the event occurred.

- *admin* events are announced to administrators listed in the *alert-names=* parameter of [server] LANMAN.INI.

The following events are some of those typically announced by the Alerter:

- Spooled print job complete

- Printer out of paper

- Server disk almost full

Chapter 10 examines the Alert APIs in more detail.

Netlogon: Distributed Logon Validation

The Netlogon service handles workstation requests to log a user on to the network. A key concept for network logon is that of a *domain,* a logical collection of workstations and servers for which the user accounts database has been centralized. (Actually, this database occurs identically on each server of the domain, but it appears to be a single database.)

When a user logs on to the network from a workstation, the logon is validated by the Netlogon service at one of the servers in the same domain. Servers can be configured to respond to the validation requests from specific users. If none of the servers are so configured, or if the specified server fails to respond, the workstation can ask any server in the domain to handle the validation. If no servers respond to this request, network logon is denied and no further access to network resources is allowed.

Stand-alone logon

A workstation can be configured to allow *stand-alone* (also known as *nonvalidated*) *logon,* which requires a special version of the WKSTA.EXE program at the workstation. In this case, if no servers respond to the validation requests, a workstation can continue as if validation had occurred. Network logon does nothing more than remember the password for future use.

After a server responds to a validation request, server security checks the username and password against its accounts database and either grants or denies network logon. This decision is based on the validity of the username and password, as well as on special information that can restrict access to certain accounts. Chapter 8 discusses the UAS and network logon in more detail.

Single system image

Users with a successful network logon can use network resources for which they have permission. Each time a session is created between the workstation and a server, the server performs a *server logon* to check that the username and password match those of an account at the server. Provided the servers that a user tries to access have the same username and password in their databases, this server logon happens transparently. Otherwise, an explicit password must be provided as each new server is accessed.

With LAN Manager you can use the Single System Image (SSI) to ensure that all servers in a domain have the same user-account information. SSI

An out-of-domain experience

What happens if a workstation tries to establish a session with a server in a different domain?

- If the server has the network logon username and password in its accounts database, the session succeeds.

- If the logon username and password aren't in the database, the user must establish the session with an explicit password.

For example, the following logon command logs *ralph* on to the network and establishes the default password as *mypass*:

```
net logon ralph mypass
```

If the server *toolbox* were in another domain, the following connection command would override the default password with the *otherpass* password:

```
net use x: \\toolbox\public otherpass
```

Remember: There is no command for establishing a session. Sessions are established automatically with your first connection to a given server.

---

gives the appearance of a single user-accounts database for all servers in a domain. In reality, a copy of the database exists at each server, but LAN Manager keeps all of them in sync with each other through a process known as *replication*.

Servers running the Netlogon service can be part of the SSI for the domain. Such servers are called *members* of the SSI domain. One server runs a special version of the Netlogon service and therefore functions as the *domain controller*. Only the domain controller can accept updates to the user-accounts database; it then replicates the changes throughout the SSI domain. One or more servers can also be configured as backup domain controllers. These servers behave exactly like members of the domain but can be promoted to be the domain controller in the event of a failure of the primary domain controller. This promotion is not automatic: An administrator must explicitly start one of the backups as the primary domain controller.

Only the primary domain controller and designated backup domain controllers can perform network logon validation. Figure 2-8 represents the SSI domain. Note that the ACLs at each server are not part of SSI: Each server has its own ACL database and can be updated independently.

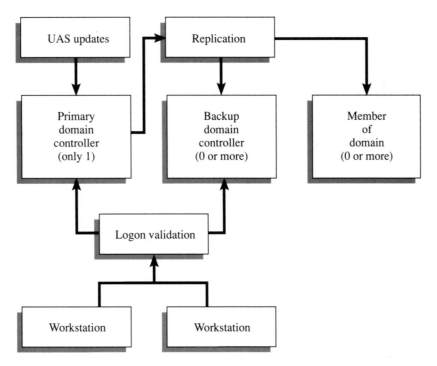

Figure 2-8.
Structure of the SSI domain.

Netrun: Remote Program Execution.

Netrun is a server-based LAN Manager service that allows remote execution of programs. When a program is executed in a file-sharing environment, the workstation loads the program from the server into its own memory and starts the program running on the workstation. When a program is remotely executed, however, it is loaded into the server memory and run at the server. Named pipes connect the program's standard input (stdin), standard output (stdout), and standard error (stderr) to the initiating workstation. The program appears to be running locally at the workstation, but it is actually mapped over the network. Programs executing remotely also map signals across the network.

> **NOTE:** *Programs executing remotely should not use the OS/2 Vio APIs to write to the screen. These calls would not be mapped across the network, and they would send the I/O to the server screen.*

Figure 2-9 shows the architecture of remote execution.

At the workstation, an auxiliary program named RUNSLAVE.EXE is executed. It opens two named pipes that connect it to the Netrun service at the server. One pipe is mapped onto the handles for standard input and standard

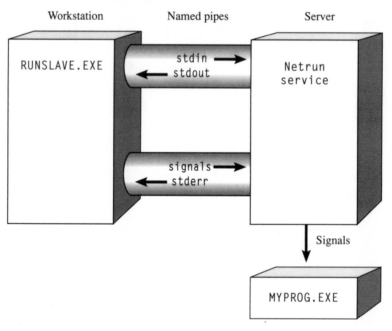

Figure 2-9.
The architecture of remote execution.

output at the workstation, and the other is mapped onto the handle for standard error. At the server, the Netrun service calls *DosExecPgm* to run the program (MYPROG.EXE in Figure 2-9) with its standard input, standard output, and standard error mapped to the named pipes. This transfers any characters at the workstation's standard input (the keyboard or a redirected input file) to the standard input of MYPROG. MYPROG executes without any knowledge that all of its standard input, standard output, and standard error are being transferred over the network. If a signal is applied at the workstation (such as a Ctrl-C from the keyboard), RUNSLAVE traps it at the workstation and transports it over the second named pipe to the server Netrun service, which then uses *DosSendSignal* to send the signal to MYPROG.

Security issues

Some security issues are relevant to remote program execution. Because the remote program is running entirely in the server environment, all of the file-system calls go directly to the server's file system and bypass the server access control system. Two things, then, are important:

- An administrator must control which programs can be executed at the server.

- Such programs should never be in danger of accidentally dealing with the wrong directories.

The best solution is to use the HPFS386 file system, which enforces local security when properly configured. In addition, consider the following security measures:

- Make the current workstation directory the server directory in which the remote program resides. By requiring the user to both connect to the directory and have permission to execute the program, LAN Manager ensures that not just any program can be remotely executed.

- Use the *runpath* parameter in LANMAN.INI to list the directories that can contain remotely executable programs. (The *runpath* parameter is similar to the OS/2 *path* environment variable.) An administrator typically places remotely executable programs in one or two secure directories (that is, directories with execute-only permission for all users).

When the Netrun service executes the named program, it does so with a clean environment, thereby preventing accidental use of a *path* or *dpath* environment variable. (Be sure that any required environment is explicitly set up for the remote process. Chapter 5 describes how to set up environments for remote programs.)

RPC vs. Netrun

Because LAN Manager allows administration to occur over the network, the server provides support for Remote Procedure Calls (RPCs), whereby server API calls can be issued at a workstation, but actually execute at and modify a server.

Remote execution is similar to RPCs. With Netrun, an entire program is executed at the server, but with RPC only a subroutine executes remotely. Netrun allows general-purpose programs to be run remotely, but RPC is limited to those API subroutines provided with LAN Manager.

THE PROGRAMMING ENVIRONMENT

When you write programs for a LAN Manager server, you must write OS/2 programs. But the programs for a LAN Manager workstation can be written to run under both MS-DOS and OS/2. Such programs are known as *bound programs* or *dual-mode executable files*. This chapter covers some of the things you need to know about the programming environments of MS-DOS and OS/2. Those sections relevant to only one environment are labeled accordingly.

> **NOTE:** *The programs shown in this book were written in Microsoft C version 5.1 and make use of the OS/2 version 1.2 API. Every effort has been made to make these programs as portable as possible; however, some OS/2-specific information could not be avoided. Keep this in mind if you port these programs to another operating system (such as UNIX) or to a different version of OS/2.*

This chapter contains information on the following topics:

- File attributes and modes

- Memory models on the Intel 80286

- Dynamic link libraries

- Calling conventions for OS/2

- Use of languages other than C

- Setting up an environment for building and executing LAN Manager programs

> **NOTE:** *This chapter is not a detailed guide to writing MS-DOS and OS/2 programs. To build these skills, refer to the following books:*

- Advanced MS-DOS Programming, 2nd edition, *by Ray Duncan (Microsoft Press, 1988)*

- Advanced OS/2 Programming, *by Ray Duncan (Microsoft Press, 1989)*

- Programming the OS/2 Presentation Manager, *by Charles Petzold (Microsoft Press, 1989)*

File-System Attributes and Modes

When you write LAN Manager programs that open files, use the *DosOpen* function so that you can include network-aware parameters with the call. Traditionally, C programmers use the *fopen* function when they want programs to be as portable as possible, but unfortunately this function doesn't include the file-attribute information available to MS-DOS and OS/2 programs in a multitasking environment. (Note: You could use the Microsoft C function *sopen*, but that is no more portable than *DosOpen*).

Every file in the OS/2 file system is associated with an attribute set by OS/2 when the file is created. The *usAttribute* parameter is set to one of the values shown in Table 3-1. A file's attribute exists as part of the file and changes only if a *DosOpen* (with create mode) or a *DosSetFileInfo* call is made.

Attribute	Value	Meaning
FILE_NORMAL	0	File can be read or written.
FILE_READONLY	0x01	Read only. Delete or open for write will fail.
FILE_HIDDEN	0x02	Hidden. Not visible to a DIR command.
FILE_SYSTEM	0x04	System. Special file used by the operating system.
FILE_ARCHIVE	0x20	Archive. File has been modified since last archive.

Table 3-1.
Possible values of the usAttribute *parameter.*

Share Mode

In a multitasking environment such as OS/2 LAN Manager, more than one program at a time might try to use the *DosOpen* call on a file. When this occurs, the *share-mode* portion of *fsOpen* dictates how the system responds to simultaneous requests. Table 3-2 lists the possible share-mode values.

Mode	Value	Meaning
OPEN_SHARE_DENYREADWRITE	0x0010	Deny-read/write share mode. The current process has exclusive access to the file. The file cannot be opened by any other process (including the current process) until the file is closed. The open fails if the file is already open by any other process.
OPEN_SHARE_DENYWRITE	0x0020	Deny-write share mode. Other processes can open the file for read-only access but cannot open it for write-only or read/write access until the file is closed.

Table 3-2.
Valid share-mode values.

(continued)

Table 3-2. *continued*

Mode	Value	Meaning
OPEN_SHARE_DENY_READ	0x0030	Deny-read share mode. Other processes can open the file for write-only access but cannot open it for read-only or read/write access until the file is closed.
OPEN_SHARE_DENY_NONE	0x0040	Deny-none share mode. Other processes can open the file for any access: read-only, write-only, or read/write.

After an open file is closed, any sharing restrictions placed on it by the opening process are canceled. In a multitasking environment such as OS/2 and in a multiuser environment such as LAN Manager, the share modes are important for preserving the integrity of the data when two or more processes (possibly on more than one workstation) want simultaneous access to the file.

Memory Models

You can write LAN Manager applications without knowing about memory models, but if you're concerned with the efficiency of the application, memory models are an important topic.

The Intel 80286 microprocessor has two modes of operation:

- *Real mode* (an emulation of the Intel 8086 microprocessor chip) gives a program access to the entire physical address space of memory (including the area containing the operating system itself).

- *Protected mode* lets a program access only that memory allocated to it by the operating system.

MS-DOS runs in real mode; OS/2 runs in protected mode.

The internal representations of memory addresses differ in the two modes, but fortunately the C compiler allows you to use a common representation, and you never need to learn the details.

The 80286 microprocessor has a *segmented* memory architecture; that is, each object in memory has a 32-bit address. Figure 3-1 shows the two parts of each address: the *segment* and the *offset*. The segment is the most significant 16 bits of the 32-bit address, and it represents an area of memory up to 64 KB in length. The offset represents the offset within the segment.

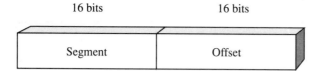

16 bits   16 bits

| Segment | Offset |

Figure 3-1.
A 32-bit address.

Whenever a program references memory, be it through a data reference or through an instruction, the microprocessor must load the segment value into a special *segment register.* A segment register exists for each of the three types of memory segment:

- *Code segments* contain instructions for the processor to execute.

- *Data segments* contain program data.

- *Stack segments* contain information from the program stack.

Unfortunately, loading a segment register can be a time-consuming operation. Whereas most microprocessor instructions take only a few machine cycles (even accounting for the memory reference through the segment register), a segment register load can require as many as 20 cycles. You can see that if a segment register were loaded every two or three instructions, the program would run at half to a third the speed of a program that had no segment register loads. (Few programs load segment registers that often, but program execution is usually dominated by a few central loops, which might contain a large number of segment register loads.)

Models of Efficiency

But LAN Manager lets you use programming models to increase the efficiency of such programs. Five models exist; each handles a different type and size of data. Table 3-3 lists the five memory models, and the paragraphs that follow it describe each in greater detail. The table is ordered by the relative size and speed cost of the memory model used. Small model produces the most efficient programs; huge model, the least efficient.

Model	*Code Segments*	*Data Segments*
Small	One	One
Medium	Many	One
Large	Many	Many (64-KB object size limit)
Huge	Many	Many (object size greater than 64 KB)
Compact	One	Many (64-KB object size limit)

Table 3-3.
The five types of memory models.

One way to make programs more efficient is to load the segment registers at the beginning of the program and ensure that all of the code, data, and stack fit in less than 64 KB apiece. All references to memory are 16-bit offsets (relative to the appropriate preloaded segment register). This removes the need to ever load a segment register again for the life of the program. The one small problem with this method is in determining whether to consider the offset relative to the data segment or to the stack segment. After all, the data could be in either place.

The small memory model
And the solution to this problem is to share the segment: Make the stack and data reside in the same segment, and have stack-segment and data-segment registers refer to the same memory. This is called the *small memory model.*

The medium memory model
As programs grow during development, they might need more than 64 KB of instructions. The code segment contains the instructions, and a program need only load a code-segment register when transferring control by a sub-routine call to another segment. In fact, the 80286 instruction set has separate instructions for performing a subroutine call within a code segment and between code segments (called *near calls* and *far calls*, respectively). Sub-routine calls are usually not as common as data references, so the cost of allowing multiple code segments should not be very high. A program with far calls, multiple code segments, and a single (shared) data and stack segment is called a *medium model program.* In practice, most programmers note a 5–10 percent cost in size and speed when going from a small to a medium model program.

The large memory model
Not surprisingly, the next step is to allow multiple code and multiple data segments in what is called the *large memory model.* Under this model, multiple data segments can exist, but no single data item can be larger than 64 KB, meaning that address calculations inside a data object (for example, an element of an array) need perform only 16-bit arithmetic.

The huge memory model
If the 64-KB limit is removed on data items, the program becomes a *huge memory model.* Manipulating memory addresses is very expensive in the huge memory model because calculations are in 32 bits and because the program must calculate both a segment and an offset within the object.

The compact memory model

For completeness, the *compact memory model* is also provided. It is the opposite of the medium memory model and allows multiple 64-KB data segments but only one code segment.

The Advantage of Mixed-Model Programming

But what if one or two large data items are the only things that keep your program from fitting into the small or medium model? It seems a shame to suffer the performance cost of going to large or huge model for the entire program. To solve this problem, Microsoft added three keywords to the C language: *near, far,* and *huge.* You can use these keywords to describe individual data items that are exceptions to the underlying memory model. The practice of using the *near, far,* and *huge* keywords is known as *mixed-model programming.*

- *near* signifies that memory references for an object will use the current value of the segment register, thus avoiding a segment register load. This can be used for both code and data references.

- *far* signifies that the object must be referenced using a full 32-bit address. Although this might involve an expensive segment register load, only the objects declared "far" require this in a small program.

- *huge,* like *far,* means that a 32-bit address is required. In addition, the object can be bigger than 64 KB and might involve expensive 32-bit address calculations. But again, only the items so declared incur the cost.

But before you can tackle mixed-model programming, you need to learn about dynamic-link libraries and OS/2 calling conventions.

Problems with pointers

If you create a small model program, all library references (such as the standard C library) must also be small model. All subroutine calls to the library are near calls, and all pointers are near (16-bit) pointers. Similarly, a large model program requires a large model library with all far calls and far pointers. Programs will not work if you mix these up. This creates a problem for mixed-model programs. If you have a small model program with a far data item, and you want to make a C library call and operate on the item, you can't pass the far pointer to it.

OS/2 Dynamic Link Libraries

Figure 3-2 shows the classic method used to create an executable program. Source files (C, ASM, etc.) are transformed by a compiler or assembler into object files (OBJ). Object files and libraries of object files are combined by the linker into an executable file (EXE). Each object file needed from the library is copied into the executable file. Thus, if you have two programs that use the C library function *strcat*, a copy of the code and data resides in each executable file. When the programs are loaded to run, the entire executable file is loaded into memory. In a multitasking system such as OS/2, several programs can execute simultaneously, all with copies of the same subroutines in memory.

But suppose that when linking, instead of placing a copy of the subroutine in the executable file, you put in a stub that calls OS/2 and informs it of an attempt to call *strcat*. When the program runs and tries to call *strcat*, OS/2 can fix up the call to point to a single copy of the subroutine. This is the process of *dynamic linking,* which has two advantages over classical linking:

- Dynamic linking requires only one copy of the subroutine code in the dynamic link library, resulting in smaller executables and decreased load times.

- Dynamic linking uses *delayed binding;* that is, the location of the code needn't be identified until a subroutine is called. With classic linking,

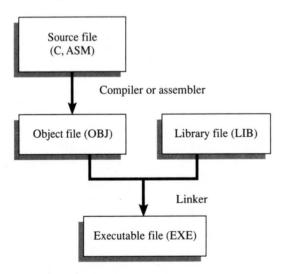

Figure 3-2.
Creating an executable program: the classic method.

the identification of the subroutine location occurred when the executable file was created. If you change the subroutine, you must relink the executable file. With a dynamic link library, you need only release a new dynamic link library.

Creating a Dynamic Link Library

Creation of a dynamic link library (DLL) is a two-part process. First the linker creates the dynamic link library file. (Dynamic link libraries are marked with a DLL extension and contain the single copy of the actual code.) Then the IMPLIB utility creates the required import library (the LIB file) for applications wanting to use the DLL. (The LIB file contains the stubs that will be put into the applications.) Figure 3-3 shows the creation of both the DLL file and the LIB file. Note that the module definition file (a text file containing segment characteristics and other information about the dynamic link library) is used by both parts of the process.

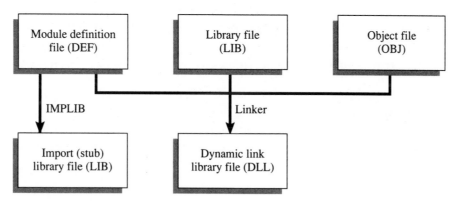

Figure 3-3.
Creating import and dynamic link libraries.

Calling Conventions

Because LAN Manager libraries can be called by a program built using any memory model, a set of conventions must govern the creation of model-independent calls. And because the program might have been written in any of several languages, a set of conventions must dictate how arguments are to be passed and returned. The greatest common denominator is reached by requiring subroutines in DLLs and LIBs to be called with a *far* call, and for all memory references to be passed as a *far* pointer. The multiple-language problem arises because languages like Pascal push their arguments on the stack from left to right (allowing use of a slightly more efficient set of instructions for call and return), but C pushes its arguments from right to left.

(Although this cannot use the more efficient instruction sequence, it allows argument lists with a variable number of arguments.) To solve the multiple-language problem you can require the use of the Pascal convention. There is a keyword in the Microsoft C compiler, "pascal" for just this purpose.

Programs must use the Pascal calling convention when making function calls. This convention, which pushes arguments on the stack from left to right, standardizes the way functions are called—important because all languages don't order arguments in the same manner. Microsoft C, for example, pushes arguments on the stack from right to left. Enforce the Pascal calling convention with the *pascal* keyword in Microsoft C programs.

Using Other Languages

Although most programmers will use C for creating LAN Manager applications, the calling conventions for LAN Manager and OS/2 APIs also allow them to be called from other high-level languages like Pascal, FORTRAN, BASIC, and assembly language. The following sections show a sample API call in Microsoft C and equivalent calls in Microsoft MASM, Microsoft FORTRAN, and Microsoft Pascal.

> **NOTE:** *Microsoft LAN Manager Programmer's Toolkit provides C header files containing LAN Manager API definitions, constants, and structures. If you are using a different language, you need to write your own declarations for the LAN Manager APIs, constants, and structures.*

Programming in Microsoft C

The LAN Manager programs in this book are primarily written in Microsoft C. Here is an example of a call to the *NetUseDel* LAN Manager API from a C program:

```
char far * servername = "\\\\ralph"; /* name of remote server */
char far * usename = "r:";            /* name of local device  */
unsigned short condition = 1;         /* use force to del      */

err = NetUseDel(servername, usename, condition);
```

Programming in Assembly Language

The following page shows what a call to the *NetUseDel* API looks like in a Microsoft Macro Assembler (MASM) program.

```
servername      db      '\\ralph',0             ; name of remote server
usename         db      'r:',0                  ; name of local device
condition       eq      1                       ; use force to del

                push    ds                      ; push server argument
                push    offset DGROUP:servername
                push    ds                      ; push use argument
                push    offset DGROUP:usename
                push    condition               ; push condition argument
                call    NETUSEDEL               ; api call

                or      ax,ax                   ; was write successful?
                jnz     error                   ; jump if call failed
```

You should keep the following items in mind when you call LAN Manager programs from assembly language:

- All pointers are far pointers, and the API call is a far call.

- The API function parameters must be pushed on the stack, the first parameter being pushed first and so on. When the function call is complete, the stack will have been adjusted so that the parameters are no longer on the stack. The return value will always be a WORD value in the AX register. This is the PLM, or *pascal*, calling convention.

- The API functions preserve values only in the following registers: DI, SI, DS, SS, and CS:IP. All other registers are volatile and therefore subject to change.

- Function names should be in all uppercase, as in NETUSEDEL.

Microsoft Macro Assembler (MASM) data types correspond directly to the data types available in Microsoft C. Table 3-4 shows how the different data types match up.

C Data Type	MASM Data Type
char	BYTE
unsigned char	BYTE
short	WORD
unsigned short	WORD
long	DWORD

Table 3-4. *(continued)*
C and MASM data types.

Table 3-4. *continued*

C Data Type	MASM Data Type
unsigned long	DWORD
char far *	DWORD PTR
unsigned int	WORD (on a 286)

Programming in Microsoft FORTRAN

A call to the *NetUseDel* API looks like this in Microsoft FORTRAN:

```
C  First declare a functional prototype of the NetUseDel API:

      INTERFACE TO INTEGER*2 FUNCTION NetUseDel
   +  (servername, usename, condition)
      CHARACTER*(*) servername, usename   ! pass args by reference
      INTEGER*2 condition[VALUE]           ! pass args by value
      END

C  Then NetUseDel can be called correctly in a program:

      PROGRAM MAIN

      INTEGER*2 NetUseDel[EXTERN]

      CHARACTER*8 server               ! name of remote server
      CHARACTER*3 usename              ! name of local device
      INTEGER*2 cond, err

      server = '\\\\ralph'C  ! C string is null-terminated
      usename = 'r:'C        ! this var has C attribute also
      cond = 1               ! use force to del

      err = NetUseDel(server, usename, cond)

      END
```

You should keep the following items in mind when you call LAN Manager programs from FORTRAN:

- All reference arguments are passed FAR, and the API call is a far call; compiling large model conforms to this by default.

- Many APIs utilize arguments passed by value; an INTERFACE block is necessary to declare the arguments correctly.

- LAN Manager programs typically expect character strings to be null-terminated; use C strings for character literals, or concatenate a null character at the end of a character expression.

Programming in Microsoft Pascal

If you are programming in Pascal, you can call the API functions directly because they use the same calling conventions as Microsoft C. A call to the *NetUseDel* API looks like this in Microsoft Pascal:

```
VAR
    serverName, useName: Cstring;      { string variables }
    srvPtr, usePtr: ^Cstring;          { pointers to strings }
    condition: Integer;                { condition integer }

BEGIN
    serverName := '\\ralph';           { name of remote server }
    useName:= 'r:';                    { name of local device }
    srvPtr := @serverName;             { address of server name }
    usePtr := @useName;                { address of device name }
    condition := 1;                    { use force to del }

    NetUseDel(srvPtr, usePtr, condition);
```

What Can Go Wrong?

One of the most common programming errors is uninitialized pointers or pointers that reference nonexistent memory. Because many LAN Manager APIs make a transition to underlying system code, it is important that no bad memory references be passed on by the API function. Each API checks the limits on all pointers and buffers to ensure that they refer to valid memory. If they don't, a General Protection Fault is generated, indicating a programming error. To fix the error, you should check all values being passed to the API.

In general, the API functions should have at least 4 KB of stack space available at the time of the function call. This provides a measure of safety even if interrupt routines are invoked while the code is in an API routine. With the Microsoft C Compiler you can use the /F switch to set the stack size. You can also reserve stack space with the STACKSIZE directive in the module definition (DEF) file.

The Programming Environment

When you build a LAN Manager application (including the examples developed in this book), you need to set up your programming environment correctly. When compiling, you need access to LAN Manager header files, and when linking, you need access to LAN Manager import libraries.

Both sets of files are available in the Microsoft LAN Manager Programmer's Toolkit. Consult the Toolkit documentation for the location of these files and information about setting your INCLUDE and LIB environment variables.

The LAN.H Header File

The constants, declarations, and data structures needed by the LAN Manager APIs appear in the Toolkit as a collection of C-language header files. You can include these files individually in your programs, or you can include the master header file LAN.H to reference some or all of them. The first method is used in this book; each API discussion contains information about the specific header file you need to include in your program and what it contains.

The master header file method is straightforward—you define constants for each API category you'll be using and then include the LAN.H file with a *#include* directive. For example, to include the functions, data types, structures, and constants associated with the Server category, put the following lines in your program:

```
#define INCL_NETSERVER
#include <lan.h>
```

Most LAN Manager programs also require the base set of OS/2 declarations and the LAN Manager error codes. To include these values along with the Server values defined above, put the following lines in your program:

```
#define INCL_BASE
#include <os2.h>

#define INCL_NETSERVER
#define INCL_NETERRORS
#include <lan.h>
```

Table 3-5 lists the constants you need to define in your program if you use the LAN.H master file method.

API Category	Constant	Header Files
All categories	INCL_NET	All header files
Access	INCL_NETACCESS	ACCESS.H
Alert	INCL_NETALERT	ALERT.H, ALERTMSG.H
Audit	INCL_NETAUDIT	AUDIT.H
NetBIOS	INCL_NETBIOS	NCB.H, NETBIOS.H

Table 3-5. *(continued)*
Constants used with the LAN.H master file method.

Table 3-5. *continued*

API Category	Constant	Header Files
Character Device	INCL_NETCHARDEV	CHARDEV.H
Configuration	INCL_NETCONFIG	CONFIG.H
Connection	INCL_NETCONNECTION	SHARES.H
Domain	INCL_NETDOMAIN	ACCESS.H
Error Logging	INCL_NETERRORLOG	ERRLOG.H
Errors, all categories	INCL_NETERRORS	NETERR.H
File	INCL_NETFILE	SHARES.H
Group	INCL_NETGROUP	ACCESS.H
Handle	INCL_NETHANDLE	CHARDEV.H
Mailslot	INCL_NETMAILSLOT	MAILSLOT.H
Message	INCL_NETMESSAGE	MESSAGE.H
Print Destination	(no LAN.H constant)	PMSPL.H
Print Job	(no LAN.H constant)	PMSPL.H
Print Queue	(no LAN.H constant)	PMSPL.H
Profile	INCL_NETPROFILE	PROFILE.H
Remote Utility	INCL_NETREMUTIL	REMUTIL.H
Server	INCL_NETSERVER	SERVER.H
Service	INCL_NETSERVICE	SERVICE.H
Session	INCL_NETSESSION	SHARES.H
Share	INCL_NETSHARE	SHARES.H
Statistics	INCL_NETSTATS	NETSTATS.H
Use	INCL_NETUSE	USE.H
User	INCL_NETUSER	ACCESS.H
Workstation	INCL_NETWKSTA	WKSTA.H

Building LAN Manager Programs

When you build programs that use the LAN Manager APIs, what commands should you use? Creating object modules from your sources is the same whether you are developing for MS-DOS or for OS/2. There are no surprises here. But linking the program is different, depending on the target environment. The following examples show the linker response files.

Linking for OS/2

If you are using the Microsoft C compiler, you must include the necessary libraries on the CL command line, for example:

```
CL prog.obj netapi.lib netoem.lib mailslot.lib
```

Chapter 4 describes the LAN Manager APIs in these libraries. If the linker is called directly, the linking dialog looks like this:

```
Object Modules [.OBJ]: prog /farcall
Run File [prog.exe]: prog.exe /noi
List File [NUL.MAP]: NUL
Libraries [.LIB]: netapi.lib +
Libraries [.LIB]: netoem.lib +
Libraries [.LIB]: mailslot.lib
Definitions File [NUL.DEF]: ;
```

Linking for MS-DOS

Most LAN Manager APIs are available for programs running under MS-DOS. Note that these programs will not run in the compatibility-mode session (the 3X box) under OS/2 but will run under MS-DOS version 3.1 or later. Using the Microsoft C compiler, the command line for linking is

```
CL prog.obj dosnet.lib
```

The linker can be invoked directly with a dialog similar to the following:

```
Object Modules [.OBJ]: prog /farcall
Run File [prog.exe]: prog.exe /noi
List File [NUL.MAP]: NUL
Libraries [.LIB]: dosnet.lib
```

When programs are linked under MS-DOS, there is no support for the OS/2 style file APIs: APIs such as *DosOpen*, *DosRead*, and *DosWrite* cannot be called. In most cases, the more portable C language routines such as *fopen*, *fread*, and *fwrite* can be used, but they don't have all of the same capabilities as the DOS APIs.

Creating Dual-Mode Executable Files

Under OS/2, you can create executable files that run under both OS/2 and MS-DOS. These programs are called *dual-mode executable files*, or *bound programs*. After building an OS/2 program as shown above, use the BIND utility to create the dual-mode program. These dual-mode programs can use all of the OS/2 APIs that are part of the Family API (FAPI) collection of functions. See your OS/2 documentation for a complete list. All DOS APIs used in this book are part of the FAPI set.

The following command line creates a bound program named PROGB.EXE:

```
BIND prog.exe syscall0.lib doscalls.lib dosnet.lib -o progb.exe
```

Note that the SYSCALL0.LIB library must be the first library on the command line.

Runtime Environment (OS/2 Only)

After an application is linked, it can be run. If it is linked with an import stub library, it will need to know where to find the associated DLL. It can find this information by checking the OS/2 configuration file, CONFIG.SYS. It contains a variable called LIBPATH, which tells OS/2 where to find dynamic link libraries. Be sure that your LIBPATH includes C:\LANMAN\NETLIB, which is where the standard LAN Manager DLLs reside. If you create DLLs for your applications (as some examples in this book do), you must add their locations to LIBPATH.

Creating a Mixed-Model Library (OS/2 Only)

Now that the calling conventions have been defined, and because you know something about the programming environment, you can create the mixed-model library mentioned earlier. For our purposes, all interfaces must have far calls and returns, pass far pointers to data, and use the Pascal calling convention. (The code generated for subroutines in this DLL is large model but can be called by programs using any memory model.)

The STRING_F.C program (Figure 3-4) is part of a mixed-model string library. The new entry points (such as *strcpy_f*) call the large model C library.

```
/*
 * STRING_F.C -- A model-independent string library for OS/2.
 */

#include <string.h>
```

Figure 3-4.
The STRING_F.C program.

(continued)

Figure 3-4. *continued*

```
char far * far pascal strtok_f(str, pat)
    char far *str;
    const char far * pat;
    {
    return(strtok(str, pat));
    }
char far * far pascal strcpy_f(dst, src)
    char far *dst;
    char far * src;
    {
    return(strcpy(dst, src));
    }
char far * far pascal strncpy_f(dst, src, cnt)
    char far *dst;
    char far * src;
    int cnt;
    {
    return(strncpy(dst, src, cnt));
    }
char far * far pascal strcat_f(dst, src)
    char far * dst;
    char far * src;
    {
    return(strcat(dst, src));
    }
int far pascal strcmp_f(dst, src)
    char far * dst;
    char far * src;
    {
    return(strcmp(dst, src));
    }
int far pascal strncmp_f(dst, src, n)
    char far * dst;
    char far * src;
    int n;
    {
    return(strncmp(dst, src, n));
    }
int far pascal stricmp_f(dst, src)
    char far * dst;
    char far * src;
    {
    return(stricmp(dst, src));
    }
```

(continued)

Figure 3-4. *continued*

```
int far pascal strlen_f(str)
    char far *str;
    {
    return(strlen(str));
    }

/* Add other routines as needed. Be sure to update the */
/* module definition (DEF) file appropriately. */
```

The STRING_F.DEF program (Figure 3-5) is the module definition file for building the DLL and LIB files:

```
LIBRARY STRING_F
DESCRIPTION 'Far String Library'
EXPORTS
STRTOK_F    @1
STRCPY_F    @2
STRCAT_F    @3
STRNCPY_F   @4
STRCMP_F    @5
STRNCMP_F   @6
STRICMP_F   @7
STRLEN_F    @8
STACKSIZE   0
PROTMODE
CODE SHARED EXECUTEREAD LOADONCALL DISCARDABLE
DATA MULTIPLE NONSHARED MOVABLE
SEGMENTS
```

Figure 3-5.
The STRING_F.DEF program.

Before you compile and link STRING_F.C and STRING_F.DEF, you must create a special assembly language module to prevent the linker from including the C runtime startup code during the link process. When the Microsoft C Compiler generates an object file, it includes an external reference to the symbol _acrtused. For your mixed-model DLL, you want the runtime to be linked, but you do not want this external reference. The following file, CRT.ASM, hides the startup code when assembled with the Microsoft Macro Assembler (MASM) and linked with STRING_F.OBJ, STRING_F.DLL, and STRING_F.DEF.

```
;****************************************************************;
;**    CRT.ASM -  startup code for a model-independent library   **;
;****************************************************************;
TITLE   crt.asm -- fake C runtime startup
NAME    CRT

;***crt -- fake C runtime startup
;
;       For dynamic link libraries, we do not want to load
;       the standard C runtime startup.  This module defines
;       a symbol that will prevent that loading.

        PUBLIC__acrtused
__acrtused = 1

        END
```

Finally, the following commands are used to build the DLL and LIB files:

```
cl /Alfu /Gs /c string_f.c
masm /Mx crt.asm;
link string_f crt,string_f.dll,,,string_f.def
implib string_f.lib string_f.def
```

The compiler flag *Alfu* generates far calls and far data references, and it forces the data-segment register to be loaded to the correct value for the DLL. The *Gs* flag disables stack-checking code. (You cannot do stack checking in a mixed-model library.) The outcome of this series of commands is STRING_F.DLL and STRING_F.LIB.

To see this library in use, you can compile a test routine. For example, if you compile the TEST_F.C program (Figure 3-6) with the command

```
cl test_f.c string_f.lib
```

and then run it, you'll display the parsed word list.

> **NOTE:** *This example works only when the STRING_F.DLL dynamic link library is placed in one of the directories named in the OS/2 LIBPATH environment variable.*

```
/*
 * TEST_F.C -- A test program for the model-independent string library.
 */

#include <stdio.h>
#include <string_f.h>

main()
{
    char far *q;
    char *p = "      a\n\t\t  mixed model \t\ntest\n";
    char buffer[64];

    q = strtok_f(p, " \t\n");
    while (q)
        {
        strcpy_f(buffer, q);
        printf("%s\n", buffer);
        q = strtok_f(NULL, " \t\n");
        }
}
```

Figure 3-6.
The TEST_F.C program.

Note that the TEST_F.C program contains a reference to the STRING_F.H
header file (Figure 3-7). STRING_F.H contains declarations for the model-
independent string routines shown in STRING_F.C and is used from time to
time in this book. Be sure to put this file in a directory specified by your
INCLUDE environment variable before you compile.

```
/* A model independent string header file for OS/2. */

char _far *_pascal _far strtok_f(char _far *str,const char _far *pat);
char _far *_pascal _far strcpy_f(char _far *dst,char _far *src);
char _far *_pascal _far strncpy_f(char _far *dst,char _far *src,int cnt);
char _far *_pascal _far strcat_f(char _far *dst,char _far *src);
int _pascal _far strcmp_f(char _far *dst,char _far *src);
int _pascal _far strncmp_f(char _far *dst,char _far *src,int  n);
int _pascal _far stricmp_f(char _far *dst,char _far *src);
int _pascal _far strlen_f(char _far *str);
```

Figure 3-7.
The STRING_F.H header file.

Mixing and Matching Models

When you work with mixed-model programs, you might need to reference far objects as near objects. Consider the following code fragment:

```
char far * p = "a string in far memory";
printf("%s\n", p);
```

This will not work if *printf* is a near model. It is expecting a near pointer for the string. The following macro helps solve this problem:

```
/* A macro for getting a far object into
 * model-dependent memory.
 */

#define MDPTR(fptr) ((char *)strcpy_f(alloca(strlen_f((char far *)fptr)),\
        (char far *)fptr))
```

Now the fragment above can be coded as

```
char far * p = "a string in far memory";
printf("%s\n", MDPTR(p));
```

If you are working in OS/2, you can use the *strlen_f* and *strcpy_f* routines from the model-independent library of the previous section. If you are working in MS-DOS, you need to use the following subroutines:

```
char far * far pascal strcpy_f(d, s)
    char far *d, far *s;
    {
    char far *q = d;
    while (*d++=*s++);
    return(q);
    }
int far pascal strlen_f(s)
    char far *s;
    {
    int len = 0;
    while (*s++)
        ++len;
    return(len);
    }
```

The Challenge of Nothingness

Many mixed-model programs encounter a subtle bug. Consider the following code fragment:

```
char * np = NULL;
char far * fp;
fp = np;
```

When the near pointer is copied to the far pointer, it must undergo a type conversion. Converting a near pointer to a far pointer means adding the segment. So the value of *fp* above is DS:0, not 0:0 as you might expect. However, the constant value 0 (or NULL) will always be converted correctly. The following macro will help you avoid this kind of bug:

```
/* A macro for converting a near pointer to a far
 * pointer without losing NULL.
 */

#define N2F(np) (np ? np : NULL)
```

THE APPLICATIONS PROGRAMMING INTERFACE

INTRODUCTION TO LAN MANAGER APIs

The Applications Programming Interface (API) is a set of well-defined interfaces that allow applications to use system services without knowing how the system actually works. This chapter provides an overview of the Microsoft LAN Manager APIs and describes their architecture. Chapters 5 through 12 describe the APIs in detail.

Using the APIs

The LAN Manager APIs exist in a set of dynamic link libraries under OS/2 and libraries under MS-DOS. The files are part of the standard LAN Manager workstation software that is installed in the C:\LANMAN directory by default. The H and LIB files required for developing LAN Manager programs are supplied in a separate product, the Microsoft LAN Manager Programmer's Toolkit. The following directories are used in the development of LAN Manager programs:

- The LANMAN\NETLIB directory, containing the DLLs used by the API. This directory must be in the LIBPATH established by the CONFIG.SYS file when OS/2 is started.

- A header file (H) directory containing the LAN Manager header files used when you compile programs using the API functions and data structures. (Chapters 5 through 12 list the header files each call requires.) This directory should be included in the path specified by the INCLUDE environment variable. Consult your LAN Manager Programmer's Toolkit for the location of this directory.

  Most LAN Manager programs will also need to include the OS2.H master header file, which contains the functions, constants, and data structures for the base OS/2 API. If you're writing programs for MS-DOS, you can't use this API and shouldn't include this header file.

  > NOTE: *If you experience problems with undefined constants when you compile LAN Manager Programs, be sure OS2.H is reading all the necessary include files. Some LAN Manager programs require values that are not part of the default OS2.H setup.*

- A library file (LIB) directory containing the dynamic link library stub modules that let you link an application that makes API calls. (Chapters 5 through 12 list which LIB files the linker must specify.) This directory should be included in the path specified by the LIB environment variable. Consult your LAN Manager Programmer's Toolkit for the location of this directory.

The following table lists the library files supplied with LAN Manager:

File	Contents
NETAPI.LIB	The majority of the LAN Manager APIs.
NETOEM.LIB	The Message APIs, the NetServerEnum API, and some of the APIs for logging the workstation on to the network. Some LAN Manager vendors will want to change these— the interfaces will remain the same, but the underlying API can be replaced.
NETSPOOL.LIB	APIs used along with the LAN Manager print spooler.
MAILSLOT.LIB	APIs for using mailslots.
NB30.LIB	APIs used for the IBM version of NetBIOS.
PMSPL.LIB	A dynamic link library that replaces the OS/2 Presentation Manager spooler.

To illustrate the use of these directories, here are some sample command lines using the SET command and the Microsoft C compiler. They assume that the C compiler include files are in the directory C:\INCLUDE and that the C compiler libraries are in C:\LIB. They also assume that LAN Manager header files are in a directory named C:\LANMAN\NETSRC\H and that the LAN Manager stub libraries are in a directory named C:\LANMAN-\NETSRC\LIB. The SOMEFILE.C file is a hypothetical C source file that uses some of the LAN Manager APIs.

```
set INCLUDE=c:\include;c:\lanman\netsrc\h
set LIB=c:\lib;c:\lanman\netsrc\lib
cl somefile.c netapi.lib
```

If the program is intended to be a dual-mode program, that is, one able to run under either OS/2 or MS-DOS, the additional step of binding must be taken. To bind SOMEFILE.EXE and place it in the \DUALMODE directory, type the following:

```
bind somefile.exe syscalls0.lib doscalls.lib dosnet.lib -o
\dualmode\somefile.exe
```

During the bind operation, the following libraries are used:

Library Name	Contents
SYSCALLS0.LIB	Special versions of *DosOpen* and *DosRead* that will work with the MS-DOS redirector. This library must be specified first on the BIND command line.
DOSCALLS.LIB	The rest of the support for OS/2 system calls.
DOSNET.LIB	The MS-DOS version of LAN Manager APIs.

Programs written for MS-DOS only should be linked with the DOSNET.LIB library.

What's in a Name?

LAN Manager API names are both straightforward and functional. The APIs are not a random collection of functions but rather are an ordered attempt to meet the needs of applications and systems programmers under LAN Manager.

The APIs use an "object-oriented" approach: Each API name contains an object and a verb. For example, one of the objects is Share, and one of the verbs is Enum. The result: An API named *NetShareEnum*. A perfectly regular architecture would offer M objects and N verbs and therefore $M \times N$ functions with names of the form *NetObjectVerb*. But, as with most real-world systems, the perfect architecture was not appropriate to the problem, so there are irregular verbs among the APIs. This principle is important, however, because the architecture follows it as much as possible.

The Objects in API Names

API names use the following objects:

Object	Purpose
Wksta	Allows programs to query and manipulate the basic data structures of the LAN Manager workstation.
Use	Allows programs to work with connections to shares at the server.
Message	Allows programs to interact with the interstation messaging service.
Profile	Allows programs to save and restore the state of the system. (A profile is a file that records a set of connections, shares, and print queues at a workstation or a server.)
Config	Allows information to be accessed from the LANMAN.INI file.
Remote	Allows the running of programs at a server.

(continued)

continued

Object	Purpose
Service	Allows manipulation of LAN Manager service programs.
Server	Manipulates some fundamental server data structures.
Share	Allows programs to work with shares at the server.
Session	Allows programs to work with sessions between a user and a server.
Connection	Allows programs to work with connections from the server end. In contrast, the Use APIs work from the workstation end.
File	Allows programs to work with open files at a server.
Audit	Allows programs to work with audit records at the server.
Error	Allows programs to work with error log records at either the workstation or the server.
Statistics	These APIs allow programs to work with system statistics at either the workstation or the server.
Access	Allows programs to work with the access control list database at a server.
Group	Allows programs to work with groups in the user-accounts database at a server.
User	Allows programs to work with user accounts at a server.
NmPipe	Allows interprocess communication using named pipes.
MailSlot	Allows interprocess communication using mailslots.
Alert	Allows interprocess communication using software events.
NetBIOS	Allows programs to use the NetBIOS directly.
CharDev	Allows programs to work with the serial communications device queues at a server.
PrintQ	Allows programs to work with spooled printer queues at a server.
PrintJob	Allows programs to work with the spooled print jobs contained in the print queues.
PrintDest	Allows programs to work with the devices to which print queues submit their jobs.

The Verbs in API Names

API names use the following verbs:

Verb	Purpose
Enum	Enumerates all instances of a particular object. For example, *NetShareEnum* enumerates the shares at a server.
GetInfo	Gets detailed information about an instance of an object. For example, *NetShareGetInfo* gets the type of a share and its remark.

(continued)

Verb	Purpose
SetInfo	Changes some of the attributes of an instance of an object. For example, *NetShareSetInfo* can change the remark of a share at a server.
Add	Adds new instances of an object. For example, *NetShareAdd* creates a new share at a server.
Del	Deletes instances of an object. For example, *NetShareDel* deletes an existing share at a server.

Data Structures

Each API object type has a set of data structures that the APIs use. The naming convention used for these structures is *object_info_#*. Each data structure has several levels of detail, signified by the number at the end of the name.

The level 0 structure generally contains only one member, which is the name of an instance of the object. For some objects, the higher-level structures contain information that is available only to users with administration (*admin*) privilege. Chapters 5 through 12 discuss the details of each level for each object type.

All API data structures are described as C language structures. The member names of these structures also have a naming convention, one that encodes the object type and level. For example, in a *share_info_1* structure, all members have names that begin with "shi1", and in a *server_info_2* structure, the member names all begin with "sv2_".

The API data structures have been designed to be independent of both language and memory model. Thus all pointers must be far pointers.

Structure Boundaries

On the 80286 microprocessor, it is more efficient to access word data on an even address boundary. Most C compilers try to align elements of data structures on even address boundaries by leaving holes in the structure. Some compilers allow structures to be packed, eliminating holes: Structure elements are not necessarily on even address boundaries. (In the Microsoft C Compiler, this is the /ZP option.)

LAN Manager API structure members always fall on even boundaries, regardless of how a program is compiled. (Members named *pad* are dummy members that force even alignment of the following member. For example, the *share_info_1* structure contains a member named shil_pad.) Whenever the data structures include text strings, they are always zero-terminated ASCII strings. Sometimes the structures contain a fixed size for holding a string, but the string will always be large enough to include the terminating zero.

Buffer Size Requirements

When data structures are returned from the API, the calling program must provide a buffer for the data. The API data structures contain a fixed-length structure, which might contain pointers to variable-length strings. The buffer must be large enough to hold the fixed-length portion of the structure:

- If the buffer can't hold all of the variable-length data, the API returns as much as will fit and indicates that the information is incomplete by using a return code of ERROR_MORE_DATA.

- If the buffer can't hold the text of a string, the pointer in the fixed-length portion is set to NULL.

- If the string does not exist (for example, if a share was not given a remark), the pointer will be to an empty string, that is, a zero-terminated string of zero length. In C, this is represented as

```
char *pointer_to_empty_string = "";
```

Members that refer to time are always encoded as long (double-word) integers representing seconds since January 1, 1970. If the API is being called remotely, the calling routine must handle any time-zone conversions. Chapter 5 demonstrates this process.

Return Code

A successful API has a return code of 0; if errors or unusual conditions occur, the return code is some other positive number. Although Appendix B lists all possible return codes—most of which are associated with specific APIs—the following paragraphs list codes that could be returned from almost any API. These return codes are in three sets: One set indicates programming errors, another indicates runtime errors, and a third set indicates internal LAN Manager errors.

Program Error Conditions

ERROR_MORE_DATA	The buffer supplied to the API is not large enough to hold the data. The API has returned as much information as will fit. Usually, a program will want to allocate a larger buffer and try again. See the NETENUM.C routine later in this chapter.
NERR_BufTooSmall	The buffer supplied to the API is not large enough to hold the fixed-length portion of the API data structure. No data has been returned, in contrast to the previous return code, which indicates partial data.
ERROR_INVALID_LEVEL	The *level* parameter, which indicates what level of information structure is being used, is invalid.
ERROR_INVALID_PARAMETER	One of the API parameters is invalid. The detailed descriptions of the APIs show where each API might return this code.

Runtime Error Conditions

NERR_ServerNotStarted	Most administration APIs require the server to be running before they can execute correctly.
NERR_WkstaNotStarted	Most workstation APIs require the workstation to be started before they can execute correctly.
NERR_NetNotStarted	Some APIs do not need the workstation to be running, but they do require that the network drivers (NETWK-STA.SYS and the NetBIOS drivers) be loaded when the operating system starts up. This error indicates that the workstation is not configured correctly.

(continued)

NERR_ACFNotLoaded	The APIs for the security system require that the workstation be started. This error indicates that it was not.
ERROR_NETWORK_ACCESS_DENIED	If an API attempts to perform an operation at a server for which the user has no permission, this error code is returned.
ERROR_NOT_ENOUGH_MEMORY	The system ran out of memory resources. Either the LAN Manager configuration is incorrect, or the program is running on a system with insufficient memory.
NERR_BrowserNotStarted	The Browser has not been started because the line *mailslots = no* is in the LANMAN.INI file.

Internal LAN Manager Error Conditions

The following error messages indicate internal errors. If these messages appear, you should contact your LAN Manager support representative.

```
NERR_ShareMem
NERR_OS2_IoctlError
NERR_InternalError
```

Locating Return Codes

Appendix B lists all codes beginning with ERROR_ and NERR_ and lists their meanings:

- ERROR_ return codes are in the range 1 through 500 and are defined in the BSEERR.H file, which is included as part of OS2.H.

- NERR_ return codes are in the range 2100 through 3000 and are listed in NETERR.H.

    NOTE: *ERROR_ codes in the range 51 through 79 are network-specific return codes and are not in BSEERR.H. They are defined in NETERR.H.*

Remote Procedure Calls

One feature that makes LAN Manager so powerful is the ability to execute API calls at a server. This allows programs running on workstations to run administrative functions at a server. Most API calls are designed to be run either locally or remotely. Those that can be run remotely always include the server name as the first argument. If the call is intended to be run locally, the server name can be one of three things: a NULL pointer, a pointer to a null string, or the computer name of the local workstation. If the server name is set to a valid computer name, the API code packages the rest of the arguments and sends them to the server, where the arguments are unpacked and the API call is executed locally (at the server). The return data is then packaged and sent back to the workstation, where it is unpacked and returned to the calling program.

As far as the calling program is concerned, no special handling is necessary to make a remote API call. For example, Figure 4-1 is an example of a code fragment that enumerates the shares. The first instance enumerates the shares on the computer that is running the code. The second instance enumerates the shares on the computer named "\\BIGDISK". Note that the server name must contain four backslash characters: two for the server name and two for the backslash characters in the C string.

```
err = NetShareEnum(NULL,           /* local execution */
                   0,              /* level 0          */
                   buff,           /* buffer for list */
                   BUFSIZ,         /* buffer size      */
                   &er,            /* entries read     */
                   &ta);           /* total available */

err = NetShareEnum("\\\\BIGDISK", /* remote execution */
                   0,              /* level 0          */
                   buff,           /* buffer for list  */
                   BUFSIZ,         /* buffer size      */
                   &er,            /* entries read     */
                   &ta);           /* total available  */
```

Figure 4-1.
Local vs. remote share enumeration.

A good example of the power of remote API calls is the LAN Manager full-screen interface. When the View Other Server option is selected for remote administration of a server, the code does nothing more than validate the server name and store it in a global variable. Wherever the code calls an API, the global variable is given to the API as the *servername* parameter. No special code exists for handling remote administration: The APIs do it for the application automatically.

Although most APIs can be called remotely, not every user can run programs that use this facility. Most APIs require the user to have *admin* or *operator* privilege at the server on which the APIs are to be executed. If the user does not have this permission, the API returns one of the following values to the calling program:

```
ERROR_NETWORK_ACCESS_DENIED
ERROR_ACCESS_DENIED
```

Chapters 5 through 12 indicate which APIs require administrative privileges for remote execution.

Conjugating the LAN Manager Verbs

This section describes the general characteristics of the common API verbs. Chapters 5 through 12 describe characteristics of specific object/verb combinations.

The Enum Verb

The Enum verb retrieves information structures that describe instances of objects such as all of the shares at a server, all of the uses at a workstation, or all of the servers on a network. Enum returns as many structures as fit in the buffer supplied by the calling program. Even if variable-length data does not fit, the fixed-length portion of a structure is still returned. Missing elements of variable-length data have NULL pointers in the structure. The typical enumeration call is of the following form:

```
unsigned far pascal
NetObjectEnum(
    char far *servername,      /* server to execute code   */
    short level,               /* info structure level     */
    char far *buf,             /* buffer for return data   */
    USHORT buflen,             /* size of buf              */
    USHORT far *entriesread,   /* number of entries
                                  actually read            */
    USHORT far *totalentries   /* total number of entries
                                  available                */
    );
```

servername is the server on which the code is intended to execute, and *level* is the information-structure level to be returned in the buffer. For example, if the level 1 structures describing open files on the server were needed, the call would look like this:

```
err = NetFileEnum(NULL, 1, buf, buflen, &er, &te);
```

buf is a buffer to hold the returned structures. The call fills the buffer with as many structures as will fit. If a structure has variable-length data as well as a fixed-length portion, the buffer must be large enough to hold both parts.

buflen is the size of the buffer pointed to by *buf*.

entriesread is a pointer to a variable that will be filled in by the API with the number of data structures that fit in *buf*. Note that if the fixed portion of the structure fits, *entriesread* counts the structure, even if no room is available for the variable-length data.

totalentries is a pointer to a variable that will be filled in by the API with the total number of instances of the structure that are available.

If the call is successful and all instances of the data structure are in the buffer, Enum returns 0. If the number of entries read is not the same as the total number of entries, Enum returns ERROR_MORE_DATA.

The most important issue in working with Enum calls is buffer management. A program usually makes the call with a buffer thought to be large enough; if ERROR_MORE_DATA is returned, the program gets a larger buffer and makes the call again. The NETENUM.C program, described at the end of this chapter, provides you with a method of buffer management.

The GetInfo Verb

The GetInfo verb retrieves a data structure describing a single instance of an object. Most GetInfo calls are of the following form:

```
unsigned far pascal
NetObjectGetInfo(
    char far *servername,    /* server to execute code  */
    char far *key,           /* which instance?         */
    short level,             /* info structure level    */
    char far *buf,           /* buffer for return data  */
    USHORT buflen,           /* size of buf             */
    USHORT far *totalavail   /* total number of bytes
                                in the structure         */
    );
```

servername is the server on which the code is to execute, and *key* identifies which instance is of interest. These keys are the same data returned by the level 0 structure for the object, so a common form of processing with the APIs is to call an Enum API at level 0 and then iterate through the keys with GetInfo calls at the appropriate higher level. Figure 4-2 shows an example of this.

level identifies the level of information desired.

buffer provides a place for the data to be returned, and *buflen* indicates the size of that place.

totalavail identifies exactly how many bytes of buffer are required to get both the fixed-length and the variable-length part of the structure. Note that Enum calls return the number of available entries, and GetInfo calls return the size required for a specific entry.

If ERROR_MORE_DATA is returned, any missing variable-length data is indicated by a NULL pointer in the fixed-length structure.

The NUSE.C program (Figure 4-2) shows how to use the Enum and GetInfo calls together to process all instances of an object. This example uses *Net-UseEnum* and *NetUseGetInfo* to print information about all uses at a workstation. It is similar to the LAN Manager user command net use.

```
/*
 * NUSE.C -- This skeleton program gets a list of all the
 * "uses" at the local workstation.  The Enum buffer is assumed
 * to be "big enough" and no attempt is made to manage memory
 * efficiently.  The program first calls a level 0 Enum, then
 * iterates through the list making level 1 GetInfo calls.
 * Add your own code as indicated below to process the use
 * information.
 *
 * Compile with:  C> cl nuse.c netapi.lib
 *
 * Usage:  C> nuse
 *
 */

#include <stdio.h>
#include <os2.h>
#include <netcons.h>
#include <use.h>

main()
    {
    USHORT eread, te, ta, err;
    char buf[BUFSIZ];      /* big enough buffer */
    char use[BUFSIZ];      /* big enough buffer */
    struct use_info_0 *p;  /* key list pointer */
    int i;
```

Figure 4-2.   *(continued)*
NUSE.C: a program that lists uses at a workstation.

Figure 4-2. *continued*

```
    /* get a list of keys to uses */
    err = NetUseEnum(NULL, 0, buf, BUFSIZ, &eread, &te);

    if (err == 0)
        {
        /* now iterate through key list */
        for (p = (struct use_info_0 *)buf, i = 0; i < te; ++i)
            {
            err = NetUseGetInfo(0, (char far *)p, 1, use, SIZ, &ta);
            /* insert USE processing code here */
            ++p;              /* get next key */
            }
        }
}
```

Figure 4-3 is a code fragment showing how buffer management might be accomplished for a *NetShareGetInfo* call. The key assumes the existence of a share named MODEM.

```
char far *p;
USHORT level = 2;
USHORT tavail;
USHORT err, len;
SEL sel;

len = sizeof(struct share_info_2 + 10);
DosAllocSeg(len, &sel, 0);

/* os2def.h pointer from selector macro */
p = (char far *)MAKEP(sel, 0);

err = NetShareGetInfo(NULL, "MODEM", 2, p, len, &tavail);
while (err == ERROR_MORE_DATA)
    {
    DosReallocSeg(tavail, sel);
    P = (char far *)MAKEP(sel, 0);
    err = NetShareGetInfo(NULL, "MODEM", 2, p, len, &tavail);
    }
return(err);
```

Figure 4-3.
Buffer management for a NetShareGetInfo *call.*

The SetInfo Verb

The SetInfo verb changes information in an instance of an object—for example, the remark on a share, the audit status of an ACL entry, or the performance heuristics at a workstation. SetInfo calls work with the same structures as do GetInfo calls, but not all members of the structure are settable. The detailed descriptions of the APIs in Chapters 5 through 12 identify exactly which items can be set for each API.

The typical SetInfo call is of the following form:

```
unsigned far pascal NetObjectSetInfo(
    char far *servername,    /* server to execute code  */
    char far *key,           /* which instance?         */
    short level,             /* info structure level    */
    char far *buf,           /* buffer contains struct  */
    USHORT buflen,           /* size of buf             */
    USHORT parmnum           /* which parameter?        */
    );
```

The *servername*, *key*, and *level* arguments are exactly like those in GetInfo and Enum. The *buf* parameter holds the structure with the information to be set, and *buflen* is the total size of *buf*.

The *parmnum* argument provides a shorthand way of setting information. When *parmnum* is set to 0, *buf* must contain an entire information structure at the designated level. All settable members of the structure must contain their intended values. Usually this is accomplished with a GetInfo call and then a change of the appropriate parts. If only one member is to be changed, *parmnum* can be used to identify which parameter is changing, and the buffer contains only that item, not the whole structure. If the changed parameter is a number, the first two or four bytes of the structure contain the binary value (depending on whether the parameter is a short or long). If the changed parameter is variable-length data, the zero-terminated ASCII text is in the buffer. The detailed sections on each API identify which parameters can be set and what their parameter numbers are.

If the fixed-length portion of the structure contains pointers to variable-length data, the calling program provides storage for the information. If the SetInfo call is a remote call (that is, if the server name is not NULL), the underlying API packs all of the information (both the fixed and the variable portions) into a single buffer for transmission to the server. If *buf* is large enough to hold both variable and fixed information, the API does not have to go to OS/2 to allocate a buffer and is thus much more efficient. Variable-length data is copied into the buffer by the API. If a remote call to GetInfo was made and that buffer is being used for SetInfo, the variable-length data is already packed into the buffer, and this will be recognized by the API.

If one of the settable items is a variable-length item and the pointer is set to NULL, the item will not change. This follows the same principle used by GetInfo when no room exists for the data.

SET.C (Figure 4-4) is a code fragment that contains four important features: a SetInfo call changing the structure provided by GetInfo; a SetInfo call filling in the structure by hand with NULL pointers (showing that data is not to change); a SetInfo call changing one integer item by using a *parmnum* argument; and a SetInfo call changing one text item by using a *parmnum* argument.

```
/*
 * SET.C -- A program fragment demonstrating SetInfo calls.
 *
 */

struct share_info_2 *pshi2;

/* the GetInfo/SetInfo method */

err = NetShareGetInfo(
                "\\\\server",   /* remote server name    */
                "binp",         /* key for share         */
                2,              /* level 2 structure     */
                buf,            /* place for data        */
                SIZ,            /* make it "big enough"   */
                &ta);           /* total bytes available  */

pshi2 = (struct share_info_2 *)buf;
pshi2->shi2_maxuses = 1;
pshi2->shi2_remark = "one user at a time";
err = NetShareSetInfo(
                "\\\\server",   /* remote server name    */
                "binp",         /* key for share         */
                2,              /* level 2 structure     */
                buf,            /* place for data        */
                SIZ,            /* make it "big enough"   */
                0);             /* parmnum: use everything */

/* fill-in-the-blanks method */

pshi2 = (struct share_info_2 *)buf;
pshi2->shi2_maxuses = 1;
pshi2->shi2_remark = NULL;        /* keep old value */
err = NetShareSetInfo(
                "\\\\server",   /* remote server name    */
                "binp",         /* key for share         */
                2,              /* level 2 structure     */
```

Figure 4-4. *(continued)*

SET.C: a code fragment demonstrating NetShareGetInfo *calls.*

Figure 4-4. *continued*

```
                        buf,          /* place for data        */
                        SIZ,          /* make it "big enough"   */
                        0);           /* parmnum: use everything */

/* use parmnum to change a single integer item */

*(* USHORT) buf) = 2;                 /* only change maxuses    */
err = NetShareSetInfo(
                "\\\\server",  /* remote server name     */
                "binp",        /* key for share          */
                2,             /* level 2 structure      */
                buf,           /* place for data         */
                sizeof(USHORT),        /* extra unnecessary  */
                SHI_MAXUSES_PARMNUM);  /* change maxuses     */

/* use parmnum to change a single text item */

strcpy(buf, "two at a time allowed now");
err = NetShareSetInfo(
                "\\\\server",  /* remote server name     */
                "binp",        /* key for share          */
                2,             /* level 2 structure      */
                buf,           /* place for data         */
                strlen(buf)+1, /* extra size unnecessary */
                SHI_MAXUSES_REMARK);   /* change remark    */
```

The Add Verb

The Add verb creates a new instance of an object. Add calls work with the same structures as do GetInfo or SetInfo calls, but not all members of the structures are settable. The detailed descriptions of the APIs in Chapters 5 through 12 identify exactly which items can be set for each API.

The typical Add call is of the following form:

```
unsigned far pascal
NetObjectAdd(
    char far *servername,      /* server to execute code */
    short level,               /* info structure level   */
    char far *buf,             /* buffer contains struct  */
    USHORT buflen              /* size of buf            */
    );
```

The arguments buffer contains the information structure at the indicated level.

The Del Verb

The Del verb removes an instance of an object. The typical Del call is of the following form:

```
unsigned far pascal
NetObjectDel(
    char far *servername,     /* server to execute code  */
    char far *key             /* which instance?         */
    );
```

A Generic Enumeration Routine

How big a buffer should a program allocate when calling a LAN Manager enumeration API? If the buffer is too small, the enumeration routines return with incomplete information and the ERROR_MORE_DATA error code. Fortunately, they also return the total number of data structures available. Because most LAN Manager enumeration APIs have identical argument structures, you can easily create a generic enumeration routine that handles the necessary buffer management. NETENUM.C (Figure 4-5) is a subroutine that can be used wherever a standard enumeration API might be used.

The NetEnum API takes arguments that are different from those of the standard enumeration APIs:

- The *api* parameter is a pointer to the real enumeration routine.

- The *server* and *level* parameters are the same as those for the ordinary enumeration APIs.

- The *pbuff* parameter is a pointer to a pointer, and the buffer with the enumeration information is returned through it.

- The *buflen* parameter is a first guess of how big to make the buffer. The routine will use this first and then allocate a larger buffer if that fails.

- The *infosize* parameter must be set to the size of the appropriate _info structure.

- The *peread* parameter is the number of entries read, exactly as in the ordinary enumeration routine. There is no need for a *totalavail* parameter because all entries will have been read.

NetEnum allocates a buffer of size *buflen* and makes the appropriate call. If the buffer proves too small, NetEnum uses the returned information to reallocate the buffer. The size of the fixed portion is known, but the code must iterate to find the size of the variable-length portion. The heuristic used is to start with 20 bytes per entry and then double the number of bytes until the buffer is large enough. If the *DosReallocSeg* function call fails, an error is returned. When a program is finished with the enumeration buffer, it must free the memory by using the *DosFreeSeg* function. The program could also get buffer space by using the C language calls *malloc* and *realloc* and release the buffer by using *free*.

```
/* NETENUM.C  -- This generic enumeration routine returns the
 * results of the Net*Enum routine.  It requires the
 * following arguments:
 *
 *    api        A pointer to the real enumeration function
 *    server     A pointer to the server name value
 *    level      The info structure level
 *    pbuff      A pointer to the data (this value is returned)
 *    buflen     An initial guess of the buffer size
 *    infosize   The size of the info structure
 *    peread     The number of entries read (this value is returned)
 *
 * IMPORTANT: The caller MUST free the returned buffer with the
 * DosFreeSeg API.
 *
 */

#include <os2.h>
#include <neterr.h>

#define ISIZE 512

USHORT NetEnum(api, server, level, pbuff, buflen, infosize, peread)
    USHORT (far pascal *  api)(const char far *, short,
            char far *, unsigned short, USHORT far *,
            USHORT far *);
    char far * server;
    USHORT level;
    char far * far * pbuff;
    USHORT buflen;
    USHORT infosize;
    USHORT *peread;
    {
    USHORT err;
    USHORT avail;      /* total available structures */
    USHORT incsize;    /* buffer size increment      */
    SEL sel;           /* receives allocated selector */
```

Figure 4-5. *(continued)*
NETENUM.C: a generic enumeration routine.

Figure 4-5. *continued*

```
    if ((err = DosAllocSeg(buflen, &sel, 0)) != 0)
        return(err);

    /* os2def.h pointer from selector macro */
    *pbuff = (char far *)MAKEP(sel, 0);

    err = api(server, level, *pbuff, buflen, peread, &avail);
    buflen = infosize * avail;
    incsize = avail * ISIZE;
    while (err == ERROR_MORE_DATA)
        {
        buflen += incsize;
        incsize *= 2;
        if ((err = DosReallocSeg(buflen, sel)) != 0)
            return(err);
        err = api(server, level, *pbuff, buflen, peread, &avail);
        }
    /* this is 0 if API was called successfully */
    return(err);
    }
```

NetEnum makes use of the EXAMPLES.H include file (Figure 4-6). Be sure you have it somewhere on the INCLUDE path when you compile the routine. Keep EXAMPLES.H handy—you'll use it again later in the book.

```
/*
 * This header file contains function prototypes for the NetEnum
 * routine and other examples developed throughout the book.
 */

#include <stdio.h>
#define TRUE 1
#define FALSE 0

FILE *dpfopen(char *, char *, char *, unsigned);
FILE *cfgfopen(char *, char *, char *, char *);
FILE *srvfopen(char *, char *, char *);
char far * cname(char far *);

unsigned short
NetEnum(
    unsigned short  (pascal far *api)
        (const char far *,
        short,
```

Figure 4-6.
The EXAMPLES.H include file.

(continued)

Figure 4-6. *continued*

```
        char far *,
        unsigned short,
        unsigned short far *,
        unsigned short far *),
    char far *server,
    unsigned short level,
    char far * far *pbuff,
    unsigned short buflen,
    unsigned short infosize,
    unsigned short *peread
    );

#define MDPTR(fptr) ((char *)strcpy_f(alloca(strlen_f((char far *)fptr)),\
        (char far *)fptr))
```

The following code fragment shows a call to the NetEnum routine:

```
#define SH_SIZE sizeof(struct share_info_1);
err = NetEnum(NetShareEnum,    /* API to call         */
              NULL,            /* server name         */
              1,               /* level               */
              &pbuff,          /* ptr to buff ptr     */
              100,             /* initial size guess  */
              SH_SIZE,         /* info struct size    */
              &totale          /* total entries read  */
              );
/* other processing */
DosFreeSeg(SELECTOR_OF(pbuff));
```

This routine can be used whenever a program calls any of the Enum API functions that have the common six-element parameter list. These functions are as follows:

NetUserEnum   *NetServiceEnum*
NetGroupEnum   *NetShareEnum*
NetCharDevEnum   *NetSessionEnum*
NetMessageNameEnum   *DosPrintDestEnum*
NetBiosEnum   *DosPrintQEnum*
NetServerEnum   *NetUseEnum*
NetServerDiskEnum

A second generic routine can be created for the rest of the enumeration APIs. These routines all take an additional argument, a *char far *, as the second argument. This routine is called *NetEnumStr*. The interface is shown in the following code fragment. The code changes simply pass the additional argument to the API call.

```
USHORT NetEnumStr(api, server, string, level, pbuff, infosize, peread)
USHORT (far pascal *  api)(const char far *,
                          short,
                          char far *,
                          unsigned short,
                          USHORT far *,
                          USHORT far *);
char far * server;
char far * string;
USHORT level;
char far * far * pbuff;
USHORT buflen;
USHORT infosize;
USHORT *peread;
```

The following API functions can use *NetEnumStr*:

NetAccessEnum

NetCharDevQEnum

NetConnectionEnum

NetFileEnum

DosPrintJobEnum

NetUseEnum

NetGroupGetUsers

Computer Names

Many of the LAN Manager APIs return computer names without the leading
backslashes required as input to other APIs. The *cname* subroutine (Figure
4-7) can be used to ensure that a computer name has a leading backslash.

```
/*
 * cname -- Some LAN Manager APIs require a computer name with
 * leading backslashes as an argument, but some LAN Manager
 * data structures return computer names without the leading
 * backslashes.  This subroutine solves this problem by converting
 * one format to the other.  It returns a pointer to a static
 * buffer that contains a computer name with backslashes.
 *
 */

#include <netcons.h>
#include <string_f.h>  /* defined in Chapter 3 */
```

Figure 4-7.
The cname *subroutine.*

(continued)

Figure 4-7. *continued*

```
char far *
cname(cname)
char far *cname;
    {
    static char buf[CNLEN + 3] = "\\\\";

    if (strncmp_f(cname, "\\\\", 2) == 0)
        strcpy_f(buf+2, cname+2);
    else
        strcpy_f(buf+2, cname);
    return(buf);
    }
```

WORKSTATION APIs

This chapter examines the LAN Manager APIs that operate in and interact with the workstation environment:

- The Wksta APIs control the basic characteristics of the workstation.

- The Use APIs work with connections to server resources.

- The Message APIs allow a simple form of interworkstation data exchange.

- The Profile APIs allow programs to save and restore the LAN Manager environment.

- The Remote APIs allow user-level programs to carry out operations on remote servers.

Although many of these APIs can be called remotely, they are primarily used at the local workstation, under both MS-DOS and OS/2.

Most APIs require *admin* privilege at the server to run remotely. The Remote APIs, described at the end of this chapter, allow workstations without *admin* privilege a limited number of remote execution capabilities.

The Wksta APIs

The Wksta APIs control the basic configuration of the workstation or redirector. The one data structure is named *wksta_info_0*. Most of the information in this structure is set by the workstation when it is started and can be changed only if you stop and restart the workstation. The information is taken either from the [wksta] section of the LANMAN.INI file or from arguments to the net start wksta command.

Table 5-1 shows the members of the *wksta_info_0* structure.

Member Name	Description
USHORT wki0_reserved_1	Reserved for future use.
ULONG wki0_reserved_2	Reserved for future use.
char far * wki0_root	The pathname to the LAN Manager root directory. The LANMAN.INI file is in this directory.
char far * wki0_computer name	The unique computer name given to the workstation when it is started.
char far * wki0_username	The name of the user currently logged in at the workstation.

Table 5-1.
The wksta_info_0 *data structure.*   (continued)

Table 5-1. *continued*

Member Name	Description
char far * wki0_langroup	The default logon domain. The actual logon domain is stored in wki1_logon_domain in the *wksta-_info_1* structure.
UCHAR wki0_ver_major	The major version number of the LAN Manager software. Versions 1.0 and 1.1 have a value of 1. Version 2.0 has a value of 2.
UCHAR wki0_ver_minor	The minor version number of the LAN Manager software. Versions 1.0 and 2.0 have a value of 0. Version 1.1 has a value of 1.
ULONG wki0_reserved_3	Reserved for future use.
USHORT wki0_charwait	When a *DosOpen* call is issued to a serial communications device over the network, this value represents the maximum number of seconds the workstation will wait for the call to succeed.
ULONG wki0_chartime	After a remote serial communications device is opened, the characters are buffered at either end. This value represents the maximum number of milliseconds the workstation should wait before sending a buffer of characters.
USHORT wki0_charcount	Represents the maximum number of characters to save in the buffer before transmitting the buffer.
USHORT wki0_reserved_4	Reserved for future use.
USHORT wki0_reserved_5	Reserved for future use.
USHORT wki0_keepconn	When UNC connections are deleted, they are not immediately disconnected: They are placed in a dormant state on the assumption that they will be used again within a specified period of time. This value represents the number of seconds these connections should stay dormant before they are actually disconnected.
USHORT wki0_keepsearch	As a performance enhancement, the redirector keeps a cache of search records returned by redirected *DosFindFirst* and *DosFindNext* calls. This value represents the maximum age, in seconds, that a cached record can exist before a new record is obtained from the server.
USHORT wki0_maxthreads	For threads to have concurrent access to the network, the redirector must allocate data structures at system boot. This value is the number of these structures—and hence the number of concurrent network accesses—allowed.

(continued)

Table 5-1. *continued*

Member Name	Description
USHORT wki0_maxcmds	When network commands are sent to the NetBIOS, the redirector must have data structures to keep track of the operation until the NetBIOS completes. This value represents the number of simultaneous NetBIOS commands that can be outstanding at any one time.
USHORT wki0_reserved_6	Reserved for future use.
USHORT wki0_numworkbuf	The redirector keeps file and search data cached when possible. This value represents the number of such buffers the redirector allocates at system boot.
USHORT wki0_sizworkbuf	This value indicates the size of each redirector cache buffer.
USHORT wki0_maxwrkcache	The redirector has a special protocol to LAN Manager servers for large data transfers. This value indicates the buffer size used for these transfers.
USHORT wki0_sesstimeout	The redirector periodically sends a test message to the server—just to be sure that the sessions are still valid. If the server does not respond, this value represents the time in seconds to wait and continue trying before assuming the server is down and deleting the session.
USHORT wki0_sizerror	Errors in the redirector cannot be logged directly to the file system: They are stored in an internal buffer until the WKSTA.EXE program retrieves them. This value controls the size of that buffer.
USHORT wki0_numalerts	This value controls the number of clients that can receive alerts. Each semaphore or mailslot registered through *NetAlertStart* is considered a separate client. If the Alerter service is installed, it automatically uses three of the possible alerts.
USHORT wki0_numservices	This value controls the maximum number of LAN Manager service programs that can be installed simultaneously.
USHORT wki0_errlogsz	This value indicates the maximum file size of the error log.
USHORT wki0_printbuftime	Many MS-DOS programs do not close the print spool file when printing is done over the network. This value is the time in seconds to wait before assuming that an inactive print spool file operation is complete. This affects print spooling only from DOS compatibility mode or under MS-DOS.

(continued)

Table 5-1. *continued*

Member Name	Description
USHORT wki0_numcharbuf	This value controls the number of named-pipe and serial communications device character buffers. It represents the number of pipe and character device operations that can occur simultaneously.
USHORT wki0_sizcharbuf	This value controls the size of named-pipe and serial communications device character buffers.
char far * wki0_logon_server	This controls the nature of logon service at the workstation. A NULL string means local logon; a server name means to use that server for centralized logon; the string "*" means to use any logon service that will respond.
char far * wki0_wrkheuristics	This value controls the performance heuristics of the redirector. See the *LAN Manager Programmer's Reference* for a description of the specifics.
USHORT wki0_mailslots	This value represents the number of second-class mailslots that can exist simultaneously at the workstation.

The *wksta_info_1* structure is the same as that of *wksta_info_0* but has the additional members shown in Table 5-2.

Member Name	Description
char far * wki1_logon_domain	A pointer to a text string with the name of the workstation's logon domain. The value is NULL if no one is logged on.
char far * wki1_oth_domains	A pointer to a list of other domains that the workstation is currently browsing. The domains are space delimited and the list is zero terminated.
USHORT wki1_numdgrambuf	The number of buffers allocated for receiving datagrams.

Table 5-2.
The wksta_info_1 *data structure.*

Although only admin-level users can use *wksta_info_0* and *wksta_info_1* structures remotely, the *wksta_info_10* structure can be used by user-level and guest-level accounts to get workstation information about a server. The members of the *wksta_info_10* structure are shown in Table 5-3.

Member Name	Description
char far * wki10_computer name	The unique computer name given to the workstation when it is started.
char far * wki10_username	The name of the user currently logged on to the workstation.
char far * wki10_langroup	The default logon domain. The actual logon domain is stored in wki10_logon_domain.
UCHAR wki10_ver_major	The major version number of the LAN Manager software. Versions 1.0 and 1.1 have a value of 1, and version 2.0 has a value of 2.
UCHAR wki10_ver_minor	The minor version number of the LAN Manager software. Versions 1.0 and 2.0 have a value of 0. Version 1.1 has a value of 1.
char far * wki10_logon_domain	A pointer to a text string with the name of the workstation's logon domain. The value is NULL if no one is logged on.
char far * wki10_oth_domains	A pointer to a list of other domains that the workstation is currently browsing. The domains are space delimited and the list is zero terminated. An empty list ("") means no other domains. For *NetWkstaSetInfo*, a NULL pointer means to leave it unchanged.

Table 5-3.
The wksta_info_10 *data structure.*

Four Wksta APIs are available to applications programs: *WkstaGetInfo*, *Net-WkstaSetInfo*, *NetWkstaSetUID*, and *NetWkstaSetUID2*. To use these APIs in a program, you must include NETCONS.H and WKSTA.H at compile time, and you must link with the NETAPI.LIB library.

NetWkstaGetInfo

Returns information about the workstation.

```
unsigned far pascal
NetWkstaGetInfo(
    char far *server,        /* where to execute    */
    USHORT level,            /* level of detail     */
    char far *buf,           /* where to return data */
    USHORT buflen,           /* size of buf         */
    USHORT far *ta           /* total bytes available */
    )
```

Levels:
Supports level 0, 1, and 10 data structures.

Local access:

The workstation must be started.

The user must be logged on.

Remote access:

Level 0 or 1 can be called by an administrator.

Level 10 can be called by any user.

Because there is only one instance of the object (the local workstation), no key argument is necessary. This also explains the absence of the Enum API.

Error returns:

If successful, *NetWkstaGetInfo* returns 0. If unsuccessful, it returns the standard GetInfo error codes or one of the following error codes:

Error Return	Meaning
NERR_WkstaNotStarted	The workstation service has not been started.
NERR_NotLoggedOn	No user is logged on.

An overview:

The *NetWkstaGetInfo* API returns information about the local workstation.

The LMFILE.C program (Figure 5-1) uses *NetWkstaGetInfo* to build a filename relative to the LAN Manager root. Note the use of the *str∗_f* routines defined in Chapter 3. This makes the *LMfile* subroutine useful under any memory model.

```
/*
 * LMFILE.C -- This subroutine takes a pathname relative to
 * the LAN Manager root and builds a fully qualified pathname.
 * If the user-supplied buffer is not large enough, an error
 * is returned.
 *
 */

#include <stdio.h>
#include <netcons.h>
#include <wksta.h>
#include <neterr.h>
#include <string_f.h>   /* defined in chapter 3 */
```

Figure 5-1.
The LMFILE.C program.

(continued)

Figure 5-1. *continued*

```
int LMfile(name, buf, buflen)
char *name;          /* relative pathname */
char *buf;           /* where to build fully qualified name */
unsigned buflen;     /* size of buf */


{
char wkbuf[BUFSIZ];

/* get workstation data */
err = NetWkstaGetInfo(NULL, 0, wkbuf, BUFSIZ, &ta);
if (!err)
    {
    /* is buf large enough? */
    if (strlen_f(pw->wki0_root) + strlen(name) + 2 > buflen)
        err = NERR_BufTooSmall;
    else
        {
        /* build fully qualified filename */
        strcpy_f(buf, pw->wki0_root);
        strcat(buf, "\\");
        strcat(buf, name);
        }
    }
return(err);
}
```

NetWkstaSetInfo

Configures a workstation.

```
unsigned far pascal
NetWkstaSetInfo(
    char far *servername,    /* where to execute        */
    USHORT level,            /* level of detail         */
    char far *buf,           /* buffer with wksta data  */
    USHORT buflen,           /* size of buf             */
    USHORT parmnum           /* which parameter to set  */
    )
```

Levels:
Supports level 0 and 1 data structures.

Local access:
The workstation must be started.

The user must be logged on.

Remote access:

Only an administrator can call *NetWkstaSetInfo* remotely.

Because there is only one instance of the object (the local workstation), no key argument is necessary.

If *parmnum* is 0, the buffer holds a *wksta_info_1* structure. The following data items (shown with their corresponding parameters) can be set:

Name	Value	Parameter
wki1_charwait	10	WKSTA_CHARWAIT_PARMNUM
wki1_chartime	11	WKSTA_CHARTIME_PARMNUM
wki1_charcount	12	WKSTA_CHARCOUNT_PARMNUM
wki1_errlogsz	27	WKSTA_ERRLOGSZ_PARMNUM
wki1_printbuftime	28	WKSTA_PRINTBUFTIME_PARMNUM
wki1_wrkheuristics	32	WKSTA_WRKHEURISTICS_PARMNUM
wki1_othdomains	35	WKSTA_OTHDOMAINS_PARMNUM

Error returns:

If successful, *NetWkstaSetInfo* returns 0. If unsuccessful, it returns the standard SetInfo error codes or one of the following error codes:

Error Return	Meaning
NERR_WkstaNotStarted	The workstation service has not been started.
NERR_NotLoggedOn	No user is logged on.

An overview:

The *NetWkstaSetInfo* API modifies the LAN Manager parameters that are currently active. This API does not change the LANMAN.INI file. Restarting the workstation resets any parameters set by this function.

NetWkstaSetUID

Logs a user on to the network.

```
unsigned far pascal
NetWkstaSetUID(
    char far *servername,   /* where to execute              */
    char far *username,     /* username to log on            */
    char far *password,     /* user's password               */
    char far *parms,        /* optional parameter string     */
    USHORT ucond            /* condition flag                */
    )
```

Local access:

The workstation must be started.

Remote access:

Only an administrator can call *NetWkstaSetUID* remotely.

An overview:

The *NetWkstaSetUID* API logs a user on to the network. Optional parameters can be included with the *parms* parameter.

> **NOTE:** *This API is obsolete and exists only for compatibility with version 1.0 of LAN Manager. Use* NetWkstaSetUID2 *if you are using LAN Manager version 2.0 or later.*

NetWkstaSetUID2

Logs a user onto the network in the specified domain.

```
unsigned far pascal
NetWkstaSetUID2(
     char far *reserved,     /* must be NULL             */
     char far *domainname,   /* which domain to log on to */
     char far *username,     /* username to log on       */
     char far *password,     /* user's password          */
     char far *parms,        /* optional parameter string */
     USHORT ucond,           /* condition flag           */
     USHORT level,           /* must be 1                */
     char far *buf,          /* where to return data     */
     USHORT buflen,          /* size of buf              */
     USHORT far *totalavail  /* total bytes available    */
     )
```

Levels:

Supports level 1 data structures.

Local access:

The workstation must be started.

Remote access:

Remote access is not allowed.

Error returns:

If successful, *NetWkstaSetUID2* returns 0. If unsuccessful, it returns the standard API error return codes or one of the following error codes:

Error Return	Meaning
NERR_ActiveConns	The *ucond* parameter is set too low. (Note that increasing the *ucond* value is a dangerous practice that requires great care.)
NERR_UnableToAddName_F	The username was not added as a message name. This is an error; logon was unsuccessful.
NERR_UnableToAddName_W	The message name could not be added. This is only a warning; logon was successful. (This message appears when the username is already in use at another workstation.)
NERR_LogonScriptError	During the network logon to the domain, a user script was executed, and an error occurred. This is only a warning; logon was successful.
NERR_LogonServerNotFound	The workstation was configured for centralized logon, and the logon failed. This is usually because there is no account for the username at the logon server or because the logon server does not exist.
ERROR_ACCESS_DENIED	Permission to log on to the network was denied.

An overview:

The *NetWkstaSetUID2* API is used to log on a username and a password to a specified domain. The internal workings of this call are often customized by LAN Manager vendors, but the API remains the same. In the uncustomized version, *NetWkstaSetUID2* communicates with one of the servers in the logon domain, validates the username and the password, adds the username as a message name by using the *NetMessageNameAdd* API, and possibly executes a logon script kept at the logon server.

username specifies the name to log on with. If this name is NULL, it means to log off the network.

domainname is an ASCII text string with the name of a domain that is to be used for network logon validation. If *domainname* is NULL, the default domain is used. This name is taken from the *langroup* parameter in the [wksta] section of the LANMAN.INI file or from the /DOMAIN: switch used when the workstation is started. The default domain can be seen as *wki0_langroup* from a *NetWkstaGetInfo* call.

password is an ASCII text string that becomes the workstation's default password, used whenever connections are made without an explicit password. If no password is intended, the argument must be a NULL string (" "). The meaning of a NULL pointer can be customized by vendors.

parms is an optional ASCII text string whose meanings can be customized by vendors. Unless your version of LAN Manager has a specific set of meanings for *parms*, you should set it to NULL.

ucond determines what happens if a user is already logged on to the workstation. If the current user has any connections established, they must be deleted before a new username can be logged on. This prevents the new user from "camping onto" the permissions of the previous user. Table 5-4 lists the possible values of the *ucond* parameter. *ucond* values above 0 must be used with great care.

Value	Meaning
0	If active connections exist, *NetWkstaSetUID2* fails. Otherwise, dormant connections are deleted, and logon proceeds. See the section "The Use APIs" later in this chapter for a description of dormant connections.
1	If any connections are made to the current drive for any process (including CMD.EXE for a screen group), or if any connections have open files, *NetWkstaSetUID2* fails. Otherwise, all connections are deleted, and the call proceeds.
2	If any connections are made to the current drive for any process, *NetWkstaSetUID2* fails. Otherwise, any open files are closed, all connections are deleted, and the call proceeds.
3	Forces all disconnections. This always succeeds.

Table 5-4.
Valid values for the ucond *parameter.*

buf is a buffer containing return data. If the call was made for logging on, *buf* contains the *user_logon_info_1* structure. If the call was made for logging off, *buf* contains the *user_logoff_info_1* structure. Table 5-5 describes the contents of the *user_logon_info_1* structure.

Member Name	Description		
USHORT usrlog1_code	A user code described in the next section.		
char usrlog1_eff_name	The name of the account the user was logged on to. In LAN Manager 2.0, it is the same as the username.		
USHORT usrlog1_priv	The user's privilege level. The values are as follows:		
	Privilege	*Value*	*Meaning*
	USER_PRIV_GUEST	0	A guest account
	USER_PRIV_USER	1	A user account
	USER_PRIV_ADMIN	2	An administrator account

Table 5-5.
The user_logon_info_1 *data structure.*

(continued)

Table 5-5. *continued*

Member Name	Description
ULONG usrlog1 _auth_flags	A set of bits indicating the operator privilege of the account. The values are as follows:

Bitmask	Value	Meaning
AF_OP_PRINT	0x1	Print operator
AF_OP_COMM	0x2	Comm operator
AF_OP_SERVER	0x4	Server operator
AF_OP_ACCOUNTS	0x8	Account operator

Member Name	Description
USHORT usrlog1 _num_logons	Number of logons for this username.
USHORT usrlog1 _bad_pw_count	Number of bad password attempts since last logon.
ULONG usrlog1 _last_logon	The time of the most recent logon.
ULONG usrlog1 _last_logoff	The time of the most recent logoff.
ULONG usrlog1 _logoff_time	The time when this logon is expected to log off. A value of 0xFFFFFFFF means no logoff is required.
ULONG usrlog1 _kickoff_time	The time when the system will force the logoff. A value of 0xFFFFFFFF means never.
long usrlog1 _password_age	The time in seconds since the password was last changed.
ULONG usrlog1 _pw_can_change	The time when the user is allowed to change the password. A value of 0xFFFFFFFF means that the password can never be changed.
ULONG usrlog1 _pw_must_change	The time when the user must change the password. A value of 0xFFFFFFFF means that no change is required.
char far * usrlog1 _computer	The computer name of the server that logged the user on to the domain.
char far * usrlog1 _domain	The domain that the user logged on to.
char far * usrlog1 _script_path	Pathname to the logon script for the user. The path is relative to the NETLOGON$ share at the logon server.
ULONG usrlog1 _reserved1	Reserved for future use.

The value in *usrlog1_code* is more information about the return value from *NetWkstaSetUID2* in the case of logon. This also determines which of the values in the returned *usr_logon_info_1* structure are valid. Table 5-6 lists the possible values for *userlog1_code*.

WkstaSetUID Return	usrlog1 _code *value*	Meaning
NERR_Success *or* NERR_UnableToAddName_W	NERR_Success	The network logon was successful, and all values in the structure are valid.
	NERR_StandaloneLogon	No domain controller was found, but the workstation was configured to allow logon anyway. None of the values in the returned structure are valid.

Table 5-6.
Values in the usrlog1 _code *field.*

(continued)

Table 5-6. *continued*

WkstaSetUID Return	**usrlog1_code** *value*	*Meaning*
	NERR_NonValidatedLogon	The logon was processed by a LAN Manager 1.x server. The computer name and the *script_path* are valid, and script processing was completed as part of the logon.
ERROR_ACCESS_DENIED	NERR_PasswordExpired	The user has an account, but the password has expired. None of the structure values are valid.
	NERR_InvalidWorkstation	The user tried to log on from a workstation other than the ones for which the account is configured. None of the structure values are valid.
	NERR_InvalidLogonHours	The time is outside the range for which logon is allowed on this account. None of the structure values are valid.
	NERR_LogonScriptError	An error occurred during processing of the logon script. None of the structure values are valid.
	ERROR_ACCESS_DENIED	No account exists, the account has expired, the account is disabled, or the password does not match. None of the structure values are valid.

For any other *NetWkstaSetUID* return values, the entire structure—including *usrlogl_code*—has no meaning.

If *username* was NULL, network logoff was attempted. *buf* returns the *usr_logoff_infol* structure, which has the following members:

Member Name	*Description*
USHORT usrlogf1_code	Described below.
ULONG usrlogf1_duration	The time in seconds that the user was logged on. The value 0xFFFFFFFF means unknown.
USHORT usrlogf1_num_logons	The number of other logons by this username. The value 0xFFFF means unknown.

The values in *usrlogfl_code* provide more information about the *NetWkstaSetUID2* return code and indicate which parts of the *user_logoff_info-l* structure are valid.

WkstaSetUID Return	usrlog1_code value	Meaning
NERR_Success *or* NERR_UnableToAddName_W	NERR_Success	The network logon was successful, and all values in the structure are valid.
	NERR_StandaloneLogon	No domain controller was found. None of the values in the returned structure are valid.
	NERR_NonValidatedLogon	The logon was processed by a LAN Manager 1.x server. None of the structure values are valid.

The Use APIs

The Use APIs let you add and delete connections to server resources. You can establish connections explicitly by using the *NetUseAdd* API or implicitly by accessing a server resource through its UNC name. Explicit connections usually have a workstation device name associated with the connection; for example, the redirected device name x: for a remote directory or LPT7: for a remote print queue. The redirector software makes implicit connections in the workstation whenever a UNC-style access occurs; for example, the command *type \\server\public\file.txt*. In either case, the workstation must establish a connection to the server resource.

Implicit Connections

Implicit connections always use the default password. If the server is running share-mode security and requires a password, the implicit connection fails if the default password does not match. Similarly, if the server is running user-mode security and this is the first connection, the server logon process (session establishment) requires a username and a password. If the default values are not correct, the implicit connection fails.

To maximize efficiency (and minimize server communication), implicit connections are not deleted upon completion. Instead, the redirector notes a completed connection as *dormant* and keeps it available for reuse:

- If the application needs the connection again, the connection is marked as active and no communication to the server is necessary.

- If the workstation needs the connection (the number available is limited), the oldest dormant connection can be deleted.

- If the connection remains dormant for a certain number of seconds, it is deleted by the redirector. You specify the number of seconds with the *keepconn* parameter in the LANMAN.INI file. (This parameter is also available in the *wksta_info_0* structure.)

Automatic Reconnection

If a connection is lost at the server end—perhaps through a server reboot—attempts to use the connection at the workstation fail. However, the redirector does not quit with the first failure: It tries to reestablish the connection. This means that if a server has been rebooted, the users rarely need know it. The workstations reconnect as each connection is needed.

There are four LAN Manager Use APIs to choose from: *NetUseAdd*, *NetUseDel*, *NetUseEnum*, and *NetUseGetInfo*. To use these APIs in a program, you must include NETCONS.H and USE.H at compile time, and you must link with the NETAPI.LIB library. Two levels of information structures are available for these functions: *use_info_0* and *use_info_1*.

The *use_info_0* structure contains the following members:

Member Name	Description
char ui0_local[DEVLEN+1]	The local device name, such as X: or LPT7:. This is a NULL string for a deviceless connection.
char far * ui0_remote	The remote resource netname, such as \\apps\public.

The *use_info_1* structure contains the following members:

Member Name	Description		
char ui1_local[DEVLEN+1]	The local device name, such as X: or LPT7:. This is a NULL string for a deviceless connection.		
char far * ui1_remote	The remote resource netname, such as \\apps\public.		
char far *ui1_password	If not a NULL string, this password is given to the server. See *NetUseAdd* for details.		
USHORT ui1_status	The status of an existing connection. The values are as follows:		
	Status	*Value*	*Meaning*
	USE_OK	0	The established connection is OK.
	USE_PAUSED	1	The connection is paused. Print queue and serial device connections can be paused. Device names revert to their local meaning while paused.

(continued)

Member Name	Description		
	Status	*Value*	*Meaning*
	USE_DISCONN	2	The connection has been dropped by the server.
	USE_SESSLOST	2	A synonym for USE_DISCONN.
	USE_NETERR	3	The connection is in an error state.
	USE_CONN	4	The connection is in the process of being established. This state usually lasts for only a few milliseconds before the status is OK.
	USE_RECONN	5	The connection is in the process of automatic reconnection. This is also a transitory state.
short ui1_asg_type	Specifies the type of server resource being accessed. The values are as follows:		
	Status	*Value*	*Meaning*
	USE_DISKDEV	0	The resource is a directory in the server file system.
	USE_SPOOLDEV	1	The resource is a print queue.
	USE_CHARDEV	2	The resource is a serial communications device.
	USE_IPC	3	The resource is a named pipe or a mailslot.
	USE_WILDCARD	−1	The resource type is unspecified. See *NetUseAdd* for details.
USHORT ui1_refcount	The reference count is the number of open files or open search buffers on the connection.		
USHORT ui1_usecount	The total number of connections, both implicit and explicit, to the server resource. (More than one is permitted.) Note that dormant connections have a *usecount* of 0.		

NetUseAdd

Establishes a connection between a workstation and a server.

```
unsigned far pascal
NetUseAdd(
    char far *server,      /* where to execute       */
    USHORT level,          /* must be 1              */
    char far *buf,         /* a use_info_1 structure */
    USHORT buflen          /* size of buf            */
    )
```

Levels:
Supports level 1 data structures.

Local access:

The workstation must be started.

The user must be logged on.

Remote access:

Only an administrator can call this remotely.

Error returns:

If successful, *NetUseAdd* returns 0. If unsuccessful, it returns one of the standard Add error codes or one of the following error codes:

Error Return	Meaning
ERROR_BAD_NET_NAME	The *uil_remote* name does not exist.
ERROR_ALREADY_ASSIGNED	The *uil_local* device name is already in use by an existing connection.
ERROR_BAD_DEV_TYPE	The *uil_asg_type* does not match the type of the shared resource at the server.
NERR_BadAsgType	The *uil_asg_type* is not a legal value.
NERR_LocalDrive	The *uil_local* device name is that of a local disk drive.
ERROR_REQ_NOT_ACCEPTED	The user limit on the share has been exceeded.

An overview:

The *NetUseAdd* API adds a connection from the workstation to a server resource. If called remotely, the connection is added from server to server and does not affect the connections on the local workstation.

buf must contain a *use_info_1* structure. The *uil_local* pointer can be to a device name, or to a NULL string if deviceless connection is being made. *uil_remotename* must be a valid server resource netname. *uil_status*, *uil_refcount*, and *uil_usecount* members are ignored. The following sections describe different connections the *NetUseAdd* API can create.

Connections and Devices

Connections to the same server resource can be added more than once, but device names cannot be reused. Thus you can have connections to \\server\name from X: and Y: and from a deviceless connection as well. Each time a connection is added to the same server resource, the *uil_usecount* structure component is incremented.

At the workstation, local device names of the form LPT*x* and COM*x* represent logical devices that correspond to printers and serial communications devices. A server can share spooled printer queues, and it can share serial communications devices. With *NetUseAdd*, LPT*x* and COM*x* can each be connected to either type of server resource. COM7 or LPT4 can be the local name of a remote spooled printer queue, just as LPT5 or COM3 can be the local name of a remote serial communications device.

The *uil_asg_type* structure component lets you indicate the type of connection to be made. If the connection has a local device name, the following rules apply to *uil_asg_type*:

- If the local name is a disk drive, *uil_asg_type* must be USE-_DISKDEV.

- If the local name is an LPT*x* or a COM*x* name, *uil_asg_type* can be either USE_SPOOLDEV or USE_CHARDEV. *uil_asg_type* must match the type of the share at the server.

Deviceless Connections

Connections called *deviceless connections* can be made to server shares that have no local workstation device name. Under MS-NET, no connections were ever made automatically. In order to allow UNC-style access to server resources, explicit connections could be made, but with no device name. These deviceless connections are also allowed under the LAN Manager *NetUseAdd* API. The most common use allows UNC filename access on connections that require a password other than the default password.

If the connection is a deviceless connection, *uil_asg_type* can be USE_DISKDEV, USE_SPOOLDEV, or USE_CHARDEV as long as it matches the type of the resource at the server; or *uil_asg_type* can be USE-_WILDCARD. This will match the type of the server resource. USE_WILD-CARD can be used only for deviceless connections.

A special case

There is one special case of a deviceless connection. Each server has a resource named IPC$. Workstations must connect to this resource in order to practice interprocess communication (use named pipes and mailslots) across the network. Ordinarily an application will try a UNC-style access to a named pipe or mailslot, creating the IPC$ connection automatically. It is also possible to call *NetUseAdd* with the *uil_remote* structure component name having the form *servername*\IPC$ and *uil_asg_type* set to USE_IPC.

Passwords and Connections

One of the components of the *use_info_1* structure processed by *NetUseAdd* is *uil_password*. It is interpreted as follows:

- A NULL pointer means to use the default logon password.

- A NULL string means that there is no password.

- Any other value must be a pointer to the text string to be used as the password.

If the server is running share-mode security (or is an MS-NET–level server), the password is checked against any password on the shared server resource.

If the server is running user-mode security, the password applies only to session establishment. If the connection is the first that the workstation has made to a particular server, the redirector logs on to the server and establishes a session before adding the connection. During session establishment, the server ensures the existence of a valid user account for the username and the password.

NetUseDel

Terminates a connection to a server resource.

```
unsigned far pascal
NetUseDel(
    char far * servername,    /* where to execute        */
    char far * usename,       /* connection to be deleted */
    USHORT ucond              /* disconnection force      */
    )
```

Local access:

The workstation must be started.

The user must be logged on.

Remote access:

Only an administrator can call this remotely.

Error returns:

If successful, *NetUseDel* returns 0. If unsuccessful, it returns the standard Del return codes or one of the error codes shown on the following page.

Error Return	Meaning
ERROR_INVALID_DRIVE	The *usename* parameter is a drive name that is not associated with a connection.
NERR_UseNotFound	Either the *usename* parameter is not recognized or the connection has a device name.
NERR_DevInUse	The drive is active as the current drive for some process.
NERR_OpenFiles	There is an open file on the connection and the *ucond* force level was not high enough.

An overview:

The *NetUseDel* API lets you delete connections to server resources. When successful, the connection is dropped at both ends. When the last connection to a particular server is deleted, the session is also deleted. Note that if called remotely, the connection deleted is from server to server and does not affect connections to the local workstation.

The *usename* parameter points to a text string that indicates which connection to delete. If a device name is associated with the connection, this string must be the device name. If it is a deviceless connection, this string must be the remote resource name.

The *ucond* parameter determines what happens when there are multiple connections to the same resource or when there are open files on the connection. If *usename* is a device name, the following are valid values for *ucond*:

ucond	Value	Meaning
USE_NOFORCE	0	Fail if open files exist on the connection.
USE_FORCE	1	Fail if open files exist on the connection.
USE_LOTS_OF_FORCE	2	Close any open files and delete the connection.

If *usename* is a deviceless connection name, the following are valid values for *ucond*:

ucond	Value	Meaning
USE_NOFORCE	0	Fail if open files exist on the connection.
USE_FORCE	1	Fail if open files exist on the connection. If connections with device names are also present, the use count is decremented by one. If only deviceless connections are present, all are deleted.

(continued)

continued

ucond	Value	Meaning
USE_LOTS_OF_FORCE	2	Close any open files. If connections with device names are present, the use count is decremented by one. If only deviceless connections are present, all are deleted.

The *NetUseDel* API never succeeds if the device name is the current device of any process or screen group.

NetUseEnum

Lists current connections between workstation and servers.

```
unsigned far pascal
NetUseEnum(
    char far * servername,   /* where to execute      */
    short level,             /* information level     */
    char far * buf,          /* space for return data */
    unsigned short buflen,   /* size of buf           */
    USHORT far * entriesread, /* number of entries read */
    USHORT far * totalentries /* total entries available */
    )
```

Levels:
Supports level 0 and 1 data structures.

Local access:
The workstation must be started.

The user must be logged on.

Remote access:
Only an administrator can call this remotely.

An overview:
The *NetUseEnum* API returns information about connections between workstations and server resources. This is a regular Enum call, as described in Chapter 4. It can be called remotely but requires *admin* privilege at the server. Note that when *NetUseEnum* is called remotely, it returns information about connections the workstation portion of the server has to other servers.

For security reasons, the password entry of a *use_info_1* structure is always a NULL string.

Error returns:

If successful, *NetUseEnum* returns 0. If unsuccessful, it returns one of the standard Enum error codes.

USEENUM.C (Figure 5-2) is a sample program that displays the highest level of detail about the connections at your workstation.

```
/*
 * USEENUM.C -- A program that displays information about the
 * connections at your workstation.
 *
 * Compile with:  C> cl useenum.c netapi.lib
 *
 */

#include <stdio.h>
#include <netcons.h>
#include <use.h>

main(argc, argv)
int argc;
char **argv;

{
    char buf[BUFSIZ], dir[PATHLEN+1], netname[RMLEN+1], *p;
    unsigned short er, te, err;
    struct use_info_1 use, *pu = (struct use_info_1 *)buf;
    char * status();
    char * asg();

    if ((err = NetUseEnum(NULL, 1, buf, BUFSIZ, &er, &te)) != 0)
        {
        printf("Cannot list existing uses: %d\n", err);
        exit(1);
        }
    while (er)
        {
        printf("remote name = %s\n", pu->uil_remote);
        printf("       local name = %s\n", pu->uil_local);
        printf("       status = %s\n", status(pu->uil_status));
        printf("       assign type = %s\n", asg(pu->uil_asg_type));
        printf("       ref count = %d\n", pu->uil_refcount);
        printf("       use count = %d\n", pu->uil_usecount);
```

Figure 5-2.
The USEENUM.C program.

(continued)

CHAPTER FIVE: WORKSTATION APIs   115

Figure 5-2. *continued*

```
            ++pu;
            --er;
            }
    exit(0);
}
char *status(stat)
int stat;
    {
    switch (stat)
        {
        case USE_OK:
            return("OK");
        case USE_PAUSED:
            return("PAUSED");
        case USE_DISCONN:
            return("DISCONNECTED");
        case USE_NETERR:
            return("ERROR");
        case USE_CONN:
            return("CONNECTING");
        case USE_RECONN:
            return("RECONNECTING");
        default:
            return("????");
        }
    }

char *asg(type)
int type;
    {
    switch(type)
        {
        case USE_WILDCARD:
            return("WILDCARD");
        case USE_DISKDEV:
            return("DISK");
        case USE_SPOOLDEV:
            return("PRINTER");
        case USE_CHARDEV:
            return("SERIAL");
        case USE_IPC:
            return("IPC");
        }
    }
```

NetUseGetInfo

Retrieves information about a connection to a shared resource.

```
unsigned far pascal
NetUseGetInfo(
    char far *server,       /* where to execute      */
    char far *usename,      /* local or remote name  */
    USHORT level,           /* level of detail       */
    char far *buf,          /* where to return data  */
    USHORT buflen,          /* size of buf           */
    USHORT far *ta          /* total bytes available */
    )
```

Levels:

Supports level 0 and 1 data structures.

Local access:

The workstation must be started.

The user must be logged on.

Remote access:

Only an administrator can call this remotely.

Error returns:

If successful, *NetUseGetInfo* returns 0. If unsuccessful, it returns one of the standard GetInfo return codes or the following error code:

Error Return	Meaning
NERR_UseNotFound	The requested use does not exist.

An overview:

The *NetUseGetInfo* API takes as a key either a local name (such as X:) or a remote name (such as \\apps\public). It returns either a *use_info_0* or a *use_info_1* structure if the connection exists.

For security reasons, the password entry of a *use_info_1* structure is always a NULL string.

An Example of the Use APIs

The NETCDX.C program (Figure 5-3) demonstrates use of the *NetUseEnum* and *NetUseAdd* functions in a network environment. NETCDX establishes a network connection and changes to the requested directory in the same step.

Because directories are an attribute of a process in OS/2, NETCDX must be called from a batch file to have a permanent effect. NETCD.CMD (Figure 5-4) shows how this can be done from a batch file. NETCDX.EXE receives the command line parameters from NETCD.CMD and writes commands to standard output (stdout), which are redirected to NETCDY.CMD to carry out the actual directory change.

NOTE: *This batch-calling technique is not necessary in MS-DOS— NETCDX can be used directly.*

A sample call to NETCD is as follows. If the call is successful, the new current directory will be \ *ralph\lanfiles* on the *apps\public* server.

```
netcd \\apps\public\ralph\lanfiles
```

```
/*
 * NETCDX.C
 *
 * This program establishes a redirected drive to the UNC-style
 * pathname supplied by the NETCD.CMD batch file and then generates
 * a batch command to change the directory.
 *
 * Compile with:  C> cl netcdx.c netapi.lib string_f.lib
 *
 * Usage:  Call this program from the NETCD.CMD batch file.
 * NETCD.CMD requires the following command line:
 *
 * C> netcd UNC_pathname [password]
 *
 */

#include <stdio.h>
#include <string.h>
#include <string_f.h>  /* defined in Chapter 3 */
#include <os2.h>
#include <netcons.h>
#include <use.h>

main(argc, argv)
int argc;
char **argv;
    {
    int i;
    char far *passwd = NULL;
    char buf[BUFSIZ], dir[PATHLEN+1], netname[RMLEN+1], *p;
```

Figure 5-3.
The NETCDX.C program.

(continued)

Figure 5-3. *continued*

```
unsigned short er, te, err, attr, curd;
unsigned long diskmap, mask;
struct use_info_1 use, *pu = (struct use_info_1 *)buf;

printf("@echo off\n");
/* argument checks */
if (argc != 2  && argc != 3)
    error("NETCD UNC-pathname [password]\n", NULL);
if (argc == 3)
    passwd = argv[2];

/* establish that the user has access to the UNC pathname */
if (DosQFileMode(argv[1], &attr, OL) != 0 !! (attr &
        FILE_DIRECTORY) == 0)
    error("Cannot access directory %s\n", argv[1]);

/* make sure it is a UNC name and parse out netname portion */
if (strncmp(argv[1], "\\\\", 2) != 0 !!
        (p = strchr(argv[1]+2, '\\')) == NULL)
    error("\"%s\" is not a UNC name\n", argv[1]);
if ((p = strchr(p+1, '\\')) != NULL)
    {
    strcpy(dir, p);
    *p = 0;
    }
else
    dir[0] = 0;
strcpy(netname, argv[1]);

/* is there already a redirected drive to it ? */
if ((err = NetUseEnum(NULL, 1, buf, BUFSIZ, &er, &te)) != 0)
    error("Cannot list existing uses: %d\n", err);
while (er)
    {
    /* names match and it is not a UNC use */
    if (stricmp_f(pu->ui1_remote, netname) == 0 &&
        pu->ui1_local [0] != 0)
        break;
    ++pu;
    --er;
    }
if (er)
    {
    /* redirected drive already exists; generate commands */
    printf("%s\n", pu->ui1_local);
    if (dir[0])                            .
```

(continued)

Figure 5-3. *continued*

```
            printf("cd %s\n", dir);
        }
    else
        {
        /* get the next available drive name (skip A and B) */
        DosQCurDisk(&curd, &diskmap);
        for (i = 2, mask = (1 << 2); i < 26; ++i, mask <<= 1)
            {
            if ((diskmap & mask) == 0)
                break;
            }
        if (i == 26)
            error("No logical drives available\n", NULL);

        /* add the use */
        sprintf(use.ui1_local, "%c:", i + 'A');
        use.ui1_remote = netname;
        use.ui1_password = passwd;
        use.ui1_asg_type = USE_DISKDEV;
        pu = &use;
        if ((err = NetUseAdd(NULL, 1, &use, sizeof(use))) != 0)
            error("Cannot add use: %d\n", err);
        /* generate commands */
        printf("%s\n", pu->ui1_local);
        if (dir[0])
            printf("cd %s\n", dir);
        }
    printf("echo changing to %s%s\n", pu->ui1_local, dir);
    exit(0);
    }

/* error -- print the error message as an Echo batch command and exit */

error(msg, arg)
char *msg;
char *arg;
    {
    printf("echo ERROR: ");
    printf(msg, arg);
    exit(1);
    }
```

```
@echo off

rem NETCD.CMD
rem
rem This OS/2 batch file accepts a UNC-style resource name from the
rem user and creates a network connection with the next available
rem virtual drive.  After the connection, the batch file changes
```

Figure 5-4.　　　　　　　　　　　　　　　　　　　　　　　　　　　*(continued)*
The NETCD.CMD batch file.

The installable file system

Under MS-DOS and OS/2 through version 1.1, the file system is based on the original MS-DOS 2.0 design—the File Allocation Table (FAT). This allows a computer to be booted in either operating system and still have access to a common file system. Under OS/2 1.2, an extension to the file system allows nonstandard devices and special-purpose file systems to be created and added to OS/2. These are known as *installable file systems* (IFSs). The redirector under MS-DOS and earlier versions of OS/2 is the model for an IFS. The redirector creates a name space of filenames (UNC filenames in this case) that can be mapped onto a virtual disk drive, and the operating system passes off all relevant file-system requests to the redirector.

Under OS/2 1.2, this ability to redirect file-system access has been generalized so that any number of specialized file systems can be installed. The LAN Manager redirector is but one of several possible IFS. For example, there might be an IFS for a CD-ROM drive or for a special partition on a hard disk that contains a high-performance ISAM file system. Each IFS has an associated file-system driver that OS/2 is configured to communicate with.

The workstation functions *NetUseAdd*, *NetUseDel*, and *NetUseGetInfo* have been generalized for use with IFS. The related OS/2 APIs are *DosFSAttach* and *DosQFSAttach*. The details of these APIs are available in the documentation for OS/2 1.2.

DosFSAttach provides the same functionality as *NetUseAdd*. So which one should you use? If your network programs are intended to run on either MS-DOS or OS/2 as dual-mode executables, use *NetUseAdd*. If your programs are exclusively for OS/2, and you want to allow for use of file systems other than the network, use *DosFSAttach*.

Figure 5-4. *continued*

```
rem directories to the specified network pathname.
rem
rem This file requires the NETCDX.EXE program and creates the
rem temporary file NETCDY.CMD in the current directory.

netcdx.exe %1 %2 > netcdy.cmd
call netcdy
del netcdy.cmd
```

The Message APIs

The Message APIs allow programs to interact with the Messenger service.
Three sets of Message APIs are available:

- Name APIs work with message names, alias names, and name forwarding.

- Send APIs send memory buffers or files to specified names.

- Log file APIs work with a log of received messages.

Any user, regardless of privilege level, can issue a Message API locally.
The key to understanding these APIs is understanding how the Messenger
service works at the workstation and server levels.

The Messenger Service

One of the properties of the NetBIOS is the ability to add unique names to
the network adapter card. The Messenger service allows messages to be
received by any name that is on the adapter card. When the workstation is
started, the computer name is added, and when the user logs on, the *Net-
WkstaSetUID* API adds the username. At this point, the Messenger service
receives messages sent to either of these names (which could be the same).
The Message APIs allow additional names, called *aliasnames,* to be added to
the adapter card, and messages can be received by these names as well.

The Messenger service also allows names to be forwarded. (The Messenger
service at each end has a copy of the name that is marked appropriately with
"forwarded to" or "forwarded from" information.) Forwarded names can
be unforwarded, which removes the remote copy of the name and restores
delivery to the original computer.

> **NOTE:** *The Message APIs take text strings that are case sensitive. The
> LAN Manager user interface uses the same APIs but always maps names
> to uppercase.*

Messenger service protocols

The following rules are enforced by the Message APIs:

- All Message APIs except *NetMessageBufferSend* and *NetMessageFile-Send* require the Messenger service to be started at the workstation.

- If the Message APIs are called remotely, the Messenger service must be started at the remote computer, with the exception of *NetMessage-BufferSend* and *NetMessageFileSend*.

- When messages are received at a workstation, they are buffered in a memory buffer whose size is controlled by the LANMAN.INI parameter *sizmessbuf*. If this buffer is too small, the message cannot be received.

- If logging is enabled (see *NetMessageLogFileSet*), the Messenger service writes the messages out to the log file.

- If the Netpopup service is started, the message is written to a pop-up screen at the receiving workstation.

Multiple networks

A workstation can maintain a NetBIOS driver for more than one network at a time. Chapter 12 shows how to configure a workstation for this. If a network is configured as a managed network, the workstation can send and receive messages on the network. If more than one managed network exists, the workstation can send and receive messages on all of them.

Using the Message APIs

To use the Message APIs in a program, you must include NETCONS.H and MESSAGE.H at compile time. *NetMessageBufferSend* and *NetMessageFile-Send* must link with the NETOEM.LIB stub library. The rest of the Message APIs must link with the NETAPI.LIB stub library. With the exception of the MessageSend APIs, the Messenger service must be started for the API call to be successful. The MessageSend APIs require only that the Workstation service be running.

The message data structures

The *NetMessageNameEnum* and *NetMessageNameGetInfo* APIs make use of the *msg_info_0* and *msg_info_1* data structures. The *msg_info_0* structure contains the following member:

Member Name	Description
char msgi0_name[CNLEN+1]	A message name up to CNLEN characters in length and a 0 terminator.

The *msg_info_1* structure contains the following members:

Member Name	Description
char msgi1_name[CNLEN+1]	A message name up to CNLEN characters in length and a 0 terminator.
UCHAR msgi1_forward_flag	These bits control the meaning of the *msgi1_forward* test string. The bit masks for checking whether a bit is set are as follows:

	Bitmask	Value	Meaning
	MSGNAME_NOT_FORWARDED	0x00	The *msgi1_name* is not forwarded.
	MSGNAME_FORWARDED_TO	0x04	The *msgi1_name* is forwarded to the name in *msgi1_forward*.
	MSGNAME_FORWARDED_FROM	0x10	The *msgi1_name* is forwarded from the name in *msgi1_forward*.

char msgi1_forward [CNLEN+1]	Depending on the setting of the bitmask in *msgi1_forward_flag*, this is either the "forwarded to" or the "forwarded from" name.

The Message Name APIs

There are six message APIs that deal with the message name table in LAN Manager: *NetMessageNameEnum*, *NetMessageNameGetInfo*, *NetMessage-NameAdd*, *NetMessageNameDel*, *NetMessageNameFwd*, and *NetMessage-NameUnFwd*.

NetMessageNameEnum

Lists information about the message name table.

```
unsigned far pascal
NetMessageNameEnum(
    char far * servername,      /* where to execute         */
    short level,                /* information level        */
    char far * buf,             /* space for return data    */
    USHORT buflen,              /* size of buf              */
    USHORT far * entriesread,   /* number of entries read   */
    USHORT far * totalentries   /* total entries available  */
    )
```

Levels:
Supports level 0 and 1 data structures.

Local access:
The message service must be started.

Remote access:

Only an administrator can call this remotely.

Error returns:

If successful, *NetMessageNameEnum* returns 0. If unsuccessful, it returns one of the standard Enum return codes or the following error code:

Error Return	Meaning
NERR_MsgNotStarted	The Messenger service has not been started.

An overview:

The *NetMessageNameEnum* API is a standard Enum call returning a buffer of *msg_info_0* or *msg_info_1* structures, depending on the level argument.

NetMessageNameGetInfo

Retrieves information about a user's entry in the message name table.

```
unsigned far pascal
NetMessageNameGetInfo(
    char far *server,        /* where to execute      */
    char far *msgname,       /* message name          */
    USHORT level,            /* level of detail       */
    char far *buf,           /* where to return data  */
    USHORT buflen,           /* size of buf           */
    USHORT far *ta           /* total bytes available */
    )
```

Levels:

Supports level 0 and 1 data structures.

Local access:

The Messenger service must be started.

Remote access:

Only an administrator can call this remotely.

Error returns:

If successful, *NetMessageNameGetInfo* returns 0. If unsuccessful, it returns one of the standard GetInfo return codes or one of the following error codes:

Error Return	Meaning
NERR_MsgNotStarted	The Messenger service has not been started.
NERR_NotLocalName	The *msgname* parameter is not recognized.

An overview:

The *NetMessageNameGetInfo* API is a standard GetInfo call that returns either a *msg_info_0* or a *msg_info_1* structure, depending on the level argument.

The *msgname* parameter is the message name for which information is to be returned.

NetMessageNameAdd

Registers a username in the message name table.

```
unsigned far pascal
NetMessageNameAdd(
    char far * servername,        /* where to execute */
    char far * msgname,           /* the message name */
    short fwd_action              /* forward action   */
    )
```

Local access:

The Messenger service must be started.

Remote access:

Only an administrator can call this remotely.

Error returns:

If successful, *NetMessageNameAdd* returns 0. If unsuccessful, it returns one of the standard Add return codes or one of the following error codes:

Error Return	Meaning
NERR_MsgNotStarted	The Messenger service has not been started.
NERR_AlreadyExists	The message name already exists on this workstation.
NERR_DuplicateName	Another workstation is using the message name.
NERR_TooManyNames	Too many message names are already in use at this workstation.
NERR_AlreadyForwarded	The name exists as a "forwarded from" name on another workstation, and the *fwd_action* flag was FALSE.

An overview:

The *NetMessageNameAdd* API adds a message name to the Messenger service, allowing messages to be received by that name. *msgname* must be a unique name on the network.

If the workstation is on more than one network at the same time, the message name is added to all managed networks.

The *fwd_action* flag dictates what happens if the name exists on another computer as a ''forwarded to'' name. This can happen if a name was forwarded and the original workstation deleted the name, either explicitly by using the *NetMessageNameDel* API or implicitly by stopping the network software. The following are the valid values for *fwd_action*:

Value	Meaning
False	Do not add the messaging name to this workstation.
True	Add the messaging name to this workstation, and mark it as being ''forwarded to.''

NetMessageNameDel

Deletes a username from the message name table.

```
unsigned far pascal
NetMessageNameDel(
    char far * servername,        /* where to execute */
    char far * msgname,           /* the message name */
    short fwd_action              /* forward action   */
    )
```

Local access:
The Messenger service must be started.

Remote access:
Only an administrator can call this remotely.

Error returns:
If successful, *NetMessageNameDel* returns 0. If unsuccessful, it returns one of the standard Del return codes or one of the following error codes:

Error Return	Meaning
NERR_MsgNotStarted	The Messenger service has not been started.
NERR_NotLocalName	The message name does not exist on this workstation.
NERR_DelComputerName	The computer name can never be deleted.
NERR_NameInUse	The Messenger service is in the middle of using the name, and it cannot be deleted right now.
NERR_AlreadyForwarded	The message name is ''forwarded to'' another workstation, and the *fwd_action* flag was FALSE.

An overview:
The *NetMessageNameDel* API deletes a message name from the Messenger service, preventing messages from being received by that name. Both the

username and alias names can be deleted, but the computer name cannot be deleted from the Messenger service. The call can be made remotely but requires *admin* privilege at the server.

The *fwd_action* flag dictates what happens if the message name is currently "forwarded to" another workstation. The following are the valid values for *fwd_action*:

Value	Meaning
False	Do not delete the message name. If this occurs, the API returns NERR_AlreadyForwarded.
True	Go ahead and delete the message name.

The XMSG.C subroutine (Figure 5-5) demonstrates the use of the *NetMessageNameDel* API.

Because OS/2 is a multitasking system, you can issue the *NetMessageNameDel* call at a time when the Messenger service is in the middle of using that message name. If this occurs, the API returns NERR_NameInUse. The following subroutine shows how you can use NERR_NameInUse to handle retries if this happens.

```
/*
 * XMSG.C -- This function demonstrates the use of the
 * NetMessageNameDel API.  Note the while loop that retries
 * the deletion up to 5 times if the message name is in use.
 * Use this function as a template for all of the other
 * functions that return the NERR_NameInUse error code.
 *
 */

#include <netcons.h>
#include <message.h>
#include <neterr.h>

unsigned far pascal
XNetMessageNameDel(
    char far * servername,      /* where to execute */
    char far * msgname,         /* the message name */
    short fwd_action)           /* forward action   */


    {
    int retry = 5;              /* retry 5 times    */
    int pause = 2000;           /* wait 2 seconds   */
    unsigned err;
```

Figure 5-5.
The XMSG.C subroutine.

(continued)

Figure 5-5. *continued*

```
while (--retry)
    {
    if ((err = NetMessageNameDel(servername, msgname,
            fwd_action)) != NERR_NameInUse)
        return(err);
    }
return (err);
}
```

NetMessageNameFwd

Forwards messages from one workstation username to another.

```
unsigned far pascal
NetMessageNameFwd(
    char far * servername,     /* where to execute       */
    char far * name,           /* name to forward        */
    char far * fwd_name,       /* where to forward it to */
    short del_for              /* already forwarded flag */
    )
```

Local access:

The Messenger service must be started.

Remote access:

Only an administrator can call this remotely.

Error returns:

If successful, *NetMessageNameFwd* returns 0. If unsuccessful, it returns one of the standard API error codes or one of the following error codes:

Error Return	*Meaning*
NERR_MsgNotStarted	The Messenger service has not been started.
NERR_NotLocalName	*name* is not a message name at the workstation.
NERR_AlreadyForwarded	*name* is already forwarded, and the *del-for* flag was FALSE.
NERR_LocalForward	*fwd_name* is on the same workstation as *name*.
ERROR_NOT_SUPPORTED	The workstation is on more than one managed network.
NERR_NameNotFound	*fwd_name* does not exist as a message name at any workstation.
NERR_RemoteFull	Too many message names already exist in the Messenger service for *fwd_name*.
NERR_NameInUse	The Messenger service is in the middle of using the name, and it cannot be deleted right now.

An overview:

The *NetMessageNameFwd* API forwards the *name* message name to the *fwd_name* message name. *name* must be a valid message name on the local workstation, and *fwd_name* must be a valid message name on another (remote) workstation.

The *del_for* flag dictates what happens if *name* has already been forwarded. The following are the valid values for *del_for*:

Value	Meaning
False	Take no action. The API fails.
True	Remove the old forwarding and establish the new one. If the workstation is on more than one managed network, *NetMessageNameFwd* fails.

To forward or not to forward

If a message name is already forwarded, the program can select whether to establish the new forward or to leave the old. The UMSG.C subroutine (Figure 5-6) prompts the user to determine what action will be taken.

```
/*
 * UMSG.C -- This function demonstrates the use of NetMessageNameFwd
 * to forward a message name.  If the name is already forwarded, it
 * will prompt the user to determine whether to override the old
 * forward or not.
 *
 */

#include <stdio.h>
#include <neterr.h>
#include <examples.h>   /* defined in Chapter 4 */

unsigned far pascal
UNetMessageNameFwd(
    char far * servername,    /* where to execute      */
    char far * name,          /* name to forward       */
    char far * fwd_name)      /* where to forward it to */


    {
    unsigned err;
```

Figure 5-6.
The UMSG.C program.

(continued)

Figure 5-6. *continued*

```
if ((err = NetMessageNameFwd(servername, name,
        fwd_name, FALSE)) == NERR_AlreadyForwarded)
    {
    printf("The name is already forwarded. ");
    printf("Do you want to continue?[Y/N]");
    fflush(stdout);
    if (getchar() == 'Y')
        err = NetMessageNameFwd(servername, name, fwd_name, TRUE);
    }
}
```

NetMessageNameUnFwd

Stops the forwarding of messages from one user to another.

```
unsigned far pascal
NetMessageNameUnFwd(
    char far * servername,      /* where to execute  */
    char far * msgname          /* name to unforward */
    )
```

Local access:
The Messenger service must be started.

Remote access:
Only an administrator can call this remotely.

Error returns:
If successful, *NetMessageNameUnFwd* returns 0. If unsuccessful, it returns one of the standard API error codes or one of the following error codes:

Error Return	Meaning
NERR_MsgNotStarted	The Messenger service has not been started.
NERR_NotLocalName	*msgname* is not a message name at the workstation.
NERR_NameNotForwarded	*msgname* is not "forwarded to" another workstation.
NERR_NameInUse	The Messenger service is in the middle of using the name, and it cannot be deleted right now.

An overview:
The *NetMessageNameUnFwd* API stops forwarding messages for the specified message name and starts receiving them at the original workstation. The *msgname* parameter must be a valid message name at the workstation and must already be forwarded.

The Message Send APIs

Two APIs let you send messages: *NetMessageBufferSend* sends the contents of a memory buffer, and *NetMessageFileSend* sends the contents of a file. Each of these functions contains a parameter indicating the name of the intended recipient.

There are two special ways to send messages. If the recipient name is the wildcard ∗, a copy of the message is sent to all network workstations running the Messenger service. If the recipient name is a domain name, the message is sent to all domain workstations running the Messenger service. Both of these special cases are called *broadcast messages*.

If a broadcast message is sent from a workstation that is on more than one network at a time, the message is sent on all networks at once. Figure 5-7 shows what happens if a workstation is configured on two networks: Workstation 1 can send and receive messages from either workstation 2 or workstation 3, but 2 and 3 cannot send or receive messages to or from each other.

Messages are assumed to be text. The presence of nonprinting characters in a message can have unpredictable effects. The size of messages is limited by the *sizmessbuf* configuration parameter at the receiving end. Note that the default value for *sizmessbuf* is 4096 bytes. Broadcast messages are limited to 128 bytes.

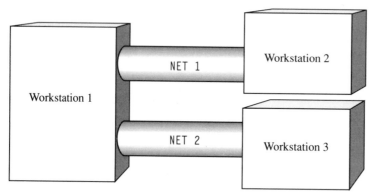

Figure 5-7.
Sending messages over two networks.

NetMessageBufferSend

Sends a buffer of data to a message name.

```
unsigned far pascal
NetMessageBufferSend(
    char far * servername,    /* where to execute   */
    char far * msgname,       /* recipient name     */
    char far * buf,           /* data to send       */
    USHORT buflen             /* size of the buffer */
    )
```

Remote access:

NetMessageBufferSend can be called remotely by an administrator or by a user with any of the following operator privileges at the server:

- accounts operator

- server operator

- print operator

- comm operator

Error returns:

If successful, *NetMessageBufferSend* returns 0. If unsuccessful, it returns one of the standard API error codes or one of the following error codes:

Error Return	Meaning
NERR_NameNotFound	*msgname* does not exist as a message name at any workstation.
NERR_BadReceive	A communication error occurred while sending the message.
NERR_TruncatedBroadcast	The broadcast message was truncated—only the first 128 bytes were sent.

An overview:

The *NetMessageBufferSend* API sends a buffer of data to the Messenger service that registered *msgname*. The buffer is limited either to the size of the message buffer at the receiving end or to 65,536 bytes.

Messages can be sent even if the Messenger service has not been started.

NetMessageFileSend

Sends a file to a message name.

```
unsigned far pascal
NetMessageFileSend(
    char far * servername,    /* where to execute    */
    char far * msgname,       /* recipient name      */
    char far * filename       /* pathname of file    */
    )
```

Remote access:

NetMessageFileSend can be called remotely by an administrator, or by a user with any of the following operator privileges at the server:

- accounts operator

- server operator

- print operator

- comm operator

Error returns:

If successful, *NetMessageFileSend* returns 0. If unsuccessful, it returns a standard file-system error code or one of the following error codes:

Error Return	*Meaning*
NERR_NameNotFound	*msgname* does not exist as a message name at any workstation.
NERR_BadReceive	A communication error occurred while sending the message.
NERR_TruncatedBroadcast	The broadcast message was truncated—only the first 128 bytes were sent.

An overview:

The *NetMessageFileSend* API sends a buffer of data to the Messenger service that registered *msgname*. The size of the file is limited to the buffer size specified by the *sizmessbuf* configuration parameter at the receiving end.

NetMessageFileSend does not require the Messenger service on the local computer, but the remote computer needs the Messenger service to be running.

Sending Message Files

With the LAN Manager net send command, you can send a file to a single network user by redirecting input to an individual's username. For example, the following command sends the contents of the file AFILE.TXT to the user *charlie*:

```
net send charlie < afile.txt
```

The implementation of net send uses a temporary file and the *Net-MessageFileSend* API. The MSGFILE.C program (Figure 5-8) allows you to send a text file to an entire list of users and avoid the extra temporary file. The MSGFILE program requires the following syntax:

```
msgfile username(s) filename
```

It is assumed that the last argument is the filename and that all of the other arguments are message names.

```c
/*
 * MSGFILE.C -- This program uses the NetMessageFileSend API
 * to send a copy of the specified file to each name in a
 * list of network users.  Each message name is converted to
 * uppercase for compatibility with the LAN Manager interface.
 *
 * Compile with:  C> cl msgfile.c netoem.lib
 *
 * Usage:  C> msgfile username(s) filename
 *
 */

#include <stdio.h>
#include <string.h>
#include <netcons.h>
#include <message.h>

main(argc, argv)
int argc;
char **argv;
    {
    unsigned len, err;
    int i, exitcode;

    if (argc < 3)
        {
        printf("syntax: msgfile username(s) filename\n");
        exit(-1);
        }
```

Figure 5-8.
The MSGFILE.C program.

(continued)

Figure 5-8. *continued*

```
exitcode = 0;
printf("%-20s%-20s\n", "NAME", "STATUS");
printf("%-20s%-20s\n", "----", "------");
for (i = 1; i < argc-1; ++i)
    {
    strupr(argv[i]);
    err = NetMessageFileSend(NULL, argv[i], argv[argc-1]);
    if (err == 0)
        printf("%-20sOK\n", argv[i]);
    else
        {
        printf("%-20s%d\n", argv[i], err);
        ++exitcode;
        }
    }
exit(exitcode);
}
```

The Message Log File APIs

When messages arrive at the workstation, they can be written out to a message log file. The *NetMessageLogFileSet* and *NetMessageLogFileGet* APIs let you query or change the logging status or the name of the log file.

NetMessageLogFileSet

Sets a log file to receive messages.

```
unsigned far pascal
NetMessageLogFileSet(
    char far * servername,    /* where to execute  */
    char far * logfile,       /* the log filename  */
    short on                  /* logging on or off? */
    )
```

Local access:
The Messenger service must be started.

Remote access:
Only an administrator can call this remotely.

Error returns:
If successful, *NetMessageLogFileSet* returns 0. If unsuccessful, it returns a standard file-system error code or one of the error codes shown on the following page.

Error Return	Meaning
NERR_MsgNotStarted	The Messenger service has not been started.
ERROR_INVALID_PARAMETER	The *logfile* parameter was CON or AUX, or one of the other parameters was invalid.
ERROR_OPEN_FAILED	The *logfile* parameter specified a file or device that could not be opened.
NERR_NoLogFile	The *logfile* parameter was NULL; there is currently no log file.

An overview

The *NetMessageLogFileSet* API changes the name of the message logging file and turns message logging on and off.

The *logfile* parameter is the new log file name. It is processed in the following manner:

- If *logfile* is NULL, do not change the log file. (This is useful if only the *on* status is to be changed.)

- If *logfile* is a device name of the form LPT*x* or COM*x*, use the device name. CON is not allowed because the Messenger service runs as a detached process.

- If the *logfile* parameter is neither of these values, assume that *logfile* is a filename.

- If the filename has no extension, add the extension LOG.

- If the filename is a relative filename, make it relative to the LOG subdirectory of the LANMAN root.

- If the filename is not a relative filename, it must be a completely specified pathname. UNC names are not allowed. (Although the current version allows redirected drive names, you should not expect this feature in future versions.)

Note that the default log file name is obtained from the *logfilename* parameter of the LANMAN.INI file when the Messenger service starts up.

The *on* parameter turns logging on and off. A value of zero turns logging off; a nonzero value turns logging on.

NetMessageLogFileGet

Retrieves the name and status of the message log file.

```
unsigned far pascal
NetMessageLogFileGet(
    char far * servername,      /* where to execute    */
    char far * buf,             /* place for data      */
    USHORT buflen,              /* size of buf         */
    short far *pon              /* returns on/off state */
    )
```

Local access:
The Messenger service must be started.

Remote access:
Only an administrator can call this remotely.

Error returns:
If successful, *NetMessageLogFileGet* returns 0. If unsuccessful, it returns a standard API error code or the following error code:

Error Return	Meaning
NERR_MsgNotStarted	The Messenger service has not been started.

An overview:
The *NetMessageLogFileGet* API returns the current message log file name and indicates whether logging is turned on or off.

The *buf* parameter must be large enough to hold the log file name. It is returned as a completely specified pathname. The *pon* parameter is zero if logging is off and nonzero if logging is on.

The Profile APIs

The Profile APIs (*NetProfileSave* and *NetProfileLoad*) let programs save and restore the LAN Manager environment. The environment settings are stored through LAN Manager user commands in a text file called a *profile file*. The following sections describe the profile file at the workstation and at the server.

NOTE: *Microsoft plans to phase out the Profile APIs as LAN Manager converges with IBM LAN Server (which does not support them). The Profile APIs should be used only in LAN Manager 1.0 programs.*

Workstation Profiles

At a workstation, the profile saves connections that have device names. Neither deviceless connections nor passwords are saved. If the connection requires passwords, they must be provided as part of the retry logic.

Figure 5-9 shows a sample workstation profile.

```
NET USE X: \\apps\public
NET USE Y: \\systems\tools
```

Figure 5-9.
A sample workstation profile.

Server Profiles

At a server, the profile saves information about shares, print queues, and comm queues:

- For shares, the remarks and user limits are saved. In the case of share-mode servers, the password and permissions for the share are saved, as are the IPC$ and ADMIN$ shares and their passwords. (These two shares are added automatically on a user-mode server.) The special shares A$–Z$ are never saved, because they are added automatically whenever the server is started.

- For print queues, the priority, print times, separator files, print processor, device assignments, and remarks are all saved.

- For comm queues, the priority is saved.

Figure 5-10 shows a sample server profile.

```
NET SHARE MODEM=COM1 /REMARK:"" /PERMISSIONS:"" /UNLIMITED  /COMM
NET COMM MODEM /PRIORITY:5
NET SHARE LASER /PRINT /REMARK:"" /PERMISSIONS:"" /UNLIMITED  /YES
NET PRINT LASER  /PRIORITY:5 /AFTER:0:0 /UNTIL:23:59 /SEPARATOR:""
/PROCESSOR:"" /ROUTE:"LPT1" /REMARK:"" /RELEASE
NET SHARE BINP=C:\BINP /REMARK:"" /PERMISSIONS:"" /USERS:4
```

Figure 5-10.
A sample server profile.

> **NOTE:** *You should not edit the profile files because the* NetProfileLoad *API depends on a specific order of commands and arguments for parsing. However, if the PRO file is to be turned into a CMD file for batch execution, there are no restrictions on editing.*

NetProfileSave

Saves the environment in a file.

```
unsigned far pascal
NetProfileSave(
    char far * servername,        /* where to execute */
    char far * pathname,          /* the profile name */
    unsigned long save_options,   /* what to save     */
    USHORT open_flags             /* flags to DosOpen */
    )
```

Local access:

The workstation service must be started.

The user must be logged on.

Remote access:

Only an administrator can call this remotely.

Error returns:

If successful, *NetProfileSave* returns 0. If unsuccessful, it returns a standard file system error code.

An overview:

The *NetProfileSave* API saves the workstation or server LAN Manager environment in the file specified by *pathname*.

save_options is a bitmap that tells the API what part of the LAN Manager environment to save:

Bitmask	Value	Meaning
PROFILE_SAVE_USES	0x01	Save only connection information.
PROFILE_SAVE_SHARES	0x02	Save only share information.
PROFILE_SAVE_PRQINFO	0x04	Save only print queue information.
PROFILE_SAVE_COMQINFO	0x08	Save only comm queue information.

If, for example, you wanted to save information about uses and shares, you would use the following bitmask:

```
(PROFILE_SAVE_USES : PROFILE_SAVE_SHARES)
```

The *open_flags* parameter is passed directly to *DosOpen* when the profile is opened. The following are the valid profile values:

Flag	Value	Meaning
FILE_TRUNC	0x02	Truncate existing file. Fail if it does not exist.
FILE_CREATE	0x10	Create the file, or fail if it exists.
	0x12	Create the file, or truncate an existing file.

NetProfileLoad

Executes commands in the profile file.

```
unsigned far pascal
NetProfileLoad(
    char far * servername,    /* where to execute     */
    char far * pathname,      /* profile to load      */
    unsigned long start,      /* offset in profile    */
    char far * buf,           /* load status info     */
    UNSHORT buflen,           /* size of buf          */
    unsigned long load_options /* add to current state? */
    )
```

Local access:
The workstation service must be started.

The user must be logged on.

Remote access:
Only an administrator can call this remotely.

Error returns:

If successful, *NetProfileLoad* returns 0. If errors in locating, opening, or reading the profile occur, *NetProfileLoad* returns a standard file system return code or one of the following error codes:

Error Return	*Meaning*
NERR_ProfileFileTooBig	The profile file was larger than 64 KB and could not be processed.
NERR_ProfileOffset	The *start* parameter is out of range.
NERR_ProfileCleanup	The profile could not delete all of the uses and shares. The API quit with the first failure, leaving things incomplete.

> **NOTE:** *If the load starts to process commands, the API returns 0 even if a command fails. The program must examine the* pli_code *value in the* profile_load_info *structure to determine whether all commands executed successfully.*

An overview:

The *NetProfileLoad* API executes the LAN Manager commands saved in the profile file.

pathname specifies the profile to be loaded. If a problem opening or reading the file occurs, a file system error code is returned.

start specifies the offset in the profile where *NetProfileLoad* starts executing.

buf returns a *profile_load_info* structure, which gives information about the success or failure of commands in the profile. This structure contains the following elements:

Member Name	*Description*
short pli_code	If zero, all commands executed successfully. If nonzero, the value is the failure code of the command that failed. A special code value— NERR_ProfileUnknownCommand—indicates corrupted lines in the profile that could not be parsed.
ULONG pli_resume_offset	If *pli_code* is nonzero, this is the offset in the profile of the failed command.
char far * pli_text	If *pli_code* is nonzero, this is the text of the failed command.
ULONG li_retry_offset	If *pli_code* is nonzero, this is the offset of the command following the one that failed.

The *load_options* parameter is a bit mask that determines what subset of the profile is to be used. The bits have the following meanings:

Bitmask	Value	Meaning
PROFILE_LOAD_USES	0x1	If 1, execute USE commands.
PROFILE_LOAD_SHARES	0x2	If 1, execute SHARE commands.
PROFILE_LOAD_PRQ_INFO	0x4	If 1, execute PRINT commands.
PROFILE_LOAD_COMQ_INFO	0x8	If 1, execute COMM commands.
PROFILE_LOAD_USE_SHARE	0x3	A combined mask for loading all uses and shares.

Two other bits defined in *load_options* indicate whether the uses and shares in the profile replace or simply append to the existing uses and shares. No bitmasks are defined for these two options:

Bit Number	Value	Meaning
8	0x100	Append USE commands.
9	0x200	Append SHARE commands.

A macro defined in PROFILE.H can be used here:

Macro	Meaning
PROFILE_LOAD_APPEND(1)	Append USE commands.
PROFILE_LOAD_APPEND(2)	Append SHARE commands.

> **NOTE:** *For programs written under LAN Manager 1.0, a* load_options *value of 0 is equivalent to the value 0xF; it causes all four categories of profile loads to be replaced.*

What Happens During Loading?

When *NetProfileLoad* executes a profile, if bit 8 of the *load_options* parameter is 0, all existing connections are deleted. Similarly, if bit 9 of *load_options* is 0, all existing shares are deleted. If any of these deletions fail, the profile load fails. The exception to this is on a share-mode server. The profile load does not try to delete the special shares IPC$ and ADMIN$. If it did delete these shares, it couldn't use the command remotely, because remote procedure calls rely on the presence of these two shares.

Each command in the profile file is checked to see if the corresponding bit in the *load_options* parameter allows that kind of command to be executed.

If so, the command is executed as if it were passed to the command-line interface. (Accordingly, you can turn profile files into batch files simply by changing their extensions to CMD.)

Retry, Retry Again

Commands in the profile are processed until one of them fails. The *profile-_load_info* structure contains information that allows a program to take corrective action and continue loading the profile. The following are some of the options available to a program:

- Stop the profile load.

- Resume loading, but skip the bad command. (Call *NetProfileLoad* again with *start* set to the value returned in *pli->pli_resume_offset*.)

- Take corrective action and resume loading with a retry of the failed command. (Call *NetProfileLoad* again with *start* set to the value returned in *pli->pli_resume_offset*.) For example, if the net share command fails because the server is not started, the application could start the server using *NetServiceStart* and then retry the command.

An Example

The PROLOAD.C program (Figure 5-11) allows a user to execute corrective commands; it then continues execution with the next line of the profile.

```
/*
 * PROLOAD.C -- A program that loads a profile file.  If an error
 * occurs, an attempt is made to recover and continue.
 *
 * Compile with:  C> cl proload.c netapi.lib
 *
 * Usage:  C> proload filename
 *
 */

#include <stdio.h>
#include <netcons.h>
#include <profile.h>

typedef struct profile_load_info PLI;
void recover_from(PLI *);
```

Figure 5-11. *(continued)*
The PROLOAD.C program.

Figure 5-11. *continued*

```
main(argc, argv)
int argc;
char **argv;
    {
    unsigned err;
    unsigned long start;
    char buf[BUFSIZ];
    PLI *pli = (PLI *)buf;

    if (argc != 2)
        {
        printf("Syntax:  proload filename\n");
        exit(1);
        }
    /* loop until file is loaded or user quits */
    start = 0;
    while (1)
        {
        /* start or continue the profile load */
        err = NetProfileLoad(NULL, argv[1], start, buf, BUFSIZ, 0L);
        if (err != 0)
            {
            printf("Profile Load failed with error %d\n", err);
            exit(1);
            }
        /* did all of the lines in the profile get loaded? */
        if (pli->pli_code == 0)
            break;  /* all done */

        /* otherwise, try to recover from the error */
        recover_from(pli);

        /* if this returned, do the next command */
        start = pli->pli_resume_offset;
        }
    exit(0);
    }

/*
 * recover_from -- Using the PLI pointer, prompt with the
 * error code and the failing line.  Allow the user to
 * type a new command line, to type "QUIT" to quit the program,
 * or to press the Enter key to skip processing of this line.
 *
 */

void recover_from(pli)
PLI *pli;
```

(continued)

Figure 5-11. *continued*

```
{
char buf[BUFSIZ];

printf("The command\n\t%s\n", pli->pli_text);
printf("failed with error code %d.\n", pli->pli_code);
printf("Type a new command line, QUIT, or press Enter to skip\n");
gets(buf);
if (*buf == 0)
    return;
else if (strnicmp(buf, "QUIT", strlen(buf)) == 0)
    exit(1);
/* otherwise, execute the command until it's right */
while (1)
    {
    system(buf);
    printf("Type a new command line or press ENTER to continue.\n");
    gets(buf);
    if (*buf == 0)
        return;
    }
}
```

The Remote APIs

Most LAN Manager APIs can be executed remotely by those having *admin* privilege at the server. The Remote APIs give remote execution capabilities to ordinary user programs. To use these APIs in a program, you must include NETCONS.H and REMUTIL.H at compile time, and you must link with the NETAPI.LIB stub library.

Different remote servers

There are two different types of remote server:

- If the remote server is running share-mode security, the user must be able to connect to IPC$ before the Remote APIs will execute at the server. This means that either there is no password on IPC$ or the user's logon password matches the IPC$ password.

- If the remote server is running user-mode security, the user must have an account at the server.

In both cases, the Remote APIs create the connection to IPC$.

NetRemoteTOD

Returns the time of day from a remote server.

```
unsigned far pascal
NetRemoteTOD(
    char far * servername,    /* where to execute   */
    char far * buf,           /* return data buffer */
    USHORT buflen             /* size of buf        */
    )
```

Remote access:
The user must have a valid UAS account at the server.

Error returns:
If successful, *NetRemoteTOD* returns 0. If unsuccessful, it returns a standard API error code.

An overview:
The *NetRemoteTOD* API returns the time of day from the specified remote server. Upon return, the *buf* buffer contains a *time_of_day_info* structure, which contains the following information:

Member Name	Description
ULONG tod_elapsedt	Seconds since January 1, 1970 (GMT)
ULONG tod_msecs	Milliseconds
UCHAR tod_hours	Current hour of the day
UCHAR tod_mins	Current minute of the hour
UCHAR tod_secs	Current second of the minute
UCHAR tod_hunds	Current hundredth of a second
USHORT tod_timezone	Time zone at the server
USHORT tod_tinterval	Server timer interval in 0.0001-second units
UCHAR tod_day	Current day of the month
UCHAR tod_month	Current month
USHORT tod_year	Current year
UCHAR tod_weekday	Current day of the week

The *tod_elapsedt*, *tod_msecs*, *tod_timezone*, and *tod_tinterval* structure members provide remote server time information. The other members are derived values. This information is identical to that returned by the OS/2 *DosGetInfoSeg* API.

The REMTOD.C program (Figure 5-12) lists the time for each server in the langroup domain. This example relies on the C language *time_t* data type.

```
/*
 * REMTOD.C  -- This program displays the current time
 * as seen at each server in the langroup domain.
 *
 * Compile:  C> cl remtod.c cname.c netapi.lib netoem.lib string_f.lib
 *
 * Usage:  C> remtod
 *
 */

#include <stdio.h>
#include <netcons.h>
#include <remutil.h>
#include <server.h>
#include <time.h>
#include <examples.h>   /* defined in Chapter 4 */

typedef struct server_info_0 SRV_0;
typedef struct time_of_day_info TOD;

main()
    {
    char tbuff[sizeof(TOD)];
    TOD * tod = (TOD *)tbuff;
    char sbuff[BUFSIZ];
    SRV_0 *psrv;
    unsigned short ser, ste, err;
    time_t rtime;

    err = NetServerEnum(NULL, 0, sbuff, sizeof(sbuff), &ser, &ste);
    if (err != 0)
        {
        printf("NetServerEnum failed with err = %d\n", err);
        exit(1);
        }

    /* for each server, get and display the time */
    for (psrv = (SRV_0 *)sbuff; ser--; ++psrv)
        {
        /* remote names require a leading \\ */
        err = NetRemoteTOD(
                          cname(psrv->sv0_name), /* server name   */
                          tbuff,                 /* return data    */
                          sizeof(tbuff)          /* length of tbuff */
                          );
```

Figure 5-12.   (continued)
The REMTOD.C program.

Figure 5-12. *continued*

```
    if (err)
        printf("RemoteTOD error for %s = %d\n",
                psrv->sv0_name, err);
    else
        {
        /* for portability, map TOD into the standard C
           time_t data type and use ctime for formatting */
        rtime = tod->tod_elapsedt;
        printf("%s: %s\n", psrv->sv0_name, ctime(&rtime));
        }
    }
}
```

NetRemoteCopy

Copies files from one location to another on a remote server.

```
unsigned far pascal
NetRemoteCopy(
    char far * sourcepath,    /* source file pathname      */
    char far * destpath,      /* destination file pathname */
    char far * sourcepass,    /* source password           */
    char far * destpass,      /* destination password      */
    USHORT oflags,            /* open flags                */
    USHORT cflags,            /* copy flags                */
    char far * buf,           /* buffer for return text    */
    USHORT buflen             /* length of buf             */
    )
```

Remote access:

NetRemoteCopy is subject to server logon and regular ACL permissions.

Error returns:

If successful, *NetRemoteCopy* returns 0. If unsuccessful, it returns a standard file-system return code, a standard API return code, or one of the following error codes:

Error Return	Meaning
NERR_BadSource	*sourcepath* is not a full UNC name.
NERR_BadDest	*destpath* is not a full UNC name.
NERR_DifferentServers	The source and destination are not on the same server.

An overview:

The *NetRemoteCopy* API provides a more efficient mechanism for copying files on a remote server than the traditional copy command. Consider the following command line:

```
copy \\apps\public\src \\apps\public\dest
```

When the copy command executes this command line, it carries out the following operations:

```
open source file (\\apps\public\src)
open destination file (\\apps\public\dest)
while not at end of file
    read a block from the source
    write the block to the destination
close source file
close destination file
```

Every one of these file-system operations would require information to be brought across the network to the machine that issued the command. The *NetRemoteCopy* API function is much more efficient. It instructs the remote machine to do the copy, and it avoids the network transfers. In the *NetRemoteCopy* API, two cases are valid:

- The source is a file, and the destination either is a file or does not exist. The source file is copied to the destination, subject to the open flags and the copy flags.

- The source is a filename, possibly containing wildcard characters, and the destination is a directory name. All matching files are copied into the directory, subject to the open flags and the copy flags.

Names and passwords

The *sourcepath* and *destpath* parameters must both be fully qualified network names, including a server name. Naturally, the server and netname portions of the pathname must name an active share at the server. In version 1.0 of LAN Manager, the source and destination must be on the same server but need not reference the same netname. Thus, it is possible to use *NetRemoteCopy* to copy *sys\public\tmp\f1* to *sys\private\f2*.

sourcepass and *destpass* are passwords to the source and destination shares. A NULL pointer in either argument indicates that the default logon password is to be used.

- If the server is running in share mode, the passwords must match the passwords of the shares, if there are any.

- If the server is running user-mode security, *sourcepass* is ignored. The password *destpass* must give the user a validated logon on the server. If a session is already established, *destpass* is also ignored.

The *oflags* and *cflags* parameters

Two additional parameters specify how the destination file will be opened and how the file will be copied. The *oflags* parameter is similar to the *DosOpen* open mode flags, although *oflags* is somewhat limited. This parameter is a set of bits that instruct the remote copy operation what to do when the destination file already exists and when it doesn't.

If the destination exists, the action is determined by *oflags* as follows:

Value	Meaning
0x0	If the destination file exists, fail.
0x1	If the destination file exists, append the source to it.

If the destination doesn't exist, the action is determined by *oflags* as follows:

Value	Meaning
0x2	If the destination file exists, truncate it. One of these three must be true.
0x00	If the destination file does not exist, fail.
0x10	If the destination file does not exist, create it. One of these two must be true.

The other bits in the *oflags* parameter must be zero. These flags are in addition to access control permissions. In order to append to or truncate a file, for example, the user must have Write (W) permission. In order to create the destination file, the user must have Create (C) permission.

The *cflags* parameter controls the interpretation of the destination pathname. It is a set of bits:

Bitmask	Value	Meaning
MUST_BE_FILE	0x01	The destination must be a file.
MUST_BE_DIR	0x02	The destination must be a directory. Only MUST_BE_FILE or MUST_BE_DIR can be set. If neither is set, the copy command assumes a file unless a directory of that name exists.
ASCIL_DEST	0x04	The destination file is ASCII. If not set, the destination file is treated as a binary.
ASCIL_SOURCE	0x08	The source file is ASCII. If not set, the source file is treated as a binary.
VERIFY	0x10	Verify all writes.

Return statusUpon return of the copy, the *buf* parameter contains the *copy_info* structure, containing the following elements:

Member Name	Description
USHORT ci_num_copied	The number of files successfully copied
char ci_err_buf[]	A text string of the filename that failed to be copied

NetRemoteMove

Moves a file from one location to another on a remote server.

```
unsigned far pascal
NetRemoteMove(
    char far * sourcepath,    /* source file pathname     */
    char far * destpath,      /* destination file pathname */
    char far * sourcepass,    /* source password          */
    char far * destpass,      /* destination password     */
    USHORT oflags,            /* open flags               */
    USHORT mflags,            /* move flags               */
    char far * buf,           /* buffer for return text   */
    USHORT buflen             /* length of buf            */
    )
```

Remote access:

NetRemoteMove is subject to server logon and regular ACL permissions.

Error returns:

If successful, *NetRemoteMove* returns 0. If unsuccessful, it returns the error codes noted in *NetRemoteCopy*.

The *NetRemoteMove* API is similar to *NetRemoteCopy*, but it deletes the source file. The *sourcepath*, *destpath*, *sourcepass*, *destpass*, *oflags*, *buf*, and *buflen* parameters have the same meaning and restrictions as they do in *NetRemoteCopy*. The *mflags* parameter is the same as the *cflags* parameter. The *move_info* structure returned in *buf* is identical to the *copy_info* structure, as shown in the following table:

Member Name	Description
USHORT mi_num_copied	The number of files successfully moved
char mi_err_buf[1]	A text string of the filename that failed to be moved

NetRemoteMove differs from *NetRemoteCopy* in the following ways:

- The source file is deleted when the destination file has been successfully written.

- The user must have delete (D) access control permission for the destination directory.

- If the source and destination files are in the same directory, no copy of data takes place; the source file is simply renamed.

NetRemoteExec

Executes a program on a remote server.

```
unsigned far pascal
NetRemoteExec(
    char far * reserved1,        /* must be 0xFFFFFFFFL     */
    char far * failname,         /* buffer for failed name  */
    unsigned failnamelen,        /* length of failname      */
    unsigned asynchtraceflags,   /* execute mode flags       */
    char far * argptr,           /* argument strings        */
    char far * envpointer,       /* environment pointer     */
    RESULTCODES far *rc,         /* OS/2 result codes       */
    char far * pgmname,          /* program filename        */
    char far * reserved2,        /* must be NULL            */
    USHORT rexflags              /* remote exec flags       */
    )
```

Remote access:

NetRemoteExec is subject to server logon and regular ACL permissions.

Error returns:

If successful, *NetRemoteExec* returns 0. If unsuccessful, it returns a standard API return code, a standard OS/2 DosExecPgm return code, or one of the following error codes:

Error Return	Meaning
NERR_ErrCommRunSrv	An error in communicating with the server occurred.
NERR_RunSrvPaused	The Netrun service at the server was paused.
ERROR_FILE_NOT_FOUND	The remote filename is not in the execution path.

An overview:

The *NetRemoteExec* API allows programs to execute subprograms at the server. It is very similar to the OS/2 *DosExecPgm* API. In the overview of

LAN Manager in Chapter 2, the Netrun service was described. Consider the following command:

```
net run dbupdate ralph barbara
```

The net run command takes the program name and arguments and passes them to the *NetRemoteExec* API. This API does all the work of remote program execution, including the use of named pipes to map the remote program's standard I/O and signals over the network.

The parameters

Most *NetRemoteExec* and *DosExecPgm* parameters have the same meanings. If the program cannot be executed at the server, the *failname* buffer is filled with the name of the file. The calling program must set *failnamelen* to the size of the buffer. *asynchtraceflags* determines whether the program is executed synchronously or asynchronously. (See the section titled ''Local or remote?'' for a list of legal values.)

The *argptr* parameter points to a buffer containing the command-line arguments for the remote process. Conventionally, the first argument is the name of the program, but it can be any zero-terminated text string. The rest of the arguments are separated by a single space and are terminated with '\0' . If the remote program is a C program, *argv[0]* points to the first string in the buffer. Each subsequent value points to the corresponding words in the buffer. Each space character is turned into the terminating 0 for each argument.

The *envptr* parameter contains a list of environment strings, each terminated with a double '\0' to mark the end of the buffer. Environment strings are usually of the form *NAME=VALUE*, but the buffer can pass arbitrary text strings. Any environment variable can be passed to the remote process, but the PATH variable is special. The remote process receives a PATH variable set to the execution path for the server.

The *rc* parameter is a pointer to the OS/2 RESULTCODES structure. It has two members. These values will be the same as for local program execution under OS/2.

Member Name	Description
USHORT codeTerminate	The process termination code
USHORT codeResult	The process result code

The *pgmname* parameter is the name of the program to be executed remotely. It must contain a legal extension and cannot contain any path characters.

The *rexflags* parameter is a bitmask containing remote execution flags. Their meanings are as follows:

Bitmask	Value	Meaning
REM_PIPE_MODE	0x01	If 0, the standard I/O pipes use message mode. If 1, they use raw mode.
REM_WAIT_MODE	0x02	If 0, a CWait function waits for the entire process tree before returning a result code. If 1, the immediate remote process is waited on.
REM_SIGL_MODE	0x04	If 0, SIGINTR and SIGBREAK signals are mapped to SIGKILL when transmitted to the remote process. If 1, no mapping occurs.

Local or remote?

The *NetRemoteExec* parameters are very similar to those used in the OS/2 *DosExecPgm* API. In fact, if the current directory is on the local workstation, the *NetRemoteExec* call simply passes the arguments to *DosExecPgm*. *NetRemoteExec* differs from *DosExecPgm* in the following ways:

■ The asynch trace flags can take only the following values:

EXEC_SYNC	Execute in foreground.
EXEC_ASYNC	Execute in background with no result code.
EXEC_ASYNCRESULT	Execute in background with a result code.

■ *NetRemoteExec* cannot take asynch flag values of EXEC_TRACE or EXEC_BACKGROUND.

■ The *envpointer* parameter cannot be NULL.

■ The program name must contain an extension. It cannot contain path separator characters (that is, only the name of the file within the current directory is allowed).

■ The remote process inherits only handles 0 (stdin), 1 (stdout), and 2 (stderr). No other open handles are inherited.

■ The *codeTerminate* member in the RESULTCODES structure has no meaning.

If *NetRemoteExec* is used with the *asynchtraceflags* parameter, indicating asynchronous execution, a PID is returned in the first word of the RESULTCODES structure. This is a valid PID and can be used with *DosFlagProcess* to send signals to the remote process. The use of *DosCWait* or *DosKillProcess* with the PID is also valid.

Some security concerns

Because the remotely executed program runs at the server, any file-system access occurs directly at the server, bypassing LAN Manager security. In order to make remote program execution somewhat safer, a number of constraints have been placed on the *NetRemoteExec* API:

- The current drive must be a redirected drive connected to the server on which you want to execute the program.

- The program name cannot have any pathname qualifiers in it. It must be the name of the EXE file only.

- The user must have execute (X) permission for the program.

- The directory containing the program must be in the server's *runpath*. The runpath variable is an item in the server's LAN-MAN.INI file that declares a list of directories from which programs can be remotely executed.

Searching for the file

NetRemoteExec has two other oddities:

- Although the current drive must be redirected to the server, no correlation between the current directory and the location of the remote executable is required. In fact, the current directory is ignored in the search for the executable: The Netrun service searches *runpath* until it finds a program with a matching name. Thus if you had two programs named PROG.EXE in two different directories, and if both directories were in *runpath*, *NetRemoteExec* would always find the program in the first directory, regardless of your current directory location. This is unlike *DosExecPgm*, which first looks in the current directory.

- The PATH environment variable for the remote program is always set to *runpath*, even if PATH is set as part of the *envp* argument to *NetRemoteExec*.

A Net Run Extender

When you use the net run command to execute a remote program, you must first use the net use command to change the current drive to the server. The NRUN program (Figure 5-13) combines these two commands: It takes a network pathname as its first argument and establishes the connection. It then changes the current drive. Note that on OS/2 the current drive is a character-istic of the process, so the current drive will be unchanged when the program terminates.

A simple extension to this program is to have it change back to the original directory and delete the network connection at the end of the program.

```
/*
 * NRUN.C -- This program remotely executes a program by establishing
 * a connection to the specified network pathname (if the connection
 * doesn't already exist), changing the current drive and directory, and
 * executing the file with the NetRemoteExec API.  If a password is
 * required, NRUN uses the default.  An argument list for the remote
 * program can be specified after the remote program name.
 *
 * Compile with:  C> cl nrun.c netapi.lib string_f.lib
 *
 * Usage:  C> nrun UNCpathname programname [arg_list]
 *
 */

#include <stdio.h>
#include <os2.h>
#include <string.h>
#include <string_f.h>   /* defined in Chapter 3 */
#include <netcons.h>
#include <remutil.h>
#include <use.h>

main(argc, argv)
int argc;
char **argv;
    {
    int i;
    char buf[BUFSIZ];
    char argbuf[BUFSIZ], envbuf[2], pgmbuf[12];
    char *p, *pgmname, *netname;
    unsigned short er, te, err, attr, curd;
    unsigned long diskmap, mask;
    RESULTCODES rc;
    struct use_info_1 use, *pu = (struct use_info_1 *)buf;

    if (argc < 3)
        error("Syntax:  nrun UNCpathname programname [arg_list]\n");
```

Figure 5-13.
The NRUN.C program.

(continued)

Figure 5-13. *continued*

```
/* check for an extension */
pgmname = argv[2];
if (strchr(pgmname, '.') == NULL)
    {
    strcpy(pgmbuf, pgmname);
    strcat(pgmbuf, ".EXE");
    pgmname = pgmbuf;
    }


/* be sure the first argument is a UNC pathname */
if (strncmp(argv[1], "\\\\", 2) != 0)
    error("\"%s\" is not a UNC pathname\n", argv[1]);
netname = argv[1];
argc -= 2;
argv += 2;

/* Is there already a redirected drive to the UNC pathname? */
if ((err = NetUseEnum(NULL, 1, buf, BUFSIZ, &er, &te)) != 0)
    error("Cannot list existing uses: %d\n", err);
while (er)
    {
    /* names match and it is not a UNC use */
    if (stricmp_f(pu->ui1_remote, netname) == 0 &&
            pu->ui1_local [0] != 0)
        break;
    ++pu;
    --er;
    }
if (!er)
    {
    /* get the next available drive name (skip A and B) */
    DosQCurDisk(&curd, &diskmap);
    for (i = 2, mask = (1 << 2); i < 26; ++i, mask <<= 1)
        {
        if ((diskmap & mask) == 0)
            break;
        }
    if (i == 26)
        error("No logical drives available\n", NULL);

    /* add the use, with default password */
    sprintf(use.ui1_local, "%c:", i + 'A');
    use.ui1_remote = netname;
    use.ui1_password = NULL;
    use.ui1_asg_type = USE_DISKDEV;
    pu = &use;
```

(continued)

Figure 5-13. *continued*

```
        if ((err = NetUseAdd(NULL, 1, (char far*)&use,
                sizeof(use))) != 0)
            error("Cannot add use: %d\n", err);
        }


    /* We have a drive letter and a (possibly null) pathname.
       Now change the current drive. */
    DosSelectDisk(*pu->uil_local - 'A' + 1);


    /* set up the environment and argument list */
    envbuf[0] = envbuf[1] = 0;
    strcpy(argbuf, pgmname);
    p = argbuf + strlen(argbuf) + 1;
    *p = 0;
    while (--argc)
        {
        strcat(p, *++argv);
        if (argc != 1)
            strcat(p, " ");
        }
    p[strlen(p) + 1] = 0;
    /* now remotely execute the program */
    err = NetRemoteExec(
            (char far *)0xffffffff, /* reserved              */
            buf,                    /* name for failed exec  */
            BUFSIZ,                 /* size                  */
            0,                      /* async flag            */
            argbuf,                 /* argument buffer       */
            envbuf,                 /* environment buffer    */
            &rc,                    /* result codes          */
            pgmname,                /* program filename      */
            NULL,                   /* reserved              */
            0);                     /* remote exec flags     */
    printf("--------\n");
    printf("ERR = %d\n", err);
    exit(0);
    }

/* error -- Print the error message as an Echo batch command
            and exit. */

error(msg, arg)
char *msg;
char *arg;
    {
    printf("ERROR:");
    printf(msg, arg);
    exit(1);
    }
```

SERVICE AND CONFIG APIs

LAN Manager is built around a set of services provided to workstations and servers. Some services are standard LAN Manager services; others are added by users. Two sets of APIs deal specifically with services:

- Service APIs allow users to control the standard services as well as create new services.

- Config APIs allow services and other LAN Manager programs to retrieve configuration information from the LANMAN.INI file.

This chapter introduces the standard LAN Manager services and describes how to use the Service and Config APIs to install, control, and configure all types of services.

What Is a Service?

A LAN Manager service is a program (or set of programs)—written to a set of specifications—that becomes an extension of the core LAN Manager. Whenever you use a LAN Manager user command to start, pause, continue, or stop a LAN Manager service, you use the simplest form of a service. You can use these commands not only on LAN Manager standard services but also on new services created with the Service APIs.

Services can be started (installed), paused, continued, and stopped (uninstalled), and each service can register its ability to perform any of these operations. Services must carry out these operations quickly (usually within ten seconds) or must notify the system that the requested operation is still in progress. (See the *NetServiceStatus* API.)

To start a service, you call the *NetServiceInstall* API, which calls *DosExec-Pgm* to start the service. If the LANMAN.INI file contains a component for the service, the component's parameters are passed to the command line of the service. During the life of the service program, other programs can send instructions and queries to the service through the *NetServiceControl* API. The service responds through the *NetServiceStatus* API.

Standard LAN Manager Services

The standard LAN Manager services let you control the functional components of the network. This section describes each of the standard LAN Manager services.

The Workstation Service

The Workstation service is the primary LAN Manager service. Because it maintains information and tables used by many APIs, it must be installed (started) before any other services can be installed. After it has been installed, it can be paused, continued, or stopped:

- The workstation can be paused and continued. This causes all PrintQ and Comm redirection to be paused. This does not affect any open handles on redirected device names, but all other PrintQ and Comm connections revert to their local meanings. For example, if LPT1 is the local name for a connection to \\srv\laser, pausing the workstation makes LPT1 refer to the first printer device until the service is continued.

- If the workstation is paused or continued, the *arg* argument is a bit-mask with the following meanings:

Bitmask	Meaning
SERVICE_CTRL_REDIR_PRINT	Pause PrintQ redirection
SERVICE_CTRL_REDIR_COMM	Pause Comm redirection

- The workstation can be stopped. However, if the server is installed, the workstation uninstall will fail.

The Message Service

The Message service lets workstations receive text messages from other workstations. With the exception of the *NetMessageBufferSend* and *NetMessageFileSend* APIs, all Message APIs require that the Message service be installed. Under OS/2 this service can be uninstalled, but it cannot be paused or continued.

The Netpopup Service

When the Message service indicates that a message has arrived, the Netpopup service uses the OS/2 Vio functions to print the message on the workstation console. Under OS/2 this service can be uninstalled, but it cannot be paused or continued.

The Server Service

The Server service is the primary service at the server. If the Server service is paused, no new sessions or new connections can be created, and no new opens are allowed. Existing sessions, connections, and opens are unaffected. The Server service can also be continued and uninstalled.

The Alerter Service

The Alerter service works with the Alert APIs (to package notification of significant events) and the Message APIs (to send messages to appropriate users or administrators). The Alerter service can be uninstalled, but it cannot be paused or continued.

The Netrun Service

The Netrun service lets a workstation execute a program on a remote server with the server's memory and system resources. Netrun uses the *NetRemoteExec* API to execute the remote application. Note that programs requiring screen output cannot be executed with Netrun.

The Netrun service must be installed at the server for *NetRemoteExec* to work. Netrun can be paused, preventing remote processes from executing at the server. (*NetRemoteExec* will return NERR_RunSrvPaused to the workstation.) Any currently executing programs are unaffected. Netrun can then be continued, restoring its ability to accept new remote executions. When Netrun is uninstalled, it issues a *DosKillProcess* function for each process it has started. Note that this can fail if the process is trapping signals.

The Netlogon Service

The Netlogon service maintains network security by verifying the username and password supplied by each person who attempts to log on to the network. Netlogon can be paused, preventing it from participating in network logon if it is a primary or backup domain controller.

Nonprogrammable Services

Four additional services are available in LAN Manager version 2.0:

- The Replicator service

- The Uninterruptible Power Supply (UPS) service

- The Remoteboot service

- The Timesource service

These services are not associated with any LAN Manager APIs, and as such, are not programmable. They are mentioned here for completeness only. For information about using these services, consult the *Microsoft LAN Manager Administrator's Guide*.

The Service APIs

Service APIs let you install and control the network service programs just described, as well as those you create on your own. Five Service APIs are available:

- *NetServiceControl*
- *NetServiceEnum*
- *NetServiceGetInfo*
- *NetServiceInstall*
- *NetServiceStatus*

To use the Service APIs in a program you must include NETCONS.H and SERVICE.H at compile time and must link with the NETOEM.LIB stub library. Three levels of information structures are available for these APIs.

The *service_info_0* structure (level 0) contains the following member:

Member Name	Description
char svci0_name[SNLEN+1]	The name of the service (e.g., "NETRUN")

The *service_info_1* structure (level 1) contains the following members:

Member Name	Description		
char svci1_name[SNLEN+1]	The name of the service (e.g., "NETRUN")		
USHORT svci1_status	A bitmasked field showing the current status of the service. In some cases, there is a fieldmask and a value within the field. In the other cases, there is just a bitmask.		
	Fieldmask	*Value*	*Meaning*
	SERVICE_INSTALL_STATE	0x03	Bits 0,1: Is the service installed?
	Fields	*Value*	*Meaning*
	SERVICE_UNINSTALLED	0x00	The service is currently not installed.
	SERVICE_INSTALL_PENDING	0x01	The service is in the process of installing.
	SERVICE_UNINSTALL_PENDING	0x02	The service is in the process of uninstalling.
	SERVICE_INSTALLED	0x03	The service is currently installed.

(continued)

Member Name	Description		
	Fieldmask	**Value**	**Meaning**
	SERVICE_PAUSE_STATE	0x0C	Bits 2,3: Is the service paused?
	Fields	**Value**	**Meaning**
	SERVICE_ACTIVE	0x0	The service is not paused.
	SERVICE_CONTINUE_PENDING	0x4	The service is in the process of continuing.
	SERVICE_PAUSE_PENDING	0x08	The service is in the process of pausing.
	SERVICE_PAUSED	0x0C	The service is paused.
	Bitmask	**Value**	**Meaning**
	SERVICE_NOT_UNINSTALLABLE	0x00	Bit 4: Once installed, the service cannot be uninstalled.
	SERVICE_UNINSTALLABLE	0x10	Bit 4: The service can be uninstalled.
	SERVICE_NOT_PAUSABLE	0x00	Bit 5: The service cannot be paused.
	SERVICE_PAUSABLE	0x20	Bit 5: The service can be paused.
ULONG svci1_code	The meaning of this field depends on the operation being performed. During installation it will carry CCP information, and during uninstallation it will carry UIC information.		
	State	**Information**	
	SERVICE_UNINSTALLED	Why the uninstall was done. This is the UIC.	
	SERVICE_UNINSTALL_PENDING	Must be 0.	
	SERVICE_INSTALL_PENDING	The continuing status of the installation. This is the CCP information.	
	SERVICE_INSTALLED	Must be 0.	
USHORT svci1_pid	The process ID of the service program.		

The *service_info_2* structure (level 2) contains all of the members of the *service_info_1* structure, with the addition of the following member:

Member Name	Description
char svci2_text[STXTLEN+1]	If the service is in the uninstalled state, this text string provides further UIC information. In all other cases, it must be a null string (zero length).

The fieldmask isolates the bits of interest, and the bitmask checks for a matching value. For example, the following C expression determines whether the installation status is in the installed state:

```
if ((status & SERVICE_INSTALL_STATE) == SERVICE_INSTALLED)
```

The bitmask checks a bit directly, as in checking whether the service can be paused or not:

```
if ((status & SERVICE_PAUSABLE) != 0)
```

NetServiceControl

Controls the operation of started (installed) services.

```
unsigned far pascal
NetServiceControl(
        char far * servername,      /* where to execute        */
        char far * service,         /* service name            */
        char opcode,                /* control command         */
        unsigned char arg,          /* control argument        */
        unsigned char far * buf,    /* buffer for return data  */
        USHORT buflen               /* size of buf             */
        )
```

Remote access:

NetServiceControl can be called remotely by an administrator, or by a user with the *server operator* privilege at the server.

NetServiceControl can be called remotely but requires *admin* privilege at the server.

Error returns:

If successful, *NetServiceControl* returns 0. If unsuccessful, it returns one of the following error codes:

Error Return	Meaning
NERR_Buf_TooSmall	The *buf* return buffer is too small to hold a *service_info_2* structure.
NERR_ServiceNotInstalled	The *service* name is not active.
NERR_ServiceTableLocked	A conflict exists over the use of an internal resource. Retry the operation.
NERR_ServiceCtlBusy	A conflict exists over the use of an internal resource. Retry the operation.
NERR_ServiceCtlNotValid	*opcode* is invalid. This can occur, for example, if the service is not pausable and *opcode* is PAUSE.
NERR_ServiceCtlTimeout	The service did not respond to the control operation within the timeout period. Usually this means that the service is no longer alive, but if the system is heavily loaded and the service is running at low priority, it might mean the service didn't have time to respond. If this is the case, lengthen the timeout period and interrogate the status to see if the control operation succeeded.
NERR_ServiceKillProc	The service did not respond to an uninstall signal, so it is stopped with *DosKillProcess* and marked as uninstalled.
NERR_ServiceNotCtrl	The service is not in the installed state, so the operation was ignored.

An overview:

Applications use the *NetServiceControl* API to interrogate or send control messages to a LAN Manager service.

The following values are valid arguments for *opcode*:

Opcode	Meaning
SERVICE_CTRL_INTERROGATE	Obtain the status of the service.
SERVICE_CTRL_PAUSE	Pause the installed service.
SERVICE_CTRL_CONTINUE	Continue the paused service.
SERVICE_CTRL_UNINSTALL	Stop (uninstall) the installed service.

NOTE: *Microsoft reserves values 4 through 127 for future expansion. OEMs can use values 128 through 255 for their own service-control opcodes.*

The service can choose to ignore pause or uninstall opcodes but should have its *svci2_status* bit set at NOT_PAUSABLE or NOT_UNINSTALLABLE, respectively. The meaning of pause and continue varies from service to service and is discussed at the beginning of this chapter. An ignored opcode is treated as if it were an interrogate request.

The *arg* argument provides the service with extra information about the opcode. The meaning of the values is arbitrary and varies from service to service. In most cases it should be 0. For standard LAN Manager services, only the Workstation service has meaningful *arg* values. (These are listed on page 163.)

The *buf* argument returns a *service_info_2* structure. *svci2_status* contains the status of the requested operation. If the operation might take longer than the timeout period, the service returns a "pending" status value (such as SERVICE_UNINSTALL_PENDING). An application would need to do subsequent *NetServiceControl* operations to interrogate the status and determine when the operation was complete.

We have ways of making you talk

The interrogate opcode is always valid, provided that the service is installed.

- If the service is in the installed or paused state, then the service itself is signaled, requesting it to update its current status with a *NetServiceStatus* call.

- If the service is in the INSTALL_PENDING, UNINSTALL_PENDING, or UNINSTALLED state, then the last known status is returned with no attempt to communicate with the service itself.

- If the service has never been installed or if the service has been uninstalled and its entry in the service table has been overwritten, then *NetServiceControl* returns an error code of NERR_ServiceNotInstalled.

Service status information is kept in a table, the size of which is determined by the *numservices* parameter in the LANMAN.INI file. Once a service is uninstalled, the last available status information remains in the table until the system needs to reuse the table entry. The information is preserved as long as possible. This allows applications to use *NetServiceControl* to get UIC information about uninstalled services.

Opcodes other than SERVICE_CTRL_INTERROGATE are valid only for services in the INSTALLED state. If the service is in the PAUSE_PENDING or UNINSTALL_PENDING state, *NetStatusControl* returns the NERR_ServiceCtlNotValid error code for such opcodes.

NetServiceEnum

Retrieves information about all started services.

```
unsigned far pascal
NetServiceEnum(
    char far * servername,    /* where to execute        */
    short level,              /* must be zero            */
    char far * buf,           /* buffer for return data  */
    USHORT buflen,            /* size of buf             */
    USHORT far *entriesread,  /* number of entries read  */
    USHORT far *totalentries, /* total entries available */
    )
```

Levels:
Supports level 0, 1, and 2 data structures.

Remote access:
NetServiceEnum can be called remotely by any user with a valid account in the UAS database. *NetServiceEnum* can be called remotely, but it requires *admin* privilege at the server.

Error returns:
If successful, *NetServiceEnum* returns 0. If unsuccessful, it returns the standard error codes for Enum calls.

An overview:
The *NetServiceEnum* API obtains information about all active LAN Manager services. No information is provided about services in the uninstalled state. This is a straightforward Enumeration call as described in Chapter 4.

NetServiceGetInfo

Retrieves information about a specific service.

```
unsigned far pascal
NetServiceGetInfo(
    char far * servername,    /* where to execute        */
    char far * service,       /* service name            */
    short level,              /* info structure level    */
    char far * buf,           /* buffer for return data  */
    USHORT buflen,            /* size of buf             */
    USHORT far *totalavail    /* total bytes available   */
    )
```

Levels:
Supports level 0, 1, and 2 data structures.

Remote access:
NetServiceGetInfo can be called remotely by any user with a valid account in the UAS database. *NetServiceGetInfo* can be called remotely, but it requires *admin* privilege at the server.

Error returns:
If successful, *NetServiceGetInfo* returns 0. If the service is uninstalled (or if its resources were reused), *NetServiceEnum* returns NERR_ServiceNot-Installed. If unsuccessful, it returns the standard error codes for GetInfo calls.

An overview:
The *NetServiceGetInfo* API returns information about a specific active LAN Manager service. Unlike *NetServiceEnum*, this API can obtain information about uninstalled services. This allows programs to examine the UIC codes to determine why the service is uninstalled. Note that if there is a lot of service installation occurring, the service resources for an uninstalled service might be reused and the UIC information lost.

NetServiceInstall

Starts a network service.

```
unsigned far pascal
NetServiceInstall(
        char far * servername,    /* where to execute         */
        char far * service,       /* service name             */
        char far * buf,           /* buffer for return data   */
        char far * cmdargs,       /* command-line arguments   */
        USHORT buflen             /* size of buf              */
        )
```

Remote access:
NetServiceInstall can be called remotely by an administrator, or by a user with *operator* privilege at the server.

Error returns:
If successful, *NetServiceInstall* returns 0. If unsuccessful, it returns an OS/2 *DosExecPgm* error or one of the error codes shown on the following page.

Error Return	Meaning
NERR_BufTooSmall	The *buf* argument was too small for a *service_info_2* structure.
NERR_BadServiceName	The *service* name does not exist in the [services] component of the LANMAN.INI file.
NERR_BadServiceProgName	The program name given in the [services] component is invalid.
NERR_LineTooLong	A service parameter in the LANMAN.INI file has a line that is longer than PATHLEN+1.
NERR_ServiceInstalled	The service is already installed.
NERR_ServiceCtlTimeout	The service program did not respond to the *NetServiceInstall* within the timeout period. The program is terminated by *DosKillProcess* and marked uninstalled.
NERR_ServiceTableLocked	A conflict exists over the use of an internal resource. Retry the installation.
NERR_ServiceEntryLocked	A conflict exists over the use of an internal resource. Retry the installation.
NERR_ServiceTableFull	When the workstation started, the LANMAN.INI parameter *numservices* determined how many services could be run simultaneously. This installation would exceed that number.
NERR_ServiceCtlBusy	A conflict exists over the use of an internal resource. Retry the installation.
ERROR_NOT_ENOUGH_MEMORY	An internal call to *DosAllocSeg* failed.

An overview:

The *NetServiceInstall* API lets you start a LAN Manager service.

The *service* argument must match the name of a service in the [services] component of the LANMAN.INI file. This section of LANMAN.INI declares service names and the corresponding programs to be executed when the service is installed. For example, the following lines declare the standard LAN Manager services for the Workstation, Server, and Messenger:

```
[services]
workstation = services\wksta.exe
server = services\netsvini.exe
messenger = services\msrvinit.exe
```

Program names on the right are relative to the LAN Manager root directory. The *NetServiceInstall* API looks up the service name (using the *NetConfigGet* API) and uses the *DosExecPgm* function to start the service program. This program can comprise the entire service, or it can execute other processes as part of the service.

The *cmdargs* argument is a set of command-line parameters passed to the service program at startup. *cmdargs* is a pointer to a buffer containing a set of end-to-end text strings (delineated by each string's terminating '\0') with a double '\0' terminator. These parameters can be of the following forms:

```
parameter_name
parameter_name=value
parameter_name:value
```

where *parameter_name* and *value* can be arbitrary text strings but are expected to be known by the service.

If the component matching the *service* parameter in LANMAN.INI exists, the parameter strings there are merged with those supplied in the *cmdargs* argument. In the case of duplication, the *cmdargs* version takes precedence.

The service program is executed with the merged parameter list passed as *execargs* to *DosExecPgm*. The program is expected to follow the service protocol presented at the end of this chapter.

When *NetServiceInstall* returns, the *buf* argument contains a *service_info_2* structure. *svci2_status* indicates the state of the service. If the status is uninstalled, *svci2_code* contains UIC information for determining why the service failed to install.

NetServiceStatus

Updates status information for a service.

```
unsigned far pascal
NetServiceStatus(
    char far * buf,          /* status data   */
    USHORT buflen            /* length of buf */
    )
```

Remote access:
The *NetServiceStatus* API cannot be called remotely.

Error returns:
If successful, *NetServiceStatus* returns 0. If unsuccessful, it returns one of the error codes shown on the following page.

Error Return	Meaning
NERR_Buf_TooSmall	The *buf* return buffer is too small to hold a *service_info_2* structure.
NERR_ServiceNotInstalled	The *service* name is not active.
NERR_ServiceTableLocked	A conflict exists over the use of an internal resource. Retry the operation.

An overview:

Installed services use the *NetServiceStatus* API to update their status information. Only those programs started with *NetServiceInstall* can use *NetServiceStatus*.

The *buf* argument must contain *service_status* structures of the following forms:

Member Name	Description
USHORT svcs_status	This information is copied directly into the *svci2_status*.
ULONG svcs_code	This information is copied directly into the *svci2_code*.
USHORT svcs_pid	The service APIs keep track of the OS/2 PID of the service program so that *DosSignal* values can be sent to the process as part of the *NetServiceControl* call. The *svcs_pid* value lets the service change the process receiving the signal. This is especially useful in a multiprocess service. Once *svcs_pid* is set, only that process can issue *NetServiceStatus* calls, which could also pass the torch on to yet another process. If 0, the PID is left unchanged.
char svcs_text[STXTLEN+1]	This information is copied directly into *svci2_text*.

A service can update its status at any time with the *NetServiceStatus* API.

Providing Status Information During Pending Operations

Each service must provide "control completion pending" (CCP) information when a pending install expects to take a long time, and "uninstall information codes" (UICs) during a pending uninstall.

Control Completion Pending (CCP) Values

If a service expects to take longer than two seconds to install or uninstall, it must periodically use the *NetServiceStatus* function to inform the system that installation is still pending. In each *NetServiceStatus* status report, the installing service sets the CCP value in *svcil_code*. A value of 0 in *svcil_code* means that no information is available.

The *svcl_code* long word is divided into three fields:

Field Name	Value	Meaning
SERVICE_IP_QUERY_HINT	0x10000	This is a bit that tells the requesting application that the CCP information is "real" and not just a wild guess.
SERVICE_IP_WAIT_TIME	0x0FF00	The time (in tenths of a second) that the installation is expected to take.
SERVICE_IP_CHKPT_NUM	0x0FF	This is a sequence number of the NetServiceStatus calls made during the pending installation.

The SERVICE.H include file defines a macro for setting the IP values:

```
SERVICE_CCP_CODE(wait, chkpt)
```

There are no macros defined for getting these values out of the *svcil_code* member, so here are three macros for that:

```
#define SERVICE_CCP_HINT_GET(psvc) (psvc->svcil_code & 0x10000)

#define SERVICE_CCP_WAIT_GET(psvc) ((psvc->svcil_code >> 8) & 0xff)

#define SERVICE_CCP_CHKPT_GET(psvc) (psvc->svcil_code & 0xff)
```

Uninstall Information Codes (UICs)

When a service completes an uninstall operation, it should fill in the *svci2_code* member with information about why the uninstall was done. If the service is doing the uninstall at the instruction of a *NetServiceControl* operation, the UIC should be set to 0. If the service is uninstalling itself because an error has occurred, the UIC lets other programs obtain information about the reason for the uninstall.

The UIC information is packed into high and low words of the long integer *svci2_code*. The high word contains the actual UIC value (the reason for uninstallation), and the low word is a modifier. The *svci2_text* array can contain an ASCIIZ string with further information about the uninstall.

The SERVICE.H file defines a macro for putting values into *svci2_code:*

```
#define SERVICE_UIC_CODE(cc,mm)
```

However, it doesn't provide a macro for other programs to extract them. Here are two macros that do this:

```
#define SERVICE_UIC_CODE_GET(uic) ((uic & 0xffff0000) >> 16)
```

```
#define SERVICE_UIC_MOD_GET(uic) (uic & 0xffff)
```

The uninstall code (the high word) can be one of the following values:

UIC	Value	Meaning
SERVICE_UIC_BADPARMVAL	3051	One of the command-line parameters has a bad value.
SERVICE_UIC_MISSPARM	3052	A required parameter is missing from the command line.
SERVICE_UIC_UNKPARM	3053	An unknown parameter was present on the command line.
SERVICE_UIC_RESOURCE	3054	There was not enough of some resource needed by the service.
SERVICE_UIC_CONFIG	3055	There was a problem with the configuration of the service.
SERVICE_UIC_SYSTEM	3056	An OS/2 system error occurred.
SERVICE_UIC_INTERNAL	3057	An internal error to the service occurred.
SERVICE_UIC_AMBIGPARM	3058	Two or more parameters provided ambiguous information.
SERVICE_UIC_DUPPARM	3059	A command-line parameter was duplicated.
SERVICE_UIC_KILL	3060	A kill signal was sent to the process.
SERVICE_UIC_EXEC	3061	There was a problem doing a program exec for part of the service.
SERVICE_UIC_SUBSERV	3062	The service tried to install another service, and the install failed.
SERVICE_UIC_CONFLPARM	3063	One or more of the command parameters conflict.

The lower word of the UIC contains a modifier for the base UIC value. The modifiers defined for each base UIC value are as follows:

UIC	Value	Meaning
SERVICE_UIC_BADPARMVAL		No modifiers are defined, but *svci2_text* is the parameter name.
SERVICE_UIC_MISSPARM		No modifiers are defined, but *svci2_text* is the parameter name.
SERVICE_UIC_UNKPARM		No modifiers are defined, but *svci2_text* is the parameter name.
SERVICE_UIC_AMBIGPARM		No modifiers are defined, but *svci2_text* is the parameter name.
SERVICE_UIC_DUPPARM		No modifiers are defined, but *svci2_text* is the parameter name.
SERVICE_UIC_RESOURCE		
SERVICE_UIC_M_MEMORY	3070	Insufficient memory.
SERVICE_UIC_M_DISK	3071	Insufficient disk space.
SERVICE_UIC_M_THREADS	3072	OS/2 is out of threads.
SERVICE_UIC_M_PROCESSES	3073	OS/2 is out of processes.
SERVICE_UIC_CONFIG		
SERVICE_UIC_M_SECURITY	3074	The security subsystem failed.
SERVICE_UIC_M_LANROOT	3075	Bad or missing LAN Manager root directory.
SERVICE_UIC_M_REDIR	3076	The redirector must be installed.
SERVICE_UIC_M_SERVER	3077	The server must be started.
SERVICE_UIC_M_FILES	3079	There are incompatible files in the LAN Manager root directory.
SERVICE_UIC_M_LOGS	3080	The LOGS directory does not exist in the LAN Manager root.
SERVICE_UIC_M_LANGROUP	3081	Bad (domain) langroup name.
SERVICE_UIC_M_MSGNAME	3082	The computer name is already in use.
SERVICE_UIC_M_ANNOUNCE	3083	The server name announcement failed.
SERVICE_UIC_SYSTEM		The OS/2 system error code is in the low word.
SERVICE_UIC_INTERNAL		No modifier or text is defined.
SERVICE_UIC_KILL		No modifier or text is defined.
SERVICE_UIC_EXEC		No modifier or text is defined.

(continued)

UIC	Value	Meaning
SERVICE_UIC_SUBSERV		No modifier, but the text is the sub-service name.
SERVICE_UIC_CONFLPARM		No modifier, but the text is a list of the conflicting parameters.

The Config APIs

The Config APIs let programs retrieve information from the LANMAN.INI configuration file. Four Config APIs are available:

- *NetConfigGet*

- *NetConfigGet2*

- *NetConfigGetAll*

- *NetConfigGetAll2*

The Config APIs do not support data structures. To use these APIs in a program, you must include NETCONS.H and CONFIG.H at compile time, and you must link with the NETAPI.LIB stub library.

The Format of LANMAN.INI

The LANMAN.INI file is a text file that contains configuration information for LAN Manager services or for other programs. This file is always located in the root directory of the LAN Manager distribution tree—typically C:\LANMAN.

The file is divided into named components, and each component contains parameters relevant to that component. Any line that has a semicolon as the first nonblank character is a comment line. Comment lines and blank lines can appear anywhere in the LANMAN.INI file and are ignored by the Config APIs.

LANMAN.INI components

Each component begins with a component name line of the following form:

[*component_name*]

component_name can be arbitrary, but for LAN Manager services it must be the same as the service name. The components supplied in the version 2.0 default LANMAN.INI file are as follows:

Component Name	Used For
[networks]	Gives the redirector information about one or more NetBIOS drivers
[workstation]	Configures the basic workstation software
[messenger]	Configures the Messenger service
[netshell]	Configures the full-screen user interface
[server]	Configures the server
[alerter]	Configures the Alerter service
[netrun]	Configures the Netrun service
[replicator]	Configures the Replicator service
[ups]	Configures the Uninterruptible Power Supply (UPS) service
[netlogon]	Configures the Netlogon service
[remoteboot]	Configures the service responsible for booting workstations remotely from the server
[services]	Informs the *NetService* APIs of the existence of LAN Manager service programs

Applications can add their own components to the LANMAN.INI file.

LANMAN.INI parameters

Each component in the LANMAN.INI file contains a (possibly empty) list of parameters. Each parameter is made up of a keyword and a value:

keyword = value

keyword is an arbitrary word meaningful to the software for which the component is intended. Each *keyword* must be unique within a component but need not be unique between components. *value* is a text string that includes all characters after the equal sign (=) to the end of the line. Values can be numbers, but they are always represented as text.

Here is an example of two hypothetical LANMAN.INI components:

```
[toast]
    ; is it wheat, white, or both?
    wheat = yes
    white = no
    slices = 4

; The flavors must be present. Jar size is optional.
[jam]
    flavor = strawberry, raspberry
    ; this number must match the number of flavors
    numflavors = 2
```

NetConfigGet

Retrieves a single entry from a local LANMAN.INI file.

```
unsigned far pascal
NetConfigGet(
    char far * component,     /* component name          */
    char far * parameter,     /* parameter keyword       */
    char far * buf,           /* place for return value  */
    USHORT buflen,            /* size of buf             */
    USHORT *len               /* actual length of value  */
    )
```

An overview:

The *NetConfigGet* API gets the value of a single entry for a given section of a local LANMAN.INI file.

> **NOTE:** *This API is obsolete and exists only for compatibility with LAN Manager version 1.0. Use* NetConfigGet2 *if you are using LAN Manager version 2.0 or later.*

NetConfigGet2

Retrieves a single entry from a local or remote LANMAN.INI file.

```
unsigned far pascal
NetConfigGet2(
    char far * servername,    /* where to execute        */
    char far * reserved,      /* must be NULL            */
    char far * component,     /* component name          */
    char far * parameter,     /* parameter keyword       */
    char far * buf,           /* place for return value  */
    USHORT buflen,            /* size of buf             */
    USHORT *parmlen,          /* actual length of value  */
    )
```

Remote access:

NetConfigGet2 can be called remotely by an administrator, or by a user with any of the following operator privileges at the server:

- accounts operator

- server operator

- print operator

- comm operator

Error returns:

If successful, *NetConfigGet2* returns 0. If unsuccessful, it returns a standard API return code, a standard file-system error code, or one of the following error codes:

Error Return	Meaning
NERR_CfgCompNotFound	The component name does not exist.
NERR_CfgParamNotFound	The parameter name does not exist.
NERR_BufTooSmall	*buflen* is too small to hold parameter data. See the *parmlen* argument for the required length.

An overview:

The *NetConfigGet2* API retrieves a specific parameter value from the LAN-MAN.INI file. Upon return the *buf* return buffer contains whatever is to the right of the equal sign in the parameter, with leading and trailing spaces stripped off. If the *buflen* value is too small for the parameter data, NERR_BufTooSmall is returned as an error code, and *parmlen* will contain the actual buffer size needed.

The *component* argument does not include the enclosing brackets. The *component* and *parameter* arguments are not case dependent. For example, in the hypothetical components previously shown, the following call would return with *buf* containing ''strawberry, raspberry'' in the *buf* array:

```
NetConfigGet2(NULL, NULL, "Jam", "FLAVOR", buf, buflen, &len);
```

NetConfigGetAll

Retrieves an entire component section of a local LANMAN.INI file.

```
unsigned far pascal
NetConfigGetAll(
    char far * component,   /* component name        */
    char far * buf,         /* place for return value */
    USHORT buflen,          /* size of buf           */
    USHORT *bread,          /* number of bytes read  */
    USHORT *bavail          /* bytes available       */
    )
```

An overview:

The *NetConfigGetAll* API gets all of the configuration information in the specified LANMAN.INI section for the specified local server.

NOTE: *This API is obsolete and exists only for compatibility with LAN Manager version 1.0. Use* NetConfigGetAll2 *if you are using LAN Manager version 2.0 or later.*

NetConfigGetAll2

Retrieves an entire component section from a local or remote LAN-MAN.INI file.

```
unsigned far pascal
NetConfigGetAll2(
    char far * servername,      /* where to execute         */
    char far * reserved,        /* must be NULL             */
    char far * component,       /* component name           */
    char far * buf,             /* place for return value   */
    USHORT buflen,              /* size of buf              */
    USHORT *bread,              /* number of bytes read     */
    USHORT *bavail              /* bytes available          */
    )
```

Remote access:

NetConfigGetAll2 can be called remotely by an administrator, or by a user with any of the following operator privileges at the server:

- accounts operator

- server operator

- print operator

- comm operator

Error returns:

If successful, *NetConfigGetAll2* returns 0. If unsuccessful, it returns a standard API return code, a standard file-system error code, or one of the following error codes:

Error Return	Meaning
NERR_CfgCompNotFound	The component name does not exist.
ERROR_MORE_DATA	*buflen* is too small. *bavail* contains the size needed.

An overview:

The *NetConfigGetAll2* API returns an entire component from the LAN-MAN.INI file in the *buf* return buffer. If *buflen* is too small to receive the entire component, as much data as will fit is returned, and the error code is set to ERROR_MORE_DATA. If this happens, the *bread* and *bavail* arguments are set with the number of bytes read and the number of bytes available, respectively. The parameters are returned as a concatenated set of text strings, each zero terminated, with an extra zero at the end of the set. Each parameter string is converted to have the parameter name in uppercase, an equal sign (with no intervening spaces), and the right side of the parameter unchanged. The component name is not case dependent. For example, the following call specifies the hypothetical components previously shown:

```
NetConfigGetAll2(NULL, NULL, "Jam", buf, buflen, &br, &ba)
```

This would return a buffer containing

```
FLAVOR=strawberry, raspberry\0NUMFLAVORS=2\0\0
```

Writing a LAN Manager Service Program

So far, this chapter has shown how to interact with the standard LAN Manager services. You can also add new services by writing them according to a few simple rules. A service program has the following characteristics:

- The program is listed as a service program in the LANMAN.INI file.

- The program runs detached from the console. (No direct console I/O is allowed.)

- At startup, the program follows the *NetServiceStatus* protocol.

- The program has a signal handler for responding to *NetServiceControl* calls.

LANMAN.INI and Services

Two aspects of the LANMAN.INI file affect services. The first is the [services] component. A parameter in this component has the following form:

```
servicename = pathname
```

This description identifies the program as a LAN Manager service. If the pathname of the program is not completely specified, it is relative to the SERVICES directory in the LAN Manager root directory.

A service program can also have configuration parameters in the LANMAN.INI file. When the service is started, the *NetServiceInstall* API looks for a component with the service name. Any parameters are passed on the command line when the program is executed.

For example, if there is a service named MYSERVICE, the LANMAN.INI file could contain the following entries:

```
[services]
    MYSERVICE = MYSER.EXE

[MYSERVICE]
    color = puce
    style = tacky
```

Using *NetServiceInstall* to install MYSERVICE executes the program LAN-MAN\SERVICE\MYSER.EXE and passes the two strings ''color = puce'' and ''style = tacky'' on the command line.

The Getting-Started Protocol

When a service starts up, the *NetServiceInstall* API waits to see if startup is successful. The service program must call *NetServiceStatus* within a reasonable amount of time, otherwise *NetServiceInstall* will return the error NERR_ServiceCtlTimeout. In practice, *NetServiceInstall* waits 60 seconds before doing the error return, but that blocks the calling program during the wait. If the service program will take more than a few seconds to initialize, it should register an INSTALL_PENDING status. For long initializations, the service program should post the INSTALL_PENDING status with *NetServiceStatus* every few seconds to let the system know that everything is all right.

When the service program is executed, *NetServiceInstall* records the process ID of the program so that subsequent *NetServiceControl* calls can communicate with the service. Often a service is a multiprocess application, and the original process will not contain the *NetServiceControl* signal handler. In such cases, the application must call the *NetServiceStatus* API to change the process ID to which control signals are sent.

The SERVICE.C program (Figure 6-1) is a skeleton service program.

```
/*
 * SERVICE.C -- A skeleton service program.  Add your
 * service program code as indicated below.  This program
 * requires the external signal handler sig_handler (SIGNAL.C).
 *
 * Compile with:  C> cl service.c signal.c netapi.lib
 *
 */
```

Figure 6-1.   *(continued)*
The SERVICE.C service program skeleton.

Figure 6-1. *continued*

```
#include <os2.h>
#include <netcons.h>
#include <service.h>

extern void far pascal sig_handler(unsigned, unsigned);

void main(argc,argv)
int argc;
char ** argv;
{
    PFNSIGHANDLER prev;
    unsigned short prevact;
    unsigned err;
    struct service_status ss;

    /* Install signal handler */
    DosSetSigHandler(
                    sig_handler,            /* function name     */
                    &prev,                  /* previous handler  */
                    &prevact,               /* previous action   */
                    SIGA_ACCEPT,            /* action            */
                    SERVICE_RCV_SIG_FLAG    /* flag #5           */
                    );

    /* notify that installation is complete */
    ss.svcs_pid = 0;
    ss.svcs_status = SERVICE_NOT_PAUSABLE !
                    SERVICE_UNINSTALLABLE !
                    SERVICE_INSTALLED;
    ss.svcs_code = 0;
    ss.svcs_text[0] = 0;

    /* These codes can be altered to whatever is appropriate
     * for the service program.  If a long delay is anticipated,
     * for example, SERVICE_INSTALLED should be changed to
     * INSTALL_PENDING, and NetServiceStatus should be called
     * after initialization is complete. */

    if ((err = NetServiceStatus( (char far *)&ss, sizeof(ss))) != 0)
        exit(err);
    /* INSERT SERVICE PROGRAM CODE HERE */
}
```

Responding to Signals

The service program must contain a signal handler for responding to *NetServiceControl* calls. Again, timeliness is important. The signals arrive as the Flag A signal, and the program must respond with a *NetServiceStatus* call. SIGNAL.C (Figure 6-2) is a template for a service signal handler.

```c
/*
 * SIGNAL.C -- A signal-handler template that the NetService APIs
 * will communicate through.  Add your own code as indicated
 * below.  This routine is used by the SERVICE.C program.
 *
 */

#include <os2.h>
#include <netcons.h>
#include <service.h>

void far pascal
sig_handler(sig_arg, sig_no)
unsigned sig_arg;
unsigned sig_no;
    {
    struct service_status ss;

    /* switch on action code */
    switch (sig_arg & 0xff)
        {
        case SERVICE_CTRL_UNINSTALL:     /* uninstall required */

            ss.svcs_status = SERVICE_NOT_PAUSABLE |
                             SERVICE_UNINSTALLABLE |
                             SERVICE_UNINSTALLED;
            ss.svcs_code = 0;
            NetServiceStatus((char far *)&ss, sizeof(ss));
            exit(0);
            break;

        case SERVICE_CTRL_PAUSE:
            /* add handle-pausing code here */

        case SERVICE_CTRL_CONTINUE:
            /* add handle-continuing code here */

        default:
            /* add handle user-defined control codes here */
```

Figure 6-2.   *(continued)*
The SIGNAL.C signal-handler template.

Figure 6-2. *continued*

```
    case SERVICE_CTRL_INTERROGATE:

        ss.svcs_status = SERVICE_NOT_PAUSABLE |
                         SERVICE_UNINSTALLABLE |
                         SERVICE_INSTALLED;
        ss.svcs_code = 0;
        NetServiceStatus((char far *)&ss, sizeof(ss));
        break;
    }

/* reenable DosSignal mechanism */
DosSetSigHandler(0, 0, 0, SIGA_ACKNOWLEDGE, sig_no);
return;
}
```

SERVER ADMINISTRATION APIs

This chapter describes the APIs used for routine server administration:

- Server APIs
- Share APIs
- Session APIs
- Connection APIs
- File APIs

These APIs let an administrator inspect the server environment and share resources. They also permit inspection and removal of sessions, connections, and open files.

The Server APIs

The Server APIs control the basic configuration of a server. To use the Server APIs in a program, you must include NETCONS.H and SERVER.H at compile time. If you use the *NetServerEnum* API, you must link with the NETOEM.LIB stub library. For the rest of the Server APIs, you must link with the NETAPI.LIB stub library.

> **NOTE:** *LAN Manager names are case significant. Because LAN Manager user-interface programs automatically map names to uppercase, you need to be on the lookout for case mismatches when using Server APIs.*

Server data structures exist at three levels. Most of the information in the highest-level structure is set by the server at startup and cannot be changed without stopping and restarting the server. Information is obtained either from the [server] section of the LANMAN.INI file or from arguments to the net start server user command.

The *server_info_0* structure contains this member:

Member Name	Description
char sv0_name[CNLEN+1]	A zero-terminated ASCII string containing the computer name of a server. Double backslashes are omitted.

The *server_info_1* structure contains these members:

Member Name	Description
char sv1_name[CNLEN+1]	A zero-terminated ASCII string containing the computer name of a server. Double backslashes are omitted.
UCHAR sv1_version_major	The major version number of the server software (2 in LAN Manager version 2.0).
UCHAR sv1_version_minor	The minor version number of the server software (0 in LAN Manager version 2.0).
ULONG sv1_type	This value identifies the type of server. Values are represented by setting bits, as follows:

Bitmask	Value	Meaning
SV_TYPE_WORKSTATION	0x00000001	This bit is always set. LAN Manager servers are also workstations.
SV_TYPE_SERVER	0x00000002	The server supports file, print, device, and IPC service.
SV_TYPE_SQLSERVER	0x00000004	The server is an SQL server.
SV_TYPE_DOMAIN_CTRL	0x00000008	The server is a Domain Controller.
SV_TYPE_DOMAIN_BAKCTRL	0x00000010	The server is a Backup Domain Controller.
SV_TYPE_TIME_SOURCE	0x00000020	The server is a Time server.
SV_TYPE_AFP	0x00000040	The server is an Apple File Protocol server.
SV_TYPE_NOVELL	0x00000080	The server is a Novell server.
SV_TYPE_ALL	0xffffffff	The server represents all types of servers.

Member Name	Description
char far * sv1_comment	This is a pointer to a text string describing the server. The comment can be a maximum of COMMENTSZ characters. The comment should be a short description of the server, such as "Marketing and Sales Printer Server."

The *server_info_2* structure contains all members of the *server_info_1* structure, as well as the following members:

Member Name	Description
ULONG sv2_ulist_mtime	If the server is running user-mode security, this is the last modification time of the user accounts data.
ULONG sv2_glist_mtime	If the server is running user-mode security, this is the last modification time of the group accounts data.

(continued)

continued

Member Name	Description
ULONG sv2_alist_mtime	If the server is running user-mode security, this is the last modification time of the access-control data.
USHORT sv2_users	The maximum number of simultaneous sessions allowed.
USHORT sv2_disc	Sessions idle longer than this value are deleted. The special value 0xFFFF means no autodisconnect.
char far * sv2_alerts	When admin alerts occur, these names are notified. *sv2_alerts* is a pointer to a string of names separated by spaces.
USHORT sv2_security	The server security mode. The values are as follows:

Mode	Value	Meaning
SV_SHARESECURITY	0	The server is running share-mode security.
SV_USERSECURITY	1	The server is running user-mode security.

Member Name	Description
USHORT sv2_auditing	Indicates whether auditing is enabled at the server: 0 indicates no, 1 indicates yes.
USHORT sv2_numadmin	The maximum number of remote administration sessions allowed into the server at one time.
USHORT sv2_lanmask	The workstation can be connected to more than one network at a time. (The LANMAN.INI file lists available networks in the [networks] section.) The "lanmask" is a bitmask indicating which networks are being served. For example, a value of 00000101b means that the server is processing SMBs from the first and third networks.
USHORT sv2_hidden	Indicates whether the server is announcing its presence to the rest of its domain. The values are as follows:

Mode	Value	Meaning
SV_VISIBLE	0	Periodic announcements are being made.
SV_HIDDEN	1	No announcements are being made.

Member Name	Description
USHORT sv2_announce	If the server is "visible," this is the rate (in seconds) of the announcements.
USHORT sv2_anndelta	A randomization factor (in milliseconds) for the announcement rate. It prevents server announcements from arriving at a workstation simultaneously.
char sv2_guestacct[UNLEN+1]	Name of the default guest logon account. To change it, you alter the *guestacct* parameter of the [server] component in LANMAN.INI.
char far * sv2_userpath	Each user account can be assigned a directory. This is the root directory of that set.
USHORT sv2_chdevs	The maximum number of shared character devices.
USHORT sv2_chdevq	The maximum number of character-device queues.

(continued)

Member Name	Description
USHORT sv2_chdevjobs	The maximum number of waiting jobs in a character-device queue.
USHORT sv2_connections	The maximum number of simultaneous connections that the server allows.
USHORT sv2_shares	The maximum number of simultaneous shares that the server allows.
USHORT sv2_openfiles	The maximum number of simultaneous open files that the server allows.
USHORT sv2_sessopens	The maximum number of simultaneous open files allowed on a single session.
USHORT sv2_sessvcs	The maximum number of virtual circuits to a client.
USHORT sv2_sessreqs	The maximum number of simultaneous file-system requests from a client that the server allows.
USHORT sv2_opensearch	The maximum number of file-system search buffers that can be open at one time.
USHORT sv2_activelocks	The maximum number of file locks that can be active at one time.
USHORT sv2_numreqbuf	The number of standard server buffers available.
USHORT sv2_sizreqbuf	The size of each standard server buffer.
USHORT sv2_numbigbuf	The number of 64-KB buffers available to the server for large-file transfer.
USHORT sv2_numfiletasks	The server can create multiple instances of its file service thread. This allows more overlapping of the processing of file-system requests. This member controls the number of these threads.
USHORT sv2_alertsched	The server raises admin alerts if certain events occur too frequently within a fixed period of time. This member defines this time period (in seconds). Some of the following members control the numbers of events within this time period that are reported.
USHORT sv2_erroralert	If the number of errors specified by *erroralert* occur within the number of minutes specified by *alertsched*, raise an admin alert.
USHORT sv2_logonalert	If the number of logon failures specified by *logonalert* occur within the number of minutes specified by *alertsched*, raise an admin alert.
USHORT sv2_accessalert	If the number of access failures specified by *accessalert* occur within the number of minutes specified by *alertsched*, raise an admin alert.
USHORT sv2_diskalert	If the free space on any disk falls below *diskalert* kilobytes, raise an admin alert.
USHORT sv2_netioalert	If the number of network I/O errors specified by *netioalert* occur within the number of minutes specified by *alertsched*, raise an admin alert.
USHORT sv2_maxauditsz	This is the maximum size (in kilobytes) of the audit file.
char far *sv2_srvheuristics	This value controls the performance heuristics in the server. See the *Microsoft LAN Manager Administrator's Guide* for specifics.

The *server_info_3* structure contains all members of the *server_info_2* structure, as well as the following members:

Member Name	Description
ULONG sv3_auditevents	This bitmask indicates what events the server is auditing. If all corresponding bits in the mask are 1, the indicated auditing is being done.

Bitmask	Value	Meaning
SVAUD_SERVICE	0x1	Starting, stopping, pausing, or continuing the server
SVAUD_GOODSESSLOGON	0x6	Successful server logon
SVAUD_BADSESSLOGON	0x18	Unsuccessful server logon attempts
SVAUD_SESSLOGON	0x1E	All server logon attempts, whether successful or not
SVAUD_GOODNETLOGON	0x60	Successful network logon at this server
SVAUD_BADNETLOGON	0x180	Unsuccessful network logon at this server
SVAUD_NETLOGON	0x1E0	All network logon attempts at this server
SVAUD_LOGON	0x1FE	All server and network logon attempts
SVAUD_GOODUSE	0x600	Successful connections
SVAUD_BADUSE	0x800	Unsuccessful connection attempts
SVAUD_USE	0x1E00	All connection attempts
SVAUD_USERLIST	0x2000	Modifications to the UAS database
SVAUD_PERMISSIONS	0x4000	Modifications to the ACL database
SVAUD_RESOURCE	0x8000	Attempts to use *DosOpen* to open any resource whose ACL is configured for auditing
SVAUD_LOGONLIM	0x10000	Attempts to log on beyond the configured user limit of the server

Member Name	Description
USHORT sv3_autoprofile	A server can be configured for automatic save of all shares at shutdown or automatic load of share information at startup. This value controls these automatic functions. The value is a bitmask indicating any combination of the following:

Member Name	Description		
	Bitmask	*Value*	*Meaning*
	SW_AUTOPROF_LOAD_MASK	0x1	Do autoload at server startup.
	SW_AUTOPROF_SAVE_MASK	0x2	Do autosave at server shutdown.
char far * sv3_autopath	The pathname indicating where to save and load the server information for autoload.		

NetServerGetInfo

Retrieves information about a server.

```
unsigned far pascal
NetServerGetInfo(
    char far * servername,   /* where to execute         */
    short level,             /* info structure level     */
    char far * buf,          /* buffer for return data   */
    USHORT buflen,           /* size of buf              */
    USHORT *totalavail,      /* total bytes available    */
    )
```

Levels:
Supports level 0, 1, 2, and 3 data structures.

Remote access:
Level 0 or level 1 can be called by a user with a valid account in the UAS database. All levels are available to an administrator or a user with the following operator privileges:

- accounts operator

- server operator

- print operator

- comm operator

Error returns:
If successful, *NetServerGetInfo* returns 0. If unsuccessful, it returns one of the standard GetInfo error codes.

An overview:
The *NetServerGetInfo* API returns the server's configuration information. No *key* argument exists because information is always about the server where the call is executed.

NetServerSetInfo

Sets configuration information at a server.

```
unsigned far pascal
NetServerSetInfo(
    char far * servername,    /* where to execute        */
    short level,              /* info structure level    */
    char far * buf,           /* buffer for return data  */
    USHORT buflen,            /* size of buf             */
    USHORT parmnum,           /* which parameter to set  */
    )
```

Levels:
Supports level 1, 2, and 3 data structures.

Remote access:
This can be called remotely only by an administrator or a user with the server operator privilege.

Error returns:
If successful, *NetServerSetInfo* returns 0. If unsuccessful, it returns one of the standard SetInfo error codes.

An overview:
The *NetServerSetInfo* API changes configuration information at the server.

If *parmnum* is 0, the buffer holds a *server_info_1* or *server_info_2* data structure, depending on the *level* argument. Otherwise, the buffer holds data corresponding to the *parmnum* argument. The following data items can be set:

Name	Value	parmnum
sv2_comment	5	SV_COMMENT_PARMNUM
sv2_disc	10	SV_DISC_PARMNUM
sv2_alerts	11	SV_ALERTS_PARMNUM
sv2_hidden	16	SV_HIDDEN_PARMNUM
sv2_announce	17	SV_ANNOUNCE_PARMNUM
sv2_anndelta	18	SV_ANNDELTA_PARMNUM
sv2_alertsched	37	SV_ALERTSCHED_PARMNUM
sv2_erroralert	38	SV_ERRORALERT_PARMNUM
sv2_logonalert	39	SV_LOGONALERT_PARMNUM
sv2_accessalert	40	SV_ACCESSALERT_PARMNUM

(continued)

Name	Value	parmnum
sv2_diskalert	41	SV_DISKALERT_PARMNUM
sv2_netioalert	42	SV_NETIOALERT_PARMNUM
sv2_maxauditsz	43	SV_MAXAUDITSZ_PARMNUM

NetServerDiskEnum

Retrieves a list of disk drives available on the server.

```
unsigned far pascal
NetServerDiskEnum(
    char far * servername,    /* where to execute       */
    short level,              /* must be zero           */
    char far * buf,           /* buffer for return data */
    USHORT buflen,            /* size of buf            */
    USHORT *entriesread,      /* number of entries read */
    USHORT *totalentries,     /* total entries available */
    )
```

Levels:
Supports a level 0 data structure.

Remote access:
This can be called remotely only by an administrator or a user with the server operator privilege.

Error returns:
If successful, *NetServerDiskEnum* returns 0. If unsuccessful, it returns one of the standard Enum error codes.

An overview:
The *NetServerDiskEnum* API returns a list of the disk drives available on the server. The information is returned as a set of consecutive three-character strings containing the drive letter, a colon, and a terminating zero. This call can be made locally even if the workstation or server is not started.

NetServerAdminCommand

Executes a command on a server.

```
unsigned far pascal
NetServerAdminCommand(
    char far * servername,    /* where to execute          */
    char far *command,        /* command to be executed    */
    short far *result,        /* result code of command    */
    char far * buf,           /* buffer for return data     */
    USHORT buflen,            /* size of buf                */
    USHORT *bytesread,        /* bytes actually returned    */
    USHORT *totalavail,       /* total bytes available      */
    )
```

Remote access:

This can be called remotely only by an administrator.

Error returns:

If successful, *NetServerAdminCommand* returns 0. If unsuccessful, it returns a standard API error code or one of the following error codes:

Error Return	Meaning
NERR_TooMuchData	The stdout and stderr output from the command produced more than 64 KB of data. The remote API mechanism cannot return more than this. *buf* contains the first *buflen* bytes of the output data.
NERR_ExecFailure	The command failed to execute.
NERR_TmpFile	The server encountered a file-system error on the temporary file it was using for output data.

An overview:

The *NetServerAdminCommand* API lets programs issue command lines for execution at a server. Using this API is equivalent to running the following command at the server:

```
cmd /C command <NUL >tmpfile 2>&1
```

The contents of *tmpfile* are returned to the workstation in the *buf* argument. The executable program specified by *command* can have a maximum of SV_CMD_LEN_MAX (80) characters. The stdout and stderr output from the command come back mixed together.

The *result* argument is the termination code of the executed command line.

NetServerAdminCommand vs. NetRemoteExec

Initially, the *NetServerAdminCommand* API seems similar to the *NetRemoteExec* API. But significant differences exist:

- *NetServerAdminCommand* returns a buffer with stdout and stderr mixed together; *NetRemoteExec* preserves the output streams as file-system handles.

- *NetServerAdminCommand* requires *admin* privilege at the server; *NetRemoteExec* requires only an account.

- *NetRemoteExec* requires that the program be in a directory specified by the *runpath* parameter in LANMAN.INI; *NetServerAdminCommand* will execute any program.

- *NetRemoteExec* maps signals and stdin to the remote process; *NetServerAdminCommand* doesn't.

The *NetRemoteExec* API is intended for general use by user programs that require remote execution and transparent mapping of I/O over the net. The *NetServerAdminCommand* API is intended for administration programs that need to execute administration commands at a server.

Browsing with the *NetServerEnum* APIs

The *NetServerEnum* APIs let you "browse" a domain. The *NetServerEnum2* API returns descriptions of all visible servers in a domain; *NetServerEnum* returns information about SV_TYPE_SERVER entries in a domain. (*NetServerEnum* is obsolete and exists only for compatibility with LAN Manager version 1.0.) Although architecturally *NetServerEnum2* is included among the Server administration APIs, it is actually a workstation API. It allows workstations to view a domain's set of servers.

The *NetServerEnum2* API, when called locally, needn't work on the network. Part of the workstation software is the "browser," which receives periodic broadcasts from all visible servers in the workstation's primary domain and up to five additional domains. This information is then stored locally. *NetServerEnum2* returns the same information that the browser has been accumulating.

The primary domain is that set by the LANMAN.INI *domain* parameter in the [workstation] section, or is the domain set with the /DOMAIN: switch at workstation startup.

To set additional domains for browsing, modify the *wkil_oth_domains* member of the *NetWkstaSetInfo* API. The workstation does not become a member of these additional domains; it simply accumulates the server broadcast information from them.

The primary domain (for browsing) is not necessarily the domain to which the user is logged on.

To use the *NetServerEnum* APIs in a program, you must include NET-CONS.H and SERVER.H and link with the NETOEM.LIB stub library.

NetServerEnum

Returns information about the visible servers and workstations on the network.

```
unsigned far pascal
NetServerEnum(
    char far * servername,    /* where to execute          */
    short level,              /* info structure level      */
    char far * buf,           /* buffer for return data    */
    USHORT buflen,            /* size of buf               */
    USHORT *entriesread,      /* number of entries read    */
    USHORT *totalentries,     /* total entries available   */
    )
```

An overview:

The *NetServerEnum* API works like *NetServerEnum2*, but it returns information about SV_TYPE_SERVER entries from domains being browsed.

> **NOTE:** *This API is obsolete and exists only for compatibility with LAN Manager version 1.0. Use NetServerEnum2 if you are using LAN Manager 2.0 or later.*

NetServerEnum2

Returns information about the visible servers and workstations in a domain.

```
unsigned far pascal
NetServerEnum2(
    char far * servername,    /* where to execute          */
    short level,              /* info structure level      */
    char far * buf,           /* buffer for return data    */
    USHORT buflen,            /* size of buf               */
    USHORT *entriesread,      /* number of entries read    */
    USHORT *totalentries,     /* total entries available   */
    ULONG servertype,         /* type mask                 */
    char far * domain         /* which domain ?            */
    )
```

Levels:

Supports level 0 and 1 data structures.

Local access:

The workstation must be started and configured for mailslots.

Remote access:

This can be called remotely only by an administrator.

Error returns:

If successful, *NetServerEnum2* returns 0. If unsuccessful, it returns one of the standard Enum API error codes or one of the following *NetServerEnum* error codes:

Error Return	Meaning
NERR_BrowserNotStarted	The local cache of server information is unavailable. This error occurs if the workstation is started with second-class mailslot support disabled. (To disable mailslot support, set ''mailslots = no'' in the LANMAN.INI file, or set ''/mailslots:no'' on the command line at workstation startup.)
NERR_NotLocalDomain	The name specified by *domain* is not being browsed. This must be either the primary domain, one of the ''other domains'' for the workstation, or the logon domain.

An overview:

The *buf* argument returns a *srver_info_0* or *srver_info_1* data structure, depending on the value of the *level* argument.

The *servertype* argument is a mask that determines what type of servers to enumerate. This allows a program to enumerate only certain classes of servers—for example, only domain controllers, or only SQL servers. The possible values are as follows:

Bitmask	Value	Meaning
SV_TYPE_WORKSTATION	0x00000001	Workstations do not make broadcasts under LAN Manager 2.0.
SV_TYPE_SERVER	0x00000002	All LAN Manager servers.
SV_TYPE_SQLSERVER	0x00000004	Any server running as an SQL server.

(continued)

Bitmask	Value	Meaning
SV_TYPE_DOMAIN_CTRL	0x00000008	Primary domain controllers.
SV_TYPE_DOMAIN_BAKCTRL	0x00000010	Backup domain controllers.
SV_TYPE_TIME_SOURCE	0x00000020	Servers running the Timesource service.
SV_TYPE_AFP	0x00000040	Apple File Protocol servers.
SV_TYPE_NOVELL	0x00000080	Novell servers.
SV_TYPE_ALL	0xFFFFFFFF	All servers.

Any combination of masks can be read to make a composite mask. A server may have set more than one type indicator in its broadcast, and a match of any one of the bits is sufficient to have the server enumerated.

The *domain* argument lists those browsed domains for which a list of a list of servers is returned. A NULL value indicates that the API should return information on all browsed domains. This name must be the primary domain, one of the other domains for the workstation, or the logon domain.

If *NetServerEnum2* is called remotely, and if the destination server is listening to the same domains as the calling workstation, then the set of servers returned by this call will be the same as the set returned for a local call.

A *NetServer* example

The SCHKDSK.C program (Figure 7-1) is an administrative program that checks all disks on each visible server in the domain. It uses *NetServerEnum2* to get a list of the servers and then uses *NetServerDiskEnum* to get a list of disk names. For each disk, it issues a remote Chkdsk command using the *NetServerAdminCommand* API.

```
/*
 * SCHKDSK.C -- This program checks the disk on each virtual drive
 * on each server in all browsed domains.  It requires that the
 * user have admin privilege at each server.
 *
 * Compile:  C> cl schkdsk.c cname.c netoem.lib netapi.lib string_f.lib
 *
 * Usage:  C> schkdsk
 *
 */
```

Figure 7-1. *(continued)*
The SCHKDSK.C program.

Figure 7-1. *continued*

```
#include <stdio.h>
#include <os2.h>
#include <netcons.h>
#include <server.h>
#include <string_f.h>   /* defined in Chapter 3 */
#include <examples.h>   /* defined in Chapter 4 */

typedef struct server_info_0 SRV_0;
main()
    {
    unsigned short ser, ste;
    unsigned short der, dte;
    unsigned short cbr, cba, res;
    unsigned err;
    char sbuf[BUFSIZ];              /* buffer for server list */
    char dbuf[3*26];               /* max number of drives   */
    char cbuf[BUFSIZ];             /* remote command output  */
    char cmd[16];                  /* buffer for CHKDSK      */
    char sname[CNLEN + 3];         /* remote server name     */
    SRV_0 *psrv = (SRV_0 *)sbuf;
    char *p, *q;

    err = NetServerEnum2(NULL, 0, sbuf, sizeof(sbuf), &ser, &ste,
            0xFFFFFFFF, NULL);
    if (err != 0)
        {
        printf("NetServerEnum2 failed with err = %d\n", err);
        exit(1);
        }

    /* for each server */
    while (ser--)
        {
        /* remote names require two backslash (\\) characters */
        strcpy_f(sname, cname(psrv->sv0_name));
        printf("***** %s *****\n", sname);

        /* get the list of available disks at the server */
        err = NetServerDiskEnum(sname, 0, dbuf, sizeof(dbuf),
                &der, &dte);
        if (err != 0)
            {
            if (err == ERROR_ACCESS_DENIED)
                printf("        Access Denied\n");
            else
                printf("        NetDiskEnum error = %d\n", err);
            }
```

(continued)

Figure 7-1. *continued*

```
        else
            {
            p = dbuf;
            while (der--)
                {
                /* create and execute the command line */
                sprintf(cmd, "CHKDSK %s", p);
                printf("          %s\n", cmd);
                err = NetServerAdminCommand(sname, cmd, &res, cbuf,
                        sizeof(cbuf), &cbr, &cba);
                if (err != 0)
                    printf("          NetServerAdmin error = %d\n", err);
                else
                    {
                    /* print the buffer indented one tab stop */
                    putchar('\t');
                    for (q = cbuf; cbr-- != 0; ++q)
                        {
                        putchar(*q);
                        if (*q == '\n' && cbr != 0)
                            putchar('\t');
                        }
                    }
                /* next drive name */
                p += 3;
                }
            }
        /* get next server name */
        ++psrv;
        }
}
```

The Share APIs

The Share APIs control resource sharing at the server. To use these APIs in
a program, you must include NETCONS.H and SHARES.H at compile time
and link with the NETAPI.LIB stub library. If the server is running share-
mode security, you should also include ACCESS.H.

NOTE: *The case of all LAN Manager names is significant. The LAN
Manager user-interface programs automatically map names to uppercase, so watch out for case mismatches when using the Share APIs.*

Three levels of data structures are available for Share APIs.

The *share_info_0* structure contains the following member:

Member Name	Description
char shi0_netname[NNLEN+1]	The public name by which the resource is to be known. This is an array of characters up to NNLEN in length plus a terminating zero. The characters must be legal file-system characters.

The *share_info_1* structure contains the following members:

Member Name	Description			
char shi1_netname[NNLEN+1]	The public name by which the resource is to be known. This is an array of characters up to NNLEN in length plus a terminating zero. The characters must be legal file-system characters.			
shi1_type	The type of resource being shared. The legal values are as follows:			
	Type	*Value*	*Meaning*	
	STYPE_DISKTREE	0	A directory in the file system.	
	STYPE_PRINTQ	1	A print queue. The queue must already exist. (See *NetPrintQAdd*.)	
	STYPE_DEVICE	2	A character-device queue.	
	STYPE_IPC	3	The special IPC$ share.	
char far *shi1_remark	An optional remark describing the share. An empty remark is indicated by a null string.			

The *share_info_2* structure contains all members of the *share_info_1* structure, as well as the following members:

Member Name	Description		
USHORT shi2_permissions	In share-mode security, this value represents the access permissions for the entire share. If a disk directory is being shared, the permissions apply to all files in all subdirectories. The value is a set of bits as defined for the Access APIs in ACCESS.H.		
	Bitmask	*Value*	*Meaning*
	ACCESS_READ	0x01	Read permission (R)
	ACCESS_WRITE	0x02	Write permission (W)
	ACCESS_CREATE	0x04	Create permission (C)
	ACCESS_EXEC	0x08	Execute permission (X)

(continued)

Member Name	Description		
	Bitmask	**Value**	**Meaning**
	ACCESS_DELETE	0x10	Delete permission (D)
	ACCESS_ATTRIB	0x20	Attribute permission (A)
	ACCESS_PERM	0x40	The user must have *admin* privilege to connect to this share. In share-mode security, a share must be given explicit permissions. If none are given, users can connect to the share, but they cannot actually use anything. In user-mode security, the shi2_permission bits are ignored, with the exception of the ACCESS_PERM bit, which indicates an *admin* share.
	ACCESS_ALL	0x7F	Permission to read, write, create, execute, and delete resources and modify their attributes and permissions.
USHORT shi2_max_uses	The maximum number of share connections allowed. The value 0xFFFF means unlimited.		
USHORT shi2_current_uses	The current number of share connections.		
char far * shi2_path	The pathname of the shared resource. For disk shares, this must be a completely specified pathname. For print shares, it is the name of the print queue. For device shares, it is one or more COMx or LPTx device names separated by a space. See Chapter 11 for a description of device pooling.		
char shi2_passwd [SHPWLEN+1]	For share-mode servers, this is the password for the share, which must be supplied when the connection is made. For user-mode servers, it is ignored.		

A Little Shared Information

The IPC$ share, which is of type STYPE_IPC, supports named pipes and mailslots across the networks. When workstations try to use the *DosOpen* function to open a named pipe or the *DosWriteMailSlot* function to write to a remote name, a connection is established to IPC$ on the server. No pathname is associated with the IPC$ share.

The ADMIN$ share, which is of type STYPE_DISKTREE, shares the root of the LAN Manager lanman subtree (typically C:\LANMAN). This is the directory that contains the LANMAN.INI file and all subdirectories used by the LAN Manager software.

Both ADMIN$ and IPC$ must be shared before remote administration can take place. The use and behavior of these two shares is different depending on whether the server is running share-mode security or user-mode security. In user-mode security, the following are true:

- IPC$ and ADMIN$ shares are automatically added when the server starts.

- Either of these shares can be deleted, but they must be added before remote administration can take place.

- Any user having an account or the same password as the GUEST account can establish a connection to IPC$. Individual pipes or mailslots can, of course, have more restrictive access control.

In share-mode security, however, the following are true:

- ADMIN$ and IPC$ shares are not automatically added. They must be added using the user interface or a program that performs *NetShareAdd* for each of them.

- ADMIN$ determines *admin* privilege for a session. If a workstation has a connection to ADMIN$, the session is an admin session. Note that if ADMIN$ is added without a password, any user can become an administrator. Beware of this potential security problem.

- Any user whose password matches that of IPC$ can establish a connection to IPC$. No password allows all users to connect to IPC$.

Note that an *admin*-level user has access to all resources.

NetShareEnum

Retrieves information about the shared resources on a server.

```
unsigned far pascal
NetShareEnum(
    char far * servername,     /* where to execute         */
    short level,               /* info structure level     */
    char far * buf,            /* buffer for return data   */
    USHORT buflen,             /* size of buf              */
    USHORT *entriesread,       /* number of entries read   */
    USHORT *totalentries,      /* total entries available  */
    )
```

Levels:
Supports level 0, 1, and 2 data structures.

Remote access:

Level 0 or 1 can be called by a user with a valid account in the UAS data-base. All levels are available to an administrator or a user with the following operator privileges:

- server operator

- print operator (only on print queues)

- comm operator (only on comm queues)

Error returns:

If successful, *NetShareEnum* returns 0. If unsuccessful, it returns one of the standard Enum error codes.

An overview:

The *NetShareEnum* API obtains a list of active shares. The *buf* argument returns a *share_info_0*, *share_info_1*, or *share_info_2* structure, depending on the level parameter.

NetShareGetInfo

Retrieves information about a specific share on the network.

```
unsigned far pascal
NetShareGetInfo(
    char far * servername,    /* where to execute       */
    char far * netname,       /* the "key"              */
    short level,              /* info structure level   */
    char far * buf,           /* buffer for return data */
    USHORT buflen,            /* size of buf            */
    USHORT *totalavail,       /* total bytes available  */
    )
```

Levels:

Supports level 0, 1, and 2 data structures.

Remote access:

Level 0 or 1 can be called by a user with a valid account in the UAS data-base. All levels are available to an administrator or a user with the following operator privileges:

- server operator

- print operator (only on print queues)

- comm operator (only on comm queues)

Error returns:

If successful, *NetShareGetInfo* returns 0. If unsuccessful, it returns one of the standard GetInfo error codes.

An overview:

The *NetShareGetInfo* API obtains information about a specific share. The *netname* argument is the share for which information is being requested. The *buf* argument returns a *share_info_1* or *share_info_2* structure, depending on the *level* parameter.

NetShareSetInfo

Changes a share's parameters.

```
unsigned far pascal
NetShareSetInfo(
    char far * servername,    /* where to execute       */
    char far * netname,       /* the "key"              */
    short level,              /* info structure level   */
    char far * buf,           /* buffer for return data */
    USHORT buflen,            /* size of buf            */
    USHORT parmnum,           /* which parameter to set */
    )
```

Levels:

Supports level 1 and 2 data structures.

Remote access:

Remote access is available only to an administrator or a user with the following operator privileges:

- server operator

- print operator (only on print queues)

- comm operator (only on comm queues)

Error returns:

If successful, *NetShareSetInfo* returns 0. If unsuccessful, it returns a standard SetInfo error code or the following error code:

Error Return	Meaning
NERR_NetNameNotFound	The share name does not exist.

An overview:

The *NetShareSetInfo* API lets you change information about an active share.

If *parmnum* is 0, the buffer holds a *share_info_1* or *share_info_2*, depending on the *level* argument. Otherwise, the buffer holds the data corresponding to the *parmnum* argument. The data items which can be set and their corresponding *parmnum* values are as follows:

Name	*Value*	**parmnum**
shi1_remark	4	SHI_REMARK_PARMNUM
shi2_remark	4	SHI_REMARK_PARMNUM
shi2_permissions	5	SHI_PERMISSIONS_PARMNUM
shi2_max_uses	6	SHI_MAX_USES_PARMNUM
shi2_passwd	9	SHI_PASSWD_PARMNUM

NetShareAdd

Creates a share to a server resource.

```
unsigned far pascal
NetShareAdd(
    char far * servername,    /* where to execute     */
    short level,              /* must be 2            */
    char far * buf,           /* buffer for return data */
    USHORT buflen             /* size of buf          */
    )
```

Remote access:

Remote access is available only to an administrator or a user with the following operator privileges:

- server operator

- print operator (only on print queues)

- comm operator (only on comm queues)

Error returns:

If successful, *NetShareAdd* returns 0. If unsuccessful, it returns a standard Add error code or one of the following error codes:

Error Return	Meaning
NERR_UnknownDevDir	The type is STYPE_DISKTREE or STYPE_DEVICE, and the pathname does not refer to an existing directory or device.
NERR_QNotFound	The type is STYPE_PRINTQ, and the print queue does not exist.
NERR_RedirectedPath	The pathname refers to a redirected device.
NERR_DuplicateShare	The specified resource is already in use at this server.
NERR_DeviceShareConflict	The device is assigned to a STYPE_PRINTQ share and also to a STYPE_DEVICE share.

An overview:

The *NetShareAdd* API adds a new instance of a share to the server. The *buf* argument must contain a *share_info_2* structure with information about the requested share. Keep the following points in mind when using the *NetShareAdd* API:

- Although server resources can be shared more than once, each instance must have a unique share name on the server.

- Because a server is also a workstation, redirected drive and device names can exist at the server. These redirected pathnames cannot be shared with *NetShareAdd*.

- If the *shi2_remark* member is a null string (""), it means there is no remark about the shared resource. If it is a NULL pointer, a default remark is used. For IPC$ and ADMIN$, the API supplies a default remark. In all other cases, the default is an empty remark.

- The *shi2_current_uses* member is ignored by *NetShareAdd*.

NetShareDel

Deletes a shared server resource.

```
unsigned far pascal
NetShareDel(
    char far * servername,    /* where to execute       */
    char far * netname,       /* the public share name  */
    USHORT reserved           /* must be zero           */
    )
```

Remote access:

Remote access is available only to an administrator or a user with the following operator privileges:

- server operator

- print operator (only on print queues)

- comm operator (only on comm queues)

Error returns:

If successful, *NetShareDel* returns 0. If unsuccessful, it returns a standard Del error code or the following error code:

Error Return	Meaning
NERR_NetNameNotFound	*netname* is not an active share.

Devices, print queues, and character queues

LPT and COM represent logical devices in OS/2. Under LAN Manager you can use logical devices in two ways: with print queues or with communications queues. These logical devices can be assigned to either kind of LAN Manager resource. This area is discussed in greater detail in Chapter 11, but for understanding how this affects shares, the following principles apply:

- Print queues are created by the DosPrintQ APIs. The print queue exists whether it is shared or not. For shares of type STYPE_PRINTQ, the *shi2_pathname* member is the queue name. This does not have to be the same as the *netname* of the share. Note that the LAN Manager user interface enforces the convention that the *netname* is same as the queue name.

- Communications queues are created by the *NetShareAdd* API and exist only as long as the share exists. The *shi2_pathname* member is a list of logical devices. Multiple devices are separated by a space character. Thus "COM1 COM4 LPT2" is a possible pathname. The *netname* is the queue name.

- A logical device can be assigned to multiple print queues or to multiple communications queues but can never be assigned to both types of shares simultaneously.

An overview:

The *NetShareDel* API lets you remove existing shares. The *netname* argument must be that of an existing share. Deleting a share also closes any open files or devices on any connections to the share and deletes the connections.

NetShareCheck

Checks whether a device is being shared by a server.

```
unsigned far pascal
NetShareCheck(
    char far * servername,    /* where to execute       */
    char far * device,        /* device name to check   */
    USHORT * type,            /* returned device type   */
    )
```

Remote access:

Remote access is available to all users with a valid account in the UAS database.

Error returns:

If successful, *NetShareCheck* returns 0. If unsuccessful, it returns a standard API error code or the following error code:

Error Return	Meaning
NERR_DeviceNotShared	The device is not shared.

An overview:

The *NetShareCheck* API determines whether a device is currently being shared. Devices of the following types are shared:

- A drive name (such as C:) that has one or more directories shared. When a server is started, the root of every drive is automatically shared as *admin* ("A$, B$, C$," and so forth). Unless these shares are deleted, *NetShareCheck* succeeds for all local server drive names.

- Devices assigned to shared print queues. Any COM or LPT device can be assigned to one or more print queues. Note that the device must be assigned to print queues that are not currently shared. This call succeeds only if at least one of the print queues to which it is assigned is shared.

- Devices shared as a pooled character device. Any COM or LPT device can be assigned to one or more character device pools (but not simultaneously to a print queue).

The *device* argument is the device name being checked. If it is a drive name, it must contain a colon. If it is a COM or LPT device, the colon is optional.

If the device is currently being shared, the *type* argument returns the share type:

Share Type	Value	Meaning
STYPE_DISKTREE	0	A disk
STYPE_PRINTQ	1	A print queue
STYPE_DEVICE	2	A character device

The Session APIs

The Session APIs allow programs to obtain information about and to delete sessions from client workstations. To use these APIs in a program, you must include NETCONS.H and SHARES.H at compile time and must link with the NETAPI.LIB stub library.

> **NOTE:** *The case of all LAN Manager names is significant. The LAN Manager user-interface programs automatically map names to upper-case, so watch out for case mismatches when using the Session APIs.*

Four levels of data structure are available for the session APIs.

The *session_info_0* structure contains the following member:

Member Name	Description
char far * sesi0_cname	The computer name for the client workstation. Double backslashes are omitted.

The *session_info_1* structure contains the following members:

Member Name	Description
char far * sesi1_cname	The computer name for the client workstation. Double backslashes are omitted.
char far * sesi1_username	The username at the workstation that established the session. This is a username even if the server is running in share mode.
USHORT sesi1_num_conns	The number of active connections on the session.
USHORT sesi1_num_opens	The number of *DosOpen* calls in effect on all of the connections on the session.

(continued)

Member Name	Description
USHORT sesi1_num_users	The number of users on the session. In LAN Manager version 2.0, this value is always 0 or 1.
ULONG sesi1_time	The number of seconds since the session began.
ULONG sesi1_idle_time	The number of seconds since there was any activity on the session.
ULONG sesi1_user_flags	A set of bits with further information about the session:

Bitmask	Value	Meaning
SESS_GUEST	0x01	The user has a guest account.
SESS_NOENCRYPT	0x02	When LAN Manager workstations establish a session with a LAN Manager server running in user mode, all password exchanges can be encrypted. This bit is set if encryption is not being used.

The *session_info_2* structure contains all members of the *session_info_1* structure, as well as the following member:

Member Name	Description
char far * sesi2_cltype_name	This is a pointer to a text string that describes the client workstation for the session. The valid text strings are as follows:

Text	Meaning
DOWN LEVEL	An MS-NET, PC-LAN, or XENIX client
DOS LM 1.0	A DOS LAN Manager 1.0 client
DOS LM 2.0	A DOS LAN Manager 2.0 client
OS/2 LM 1.0	An OS/2 LAN Manager 1.0 client
OS/2 LM 2.0	An OS/2 LAN Manager 2.0 client

The *session_info_10* structure contains the following members:

Member Name	Description
char far * sesi10_cname	The computer name for the client workstation. Double backslashes are omitted.
char far * sesi10_username	The username at the workstation that established the session. This is a username even if the server is running in share mode.
ULONG sesi10_time	The number of seconds since the session began.
ULONG sesi10_idle_time	The number of seconds since there was any activity on the session.

NetSessionEnum

Retrieves a list of all active sessions.

```
unsigned far pascal
NetSessionEnum(
    char far * servername,    /* where to execute      */
    short level,              /* info structure level  */
    char far * buf,           /* buffer for return data */
    USHORT buflen,            /* size of buf           */
    USHORT *entriesread,      /* number of entries read */
    USHORT *totalentries,     /* total entries available */
    )
```

Levels:

Supports level 0, 1, 2, and 10 data structures.

Remote access:

Level 0 or 10 can be called by a user with a valid account in the UAS database. All levels are available to an administrator or a user with the server operator privilege.

Error returns:

If successful, *NetSessionEnum* returns 0. If unsuccessful, it returns one of the standard Enum error codes.

An overview:

The *NetSessionEnum* API returns a list of active sessions. The *buf* argument returns a *session_info_0* or *session_info_1* structure, depending on the *level* parameter.

NetSessionGetInfo

Gets information about a specific server/workstation session.

```
unsigned far pascal
NetSessionGetInfo(
    char far * servername,    /* where to execute      */
    char far * clientname,    /* which session?        */
    short level,              /* session id            */
    char far * buf,           /* buffer for return data */
    USHORT buflen,            /* size of buf           */
    USHORT *totalavail,       /* total bytes available */
    )
```

Levels:

Supports level 0, 1, 2, and 10 data structures.

Remote access:

Level 0 or 10 can be called by a user with a valid account in the UAS database. All levels are available to an administrator or a user with the server operator privilege.

Error returns:

If successful, *NetSessionGetInfo* returns 0. If unsuccessful, it returns a standard GetInfo error code or one of the following error codes:

Error Return	Meaning
NERR_ClientNameNotFound	No such session exists.
ERROR_INVALID_PARAMETER	The *clientname* argument is missing the leading double backslash.

An overview:

The *NetSessionGetInfo* API takes as a *clientname* the computer name of the workstation that established the session. *clientname* must contain a leading double backslash. *NetSessionGetInfo* returns either a *session_info_0* or a *session_info_1* structure, depending on the level.

NetSessionDel

Deletes a session between a server and a workstation.

```
unsigned far pascal
NetSessionDel(
     char far * servername,   /* where to execute       */
     char far * cname,        /* client computer name   */
     short reserved           /* must be zero           */
     )
```

Remote access:

Remote access is available only to an administrator or a user with the server operator privilege.

Error returns:

If successful, *NetSessionDel* returns 0. If unsuccessful, it returns a standard Del error code or one of the following error codes:

Error Return	Meaning
NERR_ClientNameNotFound	No such session exists.
ERROR_INVALID_PARAMETER	The *clientname* argument is missing the leading double backslash.

An overview:

The *NetSessionDel* API forces a session closed, closing any open files or devices on all connections for the session and deleting the connections.

The Connection APIs

The only API available for connections is *NetConnectionEnum*. Connections are added when a workstation calls the *NetUseAdd* function. Although no API for deleting specific connections exists, you can delete an entire session with the *NetSessionDel* API. To use *NetConnectionEnum* in a program, you must include NETCONS.H and SHARES.H at compile time and must link with the NETAPI.LIB stub library.

> NOTE: *The case of all LAN Manager names is significant. The LAN Manager user-interface programs automatically map names to uppercase, so watch out for case mismatches when using the Connection API.*

Connection data structures exist at two levels.

The *connection_info_0* structure contains the following member:

Member Name	Description
USHORT coni0_id	The connection identification number (an integer) that identifies the specific connection.

The *connection_info_1* structure contains the following members:

Member Name	Description		
USHORT coni1_id	The connection identification number (an integer) that identifies the specific connection.		
USHORT coni1_type	The type of connection. These values can also appear in the *shi1_type* structure:		
	Type	*Value*	*Meaning*
	STYPE_DISKTREE	0	A directory in the file system.
	STYPE_PRINTQ	1	A print queue. The queue must already exist. (See *NetPrintQAdd*.)
	STYPE_DEVICE	2	A character-device queue.
	STYPE_IPC	3	The special IPC$ share.
USHORT coni1_num_opens	The number of open files, devices, or pipes on the connection.		

(continued)

Member Name	Description
USHORT coni1_num_users	The number of users on the connection. In LAN Manager version 2.0, this value is always 0 or 1.
ULONG coni1_time	The time in seconds since the connection was established.
char far * coni1_username	For a user-mode server, this is the connecting username. For share mode, it is the connecting computer name and does not include the double backslashes.
char far * coni1_netname	If the qualifier is a computer name, this is the network resource name. If the qualifier is a network resource name, this is a computer name and does not include the leading double backslash.

NetConnectionEnum

Lists all connections to a shared server resource or all connections at a specific computer.

```
unsigned far pascal
NetConnectionEnum(
    char far * servername,    /* where to execute        */
    char far * qualifier,     /* qualifier name          */
    short level,              /* info structure level    */
    char far * buf,           /* buffer for return data  */
    USHORT buflen,            /* size of buf             */
    USHORT *entriesread,      /* number of entries read  */
    USHORT *totalentries,     /* total entries available */
    )
```

Remote access:

Remote access is available only to an administrator or a user with the server operator privilege.

Error returns:

If successful, *NetConnectionEnum* returns 0. If unsuccessful, it returns a standard Enum error code or one of the following error codes:

Error Return	Meaning
NERR_ClientNameNotFound	No such session exists.
NERR_NetNameNotFound	The *qualifier* argument was not a computer name and did not match the network name of any of the server shares.

An overview:

The *NetConnectionEnum* API returns a list of active connections. The *buf* argument returns a *connection_info_0* or *connection_info_1* structure, depending on the *level* parameter. The *qualifier* argument allows a selective list of connections to be returned.

- If the *qualifier* argument is a computer name (for example, \\RALPH), then a list of all connections to that session is returned. The *conil_netname* member is the network name of the resource connected to. The computer name must have two backslashes leading the name. Note that computer names returned by the *NetSessionEnum* API do not have the backslashes; the program must add them.

- If the *qualifier* argument is the network name of a server resource, then all connections to that name are returned. The *conil_netname* member is the username (user mode) or the computer name (share mode) of the connecting workstation.

- The *qualifier* argument cannot be a NULL pointer or a null string.

In order to obtain a list of all connections, a program would have to call either *NetShareEnum* or *NetSessionEnum* and iterate through the entries using *NetConnectionEnum* with the qualifier set appropriately.

Listing connections

The CONNECTS.C program (Figure 7-2) creates a listing of all connections to server resources. The connections can be organized by sessions (/S) or by netname (/N). The session or share enumeration makes use of the *NetEnum* routine from Chapter 4 and the memory-model utilities from Chapter 3.

```
/*
 * CONNECTS.C -- A program that lists connections to the server.
 * Connections will be organized by sessions (/S) or by network
 * names (/N).  This program uses the NetEnum generic enumerator
 * to handle memory management for Session or Share enumeration.
 * It also illustrates model-dependent memory management with
 * the "pqual" pointer.
 *
 * Compile with:
 *
 * C> cl connects.c netenum.c cname.c netoem.lib netapi.lib string_f.lib
 *
 * Usage:  C> connects </S : /N>
 *
 */
```

Figure 7-2.
The CONNECTS.C program.

(continued)

Figure 7-2. *continued*

```
#include <stdio.h>
#include <os2.h>
#include <malloc.h>
#include <netcons.h>
#include <shares.h>
#include <string_f.h>   /* defined in Chapter 3 */
#include <examples.h>   /* defined in Chapter 4 */

/* choose between two types of pointer */
#define QNAME(a, b) (session ? (char far *)a : (char far *)b)

main(argc, argv)
int argc;
char **argv;
    {
    int session, err;
    struct share_info_0 far * psh;
    struct session_info_0 far * pse;
    struct connection_info_1 *pconn;
    char buf[BUFSIZ];
    unsigned short er, cer, cte;
    char *pqual;
    char *typestring(), *timestring();

    if (argc != 2)
        {
        printf("syntax: connects </S : /N>\n");
        exit(1);
        }

    /* parse the command-line flag */
    if (stricmp(argv[1], "/S") == 0)
        session = 1;                        /* TRUE */
    else if (stricmp(argv[1], "/N") == 0)
        session = 0;                        /* FALSE */
    else
        {
        /* none of the above */
        printf("syntax: connections < /S : /N >\n");
        exit(1);
        }
```

(continued)

Figure 7-2. *continued*

```
/* enumerate either sessions or shares */
if (session)
    err = NetEnum(
                NetSessionEnum,         /* Enum function  */
                NULL,                   /* server name    */
                0,                      /* level          */
                (char far * far *)&pse, /* buf pointer    */
                200,                    /* buffer guess   */
                sizeof(*pse),           /* structure size */
                &er);                   /* entries read   */
else
    err = NetEnum(
                NetShareEnum,           /* Enum function  */
                NULL,                   /* server name    */
                0,                      /* level          */
                (char far * far *)&psh, /* buf pointer    */
                200,                    /* buffer guess   */
                sizeof(*psh),           /* structure size */
                &er);                   /* entries read   */
if (err)
    {
    printf("Error enumerating %s = %d\n",
    session ? "sessions" : "shares", err);
    exit(1);
    }

/* print the header */
printf("%-9s%-9s%-9s%-7s%-11s%-11s%-12s\n", "ID", "Type",
        "Opens", "Users", "Time", "Username",
        session ? "Netname" : "Computername");
printf("%-9s%-9s%-9s%-7s%-11s%-11s%-11s\n", "--", "----",
        "-----", "-----", "----", "--------",
        session ? "-------" : "--------");

/* get and print the connections for each qualifier */
while (er--)
    {
    /* get a model-dependent pointer to the qualifier */
    if (session)
        pqual = MDPTR(cname(pse->sesi0_cname));
    else
        pqual = MDPTR(psh->shi0_netname);
```

(continued)

Figure 7-2. *continued*

```
        err = NetConnectionEnum(
                                NULL,          /* server name    */
                                pqual,         /* qualifier      */
                                1,             /* level          */
                                buf,           /* place for data */
                                sizeof(buf),   /* length of buf  */
                                &cer,          /* entries read   */
                                &cte);         /* total entries  */


    /* the qualifier is a computer name or network name */
    if (cer)
        printf("%s:\n", pqual);

    if (err != 0)
        printf("*** Cannot get connections for %s (%d)\n",
                pqual, err);

    /* this loop skips shares without connections */
    for (pconn = (struct connection_info_1 *)buf; cer--; ++pconn)
        {
        /* The last argument is a network name if the key was a
         * computer name, and a computer name if the key was a
         * network name. */

        printf("%-9d%-9s%-9d%-7d%-11s%-11s%-11s\n",
                pconn->coni1_id,
                typestring(pconn->coni1_type),
                pconn->coni1_num_opens,
                pconn->coni1_num_users,
                timestring(pconn->coni1_time),
                MDPTR(pconn->coni1_username),
                session ? MDPTR(pconn->coni1_netname):
                MDPTR(cname(pconn->coni1_netname))
                );
        }

    /* next session or share */
    QNAME(++pse, ++psh);
    }

/* free the memory allocated by NetEnum */
if (session)
    DosFreeSeg(SELECTOROF(pse));
else
```

(continued)

Figure 7-2. *continued*

```
            DosFreeSeg(SELECTOROF(psh));
    exit(0);
    }
/*
 * typestring -- Convert the type code to a text string.
 */

char *typestring(type)
int type;
    {
    switch(type)
        {
        case STYPE_DISKTREE:
            return("Disk");
        case STYPE_PRINTQ:
            return("PrintQ");
        case STYPE_DEVICE:
            return("Device");
        case STYPE_IPC:
            return("IPC");
        default:
            return("UNKNOWN");
        }
    }

/*
 * timestring -- Convert a (long) time to hrs:min:sec.
 */

char *timestring(time)
long time;
    {
    static char tbuf[9];
    int h, m, s;

    h = time / 3600;
    time -= h * 3600;
    m = time / 60;
    s = time - m * 60;

    sprintf(tbuf, "%02d:%02d:%02d", h, m, s);
    return(tbuf);
    }
```

The File APIs

At the client workstation, programs can use *DosOpen* calls to open files, print queues, character devices, and named pipes. The File APIs allow programs to get information about and to control open instances of all of these resources at the server. Each *DosOpen* call—even if to the same resource or from the same workstation—is considered a separate instance.

The File APIs do not deal with *DosOpen* calls to local server programs. Only server resources opened by a workstation are affected by these APIs.

There are two sets of similar APIs:

- *NetFileEnum*, *NetFileGetInfo*, and *NetFileClose* all deal with file IDs that are an unsigned short. These calls exist for compatibility with LAN Manager 1.0, and their ID size is limited to 64 KB.

- *NetFileEnum2*, *NetFileGetInfo2*, and *NetFileClose2* all deal with file IDs that are an unsigned long. These calls are compatible with LAN Manager versions 2.0 and later.

To use the File APIs in a program, you must include NETCONS.H and SHARES.H at compile time and must link with the NETAPI.LIB stub library. The access-control permission bitmasks are defined in ACCESS.H. File-data structures exist at two levels:

The *file_info_0* structure contains the following member:

Member Name	Description
USHORT fi0_id	This number identifies an instance of a *DosOpen* call to a server resource. It is the *key* argument for the *NetFileGetInfo* call.

The *file_info_1* structure contains the following members:

Member Name	Description
USHORT fi1_id	This number identifies an instance of a *DosOpen* call to a server resource. It is the *key* argument for the *NetFileGetInfo* call.
USHORT fi1_permissions	The access-control permissions granted with *DosOpen*. These are the permissions used by the NetAccess APIs described in Chapter 9, and they are as follows:

Bitmask	Value	Permission
ACCESS_READ	0x01	Read permission (R)
ACCESS_WRITE	0x02	Write permission (W)
ACCESS_CREATE	0x04	Create permission (C)

(continued)

Member Name	Description		
	Bitmask	**Value**	**Permission**
	ACCESS_EXEC	0x08	Execute permission (X)
	ACCESS_DELETE	0x10	Delete permission (D)
	ACCESS_ATRIB	0x20	Change Attribute permission (A)
	ACCESS_PERM	0x40	Change ACL permission (P)
USHORT fil_num_locks	The number of locks that this instance of *DosOpen* has on the file.		
char far * fil_pathname	The fully qualified local pathname of the server resource.		
char far * fil_username	In user-mode security, this is the client username. In share-mode security, this is the client computer name and does not include the double backslash. Case is significant.		

The *file_info_0* and *file_info_1* structures use an unsigned short integer to indicate the open file. The *file_info_2* and *file_info_3* structures are replacements for this, with an unsigned long open file indicator.

The *file_info_2* structure contains the following member:

Member Name	Description
ULONG fil_id	This number identifies an instance of a *DosOpen* call to a server resource. It is the *key* argument for the *NetFileGetInfo2* call.

The *file_info_3* structure is similar to a *file_info_1* structure except that the *fi3_id* member is an unsigned long.

NetFileEnum

Returns a list of open server resources.

```
unsigned far pascal
NetFileEnum(
    char far * servername,    /* where to execute       */
    char far * basepath,      /* filename qualifier     */
    short level,              /* info structure level   */
    char far * buf,           /* buffer for return data */
    USHORT buflen,            /* size of buf            */
    USHORT *entriesread,      /* number of entries read */
    USHORT *totalentries      /* total entries available */
    )
```

Levels:
Supports level 0, 1, 2, and 3 data structures.

Remote access:

This is available only to an administrator or a user with the server operator privilege.

Error returns:

If successful, *NetFileEnum* returns 0. If unsuccessful, it returns a standard Enum error code.

An overview:

The *NetFileEnum* API returns a list of instances of open server resources. The *buf* argument returns a *file_info_0*, *file_info_1*, *file_info_2*, or *file_info_3* structure, depending on the *level* argument. If *level* is 0 or 1, only file IDs less than 64 KB are returned.

The *basepath* argument acts as a qualifier on the returned information. If it is not NULL, then only open resource names that have *basepath* as a prefix are returned. For example, if *basepath* were \PIPE, *NetFileEnum* would return information about all open pipes but not about any files, devices, or print queues. Similarly, if *basepath* were C:\BIN, only information about open files in that directory or its subdirectories would be returned. If *basepath* is a NULL pointer, then information is returned about all open resources.

NetFileEnum2

Returns a list of open server resources. Supports file IDs larger than 64 KB.

```
unsigned far pascal
NetFileEnum2(
      char far * servername,    /* where to execute       */
      char far * basepath,      /* filename qualifier     */
      short level,              /* info structure level   */
      char far * buf,           /* buffer for return data */
      USHORT buflen,            /* size of buf            */
      USHORT *entriesread,      /* number of entries read */
      USHORT *totalentries,     /* total entries available */
      void far * resume_key     /* continue scanning key  */
      )
```

Levels:

Suports level 0, 1, 2, and 3 data structures.

Remote access:

This is available only to an administrator or a user with the server operator privilege.

Error returns:

If successful, *NetFileEnum2* returns 0. If unsuccessful, it returns a standard Enum error code.

An overview:

NetFileEnum2 is similar to *NetFileEnum*, with two differences:

- *NetFileEnum2* can return file IDs greater than 64 KB at levels 2 and 3.

- *NetFileEnum2* makes use of the *resume_key* argument.

Using *resume_key* With the *NetFileEnum* API, you can't obtain open file information when the data exceeds 64 KB. With *NetFileEnum2*, you can tell the API where to resume the enumeration on subsequent calls. To use the *resume_key* argument, a program needs to declare an FRK structure, initialize it properly, and pass a pointer to the structure as the *resume_key* argument for each subsequent call. The following program fragment shows how to do this. All relevant definitions are in the SHARES.H header file.

```
FileEnumExample()
    {
    FRK resume_key;

    FRK_INIT(resume_key);
    while ((err = NetFileEnum2(
                            server,
                            basep,
                            level,
                            buf,
                            buflen,
                            &entriesread,
                            &totalentries,
                            &resumekey)) == ERROR_MORE_DATA)
        {
        /* ... process each buffer of data ... */
        }
    }
```

resume_key should never be written to. All necessary information is put in it by the *NetFileEnum2* API.

Most Enum APIs return partial data if some of the variable-length data will not fit in the buffer. *NetFileEnum2* never returns partial data. If the fixed-length and variable-length portions of a record don't fit, the API stops and returns ERROR_MORE_DATA.

NetFileGetInfo

Gets information about an open server resource.

```
unsigned far pascal
NetFileGetInfo(
        char far * servername,   /* where to execute       */
        unsigned long fileid,    /* the "key"              */
        USHORT level,            /* info structure level   */
        char far * buf,          /* buffer for return data */
        USHORT buflen,           /* size of buf            */
        USHORT *totalavail,      /* total bytes available  */
        )
```

Levels:
Supports level 0, 1, 2, and 3 data structures.

Remote access:
This is available only to an administrator or a user with the server operator privilege.

Error returns:
If successful, *NetFileGetInfo* returns 0. If unsuccessful, it returns a standard FileGetInfo error code or the following error code:

Error Return	Meaning
NERR_FileNotFound	The *fileid* argument does not correspond to an open resource.

An overview:
The *NetFileGetInfo* API takes as a key the server file ID of the open resource. It returns either a *file_info_0*, *file_info_1*, *file_info_2*, or *file_info_3* structure, depending on the level. Because *fileid* is an unsigned short integer, only the first 64 KB open handles can be accessed.

NetFileGetInfo2

Gets information about an open server resource. Supports file handles larger than 64 KB.

```
unsigned far pascal
NetFileGetInfo2(
    char far * servername,      /* where to execute          */
    ULONG fileid,               /* the "key"                 */
    short level,                /* info structure level      */
    char far * buf,             /* buffer for return data    */
    USHORT buflen,              /* size of buf               */
    USHORT *totalavail,         /* total bytes available     */
    )
```

Levels:

Supports level 0, 1, 2, and 3 data structures.

Remote access:

This is available only to an administrator or a user with the server operator privilege.

An overview:

The *NetFileGetInfo2* API is similar to *NetFileGetInfo*, but it takes an unsigned long *fileid* argument, supporting file handles larger than 64 KB.

NetFileClose

Closes a resource.

```
unsigned far pascal
NetFileClose(
    char far * servername,      /* where to execute          */
    USHORT fileid               /* the "key"                 */
    )
```

Remote access:

This is available only to an administrator or a user with the server operator privilege.

Error returns:

If successful, *NetFileClose* returns 0. If unsuccessful, it returns a standard Del error code or the following error code:

Error Return	Meaning
NERR_FileNotFound	The *fileid* argument does not correspond to an open resource.

An overview:

The *NetFileClose* API is equivalent to the Del verb, but it has been named "Close" to make the name more intuitive. It considers a file ID an open server resource and forces it closed.

NetFileClose2

Closes a resource. Supports file handles larger than 64 KB.

```
unsigned far pascal
NetFileClose2(
    char far * servername,    /* where to execute     */
    unsigned long fileid      /* the "key"            */
    )
```

Remote access:

This is available only to an administrator or a user with the server operator privilege.

An overview:

The *NetFileClose2* API is similar to *NetFileClose*, but it takes an unsigned long as the *fileid* argument, supporting file handles larger than 64 KB.

INFORMATION APIs

One of an administrator's most important tasks is obtaining accurate information about network events. LAN Manager provides three kinds of APIs that provide information about the server or workstation:

- The Audit APIs use audit records to keep track of server operations and the people who perform them. These audit records can be created by the server software or by value-added applications.

- The Error APIs allow LAN Manager to record error conditions—particularly those errors occurring in software that has no convenient way to report errors to the user.

- The Statistics APIs provide information about workstation or server use of low-level communications. Such information helps you evaluate network performance and at the same time helps you discover inefficiencies in workstation or server configurations.

The Audit APIs

The Audit APIs provide a programming interface and an open format record structure for tracking significant server operations. The server software creates blocks of information called *audit records* to describe events such as creation or deletion of sessions, access to specific server resources, or failed attempts to use server resources. Audit records are stored in a text file called an *audit file*. The server can be configured to turn auditing off, in which case none of the server audit records are generated, or to generate audit records for specific classes of events. By default, the server performs all possible auditing.

Three main Audit APIs are available:

- *NetAuditWrite* is used to submit an audit record. It fills in a fixed header and writes the record out to the audit file.

- *NetAuditRead* allows programs to read audit records from the log file.

- *NetAuditClear* clears all audit records from the audit file and, optionally, writes the old audit records to a backup file.

The audit file lists the record length at both the beginning and the end of the audit record to make it easy for applications to scan either forward or backward in the file.

The audit records are kept in the audit file (NET.AUD by default) in the LANMAN\LOGS directory. The size of the audit log file is controlled by the *maxauditlog* parameter in LANMAN.INI. If the size of the audit log file exceeds 80 percent of *maxauditlog* (in KB), an administrative alert is issued.

If the audit log file is 100 percent full, another alert is issued, and no further audit records are written to the file.

Audit Records

Figure 8-1 shows the structure of an audit record. An audit record contains a fixed-length header, a variable-length data section, and a repetition of the record length. The data portion of the record can be defined by applications as needed, although the server uses a set of predefined record types.

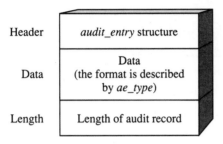

Header	*audit_entry* structure
Data	Data (the format is described by *ae_type*)
Length	Length of audit record

Figure 8-1.
The structure of an audit record.

The *audit_entry* structure is defined in AUDIT.H. Whenever it submits an audit record, *NetAuditWrite* fills in this header. The *audit_entry* structure contains the following members:

Member Name	Description
USHORT ae_len	Length of the audit record. This includes the fixed-length and the variable-length portions of the record.
USHORT ae_reserved	Not used in the current implementation.
ULONG ae_time	The time that the audit record was submitted.
USHORT ae_type	The audit record type. These are described in detail in the next section.
USHORT ae_data_offset	The offset from the beginning of the record to the data. In this implementation, the data immediately follows the offset (the offset is always 12), but this standard is not guaranteed for future versions.

The *ae_len* argument includes the fixed header (*struct audit_entry*), as well as the variable-length data section and a final repetition of the length. The data section can be empty, so the minimum size of an audit record is as follows, where the extra "unsigned short" is the repetition of the record length:

```
sizeof(struct audit_entry) + sizeof(unsigned short)
```

Predefined Audit Records

The format of *ae_data* and the value of the associated *ae_type* can be defined by applications. However, Microsoft has reserved the values 0 through 0x7FFF for *ae_type* and has defined *ae_data* formats for them. The current implementation defines these types:

Audit Type	Value	Meaning
AE_SRVSTATUS	0	Server status change
AE_SESSLOGON	1	Session logon
AE_SESSLOGOFF	2	Session logoff
AE_SESSPWERR	3	Session password error
AE_CONNSTART	4	Connection start
AE_CONNSTOP	5	Connection stop
AE_CONNREJ	6	Connection reject
AE_RESACCESS	7	Resource access
AE_RESACCESSREJ	8	Resource access denied
AE_CLOSEFILE	9	Close resource access
AE_SERVICESTAT	11	Service status
AE_ACLMOD	12	Access Control List modification
AE_UASMOD	13	User Account modification
AE_NETLOGON	14	Network logon
AE_NETLOGOFF	15	Network logoff
AE_NETLOGDENIED	16	Network logon denied
AE_ACCLIMITEXCD	17	Account limits exceeded
AE_RESACCESS2	18	Access granted (more information)
AE_ACLMODFAIL	19	Access Control List modification failed

Each audit type is associated with a data structure that describes the format of the variable-length part of the audit record. When the data is an ASCII string, the structure contains an offset into another part of the variable-length data area. This offset is from the start of the variable-length data area.

Each predefined audit type has a structure for variable-length data defined in AUDIT.H. In the 18 structures that follow, a *username* value of zero indicates that the client username is the same as the client computer name.

Type O: AE_SRVSTATUS

The server changed state. The data is in an *ae_srvstatus* structure.

Member Name	Description
USHORT ae_ss_status	The new state is one of the following:

	AE_SRVSTART	0	The server started.
	AE_SRVPAUSED	1	The server paused.
	AE_SRVCONT	2	The server continued.
	AE_SRVSTOP	3	The server stopped.

Type 1: AE_SESSLOGON

A workstation has established a session to the server. The data is in an *ae_sesslogon* structure.

Member Name	Description
USHORT ae_so_compname	An offset to a string containing the client computer name.
USHORT ae_so_username	An offset to a string containing the client username.
USHORT ae_so_privilege	The privilege of the user account. The values are as follows:

	AE_GUEST	0	guest account
	AE_USER	1	user account
	AE_ADMIN	2	admin account

Type 2: AE_SESSLOGOFF

The session has been deleted. This is submitted in all cases, whether the session delete was requested by the user or by the server. The data is in an *ae_sesslogoff* structure.

Member Name	Description
USHORT ae_sf_compname	An offset to a string containing the client computer name.
USHORT ae_sf_username	An offset to a string containing the client username.
USHORT ae_sf_reason	The reason for deleting the session. The values are as follows:

	AE_NORMAL	0	The user requested the operation.
	AE_ERROR	1	Session was dropped because an error occurred.

(continued)

continued

Member Name	Description
	AE_AUTODIS 2 Session was dropped because no activity occurred within the configured timeout period.
	AE_ADMINDIS 3 The administrator forced the session to be deleted.
	AE_ACCRESTRICT 4 Forced off by the accounts system because of restrictions, such as logon hours.

Type 3: AE_SESSPWERR

A workstation tried to establish a session, but the password was incorrect for the username. The data is in an *ae_sesspwerr* structure.

Member Name	Description
USHORT ae_sp_compname	An offset to a string containing the client computer name
USHORT ae_sp_username	An offset to a string containing the client username

Type 4: AE_CONNSTART

A workstation has established a new connection on the session to the server. This record is generated only if the number of connections (*shi2_max_uses*) on the share is not UNLIMITED. The data is in an *ae_connstart* structure.

Member Name	Description
USHORT ae_ct_compname	An offset to a string containing the client computer name
USHORT ae_ct_username	An offset to a string containing the client username
USHORT ae_ct_netname	An offset to a string containing the network name of the share
USHORT ae_ct_connid	A connection ID, unique to this server

Type 5: AE_CONNSTOP

A connection was deleted. No audit record is generated if the share has UNLIMITED uses and the connection was deleted at the user's request. The data is in an *ae_connstop* structure.

Member Name	Description
USHORT ae_cp_compname	An offset to a string containing the client computer name.
USHORT ae_cp_username	An offset to a string containing the client username.
USHORT ae_cp_netname	An offset to a string containing the network name of the share.
USHORT ae_cp_connid	A connection ID, unique to this server.
USHORT ae_cp_reason	The reason for the disconnection. The values are as follows:

AE_NORMAL	0	Normal client disconnect.
AE_SESSDIS	1	The entire session was deleted.
AE_UNSHARE	2	The share was deleted.

Type 6: AE_CONNREJ

The workstation tried to connect to a server resource but failed. The data is in an *ae_connrej* structure.

Member Name	Description
USHORT ae_cr_compname	An offset to a string containing the client computer name.
USHORT ae_cr_username	An offset to a string containing the client username.
USHORT ae_cr_netname	An offset to a string containing the network name of the share.
USHORT ae_cr_reason	The reason for the failure. The values are as follows:

AE_USERLIMIT	0	This connection exceeds the maximum use limit of the share.
AE_BADPW	1	The server is in share-mode security, and the share's password was not matched.
AE_ADMINPRIVREQD	2	*Admin* privilege is required to make this connection.
AE_NO_ACCESSPERM	3	In user mode, security devices and print queues check access permission for the connection.

Type 7: AE_RESACCESS

If the server is running user-mode security, individual resources can be configured to generate audit records when they are opened. The data is in an *ae_resaccess* structure.

Member Name	Description
USHORT ae_ra_compname	An offset to a string containing the client computer name.
USHORT ae_ra_username	An offset to a string containing the client username.
USHORT ae_ra_resname	An offset to a string containing the resource name.
USHORT ae_ra_operation	The file system operation. This is the same bitmask used in *NetAccessValidate* to determine whether a user has permission for the requested operation. The values are defined in ACCESS.H:

ACCESS_READ	0x01	Read
ACCESS_WRITE	0x02	Write
ACCESS_CREATE	0x04	Create
ACCESS_EXEC ·	0x08	Execute
ACCESS_DELETE	0x10	Delete
ACCESS_ATRIB	0x20	Change attributes
ACCESS_PERM	0x40	Change access permissions

Member Name	Description
USHORT ae_ra_returncode	The value of the return code from the operation, which might have been *DosOpen, DosMkDir, DosRmDir, PrintJobAdd*, and so on. The value is 0 if the operation was successful.
USHORT ae_ra_restype	The SMB request function code. This is for internal use only.
USHORT ae_ra_fileid	A unique file ID. This value is 0 for operations, such as *DosDelete* and *DosRmDir*, that do not create file IDs. This value is used to match an AE_RESACCESS record with its corresponding AE_CLOSEFILE record.

Type 8: AE_RESACCESSREJ

If the server is running user-mode security and the user does not have permissions to perform the requested operation, this record is generated. The data is in an *ae_resaccessrej* structure.

Member Name	Description
USHORT ae_rr_compname	An offset to a string containing the client computer name.
USHORT ae_rr_username	An offset to a string containing the client username.
USHORT ae_rr_resname	An offset to a string containing the resource name.
USHORT ae_rr_operation	The rejected file-system operation. This bitmask is the same set of values described for the type 7 *ae_ra_operation*.

Type 9: AE_CLOSEFILE

If a resource was opened and a file ID created, the corresponding close of the resource via *DosClose* generates this record. The *fileid* value can be used to match the corresponding records. The data is in an *ae_closefile* structure.

Member Name	Description
USHORT ae_cf_compname	An offset to a string containing the client computer name.
USHORT ae_cf_username	An offset to a string containing the client username.
USHORT ae_cf_resname	An offset to a string containing the resource name.
USHORT ae_cf_fileid	A unique file ID matching the *fileid* value in the corresponding AE_RESACCESS record.
ULONG ae_cf_duration	The time (in seconds) that the resource was open.
USHORT ae_cf_reason	The reason for the close. The possible values are as follows: AE_NORMAL_CLOSE 0 A normal client close. AE_SES_CLOSE 1 The underlying session was deleted. AE_ADMIN_CLOSE 2 The file was forced closed with the *NetFileClose* API.

Type 11: AE_SERVICESTAT

This record is written when service status auditing is enabled and when a service makes a *NetServiceStatus* call to one of the following states: INSTALLED, UNINSTALLED, PAUSED, CONTINUED. The data is in an *ae_servicestat* structure.

Member Name	Description
USHORT ae_ss_compname	An offset to a string containing the client computer name.
USHORT ae_ss_username	An offset to a string containing the client username.
USHORT ae_ss_svcname	An offset to a string containing the service name.
USHORT ae_ss_status	The service status being set. See Chapter 6 for the possible values.
USHORT ae_ss_code	The service code. See Chapter 6 for the possible values.
USHORT ae_ss_text	An offset to a string containing the service change text. See Chapter 6 for details.
USHORT ae_ss_returnval	The returned value.

Type 12: AE_ACLMOD

This is written when the Access Control List (ACL) is modified. This includes changes to an individual account and changes to the UAS modal values. The data is in an *ae_aclmod* structure.

Member Name	Description
USHORT ae_am_compname	An offset to a string containing the client computer name.
USHORT ae_am_username	An offset to a string containing the client username.
USHORT ae_am_resname	An offset to a string containing the resource name.
USHORT ae_am_action	The action performed on the ACL. The values are as follows: AE_MOD 0 Modified ACL AE_DELETE 1 Deleted ACL AE_ADD 2 Added new ACL
USHORT ae_am_datalen	The length of related data. For LAN Manager version 2.0, this is always 0.

Type 13: AE_UASMOD

This is written when the User Accounts System (UAS) is modified. This includes changes to an individual account and changes to the UAS modal values. The data is in an *ae_uasmod* structure.

Member Name	Description
USHORT ae_um_compname	An offset to a string containing the client computer name.
USHORT ae_um_username	An offset to a string containing the client username. This is not the name of the user account being modified but is the name of the user doing the modification.
USHORT ae_um_resname	An offset to a string containing the name of the object being modified. If this is a NUL string, the object is a UAS modal.
USHORT ae_um_rectype	The type of UAS record. The values are as follows: AE_UAS_USER 0 A user account AE_UAS_GROUP 1 A group AE_UAS_MODALS 2 UAS modals
USHORT ae_um_action	The action performed. The values are as follows: AE_MOD 0 Modified AE_DELETE 1 Deleted AE_ADD 2 Added
USHORT ae_am_datalen	The length of related data. For LAN Manager version 2.0, this is always 0.

Type 14: AE_NETLOGON

This is written by the server that processes a user's network logon. The data is in an *ae_netlogon* structure.

Member Name	Description
USHORT ae_no_compname	An offset to a string containing the client computer name.
USHORT ae_no_username	An offset to a string containing the client username.
USHORT ae_no_privilege	The privilege of the user logging on. The values are as follows:

AE_GUEST	0	Guest
AE_USER	1	User
AE_ADMIN	2	Administrator

Member Name	Description
USHORT ae_no_authflags	The authorization flags for operator privilege. These are a set of bits defined in ACCESS.H:

Bitmask	Value	Meaning
AF_OP_PRINT	0x1	Print operator
AF_OP_COMM	0x2	Comm operator
AF_OP_SERVER	0x4	Server operator
AF_OP_ACCOUNTS	0x8	Accounts operator

Type 15: AE_NETLOGOFF

This is written by the user's logon server when the user logs off. The data is in an *ae_netlogoff* structure.

Member Name	Description
USHORT ae_nf_compname	An offset to a string containing the client computer name.
USHORT ae_nf_username	An offset to a string containing the client username.
USHORT ae_nf_reason	The reason for the logoff. The values are as follows:

AE_NORMAL	0	The user requested the operation.
AE_ERROR	1	The session was dropped because an error occurred.
AE_AUTODIS	2	The domain controller determined that the user was no longer logged on.
AE_ADMINDIS	3	The administrator forced the logoff.
AE_ACCRESTRICT	4	Forced off by the accounts system because of restrictions such as logon hours.

(continued)

Member Name	Description
USHORT ae_nf_subreason	When *ae_nf_reason* is AE_ACCRESTRICT, the values for this member are as follows:

AE_LIM_UNKNOWN	0	The reason is not known.
AE_LIM_LOGONHOURS	1	The account logon hours were exceeded.
AE_LIM_EXPIRED	2	The account has expired.

Type 16: AE_NETLOGDENIED

This is written by the user's logon server when the network logon fails. The data is in an *ae_netlogdenied* structure.

Member Name	Description
USHORT ae_nd_compname	An offset to a string containing the client computer name.
USHORT ae_nd_username	An offset to a string containing the client username.
USHORT ae_nd_reason	The reason the logon failed. The values are as follows:

AE_GENERAL	0	General access denied
AE_BADPW	1	Bad password
AE_ACCRESTRICT	4	Account restrictions, such as logon hours

Member Name	Description
USHORT ae_nd_subreason	When *ae_nd_reason* is AE_ACCRESTRICT, the values for this member are as follows:

AE_LIM_UNKNOWN	0	The reason is not known.
AE_LIM_LOGONHOURS	1	The account logon hours were exceeded.
AE_LIM_EXPIRED	2	The account has expired.
AE_LIM_INVAL_WKSTA	3	The user is attempting logon from a workstation that he or she is not allowed to use.
AE_LIM_DISABLED	4	The user account has been disabled.

Type 17: AE_ACCLIMITEXCD

This is written when a user remains logged on past the time specified by the account limits. The data is in an *ae_acclim* structure.

Member Name	Description
USHORT ae_al_compname	An offset to a string containing the client computer name.
USHORT ae_al_username	An offset to a string containing the client username.

(continued)

continued

Member Name	Description
USHORT ae_al_resname	An offset to a string containing the resource name.
USHORT ae_al_limit	The limit that was exceeded. The values are as follows:

AE_LIM_UNKNOWN	0	The reason is not known.
AE_LIM_LOGONHOURS	1	Account logon hours were exceeded.

Type 18: AE_RESACCESS2

If the server is running user-mode security, individual resources can be configured to generate audit records when they are opened. The data is in an *ae_resaccess2* structure. This is similar to an *ae_resaccess* structure except that *ae_ra2_fileid* is an unsigned long integer rather than an unsigned short integer.

Member Name	Description
USHORT ae_ra2_compname	An offset to a string containing the client computer name.
USHORT ae_ra2_username	An offset to a string containing the client username.
USHORT ae_ra2_resname	An offset to a string containing the resource name.
USHORT ae_ra2_operation	The file-system operation. This is the same bitmask used by the *NetAccessValidate* API to determine whether a user has permission for the requested operation. The values are defined as follows in ACCESS.H:

ACCESS_READ	0x01	Read
ACCESS_WRITE	0x02	Write
ACCESS_CREATE	0x04	Create
ACCESS_EXEC	0x08	Execute
ACCESS_DELETE	0x10	Delete
ACCESS_ATRIB	0x20	Change attributes
ACCESS_PERM	0x40	Change access permissions

Member Name	Description
USHORT ae_ra2_returncode	The value of the return code from the operation, which might have been *DosOpen*, *DosMkDir*, *DosRmDir*, *PrintJobAdd*, and so on. The value is 0 if the operation was successful.
USHORT ae_ra2_restype	The SMB request function code (for internal use only).

(continued)

Member Name	Description
ULONG ae_ra_fileid	A unique file ID. This value is 0 for operations, such as *DosDelete* or *DosRmDir*, that do not create file IDs. The *ae_ra_fileid* value is used to match an AE_RESACCESS record with its corresponding AE_CLOSEFILE record.

Other Audit Records

The format of variable-length data in an audit record can be defined by applications. The *ae_type* value can be chosen from the range 0x8000 through 0xFFFF. When this is done, it is important to ensure that the variable-length part of the record contains all of the data. If a true pointer to a string or a substructure is put into the audit record, it cannot be used by the application that reads the audit record.

Any offsets should be specified from the start of the variable-length portion of the record.

What Do You REALLY Want To Know?

The server can be configured for the types of predefined audit records it will generate. This can range from no auditing at all to auditing everything. This configuration is determined by startup switches given to the server.

Information about events currently being audited at the server is available from the *NetServerGetInfo* API in the *sv3_auditedevents* structure member. See Chapter 7 for a description of this API.

The following sections describe the four Audit APIs.

NetAuditRead

Reads one or more records from an audit file.

```
unsigned far pascal
NetAuditRead(
    char far * servername,     /* where to execute        */
    char far * reserved1,      /* must be NULL            */
    HLOG far * ploghandle,     /* returned log handle     */
    ULONG offset,              /* offset to begin read    */
    USHORT far * reserved2,    /* must be NULL            */
```

```
ULONG reserved3,        /* must be 0L              */
ULONG flags,            /* open flags              */
char far * buf,         /* buffer for return data  */
USHORT buflen,          /* size of buf             */
USHORT far * bytesread, /* bytes read              */
USHORT far * bytesavail /* bytes actually available */
)
```

Remote access:

Remote access is available only to an administrator, or to users with the following operator privileges:

- server operator

- print operator

- comm operator

- accounts operator

Error returns:

If successful, or if no more data is available to be read, *NetAuditRead* returns 0. If unsuccessful, it returns a standard API return code, an OS/2 file-system error, or one of the following error codes:

Error Return	Meaning
NERR_BufTooSmall	The *buf* argument was too small for the audit record.
NERR_LogFileChanged	The audit file has been cleared or otherwise altered since the last call to *NetAuditRead*.
NERR_InvalidLogSeek	The audit record requested with the *offset* argument does not exist.

An overview:

The *NetAuditRead* API allows applications to read audit records without knowing the internal structure of the audit log file. Each time a buffer full of audit records is read, the *ploghandle* parameter is updated by the API so that the next call to *NetAuditRead* can pick up where the previous call left off. *NetAuditRead* also allows the audit file to be scanned either forward or backward.

The *flags* argument tells the API whether to read forward or backward and dictates the meaning of the *offset* argument. The *flags* argument is a set of bits:

Bitmask	Value	Meaning
LOGFLAGS_FORWARD	0x0	Read forward. Records are returned in chronological order (oldest first).
LOGFLAGS_BACKWARD	0x01	Read backward. Records are returned in reverse chronological order (newest first).
LOGFLAGS_SEEK	0x02	Use *offset* to determine the record number to start reading from.

If the expression *flags & LOGFLAGS_SEEK* is not true, *offset* is ignored. If it is true, the buffer of returned audit records will start at the record number indicated by *offset*.

The *buf* argument should be large enough to contain at least one audit record. Each audit record is in the format described above, with both a leading and a trailing length. *NetAuditRead* places as many records into the buffer as will fit.

The *bytesread* argument returns the number of bytes returned in the buffer.

The *bytesavail* argument indicates how many additional bytes are available.

If *bytesavail* is set to 0xFFFF on return, it means that at least 64 KB of audit record data is available. When *bytesread* and *bytesavail* both return zero, no more audit records exist. This indicates ''end of file'' if reading forward or ''beginning of file'' if reading backward.

You can dictate how *NetAuditRead* reads the audit log file:

- Passing along *ploghandle* from the previous call tells the API to get the next buffer of data.

- Initializing *ploghandle* tells the API to start at the beginning or end of the audit file (depending on the value of *flags*). Initializing can be done at any time, telling the API to start from the beginning (or end) again.

- Setting *flags | LOGFLAGS_SEEK* and setting *offset* to a specific record number tells the API to start reading (either forward or backward) from the indicated record.

The Magic Log Handle

The audit log handle is defined in the AUDIT.H file as a *loghandle* structure, also known as a "typedef HLOG." The *loghandle* structure contains the following members:

Member Name	Meaning
ULONG time	Returns the timestamp of the first record returned by the call.
ULONG last_flags	The value of *flags* from the previous call.
ULONG offset	The current file offset in bytes.
ULONG rec_offset	The record number of the most recently read record.

The *loghandle* structure contains information used by the *NetAuditRead* API so that it will know where to continue reading on each subsequent *NetAuditRead* call. Programs should not change these values with the exception of initialization.

By initializing *loghandle*, programs dictate whether *NetAuditRead* starts reading again from the beginning or from the end of the audit log. To initialize *loghandle*, set the structure members as follows:

```
HLOG lh;
lh.time = 0L;
lh.last_flags = 0L;
lh.offset = 0xffffffff;
lh.rec_offset = 0xffffffff;
```

What About a Moving Target?

What happens if another process writes to the audit log between two *NetLogFileRead* calls?

- If the read is scanning forward, the next *NetLogFileRead* gets the new data (or indicates its availability in *bytesavail* if too much exists for the buffer).

- If *NetLogFileRead* is scanning backward, or if the log file is cleared with *NetAuditClear*, the next call to *NetAuditRead* has a return code of NERR_LogFileChanged.

Whenever NERR_LogFileChanged is encountered, an application should reinitialize *loghandle* and start reading again.

NetAuditOpen

Opens an audit file for reading.

```
unsigned far pascal
NetAuditOpen(
    char far * servername,    /* where to execute      */
    unsigned far * handle,    /* returned file handle  */
    char far * reserved       /* must be NULL          */
    )
```

Remote access:
Remote access is available only to an administrator.

Error returns:
If successful, *NetAuditOpen* returns 0. If unsuccessful, it returns one of the standard API return codes or OS/2 file-system errors.

An overview:
The *NetAuditOpen* API returns to the audit log a file-system handle opened for reading. All handle-oriented API calls (*DosRead, DosChgFilePtr, DosQFSInfo*, and so on) can be made using this handle. The presence of a length at both beginning and end of the audit record makes it easy for applications to scan forward or backward.

> **NOTE:** *This API is obsolete and exists only for compatibility with LAN Manager version 1.0. Use* NetAuditRead *if you are using LAN Manager version 2.0 or later.*

NetAuditWrite

Writes a record to an audit file.

```
unsigned far pascal
NetAuditWrite(
    unsigned type            /* audit record type     */
    char far * buf,          /* audit record data     */
    USHORT buflen,           /* size of buf           */
    char far * reserved1,    /* must be NULL          */
    char far * reserved2,    /* must be NULL          */
    )
```

Remote access:
This API cannot be called remotely.

Error returns:

If successful, *NetAuditWrite* returns 0. If unsuccessful, it returns one of the standard API return codes, OS/2 file-system errors, or the following error code:

Error Return	Meaning
NERR_LogOverFlow	The audit file is 100 percent full. The size of the audit file is controlled by the *maxauditlog* parameter in the [server] component of the LANMAN.INI file. The maximum size of the audit file is also available in the *sv2_maxauditsz* structure member retrieved by the *NetServerGetInfo* API.

An overview:

The *NetAuditWrite* API writes an audit record to the audit log file.

The *type* argument contains the audit record type. Values in the range 0 through 0x7FFF are reserved for use by Microsoft. Values in the range 0x8000 through 0xFFFF can be used by applications programs.

The *buf* argument contains the data to be placed in the variable-length part of the audit record. For types not defined by Microsoft, the format of this data is determined by the applications using it.

NetAuditWrite adds the *audit_entry* structure to the front of the record and the additional length to the end. This includes filling in the timestamp.

In the following cases, *NetAuditWrite* returns an indication of success, even though the audit record is not written to the file:

- The server is not running.

- The server is running, but it was configured to turn off all auditing.

- The audit record is one of the predefined audit records, but the server is configured not to log that class of events.

Therefore, before writing audit records, an application should always do the following:

- Call *NetServerGetInfo* at level 3 to see if the server is running.

- Check *sv3_auditing* to see if auditing is enabled.

- Check *sv3_auditevents* to see which predefined audit events are actually being logged.

NetAuditClear

Deletes the entries in an audit file.

```
unsigned far pascal
NetAuditClear(
    char far * servername,    /* where to execute  */
    char far * backupfile,    /* backup filename   */
    char far * reserved       /* must be NULL      */
    )
```

Remote access:

Remote access is available only to an administrator.

Error returns:

If successful, *NetAuditClear* returns 0. If unsuccessful, it returns the standard API return codes and OS/2 file-system errors. (A file-system return code can be ambiguous because you can't determine whether the error occurred in the source or in the destination file during backup.)

An overview:

The *NetAuditClear* API clears all entries from the audit log file, setting the file size to zero.

If the *backupfile* argument is not NULL, the audit log is copied to the specified file before the clear. The save-and-clear operation is a one-step process, so no audit records are lost.

backupfile must be a valid file-system name. If the file exists, it is truncated and the new data written to it. If the name is a relative pathname, it is considered relative to the LANMAN\LOGS subdirectory. The path must be able to use the *DosMove* API, which means that it must be on the same disk drive as the LANMAN\LOGS directory, where the audit log resides.

If *NetAuditClear* is called remotely, *backupfile* is relative to the server file system.

An audit log monitor

The AUDITMON.C program (Figure 8-2) monitors the audit log in real time, looking for new audit log entries every 10 seconds. If found, they are passed to a processing routine. In this version, the processing routine is empty, but you can add your own. The following is a list of sample tasks a processing routine can accomplish:

- Format each audit record and send it to a printer. This would give an administrator a hard-copy record of auditing as it happens.

- Track failed password attempts. If too many occur on one user account, use the *NetUserSetInfo* API to disable the account.

- Process a billing system. The routine might track and bill users for logon time, connection time to a resource, one-time charges for program execution, and so forth.

This version of AUDITMON.C runs in the foreground until it is stopped. An interesting adaptation would be to make it a LAN Manager service program, as shown in Chapter 6.

```
/*
 * AUDITMON.C -- This program monitors an audit log.
 * It periodically checks the log for new entries, and if they
 * exist, it reads and passes them along to the Process routine.
 *
 * If the command line contains an argument, it is
 * assumed to be a filename, and the existing audit
 * log is copied to the file and cleared.
 *
 * Compile with:  C> cl auditmon.c netapi.lib doscalls.lib
 *
 * Usage:  C> auditmon [filename]
 *
 * The program runs in the foreground until it is stopped.
 *
 */

#include <stdio.h>
#include <os2.h>
#include <netcons.h>
#include <audit.h>
#include <neterr.h>

main(argc, argv)
int argc;
char **argv;
    {
    unsigned err;
    HLOG audlog;
    USHORT bytesread, bytesavail;
    char buf[BUFSIZ];      /* "big enough" buffer */
```

Figure 8-2.   *(continued)*
The AUDITMON.C program.

Figure 8-2. *continued*

```
    if (argc > 1)
        if ((err = NetAuditClear(NULL, argv[1], NULL)) != 0)
            {
            printf("Unable to backup audit log (%d)\n", err);
            exit(1);
            }

    /* initialize the HLOG each time through */
    ReInit:
    audlog.time = audlog.last_flags = 0L;
    audlog.offset = audlog.rec_offset = 0xffffffff;

    /* main loop -- sleep for a while, and then check for new audit
     * records and process. */

    while (1)
        {
        /* This loop reads records forward until "bytesread"
         * equals 0, indicating the end of the file.  When new entries
         * appear, they will be read. */

        do
            {
            err = NetAuditRead(
                                NULL,               /* server         */
                                NULL,               /* reserved1      */
                                &audlog,            /* handle         */
                                0L,                 /* offset (ignored) */
                                NULL,               /* reserved2      */
                                0L,                 /* reserved3      */
                                LOGFLAGS_FORWARD,   /* flags          */
                                buf,                /* data buffer    */
                                sizeof(buf),        /* buflen         */
                                &bytesread,         /* bytes returned */
                                &bytesavail         /* bytes available */
                                );
            switch (err)
                {
                case NERR_LogFileChanged:
                    /* Log was cleared.  Reinitialize the program
                     * and start over. */
                    printf("------\n");
                    goto ReInit;
```

(continued)

Figure 8-2. *continued*

```
                    default:
                        /* An unexpected error.  For simplicity in this
                         * example, report the error and get out. */
                        printf("Unexpected err %d\n", err);
                        exit(1);
                    case 0:
                        Process(buf, bytesread);
                    }
                } while (bytesread != 0);

            /* sleep for 10 seconds and check again */
            DosSleep(10000L);
            err = getch(); if (err == 'q') exit(1);
            }
        }

/*
 * Process -- A routine to process the audit record.  Place your
 * application-specific code here.  Notice the construction of the
 * pointer to the variable-length part of the record.  If bytesread
 * is 0 on entry, nothing is done.
 */

Process(ae_data, bytesread)
char *ae_data;
    {
    struct audit_entry *pae;
    union
        {
        char * init;
        struct ae_srvstatus * srvstatus;
        struct ae_sesslogon * sesslogon;
        struct ae_sesslogoff * sesslogoff;
        struct ae_sesspwerr * sesspwerr;
        struct ae_connstart * connstart;
        struct ae_connstop * connstop;
        struct ae_connrej * connrej;
        struct ae_resaccess * resaccess;
        struct ae_resaccessrej * resaccessrej;
        struct ae_closefile * closefile;
        struct ae_servicestat * servicestat;
        struct ae_aclmod * aclmod;
        struct ae_uasmod * uasmod;
        struct ae_netlogon * netlogon;
        struct ae_netlogoff * netlogoff;
```

(continued)

Figure 8-2. *continued*

```
            struct ae_netlogdenied * netlogdenied;
            struct ae_acclim * acclim;
            struct ae_resaccess2 * resaccess2;
            } pdat;

    while (bytesread > 0)
        {
        /* set up typed pointers */
        pae = (struct audit_entry *) ae_data;
        pdat.init = ae_data + pae->ae_data_offset;
        switch (pae->ae_type)
            {
            case AE_SRVSTATUS:
            case AE_SESSLOGON:
            case AE_SESSLOGOFF:
            case AE_SESSPWERR:
            case AE_CONNSTART:
            case AE_CONNSTOP:
            case AE_CONNREJ:
            case AE_RESACCESS:
            case AE_RESACCESSREJ:
            case AE_CLOSEFILE:
            case AE_SERVICESTAT:
            case AE_ACLMOD:
            case AE_UASMOD:
            case AE_NETLOGON:
            case AE_NETLOGOFF:
            case AE_NETLOGDENIED:
            case AE_ACCLIMITEXCD:
            case AE_RESACCESS2:

            /* Insert your own processing code here.
             *
             * References can be made to specific audit structures
             * through the union -- for example
             *
             * pdat.connstop->ae_cp_compname;
             */

            printf("TYPE = %d\n", pae->ae_type);
            }

    /* adjust pointers to the next record */
    ae_data += pae->ae_len;
    bytesread -= pae->ae_len;
    }
}
```

The Error APIs

Much of LAN Manager executes in the background or at the device driver level. Because of this, it's harder to obtain LAN Manager error codes than API error codes. The Error APIs and the error log file are a mechanism for noting errors on both the workstation and the server.

The Error API is very similar to the Audit API. It has an open format for the error records and three main API calls: *NetErrorLogRead*, *NetErrorLogWrite*, and *NetErrorLogClear*. The error record, shown in Figure 8-3, has a fixed structure (*error_log*), a variable-length section (data and strings), and a repeat of the record length at the end.

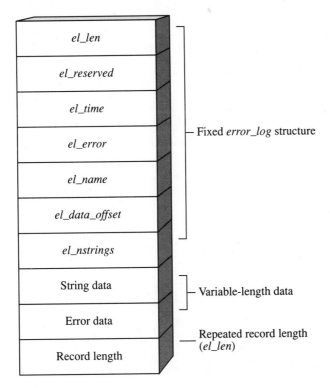

Figure 8-3.
A LAN Manager error record.

The variable-length section is in two pieces:

- Error data is raw data, usually a dump of a data structure involved in the error.

- String data is a set of ASCII strings, also called *merge strings*. Many applications, including the core LAN Manager, associate the error number (*el_error*) with a text string in an OS/2 message file. The OS/2 message strings can contain metacharacters for insertion of substrings. The merge strings are intended for this kind of substitution. For example, an error code might correspond to the following message file string:

```
Error frubdicating the %1 framish
```

The merge string could be "right" or "left" and substituted appropriately.

To use Error APIs, you must include NETCONS.H and ERRLOG.H at compile time, and you must link with the NETAPI.LIB stub library. The fixed-length *error_log* header contains the following members:

Member Name	Description
USHORT el_len	The length of the error record, including *error_log* header, raw data buffer, string buffer, and end length word.
USHORT el_reserved	Reserved for future use.
ULONG el_time	The timestamp indicating when the error record was logged.
USHORT el_error	The error number. 0x0000 through 0x7FFFF are reserved for Microsoft use. 0x8000 through 0xFFFF can be used by applications programs.
char el_name[SNLEN+1]	The service logging the error. This is a buffer SNLEN+1 characters long. The text string is zero terminated.
USHORT el_data_offset	The offset from the start of the error record to the raw data.
USHORT el_nstrings	The number of zero-terminated strings that will immediately follow the fixed-length header.

The error records are stored in the NET.ERR file in the LANMAN\LOGS directory. The size of the error log file is controlled by the LANMAN.INI configuration parameter *maxerrorlog*. If the size of the error log file exceeds this value (in KB), no additional error records are written to the file.

NetErrorLogRead

Reads an error record from the error log.

```
unsigned far pascal
NetErrorLogRead(
     char far * servername,      /* where to execute            */
     char far * reserved1,       /* must be NULL                */
     HLOG far * ploghandle,      /* returned log handle         */
     ULONG offset,               /* offset to begin read        */
     USHORT far * reserved2,     /* must be NULL                */
     ULONG reserved3,            /* must be 0L                  */
     ULONG flags,                /* open flags                  */
     char far * buf,             /* buffer for return data      */
     USHORT buflen,              /* size of buf                 */
     USHORT far * bytesread,     /* bytes read                  */
     USHORT far * bytesavail     /* bytes actually available    */
     )
```

Remote access:

Only the administrator has remote access to this API.

An overview:

The *NetErrorLogRead* API is similar to the *NetAuditRead* API, but it reads error records from the error log instead of audit records from the audit log. See the overview of the *NetAuditRead* API to learn what the arguments mean and to learn how to use the API.

NetErrorLogOpen

Returns the error log file handle.

```
unsigned far pascal
NetErrorLogOpen(
     char far * servername,      /*  where to execute            */
     unsigned far * handle,      /*  returned file handle        */
     char far * reserved         /*  must be NULL                */
     )
```

Remote access:

Remote access is available only to an administrator.

Error returns:

If successful, *NetErrorLogOpen* returns 0. If unsuccessful, it returns one of the standard API return codes or OS/2 file-system errors.

An overview:

The *NetErrorLogOpen* API returns to the error file a file-system handle opened for reading. All handle-oriented API calls (*DosRead*, *DosChgFilePtr*, *DosQFSInfo*, and so on) can be made on this handle.

> **NOTE:** *This API is obsolete and exists only for compatibility with LAN Manager 1.0. Use* NetErrorLogRead *if you are using LAN Manager version 2.0 or later.*

NetErrorLogWrite

Writes an error record to an error log file.

```
unsigned far pascal
NetErrorLogWrite(
    char far * reserved1,    /* must be NULL       */
    USHORT code,             /* error record type  */
    char far * compname,     /* service component  */
    char far * buf,          /* error record data  */
    USHORT buflen,           /* size of buf        */
    char far * insbuf,       /* string data buffer */
    USHORT nstrings,         /* number of strings  */
    char far * reserved2     /* must be NULL       */
    )
```

Remote access:

This API cannot be called remotely.

Error returns:

If successful, *NetErrorLogWrite* returns 0. If unsuccessful, it returns a standard API return code, an OS/2 file-system error, or the following error code:

Error Return	Meaning
NERR_LogOverflow	The log file is 100 percent full. The size of the error log file is controlled by the *maxerrorlog* parameter in the [wksta] component of the LANMAN.INI file.

An overview:

The *NetErrorLogWrite* API submits error records for writing to the error log file.

The *code* argument is the error record number. Microsoft reserves the range 0x0000 through 0x7FFFF. Error messages already defined are available in ERRLOG.H.

The *compname* argument is the name of the LAN Manager service submitting the error and can be any text string, up to SNLEN characters and a terminating zero.

The *buf* argument contains raw data written to the error log. Some examples of raw data are unrecognized NCBs, unrecognized SMBs, and OS/2 error-return codes.

The *insbuf* argument is a buffer of ASCII strings, each separated (and terminated) by a zero. *nstrings* is the number of strings in the buffer.

One innovative use of the *NetErrorLogWrite* API is as a debugging tool. Applications that do not have access to the console can write debugging information to the error log. See Chapter 14 for an example of this.

NetErrorLogClear

Clears an error log file.

```
unsigned far pascal
NetErrorLogClear(
    char far * servername,    /* where to execute  */
    char far * backupfile,    /* backup filename   */
    char far * reserved       /* must be NULL      */
    )
```

Remote access:
Remote access is available only to an administrator, or to a user with the server operator privilege.

Error returns:
If successful, *NetErrorLogClear* returns 0. If unsuccessful, it returns one of the standard OS/2 file-system error codes. (The return can be ambiguous because you can't determine whether the error occurred in the source or in the destination file during backup.)

An overview:
The *NetErrorLogClear* API clears all entries from the error log file. This sets the file size to zero. If the *backupfile* argument is not NULL, the error log is copied to the specified file before the clear. The save-and-clear operation is a one-step process, so no error records are lost.

The *backupfile* argument must be a valid file-system name. If the file exists, it is truncated, and the new data is written to it. If the name is a relative pathname, it is considered relative to the LANMAN\LOGS directory. The path must be able to use the *DosMove* API, which means that it must be on the same disk drive as the LANMAN\LOGS directory, where the error log resides.

Getting Messages out of the Bottle

Although the Error APIs are useful for generating and retrieving raw error records, getting error information to a user or administrator takes a bit more work. Both the command-line version and the full-screen version of the LAN Manager user interface let you format and display error log data:

- If the error number is a predefined Microsoft number, the programs can look up text in the NET.ERR message file, merge the string data, and write out the message. The descriptive text for each error message is obtained from comments in the ERRLOG.H file.

- If the error number is unrecognized, the user-interface programs simply display the raw data in a debugging format.

Application programs could do the same processing on the error log entries and use the error number to determine what message file to retrieve the text from. There is an easier way to do this, however. NELOG_OEM_Code is a generic error log entry that can be used by applications but will be properly formatted by the LAN Manager user interface programs. The error code is NELOG_OEM_Code, defined in ERRLOG.H. The text for the error message is only nine merge strings. Any of the merge strings can be empty. The suggested way to use this generic error code is as follows:

Merge String	Contents	Example
%1	System name	Generic LAN Corp
%2	Service name	GLC Mail Service
%3	Severity level	Error, warning, etc.
%4	Subidentifier	Error code, etc.
%5–%9	Text	As needed

The application must provide nine text strings in the string buffer, although they can be empty strings.

The LOGERR.C routine (Figure 8-4) provides a convenient interface for logging generic error reports. It accepts a variable number of arguments and pads the string buffer (with empty strings) to ensure the existence of nine strings.

```
/*
 * LOGERR.C -- This routine packages error messages and strings
 * for submission to the error log file. The error code will always
 * be NELOG_OEM_Code.
 *
 * Compile with:  C> cl -c logerr.c netapi.lib
 *
 */

#include <netcons.h>
#include <errlog.h>
#include <stdarg.h>
#include <malloc.h>

int logerr(compname, buf, buflen, nstrings, ...)
char *compname;
char *buf;
int buflen;
int nstrings;
    {
    va_list ps;
    int i, size, err;
    char *sbuf, *p;

    /* how much space is needed? */
    va_start(ps, nstrings);
    size = 9;
    for (i = 0; i < nstrings; ++i)
        {
        size += strlen(va_arg(ps, char *)) + 1;
        }
    sbuf = alloca(size);

    /* copy strings to sbuf */
    va_start(ps, nstrings);
    for (p = sbuf, i = 0; i < nstrings; ++i)
        {
        strcpy(p, va_arg(ps, char *));
        p += strlen(p) + 1;
        }
    va_end(ps);
```

Figure 8-4.
The LOGERR.C routine.

(continued)

Figure 8-4. *continued*

```
    /* add empty strings for unused merge strings */
    for (i = nstrings; i < 9; ++i)
        *p++ = 0;

    /* log the error */
    err = NetErrorLogWrite(
                        NULL,            /* reserved1 */
                        NELOG_OEM_Code,  /* generic error code */
                        compname,        /* component name */
                        buf,             /* raw error data */
                        buflen,          /* length of buf */
                        sbuf,            /* strings */
                        9,               /* 9 strings required */
                        NULL);           /* reserved2 */
    return(err);
}
```

For example, suppose the LOGERR.C routine were called with the following arguments in a program:

```
char * rawdata = "Raw Data";
logerr(
        "GLC Mail",          /* component name         */
        rawdata,             /* error data             */
        13,                  /* size of raw data       */
        6,                   /* number of text strings */
        "GLC LanMan",
        "Mail",
        "warning",
        "12",
        ":",
        "Framish limit");
```

The net error command would produce the following output:

```
Program              Message              Time
------------------------------------------------------------------
GLC Mail                3299                 03-09-90 12:46pm
NET3299:  GLC LanMan Mail warning 12 : Framish limit    .
       52 61 77 20 44 61 74 61 00 46 72 61 6D    Raw Data.Fram
```

The Statistics APIs

The Statistics APIs let you interrogate or clear the operating statistics of the workstation or server. Three Statistics APIs are available: *NetStatisticsGet*, *NetStatisticsGet2*, and *NetStatisticsClear*. To use these APIs in a program, you must include NETCONS.H and NETSTATS.H at compile time, and you must link with the NETAPI.LIB stub library.

NetStatisticsGet

Returns server or workstation statistics.

```
unsigned far pascal
NetStatisticsGet(
    char far * servername,    /* where to execute           */
    char far * buf,           /* statistics data            */
    USHORT buflen,            /* size of buf                */
    USHORT *bread,            /* number of bytes read       */
    USHORT *bavail            /* number of bytes available */
    )
```

Remote access:

Remote access is available only to an administrator.

Error returns:

If successful, *NetStatisticsGet* returns 0. ERROR_MORE_DATA is returned if only some of the available statistics were returned. If unsuccessful, *NetStatisticsGet* returns one of the standard LAN Manager error codes.

An overview:

The *NetStatisticsGet* API returns operating statistics for the workstation or server.

> **NOTE:** *This API is obsolete and exists only for compatibility with LAN Manager 1.0. Use* NetStatisticsGet2 *if you are using LAN Manager 2.0 or later.*

The *buf* argument returns a *statistics_info_0* structure (level 0), which contains the following members:

Member Name	Description
ULONG st0_start	A timestamp of when statistics were last cleared.
ULONG st0_wknumNCBs	The number of workstation NCBs issued.
ULONG st0_wkfiNCBs	The number of workstation NCBs that failed submission to NetBIOS.

(continued)

continued

Member Name	Description
ULONG st0_wkfcNCBs	The number of NCBs that failed to complete.
ULONG st0_wksesstart	The number of workstation sessions started.
ULONG st0_wksessfail	The number of attempted sessions that failed.
ULONG st0_wkuses	The number of successful connections made by the workstation.
ULONG st0_wkusefail	The number of failed connections attempted by the workstation.
ULONG st0_wkautorec	The number of automatic reconnections made by the workstation.
ULONG st0_rdrnumNCBs	The number of NCBs issued by the redirector.
ULONG st0_svrnumNCBs	The number of NCBs issued by the server.
ULONG st0_usrnumNCBs	The number of NCBs issued by user programs using *NetBiosSubmit* (or Int 5C/2A under an OS/2 MS-DOS partition).
ULONG st0_reserved4	Always 0xFFFF.
ULONG st0_reserved5	Always 0xFFFF.
ULONG st0_reserved6	Always 0xFFFF.
ULONG st0_reserved7	Always 0xFFFF.
ULONG st0_reserved8	Always 0xFFFF.
ULONG st0_svfopens	The number of server file opens. This includes opens of named pipes.
ULONG st0_svdevopens	The number of server device opens.
ULONG st0_svjobsqueued	The number of server print jobs spooled.
ULONG st0_svsopens	The number of server sessions started.
ULONG st0_svstimedout	The number of server sessions timed out.
ULONG st0_svserrorout	The number of server sessions deleted because of errors.
ULONG st0_svpwerrors	The number of server password violations.
ULONG st0_svpermerrors	The number of server resource permission errors.
ULONG st0_svsyserrors	The number of server system errors.
ULONG st0_svbytessent	The total number of bytes sent by the server. The special value 0xFFFFFFFE is the highest possible value and indicates that the counter has overflowed. The value 0xFFFFFFFF is reserved.
ULONG st0_svbytesrcvd	The total number of bytes received by the server. The special value 0xFFFFFFFE is the highest possible value and indicates that the counter has overflowed. The value 0xFFFFFFFF is reserved.
ULONG st0_svavresponse	The average response time, in milliseconds, of server request processing.

Values reflect statistics since the last time the statistics were cleared (the *st0_start* time).

The *statistics_info_0* structure consists entirely of double word (unsigned long) values, so the size of the required buffer is always known. However, if *buflen* is smaller than the total size of *statistics_info_0*, this API returns as much data as will fit in the buffer. This is unlike the rest of the GetInfo APIs, which never return a partial fixed-length structure. The *bread* and *bavail* arguments indicate the number of bytes read and the total number of bytes available.

If specific statistics are unavailable or—as in the case of server statistics for a workstation—not applicable, the value 0xFFFFFFFF is returned for that structure member.

NetStatisticsGet2

Returns information about a server or workstation service.

```
unsigned far pascal
NetStatisticsGet2(
    char far * servername,   /* where to execute         */
    char far * servicename,  /* which service?           */
    ULONG reserved,          /* must be 0L               */
    short level,             /* must be 0                */
    ULONG options,           /* statistics options       */
    char far * buf,          /* statistics data          */
    USHORT buflen,           /* size of buf              */
    USHORT *bavail           /* number of bytes available */
    )
```

Levels:
Supports a level 0 data structure.

Remote access:
Remote access is available only to an administrator.

Error returns:
If successful, *NetStatisticsGet2* returns 0. If unsuccessful, it returns a standard API return code or one of the following error codes:

Error Return	Meaning
ERROR_NOT_SUPPORTED	The *servicename* argument was not SERVICE_WORKSTATION or SERVICE_SERVER.
NERR_ServiceNotInstalled	The server statistics were requested, and the server is not running.
NERR_BufTooSmall	The *buf* buffer was too small for the entire set of statistics.

An overview:

The *NetStatisticsGet2* API returns statistics for a specific LAN Manager service. The following text strings are valid *servicename* arguments:

Service Name	Text String
SERVICE_WORKSTATION	"workstation"
SERVICE_SERVER	"server"

The strings are not case sensitive. Both manifest constants are defined in SERVICE.H.

The *options* parameter can receive one of the following values:

Bitmask	Value	Meaning
	0	Get the requested statistics.
STATSOPT_CLR	1	Get the requested statistics and clear the statistics at the same time. This allows the atomic operation of get/clear so that no new statistics can be accumulated in the time between getting and clearing.

If *servicename* is SERVICE_WORKSTATION, the *buf* buffer returns with a *stat_workstation_0* structure, which contains the following members:

Member	Meaning
ULONG stw0_start	The time since collection was started, typically the last time the statistics were cleared.
ULONG stw0_numNCB_r	The total number of NCBs issued by the redirector, including unsuccessful NCBs.
ULONG stw0_numNCB_s	The total number of NCBs issued by the server, including unsuccessful NCBs.
ULONG stw0_numNCB_a	The total number of NCBs issued by the applications, including unsuccessful NCBs.

(continued)

continued

Member	Meaning
ULONG stw0_fiNCB_r	The number of NCBs that failed when issued by the redirector.
ULONG stw0_fiNCB_s	The number of NCBs that failed when issued by the server.
ULONG stw0_fiNCB_a	The number of NCBs that failed when issued by applications.
ULONG stw0_fcNCB_r	The number of NCBs issued by the redirector that failed to complete.
ULONG stw0_fcNCB_s	The number of NCBs issued by the server that failed to complete.
ULONG stw0_fcNCB_a	The number of NCBs issued by applications that failed to complete.
ULONG stw0_sesstart	The number of workstation sessions started.
ULONG stw0_sessfailcon	The number of connection attempts that failed, not including cases in which the name was not found.
ULONG stw0_sessbroke	The number of sessions that failed after they had been established.
ULONG stw0_uses	The number of workstation uses.
ULONG stw0_usefail	The number of failed uses. These are cases in which the server was found but the resource didn't exist.
ULONG stw0_autorec	The number of autoreconnects.
ULONG stw0_bytessent_r_lo	The low DWORD of the number of workstation bytes sent to the network.
ULONG stw0_bytessent_r_hi	The high DWORD of the number of workstation bytes sent to the network. With the low DWORD, these two values are a 64-bit count.
ULONG stw0_bytesrcvd_r_lo	The low DWORD of the number of workstation bytes received from the network.
ULONG stw0_bytesrcvd_r_hi	The high DWORD of the number of workstation bytes received from the network. With the low DWORD, these two values are a 64-bit count.
ULONG stw0_bytessent_s_lo	The low DWORD of the number of server bytes sent to the network.
ULONG stw0_bytessent_s_hi	The high DWORD of the number of server bytes sent to the network. With the low DWORD, these two values are a 64-bit count.
ULONG stw0_bytesrcvd_s_lo	The low DWORD of the number of server bytes received from the network.
ULONG stw0_bytesrcvd_s_hi	The high DWORD of the number of server bytes received from the network. With the low DWORD, these two values are a 64-bit count.

(continued)

continued

Member	Meaning
ULONG stw0_bytessent_a_lo	The low DWORD of the number of application bytes sent to the network.
ULONG stw0_bytessent_a_hi	The high DWORD of the number of application bytes sent to the network. With the low DWORD, these two values are a 64-bit count.
ULONG stw0_bytesrcvd_a_lo	The low DWORD of the number of application bytes received from the network.
ULONG stw0_bytesrcvd_a_hi	The high DWORD of the number of application bytes received from the network. With the low DWORD, these two values are a 64-bit count.
ULONG stw0_reqbufneed	The number of times a workstation work buffer was needed but unavailable. This value helps determine whether the *numworkbuf* parameter of the [wksta] component of LANMAN.INI is large enough.
ULONG stw0_bigbufneed	The number of times a workstation request buffer was needed but unavailable. This value helps determine whether the *numworkbuf* parameter of the [wksta] component of LANMAN.INI is too large.

If *servicename* is SERVICE_SERVER, the *buf* buffer returns with a *stat-_server_0* structure, which contains the following members:

Member	Meaning
ULONG sts0_start	The time since collection was started, typically the last time the statistics were cleared.
ULONG sts0_fopens	The number of file opens, including named pipes.
ULONG sts0_devopens	The number of character device opens.
ULONG sts0_jobsqueued	The number of server print jobs spooled.
ULONG sts0_sopens	The number of sessions started.
ULONG sts0_stimedout	The number of sessions timed out.
ULONG sts0_serrorout	The number of sessions dropped because of errors.
ULONG sts0_pwerrors	The number of password violations.
ULONG sts0_permerrors	The number of access permission errors.
ULONG sts0_syserrors	The number of system errors.
ULONG sts0_bytessent_low	The low DWORD of the total number of bytes sent to the network.
ULONG sts0_bytessent_high	The high DWORD of the total number of bytes sent to the network. With the low DWORD, this is a 64-bit count.
ULONG sts0_bytesrcvd_low	The low DWORD of the total number of bytes received from the network.

(continued)

continued

Member	Meaning
ULONG sts0_bytesrcvd_high	The high DWORD of the total number of bytes received from the network. With the low DWORD, this is a 64-bit count.
ULONG sts0_avresponse	The average response time in milliseconds.
ULONG sts0_reqbufneed	The number of server request buffers that failed to be allocated. This value helps determine whether the *numreqbuf* parameter of the [server] component of LANMAN.INI is large enough.
ULONG sts0_bigbufneed	The number of times a server big buffer was needed but unavailable. This value helps determine whether the *numbigbuf* parameter of the [server] component of LANMAN.INI is large enough.

Two special values might be returned for any of the preceding statistics (with the exception of the 64-bit numbers):

Value	Meaning
0xFFFFFFFF	The value was unavailable.
0xFFFFFFFE	The value was too large for a 32-bit number; the counter overflowed.

Unlike *NetStatisticsGet*, *NetStatisticsGet2* never returns a partial structure. If *buf* is not large enough for all of the data, NERR_BufTooSmall is returned.

NetStatisticsClear

Clears workstation or server statistics.

```
unsigned far pascal
NetStatisticsClear(
    char far * servername      /* where to execute  */
    )
```

Remote access:
Remote access is available only to an administrator.

Error returns:
If successful, *NetStatisticsClear* returns 0. If unsuccessful, it returns one of the standard LAN Manager error codes.

An overview:
The *NetStatisticsClear* API sets all workstation and server statistics counters to 0 and sets the *st0_time*, *stw0_time*, and *sts0_time* structures appropriately.

PROTECTION APIs

You might remember from Chapter 2 that a user-mode security system is based on the presence of Access Control Lists (ACLs) and the User Accounts System (UAS). In this chapter, you'll learn about the Access, User, and Group APIs that let you work with the user-mode security system.

When servers in a domain participate in the Single System Image (SSI), the User and Group APIs succeed only when they execute (locally or remotely) at the primary domain controller. LAN Manager ensures that changes to the UAS are replicated on the rest of the servers in the domain, thus ensuring that they are all identical. This gives the appearance of a single UAS database throughout the domain.

In contrast, the ACL databases are all specific to each server. Each server can accept its own modifications to the ACL database.

The Access APIs

A LAN Manager server gives an administrator the ability to configure security right down to the file, queue, device, or named-pipe level. Specific users (or groups of users) can be given specific access permissions for specific resources; permissions can even be granted to entire directories or entire disk devices.

The Access APIs let you examine and modify these permissions from within a program. To use the Access APIs, you must include NETCONS.H and ACCESS.H at compile time, and you must link with the NETAPI.LIB library stub.

The Access Control List

The key structure for dealing with resource permissions is the *Access Control List* (ACL). An ACL is a structure containing the name of a resource and a list of user or group names with the access permissions allowed to each. The resource name can be any of the names shown in Table 9-1. Each must be a completely specified pathname.

Resource Name	Description
File	A completely specified filename, such as C:\BIN\WIPEDISK.EXE.
Directory	A completely specified directory name, such as C:\GOODSTUFF.
Disk device	A disk name, such as C:.

Table 9-1.   *(continued)*
Valid ACL resource names.

Table 9-1. *continued*

Resource Name	Description
Print queue	A spooled print queue. The names must be of the form \PRINT\QNAME.
All print queues	The special resource name \PRINT represents all print queues.
Print queue directories	There are no actual directories of Print queues, but the naming structure allows the appearance of directories. A name of the form \PRINT*subdir* would act as if it were the directory name for \PRINT*subdir**queuename*.
Character device	A character-device name must be of the form \COMM\LPT*x*.
All character devices	The special resource name \COMM represents all character devices.
Character device directories	There are no actual directories of character devices, but the naming structure allows the appearance of directories. A name of the form \COMM*subdir* would act as if it were the directory name for \COMM*subdir**devname*.
Named pipe	A named pipe name must be of the form \PIPE\PIPENAME.
Pipe directories	There are no actual directories of named pipes, but the naming structure allows the appearance of directories. A name of the form \PIPE*subdir* would act as if it were the directory name for \PIPE*subdir**pipename*.
All named pipes	The special resource name \PIPE represents all named pipes.

In Chapter 2, we examined an algorithm for determining access permissions. It always works from the specific toward the general. If no ACL entry exists for a file, look for an ACL entry for the directory. If that doesn't exist, look for an entry for the entire disk drive. Similarly, if a print queue entry is not found, look for \PRINT, and so on, for character devices and named pipes.

The default ACL database contains three default entries:

- \PIPE has RWC permission for the USERS group.

- \COMM has RWC permission for the USERS group.

- \PRINT has C permission for the USERS group.

These default entries can be deleted or altered using the Access APIs.

Note that the resource names refer to local server resource names. Neither the share names of resources nor their shared status affects the ACL entries.

WARNING: *An ACL record for D: represents the drive level record for the D drive, but D:\ represents the parent record for all files in the root directory of the D drive. They are similar enough that you should take care when specifying the ACL record name.*

Access Data Structures

Two basic data structures exist for the Access APIs: *struct access_info_0* and *struct access_info_1.*

The *access_info_0* structure contains the following member:

Member Name	Description
char far * acc0_resource_name	An ACL text string of the form described above.

The *access_info_1* structure contains the following members:

Member Name	Description
char far * acc1_resource_name	A text string of the form described above.
USHORT acc1_attr	Auditing attribute bits for the resource. These attributes have meaning only if the server has enabled auditing. See the *sv2_auditing* flag in the *server_info_2* structure. The values are indicated by setting bits as shown. The meaning of the bits is different if the file is a directory or if it is a file; the latter includes print queue, comm queue, or named pipe. A value of 0 indicates no auditing of the resource.

Bitmask	Value	Audit Record Generated
ACCESS_AUDIT	0x0001	AE_RESACCESS—All access attempts to the resource are to be audited. If this bit is set, it is the equivalent of setting all the rest of the bits, and an error if any other bits are set.
None defined	0x0002	Reserved
None defined	0x0004	Reserved
None defined	0x0008	Reserved
None defined	0x0010	AE_RESACCESS—For files, a successful open. For directories, reserved.
None defined	0x0020	AE_RESACCESS—For files, successful write access. This includes file truncation. If 0x0010 is also set, two audit records can be generated. For directories, a successful create.

(continued)

continued

Member Name	Description		
	Bitmask	**Value**	**Audit Record Generated**
	None defined	0x0040	AE_RESACCESS—For files, a successful file deletion. For directories, a successful directory remove.
	None defined	0x0080	AE_ACLMOD—For files or directories, a change in the ACL record for the resource.
	None defined	0x0100	AE_RESACCESS—For files, a failed open attempt. For directories, reserved.
	None defined	0x0200	AE_RESACCESS—For files, a failed write attempt. If 0x0100 is also set, two audit records can be generated. For directories, a failed attempt to create a directory.
	None defined	0x0400	AE_RESACCESS—For files, a failed attempt to delete a file. For directories, a failed attempt to remove a directory.
	None defined	0x0800	AE_ACLMOD—For files or directories, a failed attempt to modify the ACL for the resource.
USHORT acc1_count	*accl_count* specifies the number of *access_list* structures following the *access_info_1* structure. This can be 0. The maximum is MAXPERMENTRIES. Each of these structures describes a user or group and its access permissions.		

The ACL will always be represented by an *access_info_1* structure followed by an array of *_access_list* structures, each specifying permissions for a specific user or group. An *access_list* structure contains the following members:

Member Name	Description		
char acl_ugname[UNLEN+1]	The user or group name.		
USHORT acl_access	The access permissions. Permissions are indicated by setting bits. The value can be 0, meaning that no access is allowed.		
	Bitmask	**Value**	**Meaning**
	ACCESS_READ	0x01	Read permission (R)
	ACCESS_WRITE	0x02	Write permission (W)
	ACCESS_CREATE	0x04	Create permission (C)

(continued)

continued

Member Name	Description		
	Bitmask	*Value*	*Meaning*
	ACCESS_EXEC	0x08	Execute permission (X)
	ACCESS_DELETE	0x10	Delete permission (D)
	ACCESS_ATTRIB	0x20	Attribute permission (A)
	ACCESS_PERM	0x40	Permission permission (P)
	ACCESS_ALL	0x7F	All of the above (RWCXDAP).
	ACCESS_GROUP	0x8000	Is this a username (0) or a group name (1)?

The security section in Chapter 2 gives more details on the meaning of each.

NetAccessEnum

Returns information about access permission records.

```
unsigned far pascal
NetAccessEnum(
    char far * servername,    /* where to execute        */
    char far * basepath,      /* name qualifier          */
    short level,              /* level of detail         */
    char far * buf,           /* return data buffer      */
    short recursive,          /* recursive search?       */
    USHORT buflen,            /* size of buf             */
    USHORT far * eread,       /* number of entries read  */
    USHORT far * etotal       /* total entries available */
    )
```

Levels:
Supports level 0 and 1 data structures.

Remote access:
Level 0 or 1 can be called by an administrator.

Level 0 or 1 can be called by any user-level account, but *NetAccessEnum* returns records for only those files for which the user has 'P' permission.

Error returns:

If successful, *NetAccessEnum* returns 0. If unsuccessful, it returns one of the standard Enum return codes or one of the following error codes:

Error Return	Meaning
NERR_ACFNotLoaded	The server is not running user-mode security.
ERROR_INVALID_ENTRY	The *basepath* argument is illegal. In particular, a trailing backslash is never allowed.

An overview:

The *NetAccessEnum* API returns a list of *access_info_0* structures if the level is 0. If the level is 1, a list of *access_info_1* structures, each followed by 0 or more *access_list* structures, is returned. Each of the level 1 *access_info_1* structures, together with its sublist, is called an *Access Control List* (ACL).

The *basepath* argument is a qualifier on the enumeration set. If it is not NULL, *NetAccessEnum* returns only those entries whose leading pathname matches the basepath. If *basepath* is NULL, all resource names are completely specified pathnames. The *accl_resource_name* value is the part of the resource name after the basepath.

The *recursive* flag works in conjunction with *basepath*. If TRUE, *NetAccessEnum* returns all ACL entries that match *basepath*, plus all subdirectories of *basepath*. If *recursive* is FALSE, only those entries in the directory specified by *basepath* are returned. If *basepath* is not a directory (or \PRINT, \COMM, or \PIPE), only a single ACL entry can possibly match, and that is all that can be returned.

Note that *etotal* is the number of total entries that can be returned, given the values of *basepath* and *recursive*.

The *NetAccessEnum* call can be made remotely, but two rules govern the return values:

- If the user making the remote call is an administrator, all information is available.

- Otherwise, only matching entries for which the user has 'P' permission are returned. If the buffer is not large enough, *etotal* indicates the number of entries the user is allowed to see.

Clearing up the basepath

The following example will clarify the use of the *basepath* and *recursive* arguments. Suppose that a single ACL exists for C:\D1\D2\FILE.EXT. Table 9-2 shows what names to expect in *accl_resource_name* for some different basepath values:

Basepath	Recursive	accl_resource_name
(NULL)	FALSE	No entries retrieved
(NULL)	TRUE	C:\D1\D2\FILE.EXT
C:	FALSE	No entries retrieved
C:	TRUE	\D1\D2\FILE.EXT
C:\D1	FALSE	No entries retrieved
C:\D1	TRUE	\D2\FILE.EXT
C:\D1\D2\F	Either	ILE.EXT
C:\D1\D	TRUE	2\FILE.EXT

Table 9-2.
The effect of basepath *and* recursive *on* accl_resource_name.

Note the handling when the basepath contains part of a directory or filename. The completely specified pathname can always be formed by concatenating *basepath* with *accl_resource_name*.

NetAccessGetInfo

Gets permission information for a resource.

```
unsigned far pascal
NetAccessGetInfo(
    char far * servername,    /* where to execute     */
    char far * resource,      /* resource pathname    */
    short level,              /* level of detail      */
    char far * buf,           /* return data buffer   */
    USHORT buflen,            /* size of buf          */
    USHORT far * btotal       /* total bytes available */
    )
```

Levels:

Supports level 0 and 1 data structures.

Remote access:

Level 0 or 1 can be called by an administrator.

Level 0 or 1 can be called by a user-level account for only those records for which the user has 'P' permission.

Error returns:

If successful, *NetAccessGetInfo* returns 0. If unsuccessful, it returns one of the standard GetInfo error codes or one of the following error codes:

Error Return	Meaning
NERR_ACFNotLoaded	The server is not running user-mode security.
NERR_ResourceNotFound	The *resource* argument does not match any ACL.
ERROR_ACCESS_DENIED	On a remote call, the user was not an administrator and didn't have 'P' access for the resource.

An overview:

The *NetAccessGetInfo* API obtains the ACL for one resource name. The level should be 1, and the buffer will contain an *access_info_1* structure followed by zero or more *access_list* structures.

NetAccessSetInfo

Changes access permission information for a resource.

```
unsigned far pascal
NetAccessSetInfo(
    char far * servername,    /* where to execute    */
    char far * resource,      /* resource pathname   */
    short level,              /* must be 1           */
    char far * buf,           /* set data buffer     */
    USHORT buflen,            /* size of buf         */
    short parmnum             /* parameter number    */
    )
```

Levels:

Supports a level 1 data structure.

Remote access:

This API can always be called by an administrator.

This API can be called by a user-level account for only those records for which the user has 'P' permission.

Error returns:

If successful, *NetAccessSetInfo* returns 0. If unsussessful, it returns one of the standard SetInfo error codes or one of the following error codes:

Error Return	Meaning
NERR_ACFNotLoaded	The server is not running user-mode security.
NERR_ResourceNotFound	The *resource* argument name does not match any ACL.
NERR_UserNotFound	The *username* argument in one of the *access_list* structures is an invalid username or group name. If any of the usernames are bad, nothing is changed.
NERR_ACFTooManyLists	More than MAXPERMENTRIES *access_list* structures exist.
ERROR_ACCESS_DENIED	On a remote call, the user was not an administrator and didn't have 'P' access for the resource.

An overview:

The *NetAccessSetInfo* API lets you edit ACLs. If the *parmnum* form of *NetAccessSetInfo* is used, only the *accl_attr* value can be altered. For this case, set *parmnum* to ACCESS_ATTR_PARMNUM. If *parmnum* is 0, an entire ACL can be changed. Most programs will want to call the *NetAccessGetInfo* function, edit the *access_list* structures appropriately, and submit the changes with *NetAccessSetInfo*.

Note that if a user with the ACCESS_PERM bit set uses this call to set the bit to 0, he or she can't make future changes to the record. Permission to change permissions also implies permission to give this privilege to other users.

Note that redundant information is required here. The *resource* argument should be the same as the *accl_resource* argument in the *access_info_1* structure. In practice, however, the API ignores the value in the structure. Don't count on this being true in future releases. Always set the two arguments to the same value.

NetAccessAdd

Adds access permission information for a new resource.

```
unsigned far pascal
NetAccessAdd(
    char far * servername,    /* where to execute */
    short level,              /* level of detail  */
    char far * buf,           /* add data buffer  */
    USHORT buflen,            /* size of buf      */
    )
```

Levels:

Supports a level 1 data structure.

Remote access:

This API can be called only by an administrator.

Error returns:

If *NetAccessAdd* is successful, it returns 0. If unsuccessful, it returns one of the standard Add error codes or one of the following error codes:

Error Return	Meaning
NERR_ACFNotLoaded	The server is not running user-mode security.
NERR_ResourceExists	An ACL entry already exists for this resource.
NERR_UserNotFound	The *username* value in one of the *access_list* structures is an invalid username or group name. If any of the usernames are bad, nothing is changed.
NERR_ACFTooManyLists	More than MAXPERMENTRIES *access_list* structures exist.

An overview:

The *NetAccessAdd* API adds a new instance of an ACL to the database. It fails if an entry already exists for the resource. The *buf* argument must contain an *access_info_1* structure and 0 or more *access_list* structures. The *accl_count* structure indicates how many list structures follow.

A common practice is to use *NetAccessAdd* to add an ACL entry with no user or group entries and to then use *NetAccessSetInfo* to add to and modify the ACL.

NetAccessDel

Deletes access permissions for a resource.

```
unsigned far pascal
NetAccessDel(
    char far * servername,    /* where to execute  */
    char far * resource       /* resource pathname */
    )
```

Remote access:

This API can be called only by an administrator.

Error returns:

If successful, *NetAccessDel* returns 0. If unsuccessful, it returns one of the standard Del error codes or one of the following error codes:

Error Return	Meaning
NERR_ACFNotLoaded	The server is not running user-mode security.
NERR_ResourceNotFound	The *resource* argument name does not match any ACL.

An overview:

The *NetAccessDel* API removes an ACL entry from the database.

NetAccessGetUserPerms

Returns an access permission bitmap.

```
unsigned far pascal
NetAccessGetUserPerms(
    char far * servername,    /* where to execute        */
    char far * ugname,        /* username or group name  */
    char far * resource,      /* resource to check       */
    USHORT far * perms        /* returned permissions    */
    )
```

Remote access:

This API can be called by an administrator.

This API can be called by a user when one or more of the following conditions are true:

- The user must have 'P' permission for the resource.

- The *ugname* argument must be the user's own name.

- The user must belong to the group specified by *ugname*.

Error returns:

If successful, *NetAccessGetUserPerms* returns 0. If unsuccessful, it returns a standard API error code or one of the following error codes:

Error Return	Meaning
NERR_ACFNotLoaded	The server is not running user-mode security.
NERR_ResourceNotFound	The *resource* argument does not match any ACL.
NERR_UserNotFound	The *ugname* argument does not match any username or group name in the ACL database.

An overview:

The *NetAccessGetUserPerms* API returns the access bitmap for the named resource and user or group specified in *ugname* (if such an entry exists). The *perms* argument returns the same bitmask specified in the *acl_access* member of the *access_list* structure.

NetAccessCheck

Verifies that a user has permission to access a resource.

```
unsigned far pascal
NetAccessCheck(
     char far * reserved,      /* must be NULL         */
     char far * username,      /* user account name */
     char far * resource,      /* resource to check */
     USHORT operation,         /* file operation       */
     USHORT far * result       /* returned result      */
     )
```

Remote access:

This API cannot be called remotely.

Error returns:

If successful, *NetAccessCheck* returns 0. If unsuccessful, it returns a standard API return code or one of the following error codes:

Error Return	Meaning
NERR_ACFNotLoaded	The server is not running user-mode security.
NERR_UserNotFound	No user account with this name exists.

An overview:

The *NetAccessCheck* API answers the question "Does this user have permission to do this operation on this resource?" The *operation* argument is the standard set of access bitmaps defined previously. *NetAccessCheck* uses the server algorithm shown in Chapter 2. If no user account exists for *username* and if a guest account has been configured, the guest account is used.

The *result* argument returns the answer to the question "Is access allowed?" It has meaning only if the return code for *NetAccessCheck* is 0 (successful). In that case, *result* is set to either 0 (access permitted) or ERROR_ACCESS_DENIED (access denied).

A little runpath security

Chapter 5 described potential security problems with *DosRemoteExec* and the net run command. To prevent some of these problems, you can require all remotely executable programs to reside in directories configured with the LANMAN.INI *runpath* parameter. It is useful for an administrator to see who has what permissions in all of the directories named in the runpath. The ACCRUN.C program (Figure 9-1) accomplishes this. It uses *NetAccessEnum* and *NetAccessGetInfo* to get all ACL entries for all files in directories in the runpath.

This program is another good example of mixed-model programming because it uses a mix of "near" and "far" objects.

```
/*
 * ACCRUN.C -- A program that lists all of the ACL entries for
 * directories in the runpath.  All enumeration is done using a
 * 64 KB buffer for programming simplicity.  Each directory in the
 * runpath is used as a basepath argument for NetAccessEnum.
 *
 * Compile with:  C> cl accrun.c netapi.lib string_f.lib
 *
 * Usage:  C> accrun
 *
 */

#include <stdio.h>
#include <netcons.h>
#include <access.h>
#include <config.h>
#include <string.h>
#include <string_f.h>  /* described in Chapter 3 */
#include <examples.h>  /* described in Chapter 4 */

/* calculate how big the maximum GetInfo buffer must be */
#define GISZ (((PATHLEN + sizeof(struct access_info_1)) \
        / sizeof(struct access_list)) + 1)

struct access_list UserList[MAXPERMENTRIES + GISZ] = {0};
char far ResList[65535] = {0};

main()
    {
    int err;
    char rpbuf[PATHLEN], pbuf[PATHLEN], *basep;
```

Figure 9-1.
The ACCRUN.C program.

(continued)

Figure 9-1. *continued*

```
unsigned short len, er, te;
struct access_info_0 far *pai_0;
struct access_info_1 *pai_1;
struct access_list *pal;
char * permtext();

/* first get the runpath */
err = NetConfigGet(
                    "netrun",        /* component     */
                    "runpath",       /* parameter     */
                    rpbuf,           /* place for data */
                    sizeof(rpbuf),   /* buflen        */
                    &len             /* actual length */
                    );
if (err)
    {
    printf("Error getting runpath (%d)\n", err);
    exit(1);
    }

/* for each directory on the runpath */
for (basep = strtok(rpbuf, " ;"); basep; basep = strtok(NULL, " ;"))
    {
    /* get any access records in that directory */
    err = NetAccessEnum(
                    NULL,               /* server name    */
                    basep,              /* basepath       */
                    0,                  /* not recursive  */
                    0,                  /* level 0        */
                    ResList,            /* resource names */
                    sizeof(ResList),    /* buflen         */
                    &er,                /* entries read   */
                    &te                 /* total entries  */
                    );
    if (err)
        {
        printf("Error (%d) in Enum with basepath = %s\n",
                err, basep);
        continue;
        }
    else
        printf("%s:\n", basep);
```

(continued)

Figure 9-1. *continued*

```
        /* for each ACL entry, get the user/group records */
        pai_0 = (struct access_info_0 far *)ResList;
        for ( ; er--; ++pai_0)
            {
            /* the resource name is relative to the basep */
            strcpy_f(pbuf, basep);
            strcat_f(pbuf, pai_0->acc0_resource_name);

            err = NetAccessGetInfo(
                                    NULL,           /* server         */
                                    pbuf,           /* resource name  */
                                    1,              /* level          */
                                    (char far *)UserList, /* return buf */
                                    sizeof(UserList),     /* buflen    */
                                    &te             /* total avail    */
                                    );
            if (err)
                {
                printf("\t\tERR=%d for GetInfo\n", err);
                continue;
                }
            printf("\t%s\n", pbuf);

            /* for each user/group */
            pai_1 = (struct access_info_1 *)UserList;
            pal = (struct access_list *) (pai_1 + 1);
            while (pai_1->acc1_count--)
                {
                /* if it is a group, print '*' */
                printf("\t\t%s",
                pal->acl_access & ACCESS_GROUP ? "*": "");

                /* print name and permission string */
                printf("%s : %s\n", pal->acl_ugname,
                permtext(pal->acl_access));
                ++pal;
                } /* next access_list */

            } /* next ACL entry for the runpath */

        } /* next runpath entry */
}
```

(continued)

Figure 9-1. *continued*

```
/*
 * permtext -- A routine to convert the access bit patterns to text.
 * Warning! This relies on the bit order of ACCESS_*.  ACCESS_LETTERS
 * is a string that guarantees the text letters to be in the same order
 * as the bitmask.
 */

char *permtext(access)
unsigned short access;
    {
    static char buf[8];
    char *p = ACCESS_LETTERS;
    char *q = buf;
    int i;

    /* for each possible bit */
    for (i = 0; i < 7; ++i)
        {
        if (access & 1)
            *q++ = *p;

        /* next position of letter string */
        ++p;
        /* and next bit */
        access >>= 1;
        }
    *q = 0;
    return(buf);
    }
```

The UAS APIs

The User Accounts System (UAS) APIs let you update and query the user-accounts database.

For servers participating in the Single System Image (SSI) for a domain, only the primary domain controller can be updated. LAN Manager replicates changes on all servers in the domain, thus keeping UAS information identical at all of the servers. This gives the appearance of a single database for the domain, or a Single System Image.

This section describes the three sets of APIs that deal with the SSI:

- The User APIs pertain to individual user accounts.

- The Modal APIs pertain to parameters for all UAS accounts at once.

- The Group APIs pertain to groups of usernames.

This section also describes some miscellaneous workstation APIs that pertain to individual user information in the UAS.

The User APIs

The User APIs allow administration of user accounts. Each account is associated with a user logon name, which is also included in a group. This logon name is also used to check resource permissions at individual servers.

User accounts can be one of three types: *admin*, *user*, or *guest*.

- An *admin* account can access all shared resources at a server and can execute APIs remotely.

- *user* accounts have access to only those resources for which they have been granted explicit permissions. *user* accounts are members of a group named USERS, and they can be given operator privileges that allow remote execution of some APIs.

- *guest* accounts are similar to *user* accounts, but their group name is GUESTS, and they cannot be assigned operator rights.

For each account, the UAS database contains all of the information described in the *user_info_2* structure in the next section. Only a few APIs can be remotely executed without operator privilege.

To use the User APIs, you must include NETCONS.H and ACCESS.H at compile time and link with the NETAPI.LIB library stub. Several levels of data structures are available for the User APIs.

The *user_info_0* structure contains this member:

Member Name	Description
char usri0_name[UNLEN+1]	The account name. This is an array containing a zero-terminated text string.

The *user_info_1* structure contains the following members:

Member Name	Description
char usri1_name[UNLEN+1]	The account name. This is an array containing a zero-terminated text string.
char usri1_password [ENCRYPTED_PWLEN]	The regular text password. Note that this array is used only for setting the password. It can never get the password.

(continued)

continued

Member Name	Description
ULONG usri1_password_age	The time in seconds since the password was last changed.
USHORT usri1_priv	The account type. The values are as follows:

USER_PRIV_GUEST	0	A *guest* account
USER_PRIV_USER	1	A *user* account
USER_PRIV_ADMIN	2	An *admin* account

Member Name	Description
char far * usri1_home_dir	The home directory. For LAN Manager 2.0, this must be an absolute local path (e.g., C:\LANMAN\HOME) or an absolute UNC path (e.g., \\HOMEDIRS\SCRATCH). Both a NULL pointer and a null string mean no home directory.
char far * usri1_comment	An optional remark associated with the account.
USHORT usri1_flags	The account flags. Values are indicated by setting bits:

Bitmask	Value	Meaning
UF_SCRIPT	0x01	If set, the logon script specified by *usr1_script_path* will be executed during network logon processing. This must be set for LAN Manager 2.0.
UF_ACCOUNTDISABLE	0x02	If set, the account is disabled, and both network and server logon will fail.
	0x04	Reserved.
UF_HOMEDIR_REQUIRED	0x08	If set, the account is required to be configured with a home directory. This is set with the *usr1_home_dir* argument.
UF_PASSWD_NOTREQD	0x20	If set, the account can be configured with no password. (This flag exists for compatibility with LAN Manager 1.0.)
UF_PASSWD_CANT_CHANGE	0x40	If set, the account owner can change the account password.

(continued)

Member Name	Description
char far * usri1_script_path	The pathname of the user's logon script. During network logon, this script (typically a CMD, PRO, BAT, COM, or EXE file) is downloaded and executed at the user's workstation. If the filename has no extension, it is treated as a CMD file for OS/2 workstations and a BAT file for MS-DOS workstations. Both a NULL pointer and a null string mean that no script exists. The name must be a relative pathname and is taken relative to the path shared as NETLOGON by the Logon Service.

The *user_info_2* structure contains the same elements as the *user_info_1* structure, with the addition of the following members:

Member Name	Description
ULONG usri2_auth_flags	User accounts can be assigned operator rights, which permit limited administration privileges. This value is a set of bits that indicate the operator privileges of the account:

Bitmask	Value	Meaning
AF_OP_PRINT	0x01	The user is allowed remote execution of most DosPrint APIs for maintenance of the spooled print queues and jobs.
AF_OP_COMM	0x02	The user is allowed remote execution of most NetComm APIs for maintenance of character-device queues.
AF_OP_SERVER	0x04	The user is allowed remote execution of most server administration APIs.
AF_OP_ACCOUNTS	0x08	The user is allowed remote execution of most NetUser and NetGroup APIs for maintenance of the UAS database. This does not allow manipulation of administrator or operator rights for any accounts.

Member Name	Description
char far * usri2_full_name	The full name of the user (up to 48 characters).
char far * usri2_usr_comment	An account comment supplied by the user (up to 48 characters).
char far * usri2_parms	A text string for application-specific parameter information. Not used by LAN Manager.

(continued)

Member Name	Description
char far * usri2_workstations	A list of up to eight workstation names from which the user is allowed to log on. These can be LAN Manager computer names or NetBIOS permanent node names, which must contain 12 hexadecimal digits separated by periods, of the form xxx.yyy.zzz. A NULL value indicates that any workstation is allowed. Note that although computer names can be changed by the user, the permanent node names are part of the network hardware at a workstation.
long usri2_last_logon	The time of the most recent logon. A 0 value indicates that it is unknown.
long usri2_last_logoff	The time of the most recent logoff. A 0 value indicates that it is unknown.
long usri2_acct_expires	The time at which the account will expire. Expiration is the equivalent of setting the UF_ACCOUNTDISABLE bitmask in the *usri2_flags* argument. A value of −1 means the account will never expire.
ULONG usri2_max_storage	The maximum storage number of bytes the user can use from under the home directory. A value of −1 means no limit. Note that this limit is not automatically enforced by LAN Manager but can be checked using the Chkstor utility at the user's logon server.
USHORT usri2_units_per_week	The user can be allowed to log on only at certain times. This argument indicates how to interpret the next value in the structure, *usri2_logon_hours*. A week is divided into N equal parts, where N is the value in *usri2_units_per_week*. For LAN Manager version 2.0, the only valid value is 168—the number of hours in a week.
UCHAR far * usri2_logon_hours	This argument is a pointer to an array of 21 bytes (168 bits). Each bit represents one of the equal units defined by *usri2_units_per_week*. If the corresponding bit is set, the user is allowed to log on during that unit of time. For LAN Manager version 2.0, each bit corresponds to an hour and *usri2_logon_hours* represents all of the hours in a week. A NULL pointer indicates no limit on the logon.
USHORT usri2_bad_pw_count	The number of logon attempts that have failed because of a bad password. The value 0xFFFF means unknown.
USHORT usri2_num_logons	The number of logons currently active for this account. The value 0xFFFF means unknown.
char far * usri2_logon_server	When a user logs on to the network, the logon can be handled by the primary domain controller or by any backup domain controller in the domain. Because of the SSI, they all have the same UAS database. This field indicates a preference for which server should process the network logon. It allows an administrator to distribute the workload for processing network logons. If the preferred server is not available to process the logon request, one of the other domain controllers (primary or backup) can then handle the request. The text string pointed to by *usri2_logon_server* can take one of three forms:

(continued)

continued

Member Name	Description	
	Logon Server	**Meaning**
	servername	The name of the preferred logon server
	*	Any primary or backup domain controller in the domain
	NULL	Only the primary domain controller
USHORT usri2_country_code	The OS/2 country code for the user. This allows LAN Manager to print messages in the proper language wherever possible.	
USHORT usri2_code_page	The OS/2 code page for the language choice of the user.	

The *user_info_10* structure allows users to obtain a limited amount of information about other users. The meanings are the same as for the *user_info_2* structure. The *user_info_10* structure contains the following members:

```
char usri10_name[UNLEN+1]
char far * usri10_comment
char far * usri10_usr_comment
char far * usri10_full_name
```

The *user_info_11* structure allows users to obtain details about their own accounts. The meanings are the same as for the *user_info_2* structure. The *user_info_11* structure contains the following members:

```
char usri11_name[UNLEN+1]
char far * usri11_comment
char far * usri11_usr_comment
char far * usri11_full_name
char usri11_name[UNLEN+1]
char far * usri11_comment
char far * usri11_usr_comment
char far * usri11_full_name
USHORT usri11_priv
ULONG usri11_auth_flags
long usri11_password_age
char far * usri11_home_dir
char far * usri11_parms
long usri11_last_logon
long usri11_last_logoff
USHORT usri11_bad_pw_count
USHORT usri11_num_logons
char far * usri11_logon_server
```

```
USHORT usri11_country_code
char far * usri11_workstations
ULONG usri11_max_storage
USHORT usri11_units_per_week
UCHAR far * usri11_logon_hours
USHORT usrUSHORT usri11_code_page
```

Note that the order of members in *user_info_11* is not the same as in *user_info_2*, so don't try to do structure copies of the information.

NetUserEnum

Returns information for all accounts.

```
unsigned far pascal
NetUserEnum(
    char far * servername,     /* where to execute        */
    short level,               /* level of detail         */
    char far * buf,            /* return data buffer      */
    USHORT buflen,             /* size of buf             */
    USHORT far * eread,        /* number of entries read  */
    USHORT far * etotal        /* total entries available */
    )
```

Levels:
Supports level 0, 1, 2, and 10 data structures.

Remote access:
All levels can be called remotely by an administrator or by a user with accounts operator privilege.

Error returns:
If successful, *NetUserEnum* returns 0. If unsuccessful, it returns a standard Enum return code or the following error code:

Error Return	Meaning
NERR_ACFNotLoaded	The UAS has not been started.

An overview:
The *NetUserEnum* API retrieves a list of *user_info_n* structures, where *n* can be 0, 1, 2, or 10, depending on the *level* argument.

Note that the *usri2_password* parameter is not readable. It is always a null string.

Warning! Passwords ahead

You need to be aware of several important principles regarding User APIs and passwords:

Case sensitivity User APIs are sensitive to the case of passwords. However, all LAN Manager user-interface programs map passwords to uppercase before calling the APIs. This can lead to confusion if your program changes the password into a string containing lowercase characters: Because the passwords would never match, the user could never log on from the user-interface program. For safety and compatibility, ensure that your programs map passwords to uppercase before calling the APIs.

Password rules A distinction exists between "no password" and "don't change the existing password" in the *NetUserInfoSet* API. The *user_info_1* and *user_info_2* structures take the password in an array. Setting the first character of the array to 0 means "no password." Setting all characters of the array to blank means "leave the existing password unchanged." This can be done by copying the predefined string NULL_USERSETINFO_PASSWD into the array element *usri2_passwd* as follows:

```
strcpy(usri2->usri2_passwd, NULL_USERSETINFO_PASSWD);
```

NetUserAdd

Establishes an account on a server.

```
unsigned far pascal
NetUserAdd(
    char far * servername,     /* where to execute        */
    short level,               /* must be 1               */
    char far * buf,            /* a struct user_info 1 or 2 */
    USHORT buflen,             /* size of buf             */
    )
```

Levels:
Supports level 1 and 2 data structures.

Remote access:
All levels can be called remotely by an administrator, or by a user with accounts operator privilege.

Error returns:

If successful, *NetUserAdd* returns 0. If unsuccessful, it returns one of the standard Add return codes or one of the following error codes:

Error Return	Meaning
NERR_ACFNotLoaded	The UAS has not been started.
NERR_GroupExists	A group with this name already exists.
NERR_UserExists	A user with this name already exists.
NERR_BadUsername	The username contained illegal characters.
NERR_NotPrimary	The server is running the Netlogon service and participating in SSI. Only the primary domain controller is allowed to change the accounts database.
ERROR_ACCESS_DENIED	Indicates insufficient permissions or an accounts operator trying to add an *admin* account or an account with operator privileges set.
ERROR_INVALID_PARAMETER	A catchall error that can have many causes. See "What can go wrong?" below for specific information.

An overview:

The *NetUserAdd* API adds a user account to the UAS database. It fails if the account already exists or if a group with the same name already exists. Note: If remote callers have only account operator privilege, they cannot create *admin* accounts or assign operator privileges.

NetUserAdd can be called with a level 1 or 2 structure. If a level 1 structure is used, the API supplies defaults for the additional information contained in the level 2 structure, as shown in the following table. These defaults can be changed with the *NetUserSetInfo* API.

Member	Default
usri2_full_name	usri2_name
usri2_usr_comment	none (null string)
usri2_parms	none (null string)
usri2_workstations	all (null string)
usri2_acct_expires	never (0xFFFFFFFF)
usri2_max_storage	unlimited (0xFFFFFFFF)
usri2_logon_hours	anytime (all bits set)

(continued)

continued

Member	Default
usri2_logon_server	domain controller (null string)
usri2_country_code	current country code on the server
usri2_code_page	code page 0
usri2_auth_flags	none (0)

What can go wrong?

The *user_info_1* or *user_info_2* structure passed to *NetUserAdd* contains information that must be set correctly. If any single data item is incorrect, *NetUserAdd* returns ERROR_INVALID_PARAMETER without specifying what went wrong. The following errors are those most likely to return ERROR_INVALID_PARAMETER:

- Ill-formed pathnames.

- UF_SCRIPT flag bit not set.

- Operator rights granted to a guest account.

- Undefined bits set in *usri2_flags* or *usri2_auth_flags*.

- Bad privilege.

- *usri2_script_path* not a relative pathname.

- UF_HOMEDIR_REQUIRED set and no *usri2_home_dir* argument.

- Text string too long. Maximum values are as follows:

Text String	Maximum Length
usri2_parms	MAXCOMMENTSZ
usri2_logon_server	UNCLEN
usri2_usr_comment	MAXCOMMENTSZ
usri2_full_name	MAXCOMMENTSZ
usri2_workstations	8 * (CNLEN + 1)
usri2_home_dir	PATHLEN
usri2_script_path	PATHLEN
usri2_comment	MAXCOMMENTSZ

NetUserDel

Removes an account from the UAS.

```
unsigned far pascal
NetUserDel(
    char far * servername,    /* where to execute      */
    char far * username       /* user account to delete */
    )
```

Remote access:

NetUserDel can be called remotely by an administrator, or by a user with accounts operator privilege.

Error returns:

If successful, *NetUserDel* returns 0. If unsuccessful, it returns one of the standard Del return codes or one of the following error codes:

Error Return	Meaning
NERR_ACFNotLoaded	The UAS has not been started.
NERR_UserNotFound	No user account with this name exists.
NERR_NotPrimary	The server is running the Netlogon service and participating in SSI. Only the primary domain controller is allowed to change the accounts database.
NERR_LastAdmin	If this call would delete the last *admin* account, it fails. Note that without an *admin* account no new administrators can be created.
ERROR_ACCESS_DENIED	Indicates insufficient permissions or an accounts operator trying to delete an *admin* account or one with operator privileges set.

An overview:

The *NetUserDel* API deletes a user account. If the user has a session established to the server, the session is deleted. The call can be made remotely but requires *admin* privilege at the server.

A remote caller with only accounts operator privilege cannot delete *admin* accounts or any accounts that have operator privileges. The API returns ERROR_ACCESS_DENIED if such attempts are made.

NetUserGetInfo

Returns specific information for one account.

```
unsigned far pascal
NetUserGetInfo(
    char far * servername,    /* where to execute       */
    char far * username,      /* user account name      */
    short level,              /* level of detail        */
    char far * buf,           /* return data buffer     */
    USHORT buflen,            /* size of buf            */
    USHORT far * btotal       /* total bytes available  */
    )
```

Levels:
Supports level 0, 1, 2, 10, and 11 data structures.

Remote access:
All levels can be called remotely by an administrator, or by a user with accounts operator privilege. Users can get level 11 information about their own accounts and level 10 information about all accounts.

Error returns:
If successful, *NetUserGetInfo* returns 0. If unsuccessful, it returns one of the standard GetInfo return codes or one of the following error codes:

Error Return	Meaning
NERR_ACFNotLoaded	The UAS has not been started.
NERR_UserNotFound	No user account with this name exists.

An overview:
The *NetUserGetInfo* API retrieves a *user_info_N* structure, where *N* can be 0, 1, 2, 10, or 11, depending on the *level* argument.

Note that the *usri2_password* parameter is not readable. It is always a null string.

NetUserSetInfo

Modifies a user's account.

```
unsigned far pascal
NetUserSetInfo(
    char far * servername,    /* where to execute      */
    char far * username,      /* user account name     */
    short level,              /* must be 1 or 2        */
    char far * buf,           /* set data buffer       */
    USHORT buflen,            /* size of buf           */
    short parmnum             /* parameter number      */
    )
```

Levels:
Supports level 1 and 2 data structures.

Remote access:
All levels can be called remotely by an administrator, or by a user with accounts operator privilege. Users can change some of their own information.

Error returns:
If successful, *NetUserSetInfo* returns 0. If unsuccessful, it returns one of the standard SetInfo return codes or one of the following error codes:

Error Return	Meaning
NERR_ACFNotLoaded	The UAS has not been started.
NERR_UserNotFound	No user account with this name exists.
NERR_NotPrimary	The server is running the Netlogon service and participating in SSI. Only the primary domain controller is allowed to change the accounts database.
NERR_LastAdmin	If this call would downgrade the privilege or disable the last *admin* account, it fails. Note that without an *admin* account, no new administrators can be created.
ERROR_INVALID_PARAMETER	See *NetUserAdd* for a description of when this error occurs.

An overview:
The *NetUserSetInfo* API changes information about an existing account. If the *parmnum* argument is 0, the buffer holds a *user_info_1* or *user_info_2* structure as indicated by the *level* argument. Otherwise, the buffer holds data corresponding to *parmnum*. Users can change information in their own accounts, but only through those parameters noted in the "User" column of Table 9-3. User changes must use the *parmnum* method. Table 9-3 lists the data items that can be set.

Name	Value	parmnum	User
usri2_passwd	3	PARMNUM_PASSWD	
usri2_priv	5	PARMNUM_PRIV	
usri2_home_dir	6	PARMNUM_DIR	
usri2_comment	7	PARMNUM_COMMENT	
usri2_flags	8	PARMNUM_USER_FLAGS	
usri2_script_path	9	PARMNUM_SCRIPT_PATH	
usri2_auth_flags	10	PARMNUM_AUTH_FLAGS	
usri2_full_name	11	PARMNUM_FULL_NAME	
usri2_usr_comment	12	PARMNUM_USR_COMMENT	yes
usri2_parms	13	PARMNUM_PARMS	yes
usri2_workstations	14	PARMNUM_WORKSTATIONS	
usri2_acct_expires	17	PARMNUM_ACCT_EXPIRES	
usri2_max_storage	18	PARMNUM_MAX_STORAGE	
usri2_logon_hours	20	PARMNUM_LOGON_HOURS	
usri2_logon_server	23	PARMNUM_LOGON_SERVER	
usri2_country_code	24	PARMNUM_COUNTRY_CODE	yes
usri2_code_page	25	PARMNUM_CODE_PAGE	yes

Table 9-3.
Data structure values and their parmnum *equivalents.*

A user with accounts operator privilege can change any value in the table except those that grant *admin* or operator privileges. Only an *admin* account can make changes to other accounts with *admin* or operator privileges.

> **NOTE:** *Because* NetUserSetInfo *lets an administrator change the password of any user (including other administrators), it should be used carefully. The system ensures that all new passwords conform to the restrictions set by the* NetUserModals *API, discussed later in the chapter.*

NetUserPasswordSet

Changes a user's password.

```
unsigned far pascal
NetUserPasswordSet(
    char far * servername,    /* where to execute  */
    char far * username,      /* user account name */
    char far * oldpasswd,     /* old password      */
    char far * newpasswd,     /* new password      */
    )
```

Remote access:

Users can change their own passwords.

Error returns:

If successful, *NetUserPasswordSet* returns 0. If unsuccessful, it returns one of the standard API return codes or one of the following error codes:

Error Return	Meaning
NERR_ACFNotLoaded	The UAS has not been started.
NERR_UserNotFound	No user account with this name exists.
NERR_NotPrimary	The server is running the Netlogon service and participating in SSI. Only the primary domain controller is allowed to change the accounts database.
ERROR_INVALID_PASSWORD	Either the old password doesn't match the current account password, or the new and old passwords are the same.

An overview:

The *NetUserPasswordSet* API allows users to change their own passwords. It requires that the *oldpasswd* argument match the password stored in the account database. Remember that passwords are case-sensitive at the API level and that if the old password was set through the user-interface programs, it will have been mapped to uppercase.

NetUserPasswordSet is most commonly used as a remote call, changing the user's password at a specific server. It does not require *admin* privilege as long as *oldpasswd* matches the current account password. Although arguments to this API accept both the new and old passwords as regular text, all passwords are encrypted before they are transmitted over the network.

When *NetUserPasswordSet* is called remotely, it fails if the role of the server is not PRIMARY or STANDALONE. Most LAN Manager servers will be participating in the domainwide SSI, so this API usually requires the name of a primary domain controller as its *servername* argument. This name is available through the *NetGetDCName* API. If *NetUserPasswordSet* is used to successfully change the password of the domain to which the user is logged on, the system automatically changes the default password at the calling workstation.

Note that an administrator can change a password without knowing the old password by using the *NetUserSetInfo* API.

NetUserGetGroups

Lists the groups to which a user belongs.

```
unsigned far pascal
NetUserGetGroups(
    char far * servername,    /* where to execute        */
    char far * username,      /* user account name       */
    short level,              /* level of detail         */
    char far * buf,           /* return data buffer      */
    USHORT buflen,            /* size of buf             */
    USHORT far * eread,       /* number of entries read  */
    USHORT far * etotal       /* total entries available */
    )
```

Levels:
Supports a level 0 data structure.

Remote access:
NetUserGetGroups can be called remotely by an administrator or by a user with accounts operator privilege. Users can get information about their own accounts.

Error returns:
If successful, *NetUserGetGroups* returns 0. If unsuccessful, it returns a standard Enum return code or one of the following error codes:

Error Return	Meaning
NERR_ACFNotLoaded	The UAS has not been started.
NERR_UserNotFound	The user account specified by *username* does not exist.

An overview:
The *NetUserGetGroups* API is an enumeration function for obtaining a list of all groups a user belongs to. Note that the arguments are exactly like those used for an Enum function without a qualifier.

The *buf* argument returns a set of *group_info_0* structures. (See the Group APIs for a description of this structure.)

NetUserSetGroups

Sets the groups to which a user account belongs.

```
unsigned far pascal
NetUserSetGroups(
    char far * servername,      /* where to execute        */
    char far * username,        /* user account name       */
    short level,                /* must be 0               */
    char far * buf,             /* return data buffer      */
    USHORT buflen,              /* size of buf             */
    USHORT entries,             /* number of entries       */
    )
```

Levels:

Supports level 0 data structures.

Remote access:

This API can be called remotely by an administrator, or by a user with accounts operator privilege. A user can change group membership for his or her own account.

Error returns:

If successful, *NetUserSetGroups* returns 0. If unsuccessful, it returns a standard API return code or one of the following error codes:

Error Return	Meaning
NERR_ACFNotLoaded	The UAS has not been started.
NERR_UserNotFound	No user account with this name exists.
NERR_UserGroupNotFound	One or more of the groups in the list do not exist.
NERR_NotPrimary	The server is running the Netlogon service and participating in SSI. Only the primary domain controller is allowed to change the accounts database.

An overview:

The *NetUserSetGroups* API defines the set of groups to which an account belongs:

- If the list in the *buf* buffer contains groups that *username* does not belong to, *username* is added to them.

- If *username* belongs to groups not in the list, *username* is deleted from those groups.

The *buf* buffer must contain a set of *group_info_0* structures. (See the *group_info_0* discussion in the Group APIs section below.) The *entries* argument tells the API how many entries to expect.

Uncovering surprises

Occasionally an administrator can be surprised by someone gaining access to a resource when there is no apparent ACL record. Usually this means that access was granted because there is a more general record in the database, such as a parent or drive-level record.

Although *NetAccessCheck* says whether or not access is allowed, it doesn't say why. The ACCWHY.C program (Figure 9-2) implements the access-checking algorithm described in Chapter 2 and shows why access was granted or denied to a particular resource. For this program to work, you must have the User Accounts System (UAS) running.

ACCWHY takes the following syntax:

```
accwhy user permission resource
```

For example, to check whether the user Ted has read and write (RW) permission for the file C:\TMP\FILE, type

```
accwhy Ted RW C:\TMP\FILE
```

The following lines would be typical of the results returned by ACCWHY:

- Ted GRANTED RW to C:\TMP\FILE C:\TMP record (parent)

- Ted DENIED X to C:\BIN\APP.EXE
  no ACLs

- Ted GRANTED D to C:\SECRETS
  C: (drive) and group accumulation

```
/*
 * ACCWHY.C -- This program emulates the LAN Manager ACL
 * permission logic.  It answers the question "Does USER have
 * PERMISSION on RESOURCE?"  ACCWHY uses NetAccessCheck to
 * check for permission status and then displays why access was
 * granted or denied.
 *
 * Compile with:  C> cl accwhy.c netapi.c
 *
 * Usage:  C> accwhy <user> <permission> <resource>
 *
 */
```

Figure 9-2.   *(continued)*
The ACCWHY.C program.

Figure 9-2. *continued*

```c
#include <stdio.h>
#include <os2.h>
#include <netcons.h>
#include <access.h>
#include <neterr.h>
#include <string.h>

#define BSIZE 100

main(argc, argv)
int argc;
char **argv;
    {
    char *p;
    int err;

    if (argc != 4)
        {
        printf("syntax: accwhy <user> <permission> <resource>\n");
        exit(1);
        }

    /* now do the work */
    err = AccWhy(argv[1], argv[2], argv[3]);
    if (err != 0)
        printf("AccWhy error = %d\n", err);
    exit(err);
    }

/*
 * AccWhy -- This routine emulates the ACL logic.  The try
 * routine called by AccWhy might not return.  If it has found
 * an ACL entry, the permissions must pass or fail based on
 * that record. If the return code from try is nonzero, an error
 * has occurred, so exit the program.
 */

AccWhy(user, permstr, resource)
char * user;
char * permstr;
char * resource;
    {
    int err;
    char buf[BSIZE];
```

(continued)

Figure 9-2. *continued*

```
short tavail;
char rbuf[PATHLEN];
struct user_info_1 * pu;

/* first see if the user has an account */
err = NetUserGetInfo(
                    NULL,      /* server name    */
                    user,      /* username       */
                    1,         /* level          */
                    buf,
                    BSIZE,     /* buflen         */
                    &tavail);  /* available data */
if (err != 0)
    return(err);

/* is this an admin user? */
pu = (struct user_info_1 *)buf;
if (pu->usri1_priv == USER_PRIV_ADMIN)
    {
    printf("%s GRANTED %s access to %s n\t ADMIN account\n",
            user, permstr, resource);
    return(0);
    }

/* first try the resource record */
if ((err = try(user, permstr, resource, resource, "resource")) != 0)
    return (err);

/* no ACL for resource ... try parent */
parent(resource, rbuf);
if ((err = try(user, permstr, resource, rbuf, "parent")) != 0)
    return (err);

/* no ACL for parent, try drive level */
drive(resource, rbuf);
if (rbuf[0])
    if ((err = try(user, permstr, resource, rbuf, "drive")) != 0)
        return (err);

/* no ACL records => no access */
printf("%s DENIED %s access to %s\n\tno ACL records\n",
        user, permstr, resource);
return(0);
}
```

(continued)

Figure 9-2. *continued*

```
/* try -- This routine looks for an ACL.  If one is not found,
 * it returns 0.  Other error codes indicate name problems and
 * should be returned immediately for diagnostic exit.
 * If an ACL is found, look for user and use the permissions.
 * Otherwise, accumulate the group permissions and use them.
 * The routine must GRANT or DENY at this point.
 */

try(user, permstr, resource, currrec, currtype)
char *user;         /* username              */
char *permstr;      /* permission string     */
char *resource;     /* original resource name */
char *currrec;      /* current record name    */
char *currtype;     /* type of current record */
    {
    int err, i;
    char buf[BSIZE], ubuf[BSIZE];
    USHORT perms, xperms, accperms, permbits();
    short tavail, er, te;
    struct access_info_1 * pa;
    struct access_list *pl;

    perms = permbits(permstr);
    err = NetAccessGetInfo(
                        NULL,       /* server name     */
                        currrec,    /* resource name   */
                        1,          /* level           */
                        buf,
                        BSIZE,      /* buflen          */
                        &tavail);   /* available data */

    /* anything but NotFound indicates name problems */
    if (err != 0)
        return (err == NERR_ResourceNotFound ? 0 : err);

    /* now search for a username record */
    pa = (struct access_info_1 *) buf;
    pl = (struct access_list *)(pa + 1);
    for (i = 0; i < pa->accl_count; ++i)
        {
        if (stricmp(user, pl->acl_ugname) == 0)
            {
            /* There is a match! -- use these permissions.
             * First, compensate for R=>X by constructing
             * a new perms mask. */
```

(continued)

Figure 9-2. *continued*

```
                    if ((perms & ACCESS_EXEC) && (pl->acl_access & ACCESS_READ))
                        xperms = (perms & ~ACCESS_EXEC) : ACCESS_READ;
                    else
                        xperms = perms;

                    /* now check for access permission */
                    if ((xperms & pl->acl_access) == xperms)
                        printf("%s GRANTED %s access to %s\n\t%s record (%s)\n",
                                user, permstr, resource, currrec, currtype);
                    else
                        printf("%s DENIED %s access to %s\n\t%s record (%s)\n",
                                user, permstr, resource, currrec, currtype);

                    /* got an answer, so exit */
                    exit(0);
                    }
            /* next acl_list in user scan */
            ++pl;
            }

    /* A user record wasn't found, so accumulate group permissions.
     * First, get the list of groups the user is in. */

    NetUserGetGroups(
                    NULL,           /* server name     */
                    user,           /* username        */
                    0,              /* level           */
                    ubuf,           /* buffer for data */
                    BSIZE,          /* size            */
                    &er,            /* entries read    */
                    &te);           /* total entries   */

    /* Now walk through all of the ACL groups and look for a match.
     * If found, accumulate permissions. */

    pl = (struct access_list *)(pa + 1);
    accperms = 0;          /* no permission to start */
    for (i = 0; i < pa->accl_count; ++i)
        {
        if (pl->acl_access & ACCESS_GROUP)
            {
            /* Is this group in the user's list? */
            if (InGroup(ubuf, er, pl->acl_ugname))
                {
                /* Yes -- now OR the permissions into the
                 * accumulated group permissions. */
                accperms |= pl->acl_access;
```

(continued)

Figure 9-2. *continued*

```
                    /* Is this enough to grant access?  First, compensate
                     * for R=>X by constructing a new perms mask. */
                    if ((perms & ACCESS_EXEC) && (accperms & ACCESS_READ))
                        xperms = (perms & ~ACCESS_EXEC) : ACCESS_READ;
                    else
                        xperms = perms;

                    /* now check for accumulated access permission */
                    if ((xperms & accperms) == xperms)
                        {
                        printf("%s GRANTED %s access to %s\n\t%s record (%s)",
                                user, permstr, resource, currrec, currtype);
                        printf(" and group accumulation\n");
                        exit(0);
                        }
                    }
                }
        /* next acl_list in groups scan */
        ++pl;
        }

    /* Not enough permissions, even with groups. Indicate failure. */
    printf("%s DENIED %s access to %s\n\t%s record (%s)\n",
            user, permstr, resource, currrec, currtype);
    exit(0);
    }

/*
 * InGroup -- This routine determines if the gname value is among
 * the list of groups to which the user belongs.
 */

InGroup(pgi, ngi, gname)
struct group_info_0 *pgi;
int ngi;
char * gname;
    {
    while (ngi--)
        {
        if (stricmp(pgi->grpi0_name, gname) == 0)
            return(TRUE);
        ++pgi;
        }
    return(FALSE);
    }
```

(continued)

Figure 9-2. *continued*

```
/*
 * permbits -- This routine turns permission characters into a bit
 * pattern.
 */

USHORT permbits(p)
char *p;
    {
    USHORT perms = 0;

    while (*p)
        {
        switch(*p)
            {
            case 'R':
                perms |= ACCESS_READ;
                break;
            case 'W':
                perms |= ACCESS_WRITE;
                break;
            case 'C':
                perms |= ACCESS_CREATE;
                break;
            case 'X':
                perms |= ACCESS_EXEC;
                break;
            case 'D':
                perms |= ACCESS_DELETE;
                break;
            case 'A':
                perms |= ACCESS_ATRIB;
                break;
            case 'P':
                perms |= ACCESS_PERM;
                break;
            }
        ++p;
        }
    return(perms);
    }

/*
 * parent -- This routine creates the parent resource name for
 * the resource and puts it in rbuf.  The routine assumes that
 * ill-formed names will have been filtered out by the first
 * NetAccessGetInfo call above.
 */
```

(continued)

Figure 9-2. *continued*

```
parent(resource, rbuf)
char *resource;
char *rbuf;
    {
    char *p;

    /* special cases \PIPE\, \PRINT\, \COMM\ */
    if (strnicmp(resource, "\\PIPE\\", 6) == 0)
        {
        p = strrchr(resource, '\\');
        if (p != resource + 6)
            {
            strncpy(rbuf, resource, p - resource);
            rbuf[p - resource] = 0;
            }
        else
            rbuf[0] = 0;
        }
    else if (strnicmp(resource, "\\PRINT\\", 7) == 0)
        rbuf[0] = 0;
    else if (strnicmp(resource, "\\COMM\\", 6) == 0)
        rbuf[0] = 0;
    else
        {
        /* Must be a disk file. This is a special case, so
         * treat C:\ as its own parent. */

        if (resource[2] == '\\' && resource[3] == 0)
            strcpy(rbuf, resource);
        else
            {
            /* watch out for trailing backslash */
            p = strrchr(resource, '\\');
            if (p[1] == 0)
                p = strrchr(p-1, '\\');
            strncpy(rbuf, resource, p - resource + 1);
            rbuf[p - resource + 1] = 0;
            }
        }
    }

/*
 * drive -- If this is a file-system entry, get the drive-name
 * portion.  Otherwise, check for the special drive-level names.
 */
```

(continued)

Figure 9-2. *continued*

```
drive(resource, rbuf)
char *resource;
char *rbuf;
   {
   if (resource[2] == ':')
      {
      strncpy(rbuf, resource, 2);
      rbuf[2] = 0;
      }
   /* special cases \PIPE\, \PRINT\, \COMM\ */
   else if (strnicmp(resource, "\\PIPE\\", 6) == 0)
      strcpy(rbuf, "\\PIPE\\");
   else if (strnicmp(resource, "\\PRINT\\", 7) == 0)
      strcpy(rbuf, "\\PRINT\\");
   else if (strnicmp(resource, "\\COMM\\", 6) == 0)
      strcpy(rbuf, "\\COMM\\");
   else
      rbuf[0] = 0;
   }
```

The Modal APIs

The Modal APIs let an administrator or account operator get and set information that affects the entire UAS database. Three levels of information exist for these APIs and, unlike most APIs, the higher levels are not supersets of the lower levels.

A *user_modals_info_0* structure contains the following members:

Member Name	Description
USHORT usrmod0_min_passwd_len	The minimum length for all passwords. The values range from 0 (no minimum) to MAXPASSWDLEN.
ULONG usrmod0_max_passwd_age	The length of time in seconds that accounts can go without changing the password. A value of 0xFFFFFFFF (TIMEQ_FOR-EVER) means that the password need never be changed. The minimum period is one day (60 * 60 * 24 seconds). If a password has not been changed in this interval, the account cannot be accessed until the password is changed.
ULONG usrmod0_min_passwd_age	The time in seconds that must elapse before a password can be changed again. A value of 0 means that no delay is required.

(continued)

continued

Member Name	Description
ULONG usrmod0_force_logoff	Each account can be configured with a valid set of logon times (usri2_logon__hours). This value holds the time in seconds to wait after the end of a valid logon period to force a logoff. The value 0 means immediate forced logoff, and the value 0xFFFFFFFF (TIMEQ_FOR-EVER) means no forced logoff.
USHORT usrmod0_password_hist_len	The UAS database keeps a history of this many previous passwords. The password is not allowed to be changed back to any of the passwords on this list. The values range from 0 to 8 (DEF_MAX_PWHIST).
USHORT usrmod0_reserved1	Reserved for future use.

A *user_modals_info_1* structure contains the following members:

Member Name	Description		
USHORT usrmod1_role	Each server in a domain is assigned a role for network logon and the replication of account information under SSI:		
	Role	Value	Meaning
	UAS_ROLE_STANDALONE	0	This server is not part of the Single System Image. Although workstations can log on to the server, the UAS database at the server will not be kept in sync with any other servers. UAS account updates will succeed at this server.
	UAS_ROLE_MEMBER	1	This server is part of the SSI. Its database will be kept up to date with all UAS account updates made at the primary domain controller. UAS account updates will be rejected at this server.
	UAS_ROLE_BACKUP	2	This server is part of the SSI. Its database will be kept up to date with all UAS account updates made at the primary domain controller. UAS account updates will be rejected at this server. This server can also process the network logons.

(continued)

Member Name	Description		
	Role	Value	Meaning
	UAS_ROLE_PRIMARY	3	This server is the primary domain controller. Only one server in the domain can be running Netlogon in this role. This server will accept updates to the UAS accounts database and replicate them to all of the other servers in the domain. This server can also process network logons.
char far * usrmod1_primary	The name of the primary domain controller for this domain.		

NetUserModalsGet

Returns information about the UAS database.

```
unsigned far pascal
NetUserModalsGet(
    char far * servername,    /* where to execute      */
    short level,              /* must be 0, 1, or 100  */
    char far * buf,           /* return data buffer    */
    USHORT buflen,            /* size of buf           */
    USHORT far * tavail       /* total bytes available */
    )
```

Levels:

Supports level 0, 1, and 100 data structures.

Remote access:

All levels can be called remotely by an administrator, or by a user with accounts operator privilege. Users can make the call at level 0.

Error returns:

NetUserModalsGet works like a standard GetInfo call: If successful, it returns 0. If unsuccessful, it returns a standard GetInfo return code or the following error code:

Error Return	Meaning
NERR_ACFFileIOError	Access to the UAS database file failed.

An overview:

NetUserModalsGet returns a *user_modals_info_0* structure in the *buf* buffer when the *level* argument is 0, and a *user_modals_info_1* structure when *level* is 1. The special case of setting *level* to 100 returns OEM-specific information as an array of DBIDINFO_SIZE bytes. This special case allows the UAS system to link to an external database.

NetUserModalsGet can be called even if the UAS database is not running, provided the API has access to the UAS database kept in the LANMAN tree.

NetUserModalsSet

Sets global modal-related information in the UAS database.

```
unsigned far pascal
NetUserModalsSet(
    char far * servername,    /* where to execute       */
    short level,              /* must be 0, 1, or 100   */
    char far * buf,           /* return data buffer     */
    USHORT buflen,            /* size of buf            */
    short parmnum             /* parameter to change    */
    )
```

Levels:

Supports level 0, 1, and 100 data structures.

Remote access:

All levels can be called remotely by an administrator, or by a user with accounts operator privilege.

Error returns:

NetUserModalsSet works like a standard SetInfo call: If successful, it returns 0. If unsuccessful, it returns a standard SetInfo return code or the following error code:

Error Return	Meaning
NERR_ACFFileIOError	Access to the UAS database file failed.

An overview:

NetUserModalsSet changes the information common to the entire UAS accounts database. If the *parmnum* argument is 0, the *buf* buffer contains a *user_modals_info_0* structure when *level* is 0, and a *user_modals_info_1* structure when *level* is 1. The special case of setting *level* to 100 expects the buffer to contain OEM-specific information as an array of DBIDINFO-_SIZE bytes. This special case allows the UAS system to link to an external database.

Depending on what the *level* argument is, *parmnum* indicates different information in the *buf* buffer:

Name	Level	Value	parmnum
usrmod0_min_passwd_len	0	1	MODAL0_PARMNUM_MIN_LEN
usrmod0_max_passwd_age	0	2	MODAL0_PARMNUM_MAX_AGE
usrmod0_min_passwd_age	0	3	MODAL0_PARMNUM_MIN_AGE
usrmod0_force_logoff	0	4	MODAL0_PARMNUM_FORCEOFF
usrmod0_password_hist_len	0	5	MODAL0_PARMNUM_HISTLEN
usrmod1_role	1	1	MODAL1_PARMNUM_ROLE
usrmod1_primary	1	2	MODAL1_PARMNUM_PRIMARY
(not defined)	100	0	MODAL100_PARMNUM_DBID

NetUserModalsSet can be called even if the UAS database is not running, provided the API has access to the UAS database kept in the LANMAN tree.

The Group APIs

A *group* is a collection of usernames that can be given access permissions collectively. When an ACL entry is created for a group, the membership in the group can change at any time and the permission checking reflects the new makeup of the group. The Group APIs let you control user groups on a server with user-level security. Group APIs let you create or delete groups and review or adjust their membership.

Because access checking is performed from the most specific to the most general, you can easily set permissions for a group and then specify exceptions through *access control entries*. For example, user TED belongs to the SALES group. The following access control entries grant TED RW access to FEBPROFIT, but only R access to FEBLOSS:

```
C:\TMP\FEBPROFIT
    group SALES:RW
C:\TMP\FEBLOSS
    group SALES:RW
    user TED:R
```

To use the Group APIs, you must include NETCONS.H and ACCESS.H at compile time, and you must link with the NETAPI.LIB library stub. Two levels of data structure are available for the Group APIs.

The *group_info_0* structure contains the following member:

Member Name	Description
char grpi0_name[GNLEN+1]	An array holding a zero-terminated text string with the group name

The *group_info_1* structure contains the following members:

Member Name	Description
char grpi1_name[GNLEN+1]	An array holding a zero-terminated text string with the group name
char far * grpi1_comment	A comment string associated with the group

Some Group APIs use a secondary data structure called *group_users-_info_0*. This structure contains one member:

Member Name	Description
char grui0_name[UNLEN+1]	An array holding a zero-terminated text string with a username

NetGroupEnum

Lists all groups in the UAS database.

```
unsigned far pascal
NetGroupEnum(
    char far * servername,    /* where to execute          */
    short level,              /* must be 0 or 1            */
    char far * buf,           /* return data buffer        */
    USHORT buflen,            /* size of buf               */
    USHORT far * eread,       /* number of entries read    */
    USHORT far * etotal       /* total entries available   */
    )
```

Levels:
Supports level 0 and 1 structures.

Remote access:
All levels can be called remotely by an administrator or by a user with accounts operator privilege. Users can get level 0 information.

Error returns:

If successful, *NetGroupEnum* returns 0. If unsuccessful, it returns a standard Enum return code or the following error code:

Error Return	Meaning
NERR_ACFNotLoaded	The UAS has not been started.

An overview:

The *NetGroupEnum* API retrieves a list of *group_info_0* structures when the *level* argument is 0 and a list of *group_info_1* structures when the *level* argument is 1.

NetGroupAdd

Adds a new group to the UAS database.

```
unsigned far pascal
NetGroupAdd(
    char far * servername,    /* where to execute  */
    short level,              /* level of detail   */
    char far * buf,           /* load status info  */
    USHORT buflen,            /* size of buf       */
    )
```

Levels:

Supports level 0 and 1 data structures.

A little group magic

Most groups can be created, modified, and deleted. But three built-in groups cannot be edited: *admins*, *users*, and *guests*. These groups are created automatically for the following accounts:

Group Name	Members
admins	All accounts with USER_PRIV_ADMIN
users	All accounts with USER_PRIV_USER
guests	All accounts with USER_PRIV_GUEST

If editing APIs are used on any of these groups, the special error code NERR_SpeGroupOp is returned.

Remote access:

All levels can be called remotely by an administrator, or by a user with accounts operator privilege.

Error returns:

If successful, *NetGroupAdd* returns 0. If unsuccessful, it returns a standard Group return code or one of the following error codes:

Error Return	Meaning
NERR_ACFNotLoaded	The UAS has not been started.
NERR_GroupExists	A group with this name already exists.
NERR_UserExists	A user with this name already exists.
NERR_BadUserName	The group name contains illegal characters.

An overview:

The *NetGroupAdd* API adds an empty group to the database. The *buf* buffer must contain a *group_info_0* structure if the *level* argument is 0 and a *group_info_1* structure if the *level* argument is 1. This call fails if the group name already exists or if the name is already used as a username.

If *NetGroupAdd* is called at level 0, the *grpil_comment* value is set to an empty string.

NetGroupDel

Removes a group from the UAS database.

```
unsigned far pascal
NetGroupDel(
    char far * servername,    /* where to execute       */
    char far * groupname      /* name of group to delete */
    )
```

Remote access:

All levels can be called remotely by an administrator, or by a user with accounts operator privilege.

Error returns:

If successful, *NetGroupDel* returns 0. If unsuccessful, it returns a standard Del return code or one of the following error codes:

Error Return	Meaning
NERR_ACFNotLoaded	The UAS has not been started.
NERR_GroupNotFound	No group with this name exists.
NERR_SpeGroupOp	The built-in groups cannot be deleted.

An overview:

The *NetGroupDel* API removes a group from the database. The built-in groups cannot be deleted.

NetGroupAddUser

Adds a user to a group in the UAS database.

```
unsigned far pascal
NetGroupAddUser(
    char far * servername,    /* where to execute       */
    char far * groupname,     /* name of group to add to */
    char far * username       /* user to add to group    */
    )
```

Remote access:

All levels can be called remotely by an administrator, or by a user with accounts operator privilege.

Error returns:

If successful, *NetGroupAddUser* returns 0. If unsuccessful, it returns a standard API return code or one of the following error codes:

Error Return	Meaning
NERR_ACFNotLoaded	The UAS has not been started.
NERR_GroupNotFound	No group with this name exists.
NERR_UserNotFound	No user with this name exists.
NERR_UserInGroup	The user is already a member of the group.
NERR_SpeGroupOp	The built-in groups cannot have names added.

An overview:

The *NetGroupAddUser* API adds a username to an existing group. No new names can be added to the built-in groups.

NetGroupDelUser

Removes a user from a group in the UAS database.

```
unsigned far pascal
NetGroupDelUser(
    char far * servername,   /* where to execute            */
    char far * groupname,    /* name of group to delete from */
    char far * username      /* user to delete from group   */
    )
```

Remote access:

All levels can be called remotely by an administrator, or by a user with accounts operator privilege.

Error returns:

If successful, *NetGroupDelUser* returns 0. If unsuccessful, it returns a standard API return code or one of the following error codes:

Error Return	Meaning
NERR_ACFNotLoaded	The UAS has not been started.
NERR_GroupNotFound	No group with this name exists.
NERR_UserNotFound	The username is not part of the group.
NERR_UserNotInGroup	The user is not a member of the group.
NERR_SpeGroupOp	The built-in groups cannot have names deleted.

An overview:

The *NetGroupDelUser* API removes a username from a group. Users cannot be deleted from the built-in groups.

NetGroupGetUsers

Lists the members of a group in the UAS database.

```
unsigned far pascal
NetGroupGetUsers(
    char far * servername,   /* where to execute            */
    char far * groupname,    /* name of group               */
    short level,             /* must be 0                   */
    char far * buf,          /* return data buffer          */
    USHORT buflen,           /* size of buf                 */
    USHORT far * eread,      /* number of entries read      */
    USHORT far * etotal      /* total entries available     */
    )
```

Levels:
Supports a level 0 data structure.

Remote access:
All levels can be called remotely by an administrator, or by a user with accounts operator privilege. Users can get information only about groups to which they belong (with the exception of the built-in groups).

Error returns:
If successful, *NetGroupGetUsers* returns 0. If unsuccessful, it returns a standard Enum return code or the following error code:

Error Return	Meaning
NERR_GroupNotFound	No group with this name exists.

An overview:
The *NetGroupGetUsers* API is an enumeration function for listing all users that currently belong to a particular group. Note that the arguments are the same as those used for an Enum function with a qualifier.

If a user without accounts operator privilege calls *NetGroupGetUsers* remotely, the call succeeds if the user is a member of the group or if the group is one of the built-in groups.

The *buf* buffer returns a set of *group_user_info_0* structures.

NetGroupSetUsers

Defines the entire membership of a group in the UAS database.

```
unsigned far pascal
NetGroupSetUsers(
    char far * servername,    /* where to execute    */
    char far * groupname,     /* name of group       */
    short level,              /* level of detail     */
    char far * buf,           /* return data buffer  */
    USHORT buflen,            /* size of buf         */
    USHORT entries            /* how many entries?   */
    )
```

Levels:
Supports level 0 data structures.

Remote access:

All levels can be called remotely by an administrator, or by a user with accounts operator privilege.

Error returns:

If successful, *NetGroupSetUsers* returns 0. If unsuccessful, it returns a standard API return code or one of the following error codes:

Error Return	Meaning
NERR_GroupNotFound	No group with this name exists.
NERR_UserNotFound	One or more of the usernames do not exist.
NERR_SpeGroupOp	The built-in groups cannot be changed.

An overview:

The *NetGroupSetUsers* API is a function for setting the list of all users that currently belong to a particular group. Whereas *NetGroupAddUser* adds a single username to a group, *NetGroupSetUsers* defines the entire membership with one call. Changes cannot be made to the built-in groups.

The *buf* buffer returns a set of *group_user_info_0* structures. The *entries* argument tells the API how many.

NetGroupGetInfo

Returns information about the specified group.

```
unsigned far pascal
NetGroupGetInfo(
    char far * servername,      /* where to execute    */
    char far * groupname,       /* which group?        */
    short level,                /* level of detail     */
    char far * buf,             /* return data buffer  */
    USHORT buflen,              /* size of buf         */
    USHORT far * tavail         /* size needed for buf */
    )
```

Levels:

Supports level 0 and 1 data structures.

Remote access:

All levels can be called remotely by an administrator, or by a user with accounts operator privilege. Users can get level 0 information.

Error returns:

If successful, *NetGroupGetInfo* returns 0. If unsuccessful, it returns a standard GetInfo return code or the following error code:

Error Return	Meaning
NERR_ACFNotLoaded	The UAS has not been started.

An overview:

The *NetGroupGetInfo* API retrieves a list of *group_info_0* structures when the *level* argument is 0 and *group_info_1* structures when the *level* argument is 1.

NetGroupSetInfo

Sets information for the specified group.

```
unsigned far pascal
NetGroupSetInfo(
    char far * servername,    /* where to execute    */
    char far * groupname,     /* which group?        */
    short level,              /* must be 1           */
    char far * buf,           /* return data buffer  */
    USHORT buflen,            /* size of buf         */
    short parmnum             /* parameter to change */
    )
```

Levels:

Supports level 1 data structures.

Remote access:

All levels can be called remotely by an administrator, or by a user with accounts operator privilege.

Error returns:

If successful, *NetGroupSetInfo* returns 0. If unsuccessful, it returns a standard SetInfo return code or one of the following error codes:

Error Return	Meaning
NERR_ACFNotLoaded	The UAS has not been started.
NERR_GroupNotFound	No group with this name exists.

An overview:

The *NetGroupSetInfo* API changes information about a group. If *parmnum* is 0, *buf* must contain a *group_info_1* structure. The data item that can be set—and its corresponding *parmnum* value—is as follows:

Name	Value	parmnum
grpi1_comment	2	GRP1_PARMNUM_COMMENT

Other UAS APIs

Some miscellaneous API calls are part of the User Accounts System:

- *NetUserValidate* is the same logic used to validate server logon.

- *NetUserValidate2* is the same logic used by a server to validate network logon.

- *NetLogonEnum* provides a way for controller programs to get a list of all of the users logged on to a domain.

- *NetGetDCName* is an API for getting the name of the primary domain controller in a domain.

The data structures used by these APIs are defined in ACCESS.H. The *user_logon_req_1* structure contains these members:

Member Name	Description
char usrreq1_name[UNLEN+1]	The account name for which validation is requested.
char usrreq1_password[SESSION_PWLEN]	The regular text password for the account.
char far * usrreq1_workstation	A pointer to a string with the name of the workstation the user is on. A string indicates the local server, and the value 0xFFFFFFFF indicates that the workstation is unknown.

The *user_logon_info_0* structure contains the following member:

Member Name	Description
char usrlog0_eff_name[UNLEN+1]	The effective logon name. Under LAN Manager 2.0, this is the same as the username (or guest account in case of guest logon).

The *user_logon_info_1* structure contains the following members:

Member Name	Description
USHORT usrlog1_code	A possible error code. See *NetUserValidate2* for details.
char usrlog1_eff_name[UNLEN+1]	The effective logon name. Under LAN Manager 2.0, this is the same as the username.
USHORT usrlog1_priv	The user's privilege level. The values are as follows:

Privilege	Value	Meaning
USER_PRIV_GUEST	0	A guest account
USER_PRIV_USER	1	A user account
USER_PRIV_ADMIN	2	An administrator account

Member Name	Description
ULONG usrlog1_auth_flags	A set of bits indicating what operator privilege the account has. The values are as follows:

Bitmask	Value	Meaning
AF_OP_PRINT	0x1	Print operator
AF_OP_COMM	0x2	Comm operator
AF_OP_SERVER	0x4	Server operator
AF_OP_ACCOUNTS	0x8	Account operator

Member Name	Description
USHORT usrlog1_num_logons	Number of logons under this username that are currently active.
USHORT usrlog1_bad_pw_count	Number of bad password attempts since the last logon.
ULONG usrlog1_last_logon	The time of the most recent logon.
ULONG usrlog1_last_logoff	The time of the most recent logoff.
ULONG usrlog1_logoff_time	The time when this logon is expected to log off. A value of 0xFFFFFFFF means no logoff is required.
ULONG usrlog1_kickoff_time	The time when the system will force the logoff. A value of 0xFFFFFFFF means never.
long usrlog1_password_age	The time in seconds since the password was last changed.
ULONG usrlog1_pw_can_change	The time when the user is allowed to change the password. A value of 0xFFFFFFFF means that the password can never be changed.
ULONG usrlog1_pw_must_change	The time when the user must change the password. A value of 0xFFFFFFFF means that no change is required.
char far * usrlog1_computer	The computer name of the server that logged the user on to the domain.
char far * usrlog1_domain	The domain that the user logged on to.
char far * usrlog1_script_path	Pathname to the logon script for the user. The path is relative to the NETLOGON share at the logon server.
ULONG usrlog1_reserved1	Reserved by Microsoft for future use.

The *user_logon_info_2* structure contains the following members:

Member Name	Description
char usrlog1_eff_name[UNLEN+1]	The effective logon name. Under LAN Manager 2.0, this is the same as the username.
char far * usrlog2_computer	The computer name of the workstation that the user logged on from. Note that this is different from *usrlog1_computer*, which gives the server that the user logged on to.
char far * usrlog2_fullname	The full name of the user in the UAS account.
char far * usrlog2_usrcomment	The user-settable comment for the UAS account.
char far * usrlog2_logon_time	The time at which the user logged on to the network.

NetUserValidate

Validates a user's password.

```
unsigned far pascal
NetUserValidate(
    char far * reserved,    /* must be NULL         */
    char far * username,    /* user account name    */
    char far * password,    /* account password     */
    USHORT far * priv,      /* returns account type */
    )
```

Remote access:
This call cannot be made remotely.

Error returns:
If successful, *NetUserValidate* returns 0. If unsuccessful, it returns a standard API return code or one of the following error codes:

Error Return	Meaning
NERR_ACFNotLoaded	The UAS has not been started.
ERROR_INVALID_PASSWORD	The password contains illegal characters.
ERROR_ACCESS_DENIED	The username and password do not correspond to an active account.

An overview:

The *NetUserValidate* API determines whether the password is valid. If no user account exists for this name, the *guest* account is checked with the supplied password. If successful, the *priv* parameter is set to one of the following values:

priv *Parameter*	*Meaning*
USER_PRIV_ADMIN	An *admin* account
USER_PRIV_USER	A *user* account
USER_PRIV_GUEST	A *guest* account

If *NetUserValidate* fails, the *usri2_bad_pw_count* value in the account database is incremented. If it succeeds, the bad-password count is reset to zero.

Remember that passwords are case-sensitive at the API level, and that if the password was set through the user-interface programs, it will have been mapped to uppercase.

> **NOTE:** *The* NetUserValidate *API exists only for compatibility with LAN Manager 1.0. If you have LAN Manager 2.0, you should use* NetUserValidate2.

NetUserValidate2

Validates a user's password and returns a buffer of information.

```
unsigned far pascal
NetUserValidate2(
    char far * reserved1,    /* must be NULL        */
    short level,             /* must be 1           */
    char far * buf,          /* buffer for data     */
    USHORT buflen,           /* length of buf       */
    USHORT reserved2,        /* must be 0           */
    USHORT far * tavail      /* total bytes available */
    )
```

Levels:

Supports level 0 data structures.

Remote access:

This call cannot be made remotely.

Error returns:

If successful, *NetUserValidate2* returns 0. If unsuccessful, it returns a standard Enum return code or one of the following error codes:

Error Return	Meaning
NERR_ACFNotLoaded	The UAS has not been started.
ERROR_ACCESS_DENIED	The username and password do not correspond to an active account.

Note that for both *NetUserValidate* and *NetUserValidate2*, NERR_UserNot-Found is never returned: If *username* does not have an account, the server checks the password for the default *guest* account. This is the same logic used by the server logon process.

An overview:

NetUserValidate2 executes the same logic that a server does during network logon. The *buf* buffer should contain a *user_logon_req_1* structure when the API is called. It returns with the *buf* buffer containing a *user_logon_info_1* structure.

If the return code is ERROR_ACCESS_DENIED, only the *usrlog1_code* value is meaningful: It is a further indication of why network logon was not allowed. The following values are possible:

usrlog1_code Value	Meaning
NERR_Success	Network logon was successful.
NERR_PasswordExpired	The account password has not been changed in the required period of time. Logon is disabled until the password is changed.
NERR_InvalidWorkstation	The *usrreq1_workstation* value is not one of the workstations the user is allowed to log on from.
NERR_InvalidLogonHours	It is outside the time periods in which the user is allowed logon.
ERROR_ACCESS_DENIED	There is no account for the user to log on to, or the account is disabled.

If *NetUserValidate2* returns anything but 0 (NERR_Success) or ERROR-_MORE_DATA, the rest of the data in *usr_logon_info_1* is invalid.

If the *reserved1* argument is not 0, the behavior of this API is unpredictable.

If *NetUserValidate2* fails, the *usri2_bad_pw_count* value in the account database is incremented. If it succeeds, the bad-password count is reset to zero.

Remember that passwords are case-sensitive at the API level, and that if the password was set through the user-interface programs it will have been mapped to uppercase.

NetLogonEnum

Returns information about all users logged on to a server.

```
unsigned far pascal
NetLogonEnum(
    char far * servername,    /* where to execute          */
    short level,              /* level of detail           */
    char far * buf,           /* return data buffer        */
    USHORT buflen,            /* size of buf               */
    USHORT far * eread,       /* number of entries read    */
    USHORT far * etotal       /* total entries available   */
    )
```

Levels:
Supports level 0 and 2 data structures.

Remote access:
An administrator or accounts operator can make a remote call at level 1 or level 2. A user can make a remote call at level 0.

Error returns:
If successful, *NetLogonEnum* returns 0. If unsuccessful, it returns a standard Enum return code or one of the following error codes:

Error Return	Meaning
NERR_NetLogonNotStarted	The Netlogon service must be running at the server.
NERR_ACCESS_DENIED	The caller did not have sufficient permission to complete the remote API. Either no valid account existed at the server, or the user did not have privilege for the level 2 structure.

An overview:
NetLogonEnum returns information about all users who have performed a network logon at a particular server on the network. If the *level* argument is 0, the *buf* buffer returns a *user_logon_info_0* structure. If the *level* argument is 2, the *buf* buffer returns a *user_logon_info_2* structure. Only administrators and account operators can obtain level 2 information.

Logon processing can be performed by the primary domain controller or by any backup domain controller in the domain. The *usri2_logon_server* data structure indicates the preferred server for processing. *NetLogonEnum* returns the set of still-active users that have been processed by a particular server.

If the *servername* argument were in a different domain than the calling workstation, the returned information would be in terms of users logged on in the server's domain.

The returned data contains more than one structure for a particular user-name if the user is logged on to more than one workstation at once.

Is anybody out there?

NetLogonEnum returns a list of users whose network logon was processed by a specific server. To obtain a list of all users logged on in the domain, you must call the API for all backup and primary domain controllers in the domain. The WHO.C program (Figure 9-3) uses the LAN manager APIs to display this information. WHO first uses the *servertype* mask with the *NetServerEnum2* API to obtain a list of the domain controllers and then obtains a list of all logged-on users at each.

```
/*
 * WHO.C -- This program displays a list of all users logged
 * on to the specified domain.
 *
 * Compile with:  C> cl who.c netapi.lib netoem.lib
 *
 * Usage:  C> who [domain]
 *
 */

#include <stdio.h>
#include <netcons.h>
#include <access.h>
#include <server.h>

main(argc, argv)
int argc;
char **argv;
    {
    char far * domain = NULL;
    char bufS[BUFSIZ], bufL[BUFSIZ];
    char srvname[CNLEN+3];
    int err;
    unsigned short ereadS, eavailS;
```

Figure 9-3.
The WHO.C program.

(continued)

Figure 9-3. *continued*

```
unsigned short ereadL, eavailL;
struct server_info_0 * psi;
struct user_logon_info_0 * pli;

/* if no domain specified on command line, use the default */
if (argc == 2)
    domain = argv[1];
else if (argc > 2)
    {
    printf("syntax:  who [domain]\n");
    }

/* get primary and backup DCs for the domain */
err = NetServerEnum2(
                    NULL,          /* execute locally  */
                    0,             /* level            */
                    bufS,          /* for server list  */
                    sizeof(bufS),  /* buflen           */
                    &ereadS,       /* entries read     */
                    &eavailS,      /* entries available */
                    SV_TYPE_DOMAIN_CTRL : SV_TYPE_DOMAIN_BAKCTRL,
                    domain
                    );
if (err)
    {
    printf("NetServerEnum returned %d\n", err);
    exit(1);
    }

/* for each backup or primary DC */
psi = (struct server_info_0 *)bufS;
while (ereadS--)
    {
    /* the returned server names do not have backslashes */
    strcpy(srvname, "\\\\");
    strcat(srvname, psi->sv0_name);

    /* get the logon list */
    err = NetLogonEnum(
                    srvname,       /* which server     */
                    0,             /* level            */
                    bufL,          /* for server list  */
                    sizeof(bufL),  /* buflen           */
                    &ereadL,       /* entries read     */
                    &eavailL       /* entries available */
                    );
```

(continued)

Figure 9-3. *continued*

```
        if (err)
            printf("** NetLogonEnum to %s returned %d\n", srvname, err);
        else
            printf("%s:\n", srvname);

        /* for each user at the server */
        pli = (struct user_logon_info_0 *)bufL;
        while (ereadL--)
            {
            printf("    %s\n", pli->usrlog0_eff_name);
            } /* for each user */
        ++psi;
        } /* for each server */
exit(0);
}
```

NetGetDCName

Returns the primary domain controller for the specified domain.

```
unsigned far pascal
NetGetDCName(
    char far * servername,    /* where to execute */
    char far * domain,        /* which domain?    */
    char far * buffer,        /* for data return  */
    USHORT buflen             /* size of buffer   */
    )
```

Remote access:

This API can be called remotely by any user with a valid account at the server.

Error returns:

If successful, *NetGetDCName* returns 0. If unsuccessful, it returns a standard API return code or one of the following error codes:

Error Return	Meaning
NERR_DCNotFound	No primary domain controller exists in the named domain. This value is also returned if the domain does not exist.

An overview:

The *NetGetDCName* API returns the name of the server operating as the primary domain controller for the specified domain. The name is returned in *buffer* as a text string, and it includes leading backslashes, as in \\ANYSERVER.

If the *domain* argument is NULL, the workstation's primary domain is used. Note that if the *servername* argument specifies remote execution and the *domain* argument is NULL, the return string is the primary domain controller of the server's domain, which might not be the same as the workstation's domain.

Note that the primary domain controller for a domain can change, so programs should be careful about using old information. Also note that because of the way *NetGetDCName* is implemented, it can take several seconds before it returns, so programs should be careful about putting calls to this API inside time-critical portions of a program.

This API is most commonly used to obtain the name of the primary domain controller so that updates can be made to the UAS database for the domain. The following code fragment demonstrates this use:

```
err = NetGetDCName(
                    NULL,            /* execute locally */
                    NULL,            /* default domain  */
                    dcname,          /* for return data */
                    sizeof(dcname)   /* buflen          */
                    );
if (err)
    /* process the error */
else
    err = NetUserSetInfo(dcname, ...
```

INTERPROCESS COMMUNICATION APIs

One of the most powerful tools under OS/2 for creating applications is the ability to create multiple processes that communicate with each other. Under LAN Manager, communication processes can be distributed to different computers on a network; they can even be MS-DOS applications that communicate with processes running on LAN Manager servers. This chapter describes the three kinds of APIs that LAN Manager provides for interprocess communication: Named-pipe APIs and Mailslot APIs, which allow distributed interprocess communication, and Alert APIs, which allow local interprocess communication. Interprocess communication can occur in several forms:

Form	Type of API and Description
One-to-one	Named pipes allow one-to-one communication between two processes.
Many-to-one	First-class mailslots allow many workstation processes to communicate with one server process.
One-to-many	Alerts allow one process to communicate with many other processes simultaneously within a workstation or server.
Many-to-many	Second-class mailslots allow many workstation processes to communicate with many other workstation processes.

NOTE: *The direct use of NetBIOS through the NetBIOS APIs is also a form of interprocess communication and is described in Chapter 12.*

Named Pipes

Named pipes are a bidirectional interprocess communication mechanism. Two processes can use named pipes to carry out a dialog: What one process writes the other reads, and vice versa.

Named pipes have two sides: The server side creates the named pipe and waits for a client to connect to the other end; the client side uses *DosOpen* and the name of the pipe to connect. Each side obtains a file-system handle and then uses *DosRead* and *DosWrite* to communicate with the other side.

A named pipe's name is one of its most important features. Because the name can always be expressed as a UNC name, the client side can be a process running on a different machine on the network.

Buffers and Blocks

A named pipe has two data buffers associated with the pipe, as shown in Figure 10-1. Each side of the named pipe can be placed in either blocking or nonblocking mode.

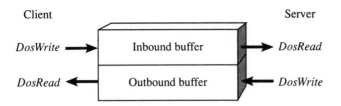

Figure 10-1.
Named-pipe buffers.

Blocking mode

In blocking mode, *DosRead* requests wait until data is available (which might be fewer than the number of bytes requested), and *DosWrite* requests return only after transferring the specified number of bytes. If *DosWrite* cannot fit all of the data into the buffer, it waits for the other end to perform a *DosRead* and make room. If a *DosWrite* is bigger than the buffer, the other end must execute *DosRead* several times to keep emptying the buffer. Figure 10-2 illustrates the blocking behavior of a byte-mode pipe (defined below) with input and output buffers of 100 bytes. Message-mode pipes (as explained below) work somewhat differently.

Client	Server
DosRead 10 bytes (blocks)	*DosWrite* 5 bytes (succeeds)
Returns with 5 bytes read	
DosRead 5 bytes (blocks)	*DosWrite* 10 bytes (succeeds)
Returns with 5 bytes read	
DosRead 5 bytes (succeeds)	
DosRead 200 bytes (blocks)	*DosWrite* 200 bytes (blocks)
Returns with 100 bytes read	Returns with 200 bytes written
DosRead 100 bytes (succeeds)	

Figure 10-2.
The blocking behavior of byte-mode pipes.

Nonblocking mode

In nonblocking mode, *DosRead* requests read only as many bytes as are currently in the buffer, which can be from zero to the buffer size. A nonblocking *DosWrite* writes only as many bytes as will fit in the buffer, which can be from zero to the buffer size.

Modes and Types

The *DosMakeNmPipe* API lets you create two kinds of pipes: *byte-mode pipes* and *message-mode pipes*.

- In a byte-mode pipe, the data is simply a collection (or stream) of data bytes; the *DosRead*s and *DosWrite*s aren't necessarily the same size.

- Message-mode pipes allow *DosWrite* and *DosRead* to deal with entire structures. This lets an application read everything at once, rather than forcing it to read an operation code indicating the size and then read the rest of the data. A *DosWrite* made to a message-mode pipe is invisibly tagged with a size so that the other end can call *DosRead* and obtain the entire message at one time.

If a *DosRead* of a named-pipe message is less than the size of the message, the partial data is read and the *DosRead* call returns ERROR-_MORE_DATA. The next *DosRead* can read up to the message boundary but no further.

Message-mode pipes can have their reading mode changed to byte mode. This allows a message to be read byte by byte if necessary. The message header is always skipped, no matter what the reading mode. Byte-mode pipes can never be read as a message.

If a message is larger than either or both the input and output buffers, the system performs the internal reads and writes required to transfer the entire message.

Two buffers or one?

Although named pipes are usually used bidirectionally, the access modes on the *DosMakeNmPipe* and *DosOpen* APIs let you create a named pipe that communicates in only one direction. For example, you might use this feature to create a server application that provides a current list of prices: A client opening the pipe could read the price list through a one-way pipe that allows *DosWrite* at the server and *DosRead* at the client. Note that the Mailslots APIs (described later in this chapter) also provide this service.

Instances of Named Pipes

Named pipes are typically used in a distributed environment; they allow many clients to use a server application. But what happens when many clients all want to use the same named pipe?

When the server creates the named pipe with the *DosMakeNmPipe* API, it specifies an "instance count." Instances are created with subsequent *DosMakeNmPipe* calls using the same pipe name. Each instance of the pipe has its own set of pipe buffers and its own file-system handle. So when clients execute a *DosOpen* on the same pipe name, each successful *DosOpen* is connected to a different instance of the pipe.

For more information on writing server applications that service many instances of a single pipe, see Chapter 13.

The Life Cycle of a Named Pipe

On the server side, a named pipe is created with the *DosMakeNmPipe* API. The server then uses the *DosConnectNmPipe* API to determine whether the client end is connected to the other end of the pipe. The client end connects to its end of the pipe by using a *DosOpen* call. After both sides are connected, they can begin the *DosRead* and *DosWrite* dialog. When the dialog is complete, the server calls the *DosDisconnectNmPipe* API, and the client performs a *DosClose* operation. The server can then execute another *DosConnectNmPipe* call and wait for the next client. Figure 10-3 illustrates this cycle.

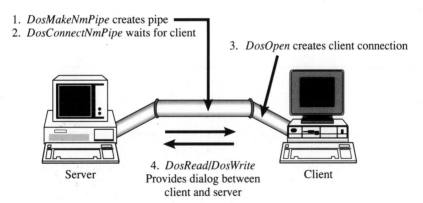

1. *DosMakeNmPipe* creates pipe
2. *DosConnectNmPipe* waits for client

3. *DosOpen* creates client connection

Server   4. *DosRead/DosWrite*   Client
          Provides dialog between
          client and server

5. *DosDisconnectNmPipe*
   deletes client connection

Figure 10-3.
The life cycle of a named pipe.

The cycle beginning with *DosConnectNmPipe* can be repeated until the application wants to stop accepting clients. The server can then execute a *DosClose* to delete the instance of the named pipe. When the last instance is deleted, the pipe no longer exists.

The Named-Pipe APIs

To use the Named-Pipe APIs, you need to include OS2.H at compile time. The standard DOSCALLS.LIB library provides library stubs. Note that in some implementations of OS/2, the DOSCALLS.LIB library is named OS2.LIB.

DosMakeNmPipe

Creates a named pipe.

```
unsigned far pascal
DosMakeNmPipe(
    char far * name,        /* pipe name              */
    unsigned far * handle,  /* returned handle        */
    USHORT omode,           /* open mode              */
    USHORT pmode,           /* pipe mode              */
    USHORT size1,           /* outgoing buffer size   */
    USHORT size2,           /* incoming buffer size   */
    long timeout            /* DosWaitNmPipe timeout  */
    )
```

Error returns:

If successful, *DosMakeNmPipe* returns 0. If unsuccessful, it returns one of the following error codes:

Error Return	Meaning
ERROR_INVALID_PARAMETER	One of the arguments contains illegal values.
ERROR_NOT_ENOUGH_MEMORY	Insufficient system memory to create the pipe buffers.
ERROR_OUT_OF_STRUCTURES	Insufficient system memory to create the internal structures used to track named pipes.
ERROR_PATH_NOT_FOUND	Invalid named-pipe pathname. Ensure that the pathname begins with \PIPE\ and consists entirely of legal file-system characters.
ERROR_PIPE_BUSY	A named pipe of this name already exists, and all available instances are being used.

An overview:

The *DosMakeNmPipe* API creates a named pipe. If the named pipe is to be used in a distributed environment, the pipe must be created by a server process. The named pipe exists until the creating process exits.

The *name* argument looks like a file-system name. It must begin with \PIPE\. The rest of the name can use any valid file-system characters, including a backslash, and is not case sensitive. By using directory names, you can avoid using the pipe name of someone else's applications. Each application can encode the application name in the pipe name. All named pipes used by LAN Manager service programs begin with \PIPE\LANMAN\. For example, the named pipes created by the Netrun service use the name \PIPE\LANMAN\NETRUN. So if the "Generic LAN Company" needed a named pipe for a database request application, it might use a name such as \PIPE\GLC\DBREQ to avoid conflict with any other DBREQ pipe.

When the pipe is created, a file-system handle is returned in the *handle* parameter. Subsequent operations on the pipe, including *DosRead* and *DosWrite*, use this handle to identify the pipe. If multiple instances of the named pipe occur, each call to *DosMakeNmPipe* with the same name returns a different handle, representing a different instance of the pipe.

The *omode* argument is the *open mode*, a set of bit values that specify the access mode, an inheritance flag, and a write-behind flag. Values for *omode* are as follows:

Bitmask	Value	Meaning
NP_ACCESS_DUPLEX	0x0002	The pipe is bidirectional. Both client and server can read and write the named pipe.
NP_ACCESS_INBOUND	0x0000	The pipe is unidirectional. The server side can read, and the client side can write.
NP_ACCESS_OUTBOUND	0x0001	The pipe is unidirectional. The server side can write, and the client side can read.
NP_INHERIT	0x0000	The named-pipe handle will be inherited by a child process.
NP_NO_INHERIT	0x0080	The named-pipe handle will not be inherited by a child process.

(continued)

continued

Bitmask	Value	Meaning
NP_WRITEBEHIND	0x4000	In remote operations, a successful return to *DosWrite* can occur before the data is actually transported over the network. This is a performance enhancement for applications that do not need synchronization with every write operation.
NP_NOWRITEBEHIND	0x0000	A successful return from *DosWrite* indicates that the data is in the named-pipe buffer on the remote computer.

The *omode* argument can specify one of the access-mode bitmasks, one of the inheritance bitmasks, and one of the write-behind bitmasks. The defaults are as follows:

```
NP_ACCESS_INBOUND : NP_INHERIT : NP_NOWRITEBEHIND
```

At minimum, most applications will likely specify NP_ACCESS-_DUPLEX. Note that the client application must open the named pipe with a file mode equivalent to the access mode used in *DosMakeNmPipe*:

Client File Mode	Server Access Mode
OPEN_ACCESS_READONLY	NP_ACCESS_OUTBOUND
OPEN_ACCESS_READWRITE	NP_ACCESS_DUPLEX
OPEN_ACCESS_WRITEONLY	NP_ACCESS_INBOUND

The *pmode* argument is a set of bits that indicates the instance count, the read mode, the type, and a wait flag. Values for *pmode* are as follows:

Bitmask	Value	Meaning
NP_WAIT	0x0000	*DosRead* calls will not return until data is available, and *DosWrite* calls will not return until there is room for the data in the pipe. This is called blocking mode.
NP_NOWAIT	0x8000	*DosRead* and *DosWrite* will return immediately if they cannot complete their operations. This is called nonblocking mode.
NP_READMODE_BYTE	0x0000	The current mode of the pipe is to read bytes.

(continued)

Bitmask	Value	Meaning
NP_READMODE_MESSAGE	0x0100	The current mode of the pipe is to read messages.
NP_TYPE_BYTE	0x0000	The pipe was created as a byte-stream named pipe.
NP_TYPE_MESSAGE	0x0400	The pipe was created as a message-stream named pipe.
NP_UNLIMITED_INSTANCES	0x00FF	An unlimited number of instances of the named pipe can exist.

The *pmode* argument should specify one of the wait options, one of the mode options, one of the type options, and an instance count. If only an instance count (1, for example) is specified, the defaults for the rest of *pmode* are as follows:

```
NP_WAIT | NP_READMODE_BYTE | NP_TYPE_BYTE | 1
```

The instance count can be from 1 through 254 (indicating a specific number of instances) or the special value NP_UNLIMITED_INSTANCES (indicating as many instances as the system can support). An instance count of 0 is a reserved value and should not be used.

The *size1* and *size2* arguments are hints to the operating system about buffering requirements for outgoing and incoming data in the pipe. Consider an application in which the client is doing blocking writes to the pipe (that is, when the NP_WAIT option is set at the client):

Client	**Server**
Write 2K	
	Read 1K, process
	Read 1K, process

If the server's incoming buffer is smaller than 2 KB, the client process must block until the server finishes its processing. Or consider a case in which the incoming buffer is 128 bytes long:

Client	**Server**
Write 2K	
	Read 2K

The server will read the first 128 bytes from the buffer and leave the client blocked, waiting to finish the write. It would take 16 *DosRead* calls for all of the data to be transferred. If this were done in a remote environment (the client and server on different computers), that would take 16 separate trips across the network. If the *size1* and *size2* arguments are big enough for the data passed through the pipe, then either end can write to the named pipe and continue processing while the data is stored safely in the named pipe. The operating system tries to create incoming and outgoing buffers of the sizes you specify, depending on the availability of system memory. In choosing the values for the size arguments, you must consider the expected pattern of reads and writes between the client and server processes and the need for buffering data in between.

The *timeout* argument is used when client processes use the *DosWaitNmPipe* API. This API allows applications to wait for the next available instance of a named pipe, up to a specified timeout period. If *DosWaitNmPipe* does not specify a timeout, it will use the *timeout* value from *DosMakeNmPipe*.

DosQNmPipeInfo

Retrieves information about a named pipe.

```
unsigned far pascal
DosQNmPipeInfo(
    unsigned handle,        /* pipe handle              */
    short level,            /* must be 1                */
    char far * buf,         /* buffer for returned info */
    USHORT buflen           /* length of buf            */
    )
```

Error returns:

If successful, *DosQNmPipeInfo* returns 0. If unsuccessful, it returns one of the following error codes:

Error Return	Meaning
ERROR_INVALID_HANDLE	The handle argument is invalid.
ERROR_BAD_PIPE	The handle is not a named pipe handle.
ERROR_INVALID_LEVEL	The level must be 1.
ERROR_BUFFER_OVERFLOW	The *buf* buffer is too small for all of the data. It will be filled with as much as will fit.

An overview:

The *DosQNmPipeInfo* API returns information about a named pipe. The *handle* argument can be the handle returned from a *DosMakeNmPipe* call for the server side or from a *DosOpen* call for the client side. The information is returned in the *buf* buffer as a _PIPEINFO structure. This structure looks like this:

Member Name	Description
USHORT cbOut	The actual size of the outgoing buffer. This is from the server's point of view and is also the client's incoming buffer.
USHORT cbIn	The actual size of the incoming buffer. This is from the server's point of view and is also the client's outgoing buffer.
BYTE cbMaxInst	The maximum number of instances allowed. If the value is NP_UNLIMITED_INSTANCE, an unlimited number of instances are allowed.
BYTE cbCurInst	The current number of instances.
BYTE cbName	The length of the name, including the terminating zero.
char szName[]	The name of the pipe follows as the next *cbName* bytes. It is zero terminated. In a remote environment, the computer name is included when the client makes this call.

DosConnectNmPipe

Waits for a client to open a named pipe.

```
unsigned far pascal
DosConnectNmPipe(
    unsigned handle            /* pipe handle */
    )
```

Error returns:

If successful, *DosConnectNmPipe* returns 0. If unsuccessful, it returns one of the following error codes:

Error Return	Meaning
ERROR_INVALID_HANDLE	The handle argument is invalid.
ERROR_BAD_PIPE	The handle is not a named-pipe handle.
ERROR_INVALID_FUNCTION	The handle is for the client side of the named pipe.
ERROR_PIPE_NOT_CONNECTED	The pipe is in nonblocking mode, and the client side has not yet performed a *DosOpen*.

(continued)

continued

Error Return	Meaning
ERROR_PIPE_BROKEN	The client end has closed or is closing the pipe. The server end must execute a *DosDisconnectNmPipe* call before *DosConnectNmPipe* can succeed.
ERROR_INTERRUPT	*DosConnectNmPipe* was interrupted while waiting for the client end to execute a *DosOpen*.

An overview:

The *DosConnectNmPipe* API is used by the server side of a named pipe to determine when the client side has connected to the pipe with a *DosOpen* call. The behavior of this call depends on whether the pipe is in blocking mode or nonblocking mode.

■ If the named pipe is in blocking mode, *DosConnectNmPipe* returns only after the client executes a *DosOpen* call. If *DosOpen* has already occurred, the call returns immediately. As soon as *DosConnectNmPipe* returns 0, the server side of the pipe can begin *DosRead* and *DosWrite* operations on the pipe handle.

■ If the named pipe is in nonblocking mode, and if the client has not yet executed a *DosOpen* call, the call returns ERROR_PIPE_NOT_CON-NECTED. Subsequent calls to *DosConnectNmPipe* will continue to fail until the client end has successfully executed *DosOpen*. As soon as *DosConnectNmPipe* returns 0, the server side of the pipe can begin *DosRead* and *DosWrite* operations on the pipe handle.

The *handle* argument is the pipe identifier returned by *DosMakeNmPipe*, either from the original named-pipe creation or from a subsequent instance creation. More than one instance of a named pipe can exist simultaneously with *DosMakeNmPipe*, but none of these instances will know whether a client exists on the other end unless a call to *DosConnectNmPipe* has been made and it has returned 0. For multiple instances, this can be done one at a time; if separate execution threads are used, more than one *DosConnectNmPipe* can run concurrently, each with its own handle of a pipe instance.

DosDisconnectNmPipe

Closes a client's connection to a named pipe.

```
unsigned far pascal
DosDisconnectNmPipe(
    unsigned handle          /* pipe handle */
    )
```

Error returns:

If successful, *DosDisconnectNmPipe* returns 0. If unsuccessful, it returns one of the following error codes:

Error Return	Meaning
ERROR_INVALID_HANDLE	The handle argument is invalid.
ERROR_BAD_PIPE	The handle is not a named-pipe handle.
ERROR_INVALID_FUNCTION	The handle is for the client side of the named pipe.

An overview:

The *DosDisconnectNmPipe* API is used by the server side of a named pipe to force the client side off the pipe. The server side must always execute a *DosDisconnectNmPipe* call before it can use *DosConnectNmPipe* to connect to a new client.

If the client end has already executed a *DosClose* call, the API returns 0 immediately. Otherwise, the client end discards any waiting data, and any subsequent *DosRead* or *DosWrite* operations by the client will fail (returning ERROR_PIPE_NOT_CONNECTED). Note that the client end must still close its side of the disconnected pipe with *DosClose*.

DosQNmpHandState

Retrieves information about the state of a named-pipe handle.

```
unsigned far pascal
DosQNmpHandState(
    unsigned handle,         /* pipe handle        */
    USHORT far * pmode       /* place for pipe mode */
    )
```

Error returns:

If successful, *DosQNmpHandState* returns 0. If unsuccessful, it returns one of the following error codes:

Error Return	Meaning
ERROR_INVALID_HANDLE	The handle argument is invalid.
ERROR_BAD_PIPE	The handle is not a named-pipe handle.
ERROR_INVALID_FUNCTION	The handle is for the client side of the named pipe.

An overview:

The *DosQNmpHandState* API returns information about the current pipe mode.

■ On the server side, the returned *pmode* contains the mode information set by the original *DosMakeNmPipe* or any subsequent *DosSetNmp-HandState* calls.

■ On the client side, the returned *pmode* contains the default modes from the original *DosOpen* call, or the modes as set by any subsequent *DosSetNmpHandState* calls.

To interpret the *pmode* value, you must check for the nondefault values as follows:

Expression	Value	Meaning
(pmode & NP_NOWAIT)	0x8000	TRUE = nonblocking
		FALSE = blocking
(pmode & NP_READMODE_MESSAGE)	0x0100	TRUE = will read in message mode
		FALSE = will read in byte mode
(pmode & NP_TYPE_MESSAGE)	0x0400	TRUE = will write in message mode
		FALSE = will write in byte mode
(pmode & NP_END_SERVER)	0x04000	TRUE = server end of named pipe
		FALSE = client end of named pipe
(pmode & NP_UNLIMITED_INSTANCES)	0xFF	The maximum number of instances

NOTE: *The maximum number of instances can be set from 1 to 254. The special value 255 (0xFF) means there can be an unlimited number of instances.*

DosSetNmpHandState

Sets the mode of a named pipe.

```
unsigned far pascal
DosSetNmpHandState(
    unsigned handle,          /* pipe handle   */
    USHORT pmode              /* new pipe mode */
    )
```

Error returns:

If successful, *DosSetNmpHandState* returns 0. If unsuccessful, it returns one of the following error codes:

Error Return	Meaning
ERROR_INVALID_HANDLE	The handle argument is invalid.
ERROR_BAD_PIPE	The handle is not a named-pipe handle.
ERROR_PIPE_NOT_CONNECTED	The client side has been forced off with a *DosDisconnectNmPipe* call.
ERROR_INVALID_FUNCTION	The *pmode* argument tried to change a pipe-mode parameter other than the blocking state or the read mode, or there was an attempt to put a byte-stream pipe into message-read mode.

An overview:

The *DosSetNmpHandState* API changes some pipe-mode parameters. Only the read mode and the blocking/nonblocking state can be changed. Watch out for the default-mode parameters when using *DosSetNmpHandState*. If, for example, the *pmode* argument were NP_READMODE_MESSAGE, the pipe would be put into the blocking state (NP_WAIT) even if the previous state were nonblocking. To change the read mode without affecting the blocking state, use the following function calls:

```
DosQNmpHandState(hdl, &pmode);
DosSetNmpHandState(hdl, (pmode & NP_NOWAIT) | NP_READMODE_MESSAGE);
```

Use (pmode & NP_READMODE_MESSAGE) to preserve the existing read mode.

When the client side executes a *DosOpen* call on the pipe, the pipe mode is NP_WAIT | NP_READMODE_BYTE. This must be changed using *DosSetNmpHandState* if the nonblocking state or message mode is needed. You can use *DosQNmpHandState* to determine what mode the server side is writing in.

Neither the client side nor the server side can change the read mode to NP_READMODE_MESSAGE if the write mode is NP_TYPE_BYTE. You can, however, change the read mode to NP_TYPE_BYTE if the write mode is NP_READMODE_MESSAGE.) If the read mode is changed to byte mode, partial messages can be read. If the mode is returned to message mode, the next *DosRead* reads the rest of the partial message.

Note that the change to the handle state applies only to the side (server or client) that issued the call.

DosPeekNmPipe

Copies a named pipe's data into a buffer for preview without removing it.

```
unsigned far pascal
DosPeekNmPipe(
    unsigned handle,      /* pipe handle      */
    char far * buffer,    /* buffer for data  */
    USHORT buflen,        /* length of buffer */
    USHORT far * bread,   /* bytes read       */
    USHORT far * bavail,  /* bytes available  */
    USHORT far * status   /* pipe status      */
    )
```

Error returns:

If successful, *DosPeekNmPipe* returns 0. If unsuccessful, it returns one of the following error codes:

Error Return	Meaning
ERROR_INVALID_HANDLE	The handle argument is invalid.
ERROR_BAD_PIPE	The handle is not a named-pipe handle.
ERROR_PIPE_NOT_CONNECTED	The client side has been forced off with a *DosDisconnectNmPipe* call.
ERROR_PIPE_BUSY	Another thread is currently reading or writing the pipe.

An overview:

The *DosPeekNmPipe* API lets you examine the contents of a named pipe without taking anything out of it. It provides a snapshot of what data is actually in the pipe's read buffer when the call is made. The results of *DosPeekNmPipe* are similar to those of a *DosRead* operation on the pipe, with these differences:

- The data is left in the pipe. As much data as will fit is copied into the *buf* buffer. The *bread* parameter returns with the number of bytes written into *buf*.

- If the pipe is in message mode, a partial message can be returned. This is similar to the behavior of *DosRead* in nonblocking mode, except that the return code is 0 for *DosPeekNmPipe* and ERROR-_MORE_DATA for *DosRead*.

- *DosPeekNmPipe* will never block, regardless of the blocking mode.

- The *bavail* and *status* arguments return additional information not available with *DosRead*.

The *bavail* argument is a pointer to an _AVAILDATA structure, which looks like this:

Member Name	Description
USHORT cbpipe	The number of bytes left in the named pipe
USHORT cbmessage	The number of bytes left in the current message

DosPeekNmPipe fills *cbpipe* with the number of bytes in the pipe, including message headers (two bytes per message) if the pipe is in message mode. Note that the bytes actually read by *DosPeekNmPipe* or *DosRead* never include the message header. *DosPeekNmPipe* fills *cbmessage* with the number of bytes available in the current message. This value will be 0 if the pipe is in byte mode.

As an example, if the pipe were in message mode, and the client had previously written two messages of lengths 20 and 30 bytes into the pipe, *DosPeekNmPipe* would return with *cbpipe* set to 54 (20 + 30 + 2 2-byte message headers) and *cbmessage* set to 20 (the size of the first message).

The *status* argument is a pointer to a USHORT that *DosPeekNmPipe* fills in with the current state of the pipe. The values are as follows:

State	Value	Meaning
NP_DISCONNECTED	1	The pipe has been created or disconnected but is not yet connected with *DosConnectNmPipe*.
NP_LISTENING	2	A *DosConnectNmPipe* call has been made, but the client end has not yet executed a *DosOpen*.
NP_CONNECTED	3	The client end has executed a *DosOpen*.
NP_CLOSING	4	Either the client has executed a *DosClose* and the server has not yet executed a *DosDisconnectNm-Pipe*, or the server has executed a *DosClose* and the client has not yet executed a *DosClose*.

DosTransactNmPipe

Performs read and write transactions on a named pipe in one step.

```
unsigned far pascal
DosTransactNmPipe(
    unsigned handle,        /* pipe handle           */
    char far * inbuf,       /* buffer for in data    */
    USHORT inlen,           /* length of in buffer   */
    char far * outbuf,      /* buffer for out data   */
    USHORT outlen,          /* length of out buffer  */
    USHORT far * bread      /* bytes read            */
    )
```

Error returns:

If successful, *DosTransactNmPipe* returns 0. If unsuccessful, it returns one of the following error codes:

Error Return	Meaning
ERROR_INVALID_HANDLE	The handle argument is invalid.
ERROR_BAD_PIPE	The handle is not a named-pipe handle.
ERROR_PIPE_NOT_CONNECTED	The client side has been forced off with a *DosDisconnectNmPipe* call.
ERROR_BAD_FORMAT	The named pipe was not created as a message-mode pipe.
ERROR_ACCESS_DENIED	The named pipe was not created with an open mode of OPEN_ACCESS_DUPLEX. *DosTransactNmPipe* cannot be used on unidirectional named pipes.
ERROR_BROKEN_PIPE	The server side of the pipe no longer exists.
ERROR_INVALID_PARAMETER	The pipe contains unread data.
ERROR_MORE_DATA	The *outlen* argument was smaller than the size of the message.

An overview:

The *DosTransactNmPipe* API is a performance enhancement for transaction-oriented dialogs. A common use of a named pipe is for the client to use *DosWrite* to send a request and to then immediately use *DosRead* to read the reply. The server end will have a *DosRead* pending for the request, which will be processed, and the reply will be sent back to the client with a *DosWrite*. This transaction is shown in Figure 10-4.

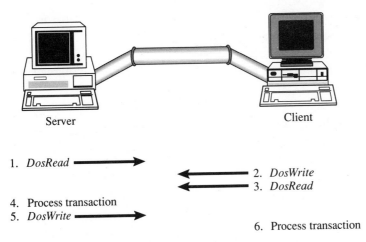

1. *DosRead* ⟶

⟵ 2. *DosWrite*
⟵ 3. *DosRead*

4. Process transaction
5. *DosWrite* ⟶

6. Process transaction

Figure 10-4.
Pipe communication with DosRead *and* DosWrite.

If the client and server ends of the pipe are distributed across a network, this dialog involves two round-trips over the network, one each for the client *DosRead* and *DosWrite*. *DosTransactNmPipe* simplifies this into a single network operation. The server doesn't change. Only the client end uses the *DosTransactNmPipe* call (Figure 10-5).

DosTransactNmPipe requires that the pipe be a message-mode pipe. (Any other type of pipe results in an ERROR_BAD_FORMAT return.) If any unread data exists at either end of the pipe, ERROR_INVALID_PARAMETER is returned. The blocking mode has no effect on this call, which always blocks until the round-trip operation is complete.

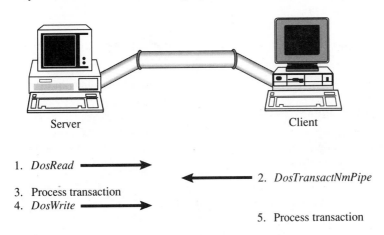

1. *DosRead* ⟶

⟵ 2. *DosTransactNmPipe*

3. Process transaction
4. *DosWrite* ⟶

5. Process transaction

Figure 10-5.
Pipe communication with DosTransactNmPipe.

DosTransactNmPipe writes a message from the *inbuf* buffer to the named pipe and reads a reply message into the *outbuf* buffer. If *outlen* is less than the message size, a partial message will be read, *bread* will be set to the actual number of bytes read, and ERROR_MORE_DATA will be returned.

DosCallNmPipe

A single call combining *DosOpen*, *DosSetNmpHandState*, *DosTransactNmPipe*, and *DosClose* operations.

```
unsigned far pascal
DosCallNmPipe(
    char far * name,        /* pipe name          */
    char far * inbuf,       /* buffer for in data */
    USHORT inlen,           /* length of in buffer */
    char far * outbuf,      /* buffer for out data */
    USHORT outlen,          /* length of out buffer */
    USHORT far * bread,     /* bytes read         */
    long timeout            /* specifier timeout  */
    )
```

Error returns:

If successful, *DosCallNmPipe* returns 0. If unsuccessful, it returns one of the following error codes:

Error Return	Meaning
ERROR_FILE_NOT_FOUND	The named pipe does not exist.
ERROR_PIPE_NOT_CONNECTED	The client side has been forced off with a *DosDisconnectNmPipe* call.
ERROR_BAD_FORMAT	The named pipe was not created as a message-mode pipe.
ERROR_ACCESS_DENIED	The named pipe was not created with an open mode of OPEN_ACCESS_DUPLEX. *DosTransactNmPipe* cannot be used on unidirectional named pipes.
ERROR_BROKEN_PIPE	The server side of the pipe no longer exists.
ERROR_MORE_DATA	The *outlen* argument was smaller than the size of the message.
ERROR_SEM_TIMEOUT	There was no available instance of the named pipe to open within *timeout* milliseconds.

(continued)

continued

Error Return	Meaning
ERROR_INTERRUPT	An interrupt occurred in the middle of a wait for a pipe instance.
ERROR_NETWORK_ACCESS_DENIED	In a network environment, the user did not have access permission to use the named pipe.

An overview:

The *DosCallNmPipe* API is a performance enhancement for applications that use single transactions. *DosCallNmPipe* is equivalent to the client side of an application calling *DosOpen*, *DosSetNmpHandState* (with message mode), *DosTransactNmPipe*, and *DosClose*.

The arguments are the same as for *DosTransactNmPipe*, with the addition of a pipe name and a timeout. If the implied *DosOpen* of the *name* argument fails because no instances of the named pipe are available, *DosCallNmPipe* waits for the number of milliseconds specified by *timeout* for an instance to become available and opens it. This is the same logic used by *DosWaitNmPipe*.

The server side must create the named pipe as a message-mode duplex pipe.

DosWaitNmPipe

Waits for a named pipe to become available.

```
unsigned far pascal
DosWaitNmPipe(
    char far * name,          /* pipe name        */
    long timeout              /* maximum wait time */
    )
```

Error returns:

If successful, *DosWaitNmPipe* returns 0. If unsuccessful, it returns one of the following error codes:

Error Return	Meaning
ERROR_FILE_NOT_FOUND	The named pipe does not exist.
ERROR_SEM_TIMEOUT	There was no available instance of the named pipe to open within *timeout* milliseconds.
ERROR_INTERRUPT	An interrupt occurred in the middle of a wait for a pipe instance.

An overview:

The *DosWaitNmPipe* API blocks until an available instance of a named pipe exists. The *timeout* argument specifies the number of milliseconds to wait for an instance of the pipe, and *name* specifies the name of the pipe. If *timeout* is 0, then the default value specified in the *timeout* argument of *DosMakeNmPipe* is used.

DosWaitNmPipe attempts to do "fair scheduling"—that is, it tries to respond to *DosWaitNmPipe* calls in the order in which clients made them. However, this order is not guaranteed.

DosWaitNmPipe should be called by a client application when *DosOpen* returns ERROR_PIPE_BUSY. There is a possible race condition between the time that *DosWaitNmPipe* returns and the time that a new *DosOpen* call can be made. The following code fragment shows how to use *DosWaitNmPipe* in a program:

```
err = DosOpen(pipename, .....
while (err == ERROR_PIPE_BUSY)
    {
    err = DosWaitNmPipe(pipename, timeout);
    if (err != 0)
        break; /* insert code to process error */
    err = DosOpen(pipename, .....
    }
```

Each time *DosOpen* returns ERROR_PIPE_BUSY, this code waits for an instance to be available and tries to open it.

DosSetNmPipeSem

Associates a semaphore with a named pipe.

```
unsigned far pascal
DosSetNmPipeSem(
    unsigned handle,            /* pipe handle      */
    long semhandle,             /* semaphore handle */
    USHORT key                  /* instance key     */
    )
```

Error returns:

If successful, *DosSetNmPipeSem* returns 0. If unsuccessful, it returns one of the following error codes:

Error Return	Meaning
ERROR_INVALID_HANDLE	The handle argument is invalid.
ERROR_BAD_PIPE	The handle is not a named-pipe handle.
ERROR_PIPE_NOT_CONNECTED	The client side has been forced off with a *DosDisconnectNmPipe* call. This will be returned only by the client side.
ERROR_INVALID_FUNCTION	The handle is for a remote named pipe.
ERROR_SEM_NOT_FOUND	The *semhandle* argument is not a valid semaphore handle.

An overview:

The *DosSetNmPipeSem* API allows an application to associate a semaphore with an instance of a named pipe. The system clears the semaphore whenever new read data is available, whenever buffer space is available for a write, or whenever the pipe has been closed by either side. Both the server side and the client side of the pipe can execute a *DosSetNmPipeSem*; they will be notified of these events separately.

The *DosSetNmPipeSem* API works only for local named pipes. If the client side attempts the call for the handle of a remote pipe, ERROR_INVALID-_FUNCTION is returned.

If a second call to *DosSetNmPipeSem* is made by the same side of the pipe, the previous semaphore is overridden, and the new semaphore is cleared when notification is made.

The *semhandle* argument is an OS/2 semaphore handle created using *DosCreateSem*. An application can wait for this event notification by calling *DosSemWait*, *DosMuxSemWait*, or *DosSemRequest*. Note that the application must first execute a *DosSetSem* to set the semaphore before waiting for the semaphore to be cleared. The semaphore should be created as a shared semaphore (CSEM_PUBLIC) so that it can be cleared by someone other than its creator.

Because a semaphore can be associated with more than one pipe handle, a *key* argument is provided to distinguish among pipe handles. This number should be unique for each pipe handle associated with a semaphore.

DosSetNmPipeSem is intended for applications that want one process thread to serve many named pipes or named-pipe instances. An application can call *DosSemWait* or *DosMuxSemWait* to know when one of its pipes needs servicing. Without this API, the application would have to either dedicate a thread per named-pipe handle and do blocking I/O or continually poll the named pipes with nonblocking I/O. *DosSetNmPipeSem* allows applications to have a small number of threads service a large number of pipes in an event-driven way.

When the application responds to the cleared semaphore, it can use the *Dos-QNmPipeSemState* API to obtain more information about what has just occurred. Chapter 12 demonstrates this strategy in a pipe server application.

DosQNmPipeSemState

Returns information about named pipes associated with semaphores that are in blocking mode.

Off to the races

When a pipe server application uses semaphores for event-driven pipe service, there are race conditions to watch out for (Figure 10-6).

The client-side *DosOpen* and *DosWrite* can succeed as soon as the server finishes *DosConnectNmPipe*. This might occur at any time before the server has finished setting up the semaphore, associating it with the pipe handle, and waiting for the clear. The server side would miss the event and continue to wait on the semaphore, despite the presence of data in the pipe. A better sequence is shown in Figure 10-7.

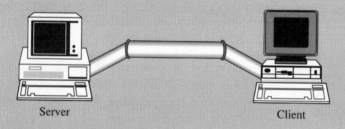

Server	Client

1. *DosMakeNmPipe* (nonblocking)
2. *DosConnectNmPipe*

                           * *DosOpen*
                           * *DosWrite*

3. *DosCreateSem*
4. *DosSemSet*
5. *DosSetNmPipeSem*
6. *DosSemWait*
7. *DosQNmPipeSemState*
8. if (state is NPSS_RDATA)
    DosRead

Figure 10-6.
Using semaphores with named pipes can produce race conditions.

```
unsigned far pascal
DosQNmPipeSemState(
    long semhandle,          /* semaphore handle          */
    char far * infobuf,      /* the _PIPESEMSTATE structure */
    USHORT infobuflen        /* infobuf length            */
    )
```

Error returns:

If successful, *DosQNmPipeSemState* returns 0. If unsuccessful, it returns one of the error codes shown on the following page.

This still leaves a small race condition. The client's *DosOpen* and *DosWrite* can succeed between the time of the server's *DosConnectNmPipe* and *DosSemWait*. It is a smaller hole than in the previous example, but a hole nonetheless.

There is no way to prevent this race condition with a single-threaded application. It is important to understand that such race conditions can occur and to make sure that the server side of the application has a chance to completely initialize before the client side can run.

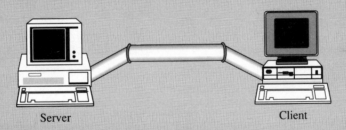

       Server   Client

1. *DosMakeNmPipe* (nonblocking)
2. *DosCreateSem*
3. *DosSemSet*
4. *DosSetNmPipeSem*
5. *DosConnectNmPipe*
                                          * *DosOpen*
                                          * *DosWrite*

6. *DosSemWait*
7. *DosQNmPipeSemState*
8. if (state is NPSS_RDATA)
       DosRead

Figure 10-7.
Reducing the chance of race conditions by delaying DosConnectNmPipe.

Error Return	Meaning
ERROR_INVALID_PARAMETER	The buffer length is invalid.
ERROR_SEM_NOT_FOUND	The *semhandle* argument is not a valid semaphore handle.
ERROR_BUFFER_OVERFLOW	The *infobuflen* value was smaller than the size of all the records to be returned.

An overview:

The *DosQNmPipeSemState* API provides information about the event that triggered the clearing of the semaphore associated with a pipe handle in *DosSetNmPipeSem*.

The *infobuf* buffer contains an array of _PIPESEMSTATE structures, with information about every pipe handle associated with the semaphore handle. More than one _PIPESEMSTATE structure per handle may exist.

The _PIPESEMSTATE structure looks like this:

Member Name	Description		
BYTE fStatus	The status of the named pipe. This can be any of the following:		
	Record Type	*Value*	*Meaning*
	NPSS_EOI	0	This is the last _PIPESEMSTATE structure in the *infobuf* buffer.
	NPSS_RDATA	1	There is data in the pipe that can be read.
	NPSS_WSPACE	2	There is room in the pipe buffer for writing.
	NPSS_CLOSE	3	The pipe is being closed.
BYTE fFlag	A set of flag bits. The only bitmask defined is NPSS_WAIT, which indicates whether a thread is waiting on the other end of the pipe. For an NPSS_WSPACE record, the client end is blocking on a *DosRead* operation or its equivalent in a *DosTransactNmPipe* or *DosCallNmPipe* call. For an NPSS_RDATA record, the client end is blocking on a *DosWrite* operation or its equivalent.		
USHORT usKey	This will match one of the keys supplied with the *DosSetNmPipeSem* call. Note that if the keys are not unique, the information is ambiguous.		
USHORT usAvail	For an NPSS_RDATA record, this is the number of bytes to a nonblocking *DosRead* call. For the NPSS_WSPACE record, this is the number of bytes that could be written to the pipe with nonblocking I/O.		

Because *DosSetNmPipeSem* can associate multiple pipes with one semaphore, you must be sure to create unique key values. In particular, a system semaphore might be used by more than one instance of the same process, so key values should take this into account. If this is likely to occur, the key values should probably be derived from the process identification number (PID).

An example in Chapter 13 shows how to use *DosSetNmPipeSem* and *Dos-QNmPipeSemState* to write applications in which many pipes are serviced by one thread (without having to poll the pipes).

DosReadAsynchNmPipe

Performs an asynchronous read of a named pipe (DOS only).

```
unsigned far pascal
DosReadAsynchNmPipe(
     unsigned handle,              /* pipe handle          */
     unsigned far pascal pfn(),    /* function to call     */
     USHORT far * perr,            /* returned error code  */
     char far *buf,                /* buffer for data      */
     USHORT buflen,                /* size of buf          */
     USHORT far * bread            /* number of bytes read */
     )
```

Error returns:

DosReadAsynchNmPipe returns immediately. If the asynchronous read is under way, the return value is 0. Otherwise, the return value is one of the following error codes:

Error Return	Meaning
ERROR_ACCESS_DENIED	Permission violation at the server.
ERROR_BROKEN_PIPE	The server end of the pipe is not in the CONNECTED state.
ERROR_BAD_PIPE	The named pipe encountered an internal error.
ERROR_INVALID_HANDLE	The handle does not correspond to an open named pipe.
ERROR_NO_PROC_SLOTS	The system ran out of resources. There are probably too many asynchronous reads pending.
ERROR_NETWORK_BUSY	The system failed in accessing the network.

An overview:

The *DosReadAsynchNmPipe* API allows applications to do asynchronous reads of a named pipe and to have the system indicate when the transfer is complete. It is available only in LAN Manager for DOS.

The *handle* argument is a named-pipe handle returned by a previous call to *DosOpen*.

The *pfn* argument is the name of the function the system calls when data transfer is complete. This function is called at interrupt level, so it cannot call any system routines.

After the function is called, *perr* contains an error code, and *bread* indicates the actual number of bytes read, which will be less than or equal to the size of the *buflen* buffer. *bread* can be 0 if the server end has closed or disconnected the pipe. *perr* is 0 if the read was successful; if the read was unsuccessful, *perr* contains any of the file-system error codes.

Using File-System APIs with Named Pipes

Although this chapter has dealt exclusively with named-pipe APIs, many OS/2 file-system APIs also work with named pipes. This section describes such file-system APIs and their interaction with named pipes. For detailed information on the specific OS/2 API arguments and return codes, consult the *Microsoft OS/2 Programmer's Reference*.

DosOpen   The client end can open a pipe by name, which can be a UNC name referencing a remote pipe. If no instance of the pipe is in LISTEN state (the state caused by a server-side *DosConnectNmPipe* call), the *DosOpen* fails with ERROR_PIPE_BUSY. A one-to-one correspondence always exists between a pipe instance and a successful *DosOpen*; that is, two processes can never simultaneously be clients on the same pipe instance. Named pipes are always opened with pipe mode (NP_WAIT ¦ NP_READ-MODE_BYTE). The client application must use *DosSetNmpHandState* to change this.

DosOpen can be used to open a pipe across the network. The name will always be of the following form:

servername\PIPE*pipename*

The open can fail under the following conditions:

- The server is running user-mode security, and the user is denied access to the pipe.

- The server is running share-mode security, and the user is unable to connect to the IPC$ share.

DosClose   Closes one end of the named-pipe instance. When a client end closes, the server end can execute *DosDisconnectNmPipe* and wait for the next client with a *DosConnectNmPipe*. When the server executes a *DosClose*, the instance of the named pipe is deleted when the client end has also closed the pipe. The pipe instance can be re-created with *DosMakeNmPipe*. When all instances of a named pipe are deleted, the pipe no longer exists.

DosQHandType   The handle type is HANDTYPE_PIPE. If the pipe is remote, the HANDTYPE_NETWORK bit will be set.

DosQFHandState For the server side, the handle state is set by the *omode* argument of *DosMakeNmPipe* or by subsequent calls to *DosFHandState*. For the client side, the handle state is set by *DosOpen* or subsequent calls to *DosSetFHandState*.

DosSetFHandState The inheritance bits and write-through bits can be changed. If the write-through bit is changed to NP_NOWRITEBEHIND, remote named-pipe writes remain incomplete until the data is completely across the network.

DosWrite In blocking mode, the call returns only when all data has been written. If the pipe buffer can't hold all of the data, *DosWrite* remains blocked until the other end reads data and makes room in the buffer. Note that a blocking *DosWrite* larger than the pipe buffer size might need more than one *DosRead* at the other end if the *DosRead* is nonblocking or if the size of the *DosRead* is less than the size of the *DosWrite*.

In nonblocking mode, *DosWrite* writes only as many bytes as will fit—up to a maximum of the pipe buffer size. The *DosWrite* byte count indicates the number of bytes actually written.

In message mode, *DosWrite* writes a message whose size is the length of the write. The size information is automatically encoded by the named pipe, so applications needn't provide lengths as part of the messages. Message-mode writes always write the entire message; even if the write is nonblocking, it blocks if the pipe buffer can't hold the entire message.

If the other end of the pipe is closed, ERROR_PIPE_BROKEN is returned.

DosWriteAsync See *DosWrite*.

DosRead The read mode is not necessarily the same as the pipe type (the write mode). The pipe can be one of three types:

- If the pipe is a byte-mode pipe (NP_TYPE_BYTE), the read mode must be NP_READMODE_BYTE.

- If the pipe is a message-mode pipe (NP_TYPE_MESSAGE), the read mode is NP_READMODE_MESSAGE, and *DosRead* tries to read an entire message up to the size of the read buffer. If the *DosRead* call requests more bytes than are in the message, only the message is read, and the "bytes read" argument is set appropriately. If the *DosRead* request is for fewer bytes than the size of the message, they are read and ERROR_MORE_DATA is returned. Subsequent *DosRead* calls continue to read the same message but do not cross over into the next message.

- If the pipe is a message-mode pipe, the read mode is NP_READ-MODE_BYTE, and the *DosRead* operation will ignore the message and read the requested number of bytes.

In blocking mode, *DosRead* will wait until some data is available in the pipe—that is, it will not return with zero bytes read except at EOF.

In nonblocking mode, a *DosRead* of a byte-mode pipe returns immediately with the number of bytes of data currently in the pipe buffer. This can range from zero to the size of the pipe buffer. The *DosRead* byte-count argument indicates how many bytes were actually read. If no data is in the pipe, a nonblocking *DosRead* call returns immediately with ERROR_NO_DATA. In message mode, a nonblocking *DosRead* call blocks if it can't read an entire message from the buffer. This can occur when the entire message has not yet been written or when the message is larger than the available buffer space. If the pipe contains no messages, the nonblocking *DosRead* call returns ERROR_NO_DATA.

DosReadAsync   See *DosRead*.

DosBufReset   If data is written to a pipe, then *DosBufReset* blocks until the other side has read all of the data. This is a way of synchronizing two processes.

Working with Handles

Instead of requiring a round-trip through the network for each byte read or written, LAN Manager buffers information and decreases the number of network accesses. The strategy for this buffering is set using two parameters from the [wksta] component of the LANMAN.INI file. The *charcount* and *charwait* parameters indicate that network data for pipes and character devices should be buffered until either *charcount* characters exist in the buffer or until *charwait* milliseconds have passed, whichever happens first. These values can be inspected and changed by using *NetWkstaGetInfo* or *NetWkstaSetInfo* with the *wki0_chartime* and *wki0_charcount* members of the *wksta_info_0* structure.

The *NetHandleGetInfo* and *NetHandleSetInfo* APIs allow applications to set the buffering strategy on a handle-by-handle basis. The default is to use the parameters from the *wksta_info_0* structure.

To use these APIs, you must include NETCONS.H and CHARDEV.H at compile time, and you must link with NETAPI.LIB. Two data structures are defined. The *handle_info_1* structure contains the following elements:

Member Name	Meaning
ULONG hdli1_chartime	The maximum time (in milliseconds) that can pass before a remote character device or remote named pipe transfers information over the network.
USHORT hdli1_charcount	The maximum number of characters that can be accumulated before a remote character device or remote named pipe transfers information over the network.

The *handle_info_2* structure contains this member:

Member Name	Meaning
char far * hdli2_username	The username of the client side of a named pipe

Note that the level 1 structure provides information for the client side to inspect or change, but the level 2 structure is available for inspection by the server side only.

NetHandleGetInfo

Returns information about network handles.

```
unsigned far pascal
NetHandleGetInfo(
    USHORT handle,       /* char dev or pipe handle  */
    short level,         /* level of information     */
    char far * buf,      /* buffer for returned data */
    USHORT buflen,       /* size of buf              */
    USHORT far * tavail  /* total bytes available    */
    )
```

Levels:
Supports level 1 and 2 data structures.

Remote access:
This API cannot be called remotely.

Error returns:
If successful, *NetHandleGetInfo* returns 0. If unsuccessful, it returns a standard GetInfo return code or the following error code:

Error Return	Meaning
ERROR_INVALID_PARAMETER	At level 1, the handle is not for a remote named pipe or character device. At level 2, the handle is not the serving side of a remote named pipe.

An overview:

The *NetHandleGetInfo* API returns information about file-system handles that are connected across the network.

If the *level* argument is 1, the *buf* buffer returns a *handle_info_1* structure. The *handle* argument is the file-system handle returned by a successful *DosOpen* call for a remote named pipe or remote character device. The caller must therefore be the client side of the connection.

If the *level* argument is 2, the *buf* buffer returns a *handle_info_2* structure. The *handle* argument must be the handle returned by a successful *DosMakeNmPipe* call. The caller must therefore be the serving side of a named pipe. If the client side of the named pipe is a local process, *NetHandleGetInfo* fails and returns ERROR_INVALID_PARAMETER.

> **NOTE:** *In MS-DOS, only level 1 is supported and only for named-pipe handles.*

NetHandleSetInfo

Sets information about network handles.

```
unsigned far pascal
NetHandleSetInfo(
    USHORT handle,      /* char dev or pipe handle  */
    short level,        /* must be 1                */
    char far * buf,     /* buffer for returned data */
    USHORT buflen,      /* size of buf              */
    USHORT parmnum      /* parameter number         */
    )
```

Levels:

Supports level 1 data structures.

Remote access:

This API cannot be called remotely.

Error returns:

If successful, *NetHandleSetInfo* returns 0. If unsuccessful, it returns a standard GetInfo return code or the following error code:

Error Return	*Meaning*
ERROR_INVALID_PARAMETER	The handle is not for a remote named pipe or character device.

An overview:

The *NetHandleSetInfo* API allows programs to change the *hdlil_chartime* or *hdlil_charcount* values for remote named pipes or character devices.

If the *parmnum* argument is 0, the *buf* buffer must contain a *handle_info_1* structure. The data items which can be set and their corresponding *parmnum* values are as follows:

Name	Value	parmnum
hdli1_chartime	1	HANDLE_SET_CHARTIME
hdli1_charcount	1	HANDLE_SET_CHARCOUNT

NOTE: *In MS-DOS, the call is supported only for named-pipe handles.*

Mailslots

Mailslots are a one-way interprocess communication. The server side of the communication creates a mailslot for receiving messages. The client side of the communication writes messages to the mailslot. Data is sent and received one message at a time, with no provision for breaking messages into bytes (as can be done with a byte-mode named pipe). The server side can read messages from the mailslot, or it can block, waiting for a message to arrive.

The creation of a mailslot is always a local call. The mailslot name is of the following form:

`\MAILSLOT\mailname`

mailname can be any set of valid characters for the file system, including the backslash. The backslash character can be used to create the appearance of directories so that different applications are not at risk of using the same mailslot names. For example, the ''Generic LAN Corporation'' might have an application that uses a mailslot for requests. The mailslot might be named

`\MAILSLOT\GLC\REQUEST`

so that it won't interfere with any other application's ''REQUEST'' mailslot. Mailslot names are always case insensitive.

Writing to a mailslot can be a remote operation. If the mailslot name is given a computer name, as in

```
\\WHOZIT\MAILSLOT\GLC\REQUEST
```

the write will go to the mailslot on the "WHOZIT" computer.

Each message is given a priority when it is sent. The receiving mailslot tries to sort all messages based on priority, with 0 being the lowest priority. Messages of the same priority are kept in the order in which they were received. The priority is only a guideline for ordering the messages in the mailslot, so this ordering is not guaranteed.

Mailslots Have Class

Messages sent to a mailslot must be associated with a mailslot class:

- First-class mail is guaranteed delivery. When the write operation is complete, the error code indicates that the data is safely in the mailslot or that it failed.

- Second-class mail indicates only that the data was sent; delivery is not guaranteed. If the mailslot has no room for the message, the second-class mailslot fails silently.

These classes have particular impact on delivery to remote mailslots in that they require you to make a trade-off between efficiency and reliability. A first-class mailslot write sends the message to the server machine and waits for a confirmation reply. A second-class mailslot write returns as soon as the message is off onto the network. Second-class mailslots are much like datagrams and, in fact, are usually implemented as such. Given a reliable network, second-class mailslot messages will reach their destination; their arrival just won't be confirmed.

For first-class mailslot communication, the mailslot must exist on a LAN Manager server. Second-class mailslots, however, can be used for communication between LAN Manager workstations.

Why use second-class mailslots? Their most important use is for workstation-to-workstation communication. Second-class mailslot writes can also be broadcast messages. If the intended recipient name is of the form

```
\\*\MAILSLOT\mailname
```

a copy of the message goes to all workstations in the langroup (domain) that have created a mailslot by that name. The example at the end of this section shows a workstation application that uses second-class mailslots and broadcast messages.

The Mailslot APIs

To use the Mailslot APIs, you must include NETCONS.H and MAIL-SLOT.H at compile time, and you must link with the MAILSLOT.LIB stub library at link time.

> **NOTE:** *Although the names of most LAN Manager APIs begin with* Net, *the Mailslot APIs are intended to become part of the OS/2 kernel API someday, so they begin with* Dos.

DosMakeMailslot

Creates a mailslot.

```
unsigned far pascal
DosMakeMailslot(
    char far *name,          /* the message-slot name */
    USHORT msgsize,          /* maximum message size  */
    USHORT mslotsize,        /* estimated mslot size  */
    unsigned far * handle    /* returned mslot handle */
    )
```

Error returns:
If successful, *DosMakeMailslot* returns 0. If unsuccessful, it returns one of the following error codes:

Error Return	Meaning
ERROR_PATH_NOT_FOUND	The mailslot name is invalid. Be sure that it begins with \MAILSLOT\ and contains only valid file-system characters.
ERROR_ALREADY_EXITS	A mailslot with this name already exists.
ERROR_INVALID_PARAMETER	Either *msgsize* or *mslotsize* has an illegal value.

An overview:
The *DosMakeMailslot* API creates a mailslot on the local computer. The mailslot exists until it is deleted with *DosDeleteMailslot* or until the creating process exits. Only the creator of the mailslot can read messages sent to it (by using *DosReadMailslot*).

The *name* argument must begin with \MAILSLOT\ and must be unique on the local computer.

The *msgsize* argument is the largest message the mailslot will accept. In LAN Manager 2.0, the maximum for this is 65,475 bytes.

The *mslotsize* argument is a hint to the system about how large to make the mailslot. It must be at least as large as the *msgsize* argument. If *mslotsize* is 0, the system will use a default system value. *mslotsize* is an advisory to the system of how many messages it wants to be able to store in the mailslot at once. Sometimes the server side of an application can't keep up with the arrival rate of messages in the mailslot, so it might need room to save some of them in the mailslot while it catches up.

The *handle* value is a returned value—much like a file-system handle—that the server side uses for subsequent mailslot operations. Although these handles are not inherited by child processes, multiple threads in one process can all use the same handle.

DosDeleteMailslot

Deletes a mailslot.

```
unsigned far pascal
DosDeleteMailslot(
    unsigned handle        /* handle of mslot to delete */
    )
```

Error returns:
If successful, *DosDeleteMailslot* returns 0. If unsuccessful, it returns the following error code:

Error Return	Meaning
ERROR_INVALID_HANDLE	The handle does not correspond to a mailslot created by this process.

An overview:
The *DosDeleteMailslot* API deletes a mailslot and discards any data it contains. Only the process that created the mailslot can delete it.

DosMailslotInfo

Returns information about a mailslot.

```
unsigned far pascal
DosMailslotInfo(
    unsigned handle,            /* mslot handle          */
    USHORT far * msgsize,       /* max msg size          */
    USHORT far * mslotsize,     /* mslot size            */
    USHORT far * nextsize,      /* next msg size         */
    USHORT far * nextpriority,  /* next msg priority     */
    USHORT far * msgcount       /* num of msgs waiting   */
    )
```

Error returns:

If successful, *DosMailslotInfo* returns 0. If unsuccessful, it returns the following error code:

Error Return	Meaning
ERROR_INVALID_HANDLE	The handle does not correspond to a mailslot created by this process.

An overview:

The *DosMailslotInfo* API returns information about the current state of the mailslot. It can be used only by the process that created the mailslot.

The *handle* value is a mailslot handle returned by a *DosMakeMailslot* call. The *mslotsize* value is the actual size of the mailslot. The *nextsize* value is the size of the next message in the mailslot, or 0 if no messages exist. The *nextpriority* value is the priority of the next message in the mailslot. The *msgcount* value is the total number of messages waiting in the mailslot.

DosReadMailslot

Reads a message in a mailslot.

```
unsigned far pascal
DosReadMailslot(
    unsigned handle,            /* mslot handle      */
    char far * buf,             /* buffer for data   */
    USHORT far * bread,         /* actual msg size   */
    USHORT far * nextsize,      /* next msg size     */
    USHORT far * nextpriority,  /* next msg priority */
    long timeout                /* maximum wait time */
    )
```

Error returns:

If successful, *DosReadMailslot* returns 0. If unsuccessful, it returns one of the following error codes:

Error Return	Meaning
ERROR_INVALID_HANDLE	The handle does not correspond to a mailslot created by this process.
ERROR_BROKEN_PIPE	The mailslot was deleted by another thread while waiting for a message to arrive.
ERROR_SEM_TIMEOUT	No message arrived within the number of milliseconds specified by *timeout*.

(continued)

continued

Error Return	Meaning
ERROR_INTERRUPT	The wait for a message to arrive was interrupted and did not last the number of milliseconds specified by *timeout*.

An overview:

The *DosReadMailslot* API is used by the creating process to read messages out of the mailslot represented by the *handle* argument. Data is transferred into the *buf* buffer, which must be large enough to hold the data. If the buffer size is not already known, it must be at least as large as the largest possible message, as specified by the *msgsize* argument to the *DosMakeMailslot* call. The *bread* argument returns with the actual message size.

Information is also returned about the next message waiting in the mailslot. The *nextsize* value returns its size, or 0 if no message exists. If a message is waiting, *nextpriority* returns its priority. (The value is undefined if no message is waiting.) Note that the next call to *DosReadMailslot* will not read this message if a higher-priority message arrives and is placed at the front of the mailslot.

If no message exists for *DosReadMailslot* to return, it blocks for the number of milliseconds specified by *timeout*, waiting for a message to arrive. A *timeout* value of 0 is a nonblocking call that returns immediately if no message is available. If no message is read because the mailslot timed out (or if *timeout* is 0), ERR_SEM_TIMEOUT is returned. If *timeout* is set to the special value −1, *DosReadMailSlot* waits until a message arrives.

DosPeekMailslot

Reads a message in a mailslot without removing it.

```
unsigned far pascal
DosPeekMailslot(
    unsigned handle,            /* mslot handle     */
    char far * buf,             /* buffer for data  */
    USHORT far * bread,         /* actual msg size  */
    USHORT far * nextsize,      /* next msg size    */
    USHORT far * nextpriority,  /* next msg priority */
    )
```

Error returns:

If successful, *DosPeekMailslot* returns 0. If unsuccessful, it returns one of the following error codes:

Error Return	Meaning
ERROR_INVALID_HANDLE	The handle does not correspond to a mailslot created by this process.
ERROR_BROKEN_PIPE	The mailslot was deleted by another thread while processing the peek.

An overview:

The *DosPeekMailslot* API reads a message from the mailslot indicated by *handle*, but it does not remove the data (as a *DosReadMailslot* call would). *DosPeekMailslot* will not wait if no message is in the mailslot.

The data is copied into the *buf* buffer, which must be large enough to hold the data. Making it at least as large as the mailslot maximum message size is safe. The *bread* value indicates the actual size of the message.

The *nextsize* and *nextpriority* values indicate the size and priority of the next message, if it exists. *nextsize* is 0 if no next message exists.

Subsequent calls to *DosReadMailslot* won't read the same data returned by *DosPeekMailslot* if a higher-priority message arrives.

DosWriteMailslot

Writes a message to a mailslot.

```
unsigned far pascal
DosWriteMailslot(
    char far * name,        /* mailslot name      */
    char far * message,     /* pointer to message */
    USHORT size,            /* msg size           */
    USHORT priority,        /* msg priority       */
    USHORT class,           /* 1 or 2 class msg   */
    long timeout            /* max wait for room  */
    )
```

Error Returns

If successful, *DosWriteMailslot* returns 0. If unsuccessful, it returns one of the following error codes:

Error Return	Meaning
ERROR_PATH_NOT_FOUND	The mailslot name is not valid. Be sure that it begins with \MAILSLOT\ or *servername*-\MAILSLOT and that it contains only valid file-system characters.

(continued)

Error Return	Meaning
ERROR_INVALID_PARAMETER	The *priority* or *class* argument contains an illegal value, or the message size is larger than the mailslot maximum message size.
ERROR_BROKEN_PIPE	The mailslot does not exist. It might have been deleted.
ERROR_BAD_NETNAME	A broadcast cannot be made unless the *class* argument is 2.

An overview:

The *DosWriteMailslot* API is used by client processes to write messages into the mailslot. The *name* argument must be a mailslot already created by a call to *DosMakeMailslot*. The mailslot can be created by another process which can even be running on another computer on the network. If the mailslot is local, the name is of the following form:

`\MAILSLOT\`*mailname*

If the mailslot is remote, the name is of the following form:

`\\`*computername*`\MAILSLOT\`*mailname*

A special form of the remote name allows a broadcast message to be sent. If the name is of the following form, the * indicates that the message is to be written to a mailslot on all computers in the domain (langroup) that have created a mailslot of this name:

`\\*\MAILSLOT\`*mailname*

You could also use the form

`\\`*domain*`\MAILSLOT\`*mailname*

to broadcast into the specified domain.

The broadcast can be done only for second-class mail.

The *priority* of a message ranges from 0, the lowest priority, to 9, the highest priority. Higher-priority messages will generally be delivered ahead of lower-priority ones, although this will not be true when the mailslot is already full.

There are two classes of messages, indicated by the *class* argument:

- If *class* is 1, the message is transported reliably and returns an error if it cannot be written into the mailslot. The *DosWriteMailslot* call will block until the write completes or until the failure condition is detected.

- If *class* is 2, there will be no indication if delivery fails.

First-class messages can be sent only to mailslots on LAN Manager servers. Second-class messages can be sent to mailslots on workstations and can be broadcast to the entire domain (langroup). Second-class mail is limited in size. LAN Manager version 2.0 allows a maximum of 444 bytes less the size of the full UNC name for the mailslot.

The *timeout* argument tells the *DosWriteMailslot* call how long to wait for room in the mailslot. The special value 0xFFFFFFFF means to wait indefinitely.

Modeling the Messenger Service

The LAN Manager Messenger service is implemented using a special SMB protocol and direct calls to NetBIOS. This gives it compatibility with older PC-LAN and MS-NET systems. You could also use mailslots to implement Messenger service functions, but this would not be interoperable with PC-LAN or MS-NET messaging.

The following programs are not a complete messaging service, but they do illustrate the use of mailslots for this purpose. MMESG.C (Figure 10-8) is a LAN Manager service program. If you add the statement

```
MMESG=service\mmesg.exe
```

to your LANMAN.INI file and put the executable file in the SERVICE directory of the LANMAN root directory, this new service can be started using the command

```
net start mmesg
```

The MSEND.C program (Figure 10-9) uses the MMESG service. It assumes that the first argument is a workstation name (or * for a domain broadcast) and sends the rest of the command line as a message. Messages are sent by constructing a remote mailslot name from the first argument and the name \MAILSLOT\EXAMPLE\MSG and then using *DosWriteMailslot* to send a second-class message. A header on the front of the message contains the sender's name.

When the MMESG service gets a message using *DosReadMailslot*, it uses the existing Netpopup service to put the message onto the screen. This is done using the Alert APIs described in the next section.

```c
/*
 * MMESG.C -- A service for receiving interstation messages.
 *
 * Compile with:  C> cl mmesg.c netapi.lib mailslot.lib
 *
 * Usage:   Install as a LAN Manager service by adding the line
 *          "MMESG=service\mmesg.exe" to your LANMAN.INI file.
 *          After installation, create a mailslot and send all
 *          received messages to the NetPopup service using
 *          NetAlertRaise.
 */

#include <stdio.h>
#include <os2.h>
#include <netcons.h>
#include <service.h>
#include <mailslot.h>
#include <alert.h>

extern void far pascal sig_handler(unsigned, unsigned);

#define MAXMSG 400
char buf[BUFSIZ] = {0};

void main(argc,argv)
int argc;
char ** argv;
    {
    PFNSIGHANDLER prev;
    USHORT prevact, hdl;
    USHORT bread, nsize, npri;
    unsigned err;
    struct service_status ss;
    char *p = buf + sizeof(struct std_alert);

    /* Install signal handler */
    DosSetSigHandler(
                sig_handler,            /* function name */
                &prev,                  /* previous handler */
                &prevact,               /* previous action */
                SIGA_ACCEPT,            /* action */
                SERVICE_RCV_SIG_FLAG    /* flag #5 */
                );
```

Figure 10-8.   *(continued)*
The MMESG.C service program.

Figure 10-8. *continued*

```
    DosMakeMailslot(
                    "\\MAILSLOT\\EXAMPLE\\MSG",   /* name */
                    MAXMSG,                       /* max message size */
                    10*MAXMSG,                    /* mailslot size */
                    &hdl                          /* handle */
                    );

    /* notify that installation is complete */
    ss.svcs_pid = 0;
    ss.svcs_status = SERVICE_NOT_PAUSABLE :
                    SERVICE_UNINSTALLABLE :
                    SERVICE_INSTALLED;
    ss.svcs_code = 0;
    ss.svcs_text[0] = 0;

    if (NetServiceStatus((char far *)&ss, sizeof(ss)) != 0)
        exit(err);

    /* process received messages */
    while (TRUE)
        {
        DosReadMailslot(hdl,
                    p,            /* message buffer */
                    &bread,       /* message size */
                    &nsize,       /* next size */
                    &npri,        /* next priority */
                    0xffffffff    /* timeout */
                    );

        /* Send text to NetPopup. The front of the
         * buffer contains sizeof(struct std_alert)
         * characters that are ignored by NetPopup.
         */

        buf[bread] = 0;
        NetAlertRaise("MESSAGE",
                    buf,
                    sizeof(struct std_alert) + bread,
                    1000L);
        }
    }

/*
 * The NetService APIs communicate through this signal handler.
 */
```

(continued)

Figure 10-8. *continued*

```
void far pascal
sig_handler(sig_arg, sig_no)
unsigned sig_arg;
unsigned sig_no;
    {
    struct service_status ss;
    switch (sig_arg & 0xff)    /* switch on action code */
        {
        case SERVICE_CTRL_UNINSTALL:

            ss.svcs_status = SERVICE_NOT_PAUSABLE :
                             SERVICE_UNINSTALLABLE :
                             SERVICE_UNINSTALLED;
            ss.svcs_code = 0;
            NetServiceStatus((char far *)&ss, sizeof(ss));
            exit(0);
            break;

        default:
            /* no other actions -- default to interrogate */
        case SERVICE_CTRL_INTERROGATE:
            ss.svcs_status = SERVICE_NOT_PAUSABLE :
                             SERVICE_UNINSTALLABLE :
                             SERVICE_INSTALLED;
            ss.svcs_code = 0;
            NetServiceStatus((char far *)&ss, sizeof(ss));
            break;
        }
    /* Enable next communication */
    DosSetSigHandler(0, 0, 0, SIGA_ACKNOWLEDGE, sig_no);
    return;
    }
```

```
/*
 * MSEND.C -- This program sends a message via the MMESG service.
 * The first argument is a computer name (or "*" for broadcast),
 * and the rest of the command line is the message.
 *
 * Compile with:  C> cl msend.c netapi.lib mailslot.lib
 *
 * Usage:  C> msend <computername> <message>
 *         The MMESG service must be installed.
 *
 *
 */
```

Figure 10-9.
The MSEND.C mailslot program.

(continued)

Figure 10-9. *continued*

```
#include <os2.h>
#include <stdio.h>
#include <netcons.h>
#include <wksta.h>
#include <mailslot.h>

main(argc, argv)
int argc;
char **argv;
    {
    char buf[BUFSIZ];
    char name[PATHLEN];
    USHORT ta;
    struct wksta_info_0 *pw = (struct wksta_info_0 *)buf;
    int err;

    if (argc < 3)
        {
        printf("syntax:  msend <computername> <message>\n");
        exit(1);
        }

    /* create the UNC mailslot name */
    sprintf(name, "\\\\%s\\MAILSLOT\\EXAMPLE\\MSG", argv[1]);

    /* put the computer name at the front of the message */
    err = NetWkstaGetInfo ( NULL, 0, buf, BUFSIZ, &ta);
    if (err)
        {
        printf("MSEND error = %d\n", err);
        exit(1);
        }
    sprintf(buf, "From %s\n", pw->wki0_computername);

    /* put the rest of the command line in the message */
    argv += 2;
    argc -= 2;
    while (argc--)
        {
        strcat(buf, *argv++);
        if (argc)
            strcat(buf, " ");
        }
```

(continued)

Figure 10-9. *continued*

```
err = DosWriteMailslot(
                        name,         /* destination mailslot name */
                        buf,          /* message buffer */
                        strlen(buf),  /* message size */
                        1,            /* priority */
                        2,            /* second-class mailslot */
                        -1L);         /* timeout */
printf("MSEND status = %d\n", err);
}
```

Alerts

Alerts are software "events." Processes register their interest in knowing when the event has occurred by calling the *NetAlertStart* API. A process can declare the event as happening by calling the *NetAlertRaise* API and passing a buffer of data describing the event. The Alert APIs offer a "one-to-many" interprocess communications mechanism, in which one call to *NetAlertRaise* communicates with one or more processes or threads that have indicated interest through the *NetAlertStart* API.

What is an event? It is simply a text string that applications agree will indicate that something has happened. Applications can choose any text string to indicate an event. However, the LAN Manager software has a set of standard event names. (See "Standard Alerts," later in this chapter.)

Waiting for an Event

When a call is made to *NetAlertStart*, the arguments include the name of the event and a "recipient." The recipient is the name of a semaphore or a mailslot that will be used for communication whenever the event occurs. A process can register its interest in the event with *NetAlertStart* and then wait for the semaphore or the mailslot to have data written to it.

If the recipient is a semaphore, it must be created in nonexclusive mode with the *DosCreateSem* API. After registering the event and semaphore through the *NetAlertStart* API call, the process can execute a *DosSemWait* or *DosMuxSemWait* API to wait for the event. When a *DosAlertRaise* call is made for this event, all registered semaphores are strobed (put through a sequence of *DosSemOpen, DosSemClear, DosSemSet, DosCloseSem* calls).

If the recipient is a mailslot, it must be created using the *DosMakeMailslot* API. Once interest in the event is registered using the *NetAlertStart* API, the process can execute a *DosReadMailslot* call to wait for the event. When a *DosAlertRaise* call is made for this event, it includes a buffer of data, and all registered mailslots will have the data written to the mailslot with a *DosWriteMailslot* call. The structure of the data is not specified, although the standard events have a specific format for the data buffer.

Here be errors

Because the *NetAlertStart* API call doesn't require that the system perform checks on the existence of the semaphore or the mailslot, you need to ensure that the recipient name in the *NetAlertStart* call is the same as the name of the semaphore or mailslot that the program will wait on. If the names don't match, the event will go undetected and will cause a subtle programming bug.

The event names are case sensitive, so cooperating processes need to use exactly the same text string. The LAN Manager standard alerts have macro names defined in ALERT.H.

The Alert APIs

To use the Alert APIs, you must include NETCONS.H and ALERT.H at compile time, and you must link with the NETAPI.LIB stub library at link time.

NetAlertStart

Registers a client for an event.

```
unsigned far pascal
NetAlertStart(
    char far * event,      /* the event of interest      */
    char far * recipient,  /* sem or mailslot name       */
    USHORT maxdata         /* max amount of event data */
    )
```

Error returns:

If successful, *NetAlertStart* returns 0. If unsuccessful, it returns one of the following error codes:

Error Return	Meaning
ERROR_INVALID_NAME	The event name is not well formed. Note that *NetAlertRaise* returns a different error code for this.
NERR_BadRecipient	Recipient is not a semaphore or a local mailslot.

(continued)

continued

Error Return	Meaning
NERR_WkstaNotStarted	The workstation must be started for alerts to be registered.
NERR_AlertExists	A *NetAlertStart* is already registered for this event and recipient.
NERR_TooManyAlerts	The system has run out of alert resources. This is controlled by the *numalerts* parameter in the LANMAN.INI configuration file.

An overview:

The *NetAlertStart* API registers the client for an event of interest, specified by the *event* argument. *event* is a text string with a maximum of 16 characters. Case is significant.

The *recipient* argument is a string indicating a semaphore or a mailslot. Semaphores always have a name of the following form:

\SEM*semaphorename*

Mailslots are always local, with a name of the following form:

\MAILSLOT*mailslotname*

No other form of recipient name can be used.

The *maxdata* argument is applicable only when *recipient* is a mailslot. It limits the amount of data written into this mailslot. Each instance of *NetAlertStart* can register its own mailslot with its own *maxdata* value.

A process or thread can register interest in an event with *NetAlertStart* more than once, but never more than once with the same event and recipient. The total number of registrations in effect at one time is limited. The information about the event and the recipient is kept in a fixed-size table created when the workstation is started. The LANMAN.INI *numalerts* parameter controls the number of entries in this table. Accordingly, the workstation must be started before the Alert APIs can be used.

NetAlertRaise

Notifies registered clients that an event has occurred.

```
unsigned far pascal
NetAlertRaise(
    char far * event,        /* the event of interest    */
    char far *buf,           /* buffer of event data     */
    USHORT buflen,           /* length of buf            */
    unsigned long timeout    /* time to wait on mailslot */
    )
```

Error returns:

If successful, *NetAlertRaise* returns 0. If unsuccessful, it returns one of the following error codes:

Error Return	Meaning
ERROR_INVALID_PARAMETER	The event name is not well formed. Note that *NetAlertStart* returns a different error code for this.
NERR_NoSuchAlert	No clients are waiting for this event.
NERR_WkstaNotStarted	The workstation must be started for alerts to be registered.

An overview:

The *NetAlertRaise* API declares that an event has just occurred. All instances of *NetAlertStart* for this event will have their semaphores strobed or the data buffer written to their mailslots. No restrictions limit how much time must pass before the same event can occur and the *NetAlertRaise* API can be called again.

The *buf* buffer contains *buflen* bytes of data to be written to the mailslot of each *NetAlertStart* registration that declared a mailslot as the recipient. Data is written with the *DosWriteMailslot* API. The actual number of bytes written to each mailslot is the lesser of the *buflen* value or the *maxdata* value declared for that mailslot with *NetAlertStart*.

Data in *buf* has no required format; applications can organize the alert data as needed. However, the standard events described in the next section do have a prescribed format.

The *timeout* argument is used as the *DosWriteMailslot* timeout for each registered mailslot write and can be used to keep *NetAlertRaise* from blocking indefinitely when one of the mailslots is full. If *timeout* is set to 0xFFFFFFFF, each *DosWriteMailslot* call blocks until the application that created the mailslot makes room for the message. Three timeout values are defined in the ALERT.H file, as shown on the following page.

Name	Timeout
ALERT_SHORT_WAIT	100 ms
ALERT_MED_WAIT	1 sec
ALERT_LONG_WAIT	10 sec

NetAlertStop

Cancels an event alert.

```
unsigned far pascal
NetAlertStop(
    char far * event,      /* the event of interest */
    char far * recipient   /* sem or mailslot name  */
    )
```

Error returns:

If successful, *NetAlertStop* returns 0. If unsuccessful, it returns one of the following error codes:

Error Return	Meaning
NERR_NoSuchAlert	This event recipient pair was never registered.
NERR_WkstaNotStarted	The workstation must be started for alerts to be registered.

An overview:

The *NetAlertStop* API cancels interest in a particular event. The *event* and *recipient* arguments must match a pair registered by a call to *NetAlertStart*. Note that *NetAlertStop* can be issued by a different process than the one that registered interest using *NetAlertStart*.

Standard Alerts

Although the event name for alerts can be any text string, LAN Manager has five predefined events and an associated structure for the data buffer of each:

- ALERT_PRINT_EVENT

- ALERT_ADMIN_EVENT

- ALERT_MESSAGE_EVENT

- ALERT_USER_EVENT

- ALERT_ERRORLOG_EVENT

Whenever one of these standard alerts is raised, the data buffer consists of a standard header—a *std_alert* structure—followed by a fixed-length structure specific to the type of alert and (optionally) variable-length data in the remainder of the alert data buffer.

The *std_alert* structure contains these elements:

Member Name	Description
alrt_timestamp	The time the alert was raised
alert_eventname	The event name
alrt_servicename	The LAN Manager service that raised the alert

The ALERT_PRINT_EVENT alert

The ALERT_PRINT_EVENT alert is raised by the spooler when a job is finished printing or when a printer needs human intervention. The ALERT_PRINT_EVENT-specific information in the data buffer is a *print_other_info* structure, which contains the following elements:

Member Name	Description
alrtpr_jobid	Spooler print job ID.
alrtpr_status	The status of the job. See the *DosPrintJobStatus* API for a description of these.
alrtpr_submitted	The time the job was submitted.
alrtpr_size	The size of the print job.

This structure is followed by variable-length information in the form of contiguous zero-terminated text strings:

Text String	Description
computername	The computer that submitted the print job
username	The user who submitted the print job
queuename	The print queue to which the job was submitted
destination	The printer destination (device) to which the print job was routed
status string	The status of the print job

See the DosPrint APIs for more information on these strings.

The ALERT_ADMIN_EVENT alert

The ALERT_ADMIN_EVENT alert is raised by the server whenever something has occurred that an administrator might want to know about. The ALERT_ADMIN_EVENT-specific information in the data buffer is an *admin_other_info* structure, which contains the following elements:

Member Name	Description
alrtad_errcode	The error code of the *admin* condition. This will be an error number in the LAN Manager error-message file. See Chapter 13 for details on how to use the message file.
alrtad_numstrings	The number of strings in the variable-length portion of the data buffer. This will be in the range 0 through 9.

This fixed-length structure is followed by up to nine contiguous zero-terminated text strings that provide more information about the alert condition. These strings are intended to be passed as a "merge string" buffer to the *DosGetMessage* API.

The ALERT_MESSAGE_EVENT alert

The ALERT_MESSAGE_EVENT alert is raised whenever the Messenger service receives a message. No fixed-length structure exists. There is only a variable-length section containing the message.

The ALERT_USER_EVENT alert

The ALERT_USER_EVENT alert is raised by the server whenever a condition occurs that a user might want to know about. The ALERT_USER_EVENT-specific information in the data buffer is a *user_other_info* structure, which contains the following elements:

Member Name	Description
alrtus_errcode	The error code of the *admin* condition. This will be an error number in the LAN Manager error-message file. See Chapter 13 for details on how to use the message file.
alrtus_numstrings	The number of strings in the variable-length portion of the data buffer. This will be in the range 0 through 9.

This fixed-length structure is followed by up to nine contiguous zero-terminated text strings that provide more information about the alert condition. These strings are intended to be passed as a "merge string" buffer to the *DosGetMessage* API.

This structure is followed by variable-length information in the form of contiguous zero-terminated text strings, as shown on the next page.

Text String	Description
username	The user that created the session
computername	The computer that created the session

The ALERT_ERRORLOG_EVENT alert

The ALERT_ERRLOG_EVENT alert is raised by the server whenever a new entry is made into the error log. The ALERT_ERRORLOG_EVENT-specific information in the data buffer is an *errlog_other_info* structure, which contains these members:

Member Name	Description
alrter_errcode	The error code of the logged error
alrter_offset	The offset in the error log file

Replacing the Alerter Service

One of the standard LAN Manager services is the Alerter service that runs at the server. This service sends interstation messages to appropriate people whenever any of the following standard alerts is raised at the server:

- ALERT_ADMIN_EVENT

- ALERT_USER_EVENT

- ALERT_PRINT_EVENT

The Alerter is conceptually a very simple application, as demonstrated by the following pseudocode:

```
DosMakeMailslot(mailslot ...);
DosAlertRaise(ALERT_PRINT_EVENT, mailslot ...);
DosAlertRaise(ALERT_USER_EVENT, mailslot ...);
while not stopped
    DosReadMailslot ...
    switch on type of alert
        PRINT:
            format message to user
            NetMessageSendBuffer ...
            break;
        USER:
            format message to user
            NetMessageSendBuffer ...
            break;
```

```
        ADMIN:
            format message to administrator
            for each name in alertnames=
                NetMessageSendBuffer ...
            break;
```

Because the format of the standard alerts is documented, it is possible to write a replacement Alerter service. The ERRLOG.C program (Figure 10-10) causes a screen popup whenever an entry is made to the LAN Manager error log with the *NetErrorWrite* API. This program could easily be modified to be a LAN Manager service program.

```
/*
 * ERRLOG.C -- This program will cause a popup whenever
 * an entry is written to the error log.  It can be adapted
 * into a LAN Manager service program and installed as an
 * auxiliary to the Alerter service.
 *
 * Compile with:  C> cl errlog.c popup.c netapi.lib mailslot.lib
 *
 * Usage:  C> errlog
 *
 */

#include <os2.h>
#include <stdio.h>
#include <netcons.h>
#include <alert.h>
#include <mailslot.h>

#define MAXSZ 512 /* maximum alert data size */

main()
    {
    unsigned err, hdl;
    USHORT bread, nsize, npri;
    char buf[MAXSZ], data[MAXSZ];
    struct std_alert * pa;
    struct errlog_other_info *pe;

    if (err = DosMakeMailslot(
            "\\MAILSLOT\\ERRLOG",    /* name          */
            MAXSZ,                    /* max msg size  */
```

Figure 10-10.
The ERRLOG.C program.

(continued)

Figure 10-10. *continued*

```
            4*MAXSZ,                 /* mailslot size */
            &hdl                     /* handle        */
            ) != 0)
   if (err)
      {
      printf("DosMakeMailslot error = %d\n", err);
      exit(1);
      }

   if (err = NetAlertStart(
            ALERT_ERRORLOG_EVENT,   /* "ERRORLOG" event */
            "\\MAILSLOT\\ERRLOG",   /* recipient        */
            MAXSZ                    /* max msg size     */
            ) != 0)
   if (err)
      {
      printf("NetAlertStart error = %d\n", err);
      exit(1);
      }

   /* forever ... */
   while (1)
      {
      /* wait for an error-log entry */
      DosReadMailslot(hdl, data, &bread, &nsize, &npri, 0xffffffff);

      /* format the information */
      pa = (struct std_alert *)data;
      pe = (struct errlog_other_info *)ALERT_OTHER_INFO(data);
      sprintf(buf, "%s reports error %d\n",
            pa->alrt_servicename, pe->alrter_errcode);

      /* send it to NetPopup */
      Popup(buf, strlen(buf));
      }
   }
```

Making Alerting Easier

To make it easy to deal with standard alerts, two macros are defined in
ALERT.H:

ALERT_OTHER_INFO(p)—If *p* is a pointer to the beginning of the alert
data buffer, this macro returns a pointer to the start of the *other_info*
structure.

ALERT_VAR_DATA(p)—If *p* is a pointer to the beginning of the *other _info* structure and if it is declared to be a pointer to that type, this macro returns a pointer to the start of the variable-length data.

Alerts as IPC to Netpopup

The Netpopup service program displays messages on the screen when they arrive at the workstation. The program carries out the following actions:

```
DosMakeMailslot(mailslot ...);
DosAlertRaise(ALERT_MESSAGE_EVENT, mailslot ...);
while not stopped
    DosReadMailslot ...
    format message buffer
    use VioPopup to display
```

We can use Netpopup to create a general-purpose screen pop-up subroutine called POPUP.C (Figure 10-11). Whenever an application wants to write a message to the screen, it can call POPUP, which will pass the text to the Netpopup service by pretending to be a message alert.

```
/*
 * POPUP.C -- A subroutine for passing a buffer of data to the
 * Netpopup service. It relies on Netpopup using the
 * "MESSAGE" alert for getting data to display.
 */

#include <os2.h>
#include <netcons.h>
#include <service.h>
#include <alert.h>
#include <malloc.h>

Popup(buf, buflen, wait)
char *buf;              /* text to be printed     */
unsigned buflen;        /* length                 */
unsigned long wait;     /* WriteMailslot wait time */
    {
    char tbuf[100];
    char *p;
    USHORT avail;
    int err;
```

Figure 10-11.
The POPUP.C subroutine.

(continued)

Figure 10-11. *continued*

```
         /* make sure that Netpopup is installed */
         err = NetServiceGetInfo(
                                 NULL,          /* server name */
                                 "netpopup",    /* service name */
                                 0,             /* level of detail */
                                 tbuf,          /* data buffer */
                                 sizeof(tbuf),  /* size */
                                 &avail         /* available data */
                                 );
         if (err)
            return(err);

         /* Netpopup ignores the standard alert header, but it
          * must be there. */

         p = malloc(buflen + sizeof(struct std_alert));
         memcpy(ALERT_OTHER_INFO(p), buf, buflen);
         buflen += sizeof(struct std_alert);

         /* send to Netpopup by raising the MESSAGE alert */
         err = NetAlertRaise(
                            ALERT_MESSAGE_EVENT,
                            p,                  /* popup text */
                            buflen,             /* length    */
                            wait                /* wait time */
                            );
         free(p);
         return(err);
         }
```

PRINTING AND CHARACTER DEVICE APIs

One of the most basic functions of the LAN Manager server is to allow workstations to share printers or other communications devices without getting in each other's way. This chapter describes the two types of APIs that make device sharing possible:

- The CharDev APIs

- The DosPrint APIs

Two server resources are associated with devices: *spooled print queues* and *character device queues.*

- Spooled print queues buffer an entire print job in a temporary file and then gain exclusive access to a printer just long enough to print the file.

- Character device queues hold *DosOpen* calls until they can gain exclusive access to a device, after which they can read and write to the device at their own pace. The queue owns the device until a call is issued on the open handle.

Server devices, whether LPT*x* or COM*x*, can be assigned to either spooled print queues or character device queues, but never to both at the same time.

The following lists summarize the differences between spooled print devices and serial character devices.

Spooled print devices have the following characteristics:

- Data can only be written to the device; it cannot be read.

- Although the workstation application executes a *DosOpen* call on a device name, the data is actually written into a temporary file. The OS/2 spooler can then schedule the temporary file to be printed at a later time.

- A *DosOpen* call returns as soon as a temporary file is created and opened. The returned handle is that of the temporary file.

- The temporary file, called a *print job,* is tracked in a print queue. This queue can be created and manipulated through a special set of APIs. Even when the queue is not shared, the queue and the job still exist.

- The server shares the print queue as type STYPE_PRINTQ.

Character devices have slightly different characteristics:

- Data can be both written to and read from the device.

- When the *DosOpen* call succeeds, reads and writes are made directly to the remote device driver. No temporary file is involved.

- *DosOpen* requests are queued by the server until a device is available. The *DosOpen* requests can time out if they do not succeed within a configurable period of time.

- The queues holding the pending *DosOpen* requests exist as long as the share exists. When the share is deleted, the queue disappears, and all pending DosOpen requests in the queue fail.

- *DosDevIoctl* calls can be made on the open device handle to change baud rate, stop bits, and so on.

- The server shares the character device as type STYPE_DEVICE.

Character Devices and Queues

A *character device* is an OS/2 device driver accessed directly through a byte stream. A character device can be read from or written to through a handle returned by a successful *DosOpen* call on its name. Any of the COM*x* or LPT*x* logical devices can be used as character devices. Some examples of character devices might be COM1 attached to a modem, COM2 attached to a scanner, LPT1 attached to a fax machine, or LPT2 attached to a printer. Note that the use of a printer as a character device allows data to go to the printer as it is written to the handle, in contrast to spooled printing, which stores all of the data in a temporary file and then accesses the printer.

Under LAN Manager, a character device queue is a queue of *DosOpen* calls, each awaiting exclusive access to a character device. Each device queue can be associated with multiple character devices. When a *NetShareAdd* API with a device type of STYPE_DEVICE is executed at a server, a character device queue is created. The name of the queue is the same as the public share name. Initially, a single character device is associated with the queue, but subsequent *NetCharDevQSetInfo* calls can associate additional character devices with the queue. The character device queue disappears when the share is deleted, and any waiting *DosOpen* calls return a failure code to their originators.

The set of character devices associated with a character device queue is the *device pool*. Device pools can be overlapping. For example, the pool for MODEM1 might include COM1 and COM2, and the pool for MODEM2 might include COM2 and COM3. When a character device becomes available, the server selects a waiting *DosOpen* call from one of the character device queues whose device pool contains the free device.

The Character Device APIs

Two sets of APIs deal with character devices:

- The CharDev APIs provide information and control for individual devices.

- The CharDevQ APIs allow information and control of character device queues. The queues are automatically created when a character device is shared. The *NetShareAdd* call fails if the device does not exist.

The LANMAN.INI file contains two configuration parameters that control character queues. In the [server] component, *maxchdevq* limits the number of device queues, and *maxchdevs* limits the number of devices in a device pool.

To use the CharDev APIs you must include NETCONS.H and CHARDEV.H at compile time and link with the NETAPI.LIB stub library.

The basic information structures for the CharDev APIs exist at two levels. The *chardev_info_0* structure contains this member:

Member Name	Description
char ch0_dev[DEVLEN+1]	This array contains the zero-terminated device name. It is of the form COM*x* or LPT*x*.

The *chardev_info_1* structure contains the following members:

Member Name	Description			
char ch1_dev[DEVLEN+1]	This array contains the zero-terminated device name. It is of the form COM*x* or LPT*x*.			
USHORT ch1_status	This is a bitmask showing the current status of the device. The values are as follows:			
	Bitmask	*Value*	*Meaning*	
	CHARDEV_STAT_OPENED	0x02	TRUE = device is opened	
			FALSE = device is closed	
	CHARDEV_STAT_ERROR	0x04	TRUE = device in error state	
			FALSE = device in OK state	
char ch1_username[UNLEN+1]	If the device is currently open, this array contains the zero-terminated user name. If the device is not open, this array contains a NULL string.			
ULONG ch1_time	The time, in seconds, that the current user has had the device opened.			

The basic information structures for the CharDevQ APIs exist at two levels. The *chardevQ_info_0* structure contains this member:

Member Name	Description
char cq0_dev[NNLEN+1]	This array contains the zero-terminated queue name. This is the same as the share name.

The *chardevQ_info_1* structure contains the following members:

Member Name	Description
char cq1_dev[NNLEN+1]	This array contains the zero-terminated queue name. This is the same as the share name.
USHORT cq1_priority	The queue priority, from 0 (low) to 9 (high). Whenever a device is in the device pool of two different queues, the pending *DosOpen* in the highest-priority queue is selected. When the queue is created by the *NetShareAdd* API, the priority defaults to 5. Three symbolically defined priorities exist:

Priority	Value	Meaning
CHARDEV_MAX_PRIORITY	9	Maximum priority
CHARDEV_MIN_PRIORITY	1	Minimum priority
CHARDEV_DEF_PRIORITY	5	Default priority

Member Name	Description
char far *cq1_devs	This pointer to a text string is a list of the device pool. It is a list of space-separated device names, such as "COM1 COM2".
USHORT cq1_numusers	The number of *DosOpen* requests waiting in the queue. This includes any current open device.
USHORT cq1_numahead	The number of *DosOpen* requests waiting in the queue ahead of the user specified in the *NetCharDevQEnum* or *NetCharDevQGetInfo* call.

NetCharDevEnum

Returns information about all devices that are part of any device pool.

```
unsigned far pascal
NetCharDevEnum(
    char far * servername,    /* where to execute        */
    short level,              /* information level       */
    char far * buf,           /* data buffer             */
    USHORT buflen,            /* buffer length           */
    USHORT eread,             /* number of entries read  */
    USHORT etotal             /* total entries available */
    )
```

Levels:
Supports level 0 and 1 data structures.

Remote access:

Any user with a valid account at the server can call this API remotely.

Error returns:

If successful, *NetCharDevEnum* returns 0. If unsuccessful, it returns one of the standard Enum return codes or the following error code:

Error Return	Meaning
NERR_ServerNotStarted	The server must be running.

An overview:

The *NetCharDevEnum* API returns information about all devices that are part of any device pool. This is a straightforward Enum call, returning a list of *chardev_info_0* or *chardev_info_1* structures, depending on the level argument.

NetCharDevGetInfo

Returns information about a specific device.

```
unsigned far pascal
NetCharDevGetInfo(
    char far * servername,      /* where to execute      */
    char far * devname,         /* device name           */
    short level,                /* information level     */
    char far * buf,             /* data buffer           */
    USHORT buflen,              /* buffer length         */
    USHORT far * btotal         /* total bytes available */
    )
```

Levels:

Supports level 0 and 1 data structures.

Remote access:

Any user with a valid account at the server can call this API remotely.

Error returns:

If successful, *NetCharDevGetInfo* returns 0. If unsuccessful, it returns one of the standard GetInfo return codes or one of the following error codes:

Error Return	Meaning
NERR_ServerNotStarted	The server must be running.
NERR_DevNotFound	The *devname* argument is not in any device pool.

An overview:

The *NetCharDevGetInfo* API returns information about a specific device. The *devname* argument must be a device that is in a device pool of one of the character device queues. This is a straightforward GetInfo call, returning a *chardev_info_0* or *chardev_info_1* structure, depending on the *level* argument.

NetCharDevControl

Allows administration of character devices.

```
unsigned far pascal
NetCharDevControl(
    char far * servername,    /* where to execute      */
    char far * devname,       /* device name           */
    short opcode              /* operation to perform  */
    )
```

Remote access:

This API can be called remotely by an administrator or by a comm operator.

Error returns:

If successful, *NetCharDevControl* returns 0. If unsuccessful, it returns one of the standard API return codes or one of the following error codes:

Error Return	Meaning
NERR_ServerNotStarted	The server must be running.
NERR_DevNotFound	The *devname* argument is not in any device pool.
NERR_DevInvalidOpcode	The opcode is not defined.

An overview:

The *NetCharDevControl* API allows administration programs to control character devices opened by another process.

The *devname* argument must be a device that is in a device pool of a character device queue. Only one value is currently defined:

opcode	Value	Meaning
CHARDEV_CLOSE	0	Force the device closed. The client process will get errors on subsequent reads or writes.

NetCharDevQEnum

Returns information about all device queues on a server.

```
unsigned far pascal
NetCharDevQEnum(
    char far * servername,     /* where to execute         */
    char far * username,       /* username                 */
    short level,               /* information level        */
    char far * buf,            /* data buffer              */
    USHORT buflen,             /* buffer length            */
    USHORT far * eread,        /* number of entries read   */
    USHORT far * etotal        /* total entries available  */
    )
```

Levels:
Supports level 0 and 1 data structures.

Remote access:
Any user with a valid account at the server can call this API remotely.

Error returns:
If successful, *NetCharDevQEnum* returns 0. If unsuccessful, it returns one of
the standard Enum return codes or one of the following error codes:

Error Return	Meaning
NERR_ServerNotStarted	The server must be running.
ERROR_INVALID_NAME	Ill-formed username.

An overview:
The *NetCharDevQEnum* API returns information about all character device
pools. This is a straightforward Enum call, returning a list of *chardev-
Q_info_0* or *chardevQ_info_1* structures, depending on the *level* argument.

The *username* argument is optional. If not a NULL pointer, it is the user
name used for the *cql_numahead* value in the *chardevQ_info_1* structure.

NetCharDevQGetInfo

Retrieves information about a particular server device queue.

```
unsigned far pascal
NetCharDevQGetInfo(
    char far * servername,    /* where to execute        */
    char far * queuename,     /* device queue name       */
    char far * username,      /* username                */
    short level,              /* information level       */
    char far * buf,           /* data buffer             */
    USHORT buflen,            /* buffer length           */
    USHORT btotal             /* total bytes available   */
    )
```

Levels:
Supports level 0 and 1 data structures.

Remote access:
Any user with a valid account at the server can call this API remotely.

Error returns:
If successful, *NetCharDevQGetInfo* returns 0. If unsuccessful, it returns one of the standard GetInfo return codes or one of the following error codes:

Error Return	Meaning
NERR_ServerNotStarted	The server must be running.
NERR_QueueNotFound	The device queue does not exist.
ERROR_INVALID_NAME	Ill-formed username.

An overview:
The *NetCharDevQGetInfo* call returns information about a specific device queue. The *queuename* argument is the same as the share name of an existing device queue. This is a straightforward GetInfo call, returning a *chardevQ_info_0* or a *chardevQ_info_1* structure, depending on the *level* argument. The *username* argument is optional. If not a NULL pointer, it is the user name used for the *cq1_numahead* value in the *chardevQ_info_1* structure.

NetCharDevQSetInfo

Sets information for a particular server device queue.

```
unsigned far pascal
NetCharDevQSetInfo(
    char far * servername,    /* where to execute  */
    char far * queuename,     /* device queue name */
    short level,              /* must be 1         */
    char far * buf,           /* data buffer       */
    USHORT buflen,            /* buffer length     */
    short parmnum             /* parameter to set  */
    )
```

Remote access:

This API can be called remotely by an administrator or by a comm
operator.

Error returns:

If successful, *NetCharDevQSetInfo* returns 0. If unsuccessful, it returns one
of the standard SetInfo return codes or one of the following error codes:

Error Return	Meaning
NERR_ServerNotStarted	The server must be running.
NERR_QueueNotFound	The device queue does not exist.
NERR_BadQueuePriority	The priority must be in the range 0–9.
NERR_BadDev	One of the device names is not an actual server device.
NERR_NoRoom	Too many device names are in the device list.
NERR_RedirectedPath	One device name is redirected to another server. The *NetShareCheck* API lets you determine whether a device is redirected.
NERR_InUseBySpooler	One of the devices is already assigned to a spooled print queue.
NERR_BadDevString	The device string is ill-formed.

An overview:

The *NetCharDevQSetInfo* API lets you change configuration information for
a device queue.

If the *parmnum* argument is 0, the *level* argument must be 1 and the buffer
holds a *chardevQ_info_1* structure. Otherwise, the buffer holds the data corresponding to *parmnum*. The data items that can be set and their corresponding *parmnum* values are as follows:

Name	Value	parmnum
CHARDEVQ_PRIORITY_PARMNUM	2	The device queue priority. The priority is 5 when the queue is created by *NetShareAdd*.
CHARDEVQ_DEVICES_PARMNUM	3	The device list. This is a zero-terminated list of device names separated by spaces. All names in the list must be names of existing devices of the form LPT*x* or COM*x*. The number of devices allowed is controlled by the *maxchdev* configuration parameter.

NetCharDevQPurge

Deletes all pending requests on a device queue.

```
unsigned far pascal
NetCharDevQPurge(
    char far * servername,    /* where to execute  */
    char far * queuename      /* device queue name */
    )
```

Remote access:

This API can be called remotely by an administrator or a comm operator.

Error returns:

If successful, *NetCharDevQPurge* returns 0. If unsuccessful, it returns one of the standard API return codes or one of the following error codes:

Error Return	Meaning
NERR_ServerNotStarted	The server must be running.
NERR_QueueNotFound	The device queue does not exist.

An overview:

The *NetCharDevQPurge* API is used to purge a character device queue. It causes all pending *DosOpen* calls to return a failure code to their originator. This API has no effect on *DosOpen* calls that have already opened a device. Such calls can be terminated with *NetCharDevControl*.

NetCharDevQPurgeSelf

Deletes pending device queue requests from the specified workstation.

```
unsigned far pascal
NetCharDevQPurgeSelf(
    char far * servername,     /* where to execute  */
    char far * queuename,      /* device queue name */
    char far * computername    /* computer name     */
    )
```

Remote access:

This API can be called remotely by any user, but only on queues in which they have pending *DosOpen* calls.

Error returns:

If successful, *NetCharDevQPurgeSelf* returns 0. If unsuccessful, it returns one of the standard API return codes or one of the following error codes:

Error Return	Meaning
NERR_ServerNotStarted	The server must be running.
NERR_QueueNotFound	The device queue does not exist.
NERR_InvalidComputer	The computername argument is ill-formed.
NERR_ItemNotFound	No pending *DosOpen* calls exist for the workstation specified in this device queue.
ERROR_ACCESS_DENIED	An attempt was made to purge another computer's *DosOpen* requests.

Working with handles

Character devices are usually used *serially,* meaning that bytes are read and written one at a time. When the character device is across the network at the server, making network transfers for every byte is inefficient. The LAN Manager uses a character buffer at both ends of the connection and transfers data only when a configurable number of characters are available or after a configurable period of time has elapsed. See the section on handles in Chapter 10 for more information both on buffering and on the *NetHandleGetInfo* and *NetHandle-SetInfo* APIs, which allow you to customize the buffering strategy.

An overview:

A workstation uses the *NetCharDevQPurgeSelf* API to purge its own *DosOpen* calls from a character device queue. This API causes all pending *DosOpen* calls to return a failure code to their originators. The API has no effect on *DosOpen* calls that have opened a device. Such calls can be terminated with *NetCharDevControl*, which requires *admin* or *comm* privilege.

The *computername* argument does not contain leading backslashes. It can be the same string returned by *NetWkstaGetInfo* in the *wki0_computername* structure member.

The Spooler

LAN Manager version 2.0 uses the OS/2 Presentation Manager spooler. Although a complete set of Spl APIs is part of the OS/2 Presentation Manager, the LAN Manager APIs provide a simplified alternative to these routines: the DosPrint APIs.

The DosPrint APIs

Three types of DosPrint APIs work with spooled print devices:

- The DosPrintQ APIs work with queues—a prioritized list of jobs waiting for exclusive access to a destination.

- The DosPrintJob APIs work with jobs—temporary files that contain the data that a workstation program has written to a spooled print device.

- The DosPrintDest APIs work with destinations—representations of the devices that do the actual printing.

A queue can be configured to pass jobs to several different destinations, and destinations can receive jobs from several different queues.

The OS/2 spooler performs all scheduling. Whenever a destination is free, the spooler selects a job from one of the queues associated with the destination and grants it exclusive access to the destination.

When a workstation connects to a spooled print device, it actually connects to a queue. When the workstation executes a *DosOpen* call on the associated device name (or on the UNC share name of the queue), the open request is passed to the server, which obtains a temporary file from the spooler. All of the workstation's subsequent write requests to the open device are written to the temporary file instead. When the workstation issues a *DosClose* call, the server notifies the spooler that the job can be scheduled for printing.

To use the DosPrint APIs, you must include NETCONS.H and PMSPL.H at compile time and link with the NETAPI.LIB stub library.

The DosPrintQ APIs

Spooled print queues are created, listed, deleted, and manipulated with the DosPrintQ APIs. Each queue exists whether it is shared or not. When a *NetShareAdd* call is executed with a share type of STYPE_PRINTQ, it associates a public share name with the private queue name. These names do not need to be the same, but the LAN Manager user-interface programs make the names the same by convention.

Each queue can be associated with a print processor. This is a dynamic link library (DLL) of subroutines that are executed whenever the spooler schedules a job for printing. The print processor is provided with information about the queue, the job, and the destination, and it is responsible for printing the data. The print processor lets you put a program into the printer data stream to do any necessary filtering of data or any dialog with the printer device. For example, a PostScript interpreter needs a two-way dialog with the printer; the print processor handles this. If the queue is configured without a print processor, a default processor built into the spooler simply copies data from the temporary file to the print destination. Print processors are a standard feature of the OS/2 spooler.

Each queue is also configured with a list of print destinations. These destinations are simply text strings that typically represent logical devices such as LPT*x* and COM*x*. But they can be anything. The print processor is responsible for interpreting the meaning of the destination. The names must have previously been given to the spooler through the Print Manager control panel at the server.

The DosPrintQ APIs are case sensitive. And because the user-interface programs always map names to uppercase, applications must take care when manipulating queues created by the user-interface programs.

Two basic data structures are used by the DosPrintQ APIs. A _PRQINFO structure, which is also defined as a PRQINFO type, contains these members:

Member Name	Description
CHAR szName[QNLEN+1]	An array containing a zero-terminated string that is the queue name.
USHORT uPriority	Each queue has a priority that is used as a factor in determining a job priority. The formula is *JobPriority = 100 − 10 ∗ QuePriority*. If a destination can be given a job from more than one queue, the spooler selects the job with the highest priority. The values of the queue priority range from 1 (low) through 9 (high). Four symbolically defined priorities exist:

Priority	Value	Meaning
PRQ_MAX_PRIORITY	9	Maximum priority
PRQ_MIN_PRIORITY	1	Minimum priority
PRQ_DEF_PRIORITY	5	Default priority
PRQ_NO_PRIORITY	0	No priority

Member Name	Description
USHORT uStartTime	No print jobs are scheduled until after this time. Time is represented as minutes since midnight. For example, 1:01 A.M. is represented as 61. This value has no effect on a spooler running without LAN Manager.
USHORT uUntilTime	Print jobs are scheduled until this time. After this time, jobs are still accepted in the queue but are not scheduled for printing. If the *uStartTime* is the same as *uUntilTime*, printing is always enabled. This value has no effect on a spooler running without LAN Manager.
PSZ pszSepFile	Queues can have a configurable separator page printed between each job. This is a pointer to a filename that contains the separator information. A separator language is described in the *LAN Manager Administrator's Guide*. The pathname must be an absolute pathname. This value has no effect on a spooler running without LAN Manager.
PSZ pszPrProc	The name of the print processor DLL. If NULL, the spooler uses the default print processor (PMPRINT). The print processor must already be configured in the OS2SYS.INI file, PM_SPOOLER_QP. Currently, the only print processors are PMPRINT.QPR and LMPRINT.QPR (a superset with separator page support).
PSZ pszDestinations	A zero-terminated string that lists print destinations. Each destination is separated by a space. These names must already be configured into the PM_SPOOLER_PORTS section of OS2SYS.INI.
PSZ pszParms	A zero-terminated parameter string. See the following section.
PSZ pszComment	A zero-terminated comment string. This is an optional description of the queue. For example, ''After Midnight Queue''.

(continued)

Member Name	Description		
USHORT fsStatus	The current status of the queue. The values are as follows:		
	Status	**Value**	**Meaning**
	PRQ_ACTIVE	0	The queue is accepting jobs and scheduling them for printing.
	PRQ_PAUSE	1	The queue is paused. New jobs are accepted but are not scheduled for printing.
	PRQ_ERROR	2	The queue is in an error state.
	PRQ_PENDING	3	The queue has been marked to be deleted. It will finish printing its jobs before it is deleted.
USHORT cJobs	For level 2 or 3 *DosPrintQEnum* or *DosPrintQGetInfo* calls, the number of *prjob_info* structures that follow.		

A *_PRQINFO3* structure, which is also defined as a PRQINFO3 type, is identical to a PRQINFO structure with the addition of the following elements:

Member Name	Description
PSZ pszPrinters	The list of printers that can print jobs from this queue. They must all be previously configured in the PM_SPOOLER_PRINTER section of OS2SYS.INI.
PSZ pszDriverName	The default device driver for the print queue. It must be previously configured in the PM_SPOOLER_DD section of OS2SYS.INI.
PDRIVDATA pDriverData	Data specific to the device driver.

pszDriverName and *pszDriverData* are for use by applications that want to create print jobs based on the queue name and construct calls to *DevOpenDC*. For details on how to do this, see the *Microsoft OS/2 Presentation Manager Programmer's Reference*.

The parameter string is an optional configuration string. It is available to the print processor and need have meaning only to that program. The parameter string is a list of parameters, each of the following form:

```
parametername=value
```

Each instance of a parameter is separated by a space, so the value must be a single word. The only parameter string currently defined is as follows:

```
TYPES=xxx
```

where *xxx* is one or more spool file data type names separated by commas. The two defined types are

```
TYPES=PM_Q_STD,PM_Q_RAW
```

An application can check this parameter using *DosPrintQGetInfo* at level 1 to determine which queues can handle a given metafile format. The first type is assumed to be the default type for the queue, and a missing TYPES parameter means only the default type. When LAN Manager attempts to add a job to a queue, it fails if the job parameter string contains a type that doesn't match one of the types in the queue parameter string. The matching is done as a case-sensitive comparison. Note that if neither the queue nor the job has a parameter string, they are both considered the default and will match.

The _PRQINFO structure exists for compatibility with older versions of LAN Manager. New applications should use the _PRQINFO3 structure.

DosPrintQEnum

Lists all printer queues on a server.

```
unsigned far pascal
DosPrintQEnum(
    char far * servername,    /* where to execute         */
    short level,              /* information level        */
    char far * buf,           /* data buffer              */
    USHORT buflen,            /* buffer length            */
    USHORT far * eread,       /* number of entries read   */
    USHORT far * etotal       /* total entries available  */
    )
```

Levels:
Supports level 0, 1, 2, 3, and 4 data structures.

Remote access:
Any user with a valid account at the server can call this API remotely.

Error returns:
If successful, *DosPrintQEnum* returns 0. If unsuccessful, it returns a standard Enum return code or one of the error codes shown on the next page.

Error Return	Meaning
NERR_SpoolerNotLoaded	The spooler must be running.
NERR_NetNotStarted	In addition to the usual meaning that the network driver is not running, this error can also be returned if the call is made locally and the local spooler cannot find the SPL1A.DLL.

An overview:

The *DosPrintQEnum* API returns information about all spooled print queues at levels 0 through 4.

Level 0 Level 0 returns an array of queue names. Each queue name is zero-terminated but is allowed QNLEN+1 characters. Unlike most of the APIs, no level 0 structure is defined, so a program must step through the level 0 return itself. Here is some pseudocode for level 0 processing:

```
char *p = buf;
    /* for each queue */
while (eread--)
    {
    process queuename ...
    p += QNLEN + 1;
    }
```

Level 1 Level 1 returns an array of _PRQINFO structures. To process these, simply step a pointer through the array of _PRQINFO structures. Here is some psuedocode for processing at level 1:

```
PRQINFO *pq1 = (PRQINFO * buf);
/* for each queue */
while (eread--)
    {
    process queuename ...
    ++pq1;
    }
```

Level 2 Level 2 returns an array of _PRQINFO structures, each followed by a list of _PRJINFO structures (defined later in the chapter)— one for each job in the queue. Here is some pseudocode for processing at level 2:

```
PRQINFO * prq2 = buf;
PRJOB * pj;
/* for each queue */
while (eread--)
```

```
{
process queue ...
/* for each job */
pj = (PRJINFO *)(pq2 + 1);
while (pq2->cJobs--)
    {
    process job ...
    ++pj;
    }
pq2 = (PRQINFO *)(pj);
}
```

Level 3   Level 3 returns an array of _PRQINFO3 structures. To process these, simply step a pointer through the array of _PRQINFO3 structures. Here is some psuedocode for processing at level 3:

```
PRQINFO3 *pq3 = (PRQINFO3 * buf);
/* for each queue */
while (eread--)
    {
    process queuename ...
    ++pq3;
    }
```

Level 4   Level 4 returns an array of _PRQINFO3 structures, each followed by a list of _PRJINFO2 structures (defined later in the chapter)—one for each job in the queue. Here is some pseudocode for processing at level 4:

```
PRQINFO * prq4 = buf;
PRJINFO2 * pj2;

/* for each queue */
while (eread--)
    {
    process queue ...
    /* for each job */
    pj2 = (PRJINF2O *)(pq4 + 1);
    while (pq4->cJobs--)
        {
        process job ...
        ++pj2;
        }
    pq4 = (PRQINFO3 *)(pj2);
    }
```

Calling the *NetPrintQEnum* API at levels 2 or 4 presents some difficult buffer size problems. If ERR_MORE_DATA is returned, the *etotal* argument indicates only the number of _PRQINFO or _PRQINFO3 structures, it contains no information about the number of _PRJOB or _PRJINFO2 structures. There are also a number of variable-length strings in the _PRQINFO and _PRQINFO3 structures. Subject to system memory constraints, an application should probably provide as large a buffer as it can when the ERROR_MORE_DATA condition occurs. A better strategy is to issue level-0 *DosPrintQEnum* calls and then iterate through level-4 *DosPrintQGetInfo* calls. Each of these will indicate exactly how much memory it needs to succeed.

The structures returned by this call describe each queue created with a *DosPrintQAdd* call. It doesn't matter whether the queue is currently shared or not.

DosPrintQEnum can be called remotely at all levels. As long as the user has access to the server, the call will succeed. A server running user-mode security requires an account, even if only as a guest. The access rights of individual users for each queue are not taken into account. In share-mode security, the user must be able to connect to the IPC$ connection.

DosPrintQGetInfo

Retrieves information about a specific printer queue.

```
unsigned far pascal
DosPrintQGetInfo(
        char far * servername,    /* where to execute        */
        char far * queuename,     /* print queue name        */
        short level,              /* information level       */
        char far * buf,           /* data buffer             */
        USHORT buflen,            /* buffer length           */
        USHORT far * btotal       /* total bytes available   */
        )
```

Levels:
Supports level 0, 1, 2, 3, and 4 data structures.

Remote access:
Any user with a valid account at the server can call this API remotely.

Error returns:

If successful, *DosPrintQGetInfo* returns 0. If unsuccessful, it returns one of the standard GetInfo return codes or one of the following error codes:

Error Return	Meaning
NERR_SpoolerNotLoaded	The spooler service must be running.
NERR_QNotFound	The queue name does not exist.
NERR_NetNotStarted	In addition to indicating that the network driver is not running, this error is returned if the call is made locally and the local spooler cannot find the SPL1A.DLL.

An overview:

The *DosPrintQGetInfo* API returns information about a specific spooled print queue. At each level, the *buf* buffer returns with the following information:

Level	Buffer Contents
0	An szName[QNLEN+1]
1	A PRQINFO structure
2	A PRQINFO structure followed by an array of PRJINFO structures
3	A PRQINFO2 structure
4	A PRQINFO2 structure followed by an array of PRJINFO2 structures

The buffer requirements can be determined by calling the routine with *buflen* set to 0 and then calling it again with a buffer of the size indicated by *btotal*.

DosPrintQSetInfo

Sets the configuration of a printer queue.

```
unsigned far pascal
DosPrintQSetInfo(
    char far * servername,      /* where to execute */
    char far * queuename,       /* print queue name */
    short level,                /* must be 1 or 3   */
    char far * buf,             /* data buffer      */
    USHORT buflen,              /* buffer length    */
    short parmnum               /* parameter to set */
    )
```

Levels:

Supports level 1 and 3 data structures.

Remote access:

This API can be called remotely by an administrator or a print operator.

Error returns:

If successful, *DosPrintQSetInfo* returns 0. If unsuccessful, it returns one of the standard SetInfo return codes or one of the following error codes:

Error Return	Meaning
NERR_SpoolerNotLoaded	The spooler service must be running.
NERR_QNotFound	The queue name does not exist.
NERR_RedirectedPath	One of the destinations is a redirected device name.
NERR_CommDevInUse	One of the destinations is already assigned to a character device queue.
NERR_BadDev	One of the destination names was not previously configured into the PM_SPOOLER_PORTS section.
NERR_ProcNotFound	The *pszPrProc* member is not an available DLL.
NERR_DataTypeInvalid	The *TYPES=* directive in the *pszParameters* member was set to an illegal value. Only PM_Q_STD and PM_Q_RAW are valid.

An overview:

The *DosPrintQSetInfo* API changes configuration information about a spooled print queue. If *parmnum* is 0, *level* must be 1 or 3, and the buffer must hold a _PRQINFO or _PRQINFO3 structure. Otherwise, the buffer holds the data corresponding to the *parmnum* value. The data items that can be set and their corresponding PARMNUMs are as follows:

Name	parmnum	Value
uPriority	PRQ_PRIORITY_PARMNUM	2
uStartTime	PRQ_STARTTIME_PARMNUM	3
uUntilTime	PRQ_UNTILTIME_PARMNUM	4
pszSepFile	PRQ_SEPARATOR_PARMNUM	5
pszPrProc	PRQ_PROCESSOR_PARMNUM	6
pszDestinations	PRQ_DESTINATIONS_PARMNUM	7
pszParms	PRQ_PARMS_PARMNUM	8
pszComment	PRQ_COMMENT_PARMNUM	9
pszPrinters	PRQ_PRINTERS_PARMNUM	12
pszDriverName	PRQ_DRIVERNAME_PARMNUM	13
pszDriverData	PRQ_DRIVERDATA_PARMNUM	14

If no print processor exists, the Spooler uses its internal print processor; the destinations must all be names already configured into the PM_SPOOLER-_PORTS section through the spooler control panel.

If the value of *pszSeparator*, *pszDestinations*, *pszPrProc*, *pszParms*, *pszComment*, *pszPrinters*, *pszDriverName*, or *pszDriverData* is a NULL pointer, the previous value is unchanged. To set any of these to ''no value'', use an empty string (""). Note that in contrast, the *DosPrintQGetInfo* call returns a NULL pointer to indicate ''no value'' for each of these.

If the *uPriority* member is PRQ_NO_PRIORITY (0), the value is unchanged.

DosPrintQAdd

Creates a print queue on a server.

```
unsigned far pascal
DosPrintQAdd(
    char far * servername,    /* where to execute */
    short level,              /* must be 1 or 3   */
    char far * buf,           /* data buffer      */
    USHORT buflen             /* buffer length    */
    )
```

Levels:
Supports level 1 and 3 data structures.

Remote access:
This API can be called remotely by an administrator or a print operator.

Error returns:
If successful, *DosPrintQAdd* returns 0. If unsuccessful, it returns one of the standard Add return codes or one of the following error codes:

Error Return	Meaning
NERR_SpoolerNotLoaded	The spooler service must be running.
NERR_QExists	The queue name already exists.
NERR_QNoRoom	The maximum number of queues already exist. This is controlled by the *maxqueues* parameter in the [spooler] component of LANMAN.INI.
NERR_RedirectedPath	One of the destinations is a redirected device name.
NERR_CommDevInUse	One of the destinations is already assigned to a character device queue.

(continued)

Error Return	Meaning
NERR_BadDev	One of the destination names was not previously configured into the PM_SPOOLER_PORTS.
NERR_ProcNotFound	The *pszPrProc* member is not an available DLL.
NERR_DataTypeInvalid	The *TYPES=* directive in the *pszParameters* value was set to an illegal value. Only PM_Q_STD and PM_Q_RAW are valid.

An overview:

The *DosPrintQAdd* API creates a new spooled print queue. Creating the queue does not share the queue. Sharing is accomplished only through a separate call to *NetShareAdd*. The *buf* buffer must contain a _PRQINFO or _PRQINFO3 structure, and the *level* argument must be 1 or 3. If *level* is 1, the extra level-3 fields are set to system defaults. The *szName* value must be set to the queue name and is limited to eight characters.

The other spool configuration values that must be set are the same as those that are changeable with *DosPrintQSetInfo*. If any string pointer values are set to NULL, it indicates "no value". Be careful about setting any to an empty string (" "), because the API will accept that and use it as the value.

DosPrintQDel

Deletes a printer queue from a server.

```
unsigned far pascal
DosPrintQDel(
    char far * servername,    /* where to execute */
    char far * queuename,     /* print queue name */
    )
```

Remote access:

This API can be called remotely by an administrator or a print operator.

Error returns:

If successful, *DosPrintQDel* returns 0. If unsuccessful, it returns one of the standard Del return codes or one of the following error codes:

Error Return	Meaning
NERR_SpoolerNotLoaded	The spooler service must be running.
NERR_QNotFound	The queue name does not exist.

An overview:

The *DosPrintQDel* API deletes a spooled print queue. If the queue is shared, a *NetShareDel* call is made automatically. If jobs in the queue are waiting to be scheduled, the queue is placed in a PRQ_PENDING state. It will not accept jobs and will be deleted once the last job has finished printing. If the queue is in the PRQ_PAUSE state and print jobs are pending, the queue is not marked as PRQ_PENDING until it is "continued" with the *DosPrintQContinue* API.

A PRQ_PENDING queue can be paused and continued, and the jobs can be manipulated with the DosPrintJob APIs. No new jobs will be accepted by the queue.

DosPrintQPurge

Removes all but the current job from a print queue.

```
unsigned far pascal
DosPrintQPurge(
    char far * servername,     /* where to execute */
    char far * queuename,      /* print queue name */
    )
```

Remote access:

This API can be called remotely by an administrator or a print operator.

Error returns:

If successful, *DosPrintQPurge* returns 0. If unsuccessful, it returns one of the standard API return codes or one of the following error codes:

Error Return	Meaning
NERR_SpoolerNotLoaded	The spooler service must be running.
NERR_QNotFound	The queue name does not exist.

An overview:

The *DosPrintQPurge* API deletes all pending jobs from the queue. Any currently printing jobs are unaffected. Ordinarily, the spooler raises an alert when a print job is deleted, but it will not do so for jobs deleted with *DosPrintQPurge*.

DosPrintQPause

Pauses a print queue.

```
unsigned far pascal
DosPrintQPause(
    char far * servername,     /* where to execute */
    char far * queuename,      /* print queue name */
    )
```

Remote access:
This API can be called remotely by an administrator or a print operator.

Error returns:
If successful, *DosPrintQPause* returns 0. If unsuccessful, it returns one of the standard API return codes or one of the following error codes:

Error Return	Meaning
NERR_SpoolerNotLoaded	The spooler service must be running.
NERR_QNotFound	The queue name does not exist.

An overview:
The *DosPrintQPause* API puts a spooled print queue in the PRQ_PAUSE state. While paused, the queue accepts print jobs but doesn't schedule any of them to be printed. Any currently printing jobs are unaffected by this call. If a queue is in the PRQ_PENDING state and is marked for deletion, *DosPrintQPause* pauses the queue but doesn't accept any new print jobs. When the queue is continued using the *DosPrintQContinue* API, it reenters the PRQ_PENDING state.

DosPrintQContinue

Restarts a paused print queue.

```
unsigned far pascal
DosPrintQContinue(
    char far * servername,     /* where to execute */
    char far * queuename,      /* print queue name */
    )
```

Remote access:
This API can be called remotely by an administrator or a print operator.

Error returns:

If successful, *DosPrintQContinue* returns 0. If unsuccessful, it returns one of the standard API return codes or one of the following error codes:

Error Return	Meaning
NERR_SpoolerNotLoaded	The spooler service must be running.
NERR_QNotFound	The queue name does not exist.

An overview:

The *DosPrintQContinue* API continues a paused queue. If the queue is not in the PRQ_ERROR state, it starts scheduling print jobs again.

The DosPrintJob APIs

Print jobs are temporary files that hold data until the spooler schedules a destination. A print job has an identifying number, the *job ID,* which is unique to the server. The DosPrintJob APIs allow listing and control of the print jobs. There is no API for adding a job; this is done automatically by the server when a workstation issues a *DosOpen* call on the print queue UNC name or on a redirected device name connected to the print queue.

The DosPrintJob APIs use three basic data structures.

A _PRJINFO structure—also defined as a PRJINFO type—contains the following members:

Member Name	Description
USHORT uJobId	A number identifying the print job on this server. Each print job has a unique *prjob_id* value within the server, even if submitted to different queues.
CHAR szUserName[UNLEN+1]	The user that submitted the job.
CHAR szNotifyName[CNLEN+1]	A name to receive a message about completion or errors in printing the job. Initially this is the same as the username but can be changed with *DosPrintJobSetInfo.*
CHAR szDataType[DTLEN+1]	An array with an optional type string of the form TYPES=*xxx.* See the description of type matching in the discussion of the TYPES= parameter of the PRQINFO structure member *szParams.*

(continued)

continued

Member Name	Description
PSZ pszParms	Any further parameter information that might be of use to a print processor.
USHORT uPosition	The position of the job in the queue. A value of 1 indicates that it is the next job to print (top of the queue).
USHORT fsStatus	The status of the print job. This is discussed below.
PSZ pszStatus	A zero-terminated string explaining the current status of the job. This is set by the print processor to expound on the status. The default print processor sets this to NULL.
ULONG ulSubmitted	The time the job was submitted.
ULONG ulSize	The size of the job temporary file.
PSZ pszComment	An optional comment string.

The *fsStatus* member is a set of bit-encoded values that indicate the status of the job. The overall status of the job is checked using an expression such as

```
if ((pj.fsStatus & PRJOB_QSTATUS) == PRJOB_QS_*)
```

The possible values are encoded in bits 0 and 1 of *fsStatus*:

Expression	Value	Meaning
PRJ_QS_QUEUED	0	The job is in the queue waiting for a destination to be scheduled.
PRJ_QS_PAUSED	1	The job is in the queue but paused. A destination will not be scheduled while it is paused.
PRJ_QS_SPOOLING	2	The data is being written to the temporary file. After this file is closed, the status can go to QUEUED.
PRJ_QS_PRINTING	3	The job is currently printing to a destination. If this is the state, bits 2 through 15 are meaningful.

If the job is in the PRJ_QS_PRINTING state, bits 2 through 15 of *fsStatus* can be checked with an expression such as

```
if (pj->fsStatus & PRJ_*)
```

The bitmasks are as follows:

Bitmask	Value	Meaning
PRJ_COMPLETE	0x04	Bit 2: The destination has completed printing the job.
PRJ_INTERV	0x08	Bit 3: The destination requires human intervention. For example, a paper tray might need to be changed.
PRJ_ERROR	0x10	Bit 4: The destination is in an error state.
PRJ_DESTOFFLINE	0x20	Bit 5: The destination is off line.
PRJ_DESTPAUSED	0x40	Bit 6: The destination is paused.
PRJ_NOTIFY	0x80	Bit 7: A printing alert should be raised. This can be set by the print processor.
PRJ_DESTNOPAPER	0x100	Bit 8: The destination is out of paper.
PRJ_DESTFORMCHG	0x200	Bit 9: The printer is waiting for a forms change.
PRJ_DESTCRTCHG	0x400	Bit 10: The printer is waiting for a cartridge change.
PRJ_DESTPENCHG	0x800	Bit 11: The printer is waiting for a pen change.
PRJ_DELETED	0x8000	Bit 15: The job is being deleted. This is set by the spooler to tell the Alerter service that the job was deleted with the *DosPrintJobDel* API.

A _PRJINFO2 structure—also defined as a PRJINFO2 type—contains the following members:

Member Name	Description
USHORT uJobId	Same as for PRJINFO.
USHORT uPriority	The print-job priority. This is a number in the range 1 (low) through 99 (high). If the value is 0, the queue priority (see the PRQINFO *uPriority* value) will be used to determine the job priority.
CHAR szUserName[UNLEN+1]	Same as for PRJINFO.
USHORT uPosition	Same as for PRJINFO.
USHORT fsStatus	Same as for PRJINFO.
ULONG ulSubmitted	Same as for PRJINFO.
ULONG ulSize	Same as for PRJINFO.
PSZ pszComment	Same as for PRJINFO.
PSZ pszDocument	A string with the document name of the print job. This is set by the printing application. The SMPR.C program (Figure 11-1) shows how to set print-job parameters.

A _PRJINFO3 structure—also defined as a PRJINFO3 type—contains the following members:

Member Name	Description
USHORT uJobId	Same as for PRJINFO
USHORT uPriority	Same as for PRJINFO2
CHAR szUserName[UNLEN+1]	Same as for PRJINFO
USHORT uPosition	Same as for PRJINFO
USHORT fsStatus	Same as for PRJINFO
ULONG ulSubmitted	Same as for PRJINFO
ULONG ulSize	Same as for PRJINFO
PSZ pszComment	Same as for PRJINFO
PSZ pszDocument	Same as for PRJINFO2
PSZ pszNotifyName	Same as for PRJINFO
PSZ pszDataType	Same as for PRJINFO
PSZ pszParms	Same as for PRJINFO
PSZ pszStatus	Same as for PRJINFO
PSZ pszQueue	The name of the queue containing the job
PSZ pszProcName	The print processor for the queue
PSZ pszProcParms	Any parameters to be passed to the print processor when it is called
PSZ pszDriverName	The queue printer-driver name
PDRIVERDATA pDriverData	Any driver data associated with the print driver
PSZ pszPrinterName	The name of the printer that the job is printing on if it is in the PRJ_QS_PRINTING state

The _PRJINFO structure exists for compatibility with older versions of LAN Manager. New applications should use the _PRJINFO3 structure.

DosPrintJobEnum

Retrieves information about all the print jobs in a print queue.

```
unsigned far pascal
DosPrintJobEnum(
    char far * servername,    /* where to execute        */
    char far * queuename,     /* print queue name        */
    short level,              /* information level       */
    char far * buf,           /* data buffer             */
    USHORT buflen,            /* buffer length           */
    USHORT far * eread,       /* number of entries read  */
    USHORT far * etotal       /* total entries available */
    )
```

Levels:
Supports level 0, 1, 2, and 3 data structures.

Remote access:
Any user with a valid account at the server can call this API remotely.

Error returns:
If successful, *DosPrintJobEnum* returns 0. If unsuccessful, it returns one of the standard Enum return codes or one of the following error codes:

Error Return	Meaning
NERR_SpoolerNotLoaded	The spooler service must be running.
NERR_QNotFound	The queue name does not exist.

An overview:
The *DosPrintJobEnum* API returns a list of print jobs in the specified queue. The information can be at four levels, with buffer contents as shown:

Level	Buffer Contents
0	An array of USHORT *uJobId* values
1	An array of PRJINFO structures
2	An array of PRJINFO2 structures
3	An array of PRJINFO3 structures

Because the structures contain several variable-length items, calculating the buffer size can be difficult. As with the *DosPrintQEnum* API at level 2 or 4, the best strategy is to enumerate at level 0 and then iterate *DosPrintJobGetInfo* calls on each job. Note that if *buflen* is 0, *etotal* returns the total number of jobs in the queue without returning anything in the *buf* buffer.

DosPrintJobGetInfo

Returns information about a specific print job in a print queue.

```
unsigned far pascal
DosPrintJobGetInfo(
    char far * servername,    /* where to execute       */
    USHORT jobid,             /* job identifier         */
    short level,              /* information level      */
    char far * buf,           /* data buffer            */
    USHORT buflen,            /* buffer length          */
    USHORT btotal             /* total bytes available */
    )
```

Levels:

Supports level 0, 1, 2, and 3 data structures.

Remote access:

Any user with a valid account at the server can call this API remotely.

Error returns:

If successful, *DosPrintJobGetInfo* returns 0. If unsuccessful, it returns one of the standard GetInfo return codes or one of the following error codes:

Error Return	Meaning
NERR_SpoolerNotLoaded	The spooler service must be running.
NERR_JobNotFound	The job ID does not exist.

An overview:

The *DosPrintJobGetInfo* API returns information about a print job identified by the *jobid* argument. This *jobid* argument can be obtained with a *DosPrint-JobEnum* call or with a *DosPrintJobGetID* call. The information can be at four levels, with buffer contents as shown:

Level	Buffer Contents
0	A USHORT *uJobId* value
1	A PRJINFO structure
2	A PRJINFO2 structure
3	A PRJINFO3 structure

DosPrintJobSetInfo

Changes the instructions for a job in the print queue.

```
unsigned far pascal
DosPrintJobSetInfo(
    char far * servername,    /* where to execute  */
    USHORT jobid,             /* job identifier    */
    short level,              /* information level */
    char far * buf,           /* data buffer       */
    USHORT buflen,            /* buffer length     */
    short parmnum             /* parameter to set  */
    )
```

Levels:

Supports level 1 and 3 data structures.

Remote access:

This API can be called remotely by an administrator or by a print operator. It can also be called remotely by users for their own jobs.

Error returns:

If successful, *DosPrintJobSetInfo* returns 0. If unsuccessful, it returns one of the standard SetInfo return codes or one of the following error codes:

Error Return	Meaning
NERR_SpoolerNotLoaded	The spooler service must be running.
NERR_JobNotFound	The job ID does not exist.
NERR_InvalidState	If the job is currently printing, the parameters cannot be changed.

An overview:

The *DosPrintJobSetInfo* API changes the parameters of the spooled print job indicated by the *jobid* argument. If *parmnum* is 0, *level* must be 1 or 3 and the buffer holds a PRJINFO or PRJINFO3 structure. Otherwise, the buffer holds the data corresponding to the *parmnum* argument. The data items that can be set and their corresponding *parmnum* values are as follows:

Name	parmnum	Value
pszNotifyName	PRJOB_NOTIFYNAME_PARMNUM	3
pszDataType	PRJOB_DATATYPE_PARMNUM	4
pszParms	PRJOB_PARMS_PARMNUM	5
uPosition	PRJOB_POSITION_PARMNUM	6
pszComment	PRJOB_COMMENT_PARMNUM	11
pszDocument	PRJ_DOCUMENT_PARMNUM	12
uPriority	PRJ_PRIORITY_PARMNUM	14
pszProcParms	PRJ_PROCPARMS_PARMNUM	16
pDriverData	PRJ_DRIVERDATA_PARMNUM	18

If the *uPosition* value has changed, the values have the following meaning:

Position	Meaning
0	Do not change the position.
1	Make the job first in the queue.
n	Move to nth position in the queue.

If the position is larger than the number of jobs in the queue, it means to put the job last in the queue.

Users with *admin* or *print* operator privilege can change the parameters only on their own jobs. The *uPosition* value can only be changed to a later position in the queue.

DosPrintJobDel

Deletes a print job from the print queue.

```
unsigned far pascal
DosPrintJobDel(
    char far * servername,    /* where to execute */
    USHORT jobid,             /* job identifier   */
    )
```

Remote access:

This API can be called remotely by an administrator or by a print operator. It can also be called remotely by users for their own jobs.

Error returns:

If successful, *DosPrintJobDel* returns 0. If unsuccessful, it returns one of the standard Del return codes or one of the following error codes:

Error Return	Meaning
NERR_SpoolerNotLoaded	The spooler service must be running.
NERR_JobNotFound	The job ID does not exist.
NERR_ProcNotRespond	The job is currently printing, but the print processor is not responding to the *DosPrintDestControl* API. The job cannot be stopped at the printer.
ERROR_NETWORK_ACCESS_DENIED	A user without *admin* privilege at the server tried to delete another user's job.

An overview:

The *DosPrintJobDel* API deletes a print job. If the job is currently printing, the spooler issues a *DosPrintDestControl* call to the print processor to stop the printing.

DosPrintJobPause

Pauses a print job in the print queue.

```
unsigned far pascal
DosPrintJobPause(
    char far * servername,    /* where to execute */
    USHORT jobid,             /* job identifier   */
    )
```

Remote access:

This API can be called remotely by an administrator or by a print operator. It can also be called remotely by users for their own jobs.

Error returns:

If successful, *DosPrintJobPause* returns 0. If unsuccessful, it returns one of the standard API return codes or one of the following error codes:

Error Return	Meaning
NERR_SpoolerNotLoaded	The spooler service must be running.
NERR_JobNotFound	The job ID does not exist.
ERROR_NETWORK_ACCESS_DENIED	A user without *admin* privilege at the server tried to delete another user's job.
NERR_InvalidState	If the job is currently printing, it cannot be paused.

An overview:

The *DosPrintJobPause* API holds a job in the print queue. The job continues to move to the front of the queue but isn't scheduled for a destination until it is continued with the *DosPrintJobContinue* API. If the job is currently printing, the printing continues and the API fails.

DosPrintJobContinue

Continues a paused print job.

```
unsigned far pascal
DosPrintJobContinue(
    char far * servername,    /* where to execute */
    USHORT jobid,             /* job identifier  */
    )
```

Remote access:

This API can be called remotely by an administrator or by a print operator. It can also be called remotely by users for their own jobs.

Error returns:

If successful, *DosPrintJobContinue* returns 0. If unsuccessful, it returns one of the standard API return codes or one of the error codes shown on the next page.

Error Return	Meaning
NERR_SpoolerNotLoaded	The spooler service must be running.
NERR_JobNotFound	The job ID does not exist.
ERROR_NETWORK_ACCESS_DENIED	A user without *admin* privilege at the server tried to delete another user's job.
NERR_InvalidState	If the job is currently printing, it cannot be continued.

An overview:

The *DosPrintJobContinue* API continues a paused job. It is not an error to continue a job that is not paused.

DosPrintJobGetId

Gets information about a print job in a print queue.

```
unsigned far pascal
DosPrintJobGetId(
    USHORT handle,          /* DosOpen file handle */
    char far * buf,         /* data buffer        */
    USHORT buflen,          /* buffer length      */
    )
```

Remote access:

This API cannot be called remotely.

Error returns:

If successful, *DosPrintJobGetId* returns 0. If unsuccessful, it returns one of the standard API return codes or the following error code:

Error Return	Meaning
NERR_DevNotRedirected	The file handle is not a redirected spooled print device.

An overview:

The *DosPrintJobGetId* API allows a workstation to translate an open file handle into a Printjob id. This is useful when an application has opened a redirected print device or UNC spooled print queue and wants to use the DosPrintJob APIs on the print job. The *buf* buffer returns with a _PRIDINFO structure. This structure is also defined as a PRIDINFO type, which contains the following elements:

Member Name	Description
USHORT uJobId	The job id.
CHAR szServer[CNLEN+1]	An array containing the server name. It does not contain leading backslashes.
CHAR szQName[QNLEN+1]	An array containing the queue name. This is also the share name.

This API will not work for job handles for a local spooler. If the handle is not to a redirected device, *DosPrintJobGetId* returns NERR_DevNot-Redirected.

Smart Printing with DosPrintJob APIs

By using the print job APIs, you can create a program that passes additional information to the print processor. The SMPR.C program (Figure 11-1) takes the filename and the redirected device name from the command line and copies the information to the spooler file. Before closing the file (which would schedule the job to print), the program copies the rest of the command line to the *pszParms* value for the print job. This information could be anything of interest to the print processor, such as a phone number for fax transfer or a destination name for file transfer. Any settable job parameters can be set at this time.

```
/*
 * SMPR.C -- This smart printing utility copies the input
 * file to the redirected device name. It sets the
 * print-job "szParms" value to a string containing
 * the rest of the command line.
 *
 * Compile with:  C> cl smpr.c netapi.lib
 *
 * Usage:  C> smpr <file> <device> [rest of command ...]
 *
 */

#include <stdio.h>
#include <os2.h>
#include <netcons.h>
#include <pmspl.h>    /* requires LAN Manager 2.0 or later */
#include <malloc.h>
```

Figure 11-1.
The SMPR.C program.

(continued)

Figure 11-1. *continued*

```
main(argc, argv)
int argc;
char **argv;
    {
    int err, size, i;
    HFILE fhdl, dhdl;
    USHORT action, inum, onum;
    PRIDINFO pi;
    char buf[BUFSIZ], *p;
    char * msgstr = "Parameter string set by SMPR.EXE";

    if (argc < 3)
        {
        printf("syntax:  smpr <file> <device> ...\n");
        exit(1);
        }

    /* open the input file */
    err = DosOpen(
                    argv[1],                /* filename */
                    &fhdl,                  /* handle */
                    &action,                /* for error info */
                    0L,                     /* size not needed */
                    0,                      /* attribute not needed */
                    FILE_OPEN,              /* file must exist */
                    OPEN_ACCESS_READONLY :
                    OPEN_SHARE_DENYNONE,    /* open mode */
                    0L                      /* reserved */
                    );
    if (err)
        {
        printf("DosOpen of %s fails (%d)\n", argv[1], err);
        exit(1);
        }

    /* open redirected device */
    err = DosOpen(
                    argv[2],                /* device name */
                    &dhdl,                  /* handle */
                    &action,                /* for error info */
                    0L,                     /* size not needed */
                    0,                      /* attribute not needed */
                    FILE_OPEN,              /* device must exist */
                    OPEN_ACCESS_READWRITE :
                    OPEN_SHARE_DENYNONE,    /* open mode */
                    0L                      /* reserved */
                    );
```

(continued)

Figure 11-1. *continued*

```
if (err)
   {
   printf("DosOpen of %s fails (%d)\n", argv[2], err);
   exit(1);
   }

/* be sure that there is a PrintQ on the other end */
err = DosPrintJobGetId(dhdl, (char far *)&pi, sizeof(pi));
if (err)
   {
   printf("DosPrintJobGetId of fails (%d)\n", err);
   exit(1);
   }

/* package the command line into one string */
for (i = 3, size = 0; i < argc; ++i)
   size += strlen(argv[i]) + 1;
if (size)
   {
   p = malloc(size);
   *p = 0;
   for (i = 3; i < argc; ++i)
      {
      strcat(p, argv[i]);
      if (i != argc-1)
         strcat(p, " ");
      }
   }
/* set the prjob_parms */
if (size)
   {
   err = DosPrintJobSetInfo(
                        NULL,               /* server name */
                        pi.uJobId,          /* job id      */
                        1,                  /* level       */
                        p,                  /* buffer      */
                        size,               /* buflen      */
                        PRJOB_PARMS_PARMNUM); /* parameter  */
   if (err)
      {
      printf("DosPrintJobSetInfo fails (%d)\n", err);
      exit(1);
      }
```

(continued)

Figure 11-1. *continued*

```
    /* also set the job comment */
        err = DosPrintJobSetInfo(
                              NULL,             /* server name */
                              pi.uJobId,        /* job id      */
                              1,                /* level       */
                              msg_string,       /* buffer      */
                              size,             /* buflen      */
                              PRJOB_COMMENT_PARMNUM);
        if (err)
            {
            printf("DosPrintJobSetInfo fails (%d)\n", err);
            exit(1);
            }
        }

    /* now copy the information */
    do
        {
        DosRead(fhdl, buf, BUFSIZ, &inum);
        DosWrite(dhdl, buf, BUFSIZ, &onum);
        } while (inum == BUFSIZ);
    /* exit will close device and cause scheduling */
    exit(0);
    }
```

The DosPrintDest APIs

The DosPrintDest APIs let you list and control *print destinations*. A print destination is any spooled device, such as a laser printer, that is physically connected to a server. Print destinations are a LAN Manager concept similar to the OS/2 Presentation Manager concept of a "spooler printer," which is configured in the PM_SPOOLER_PRINTER section of OS2SYS.INI. Each "spooler printer" maps one to one to a logical address called PM_SPOOLER_PORTS. LAN Manager destinations always use these logical addresses. Note that in the DOS world, the concept of logical addresses corresponds to the logical devices LPT*x* and COM*x*.

An application can send control signals to a print destination, telling it to kill the job, pause, continue, or restart the job. These control signals are sent with the *DosPrintDestControl* API and are actually signals to the print processor, which performs the appropriate action on the logical address.

The DosPrintDest APIs use two main data structures.

A _PRDINFO structure—also defined as a PRDINFO type—contains the following members:

Member Name	Description
CHAR szName[PDLEN+1]	An array containing the zero-terminated destination name.
CHAR szUserName[UNLEN+1]	An array containing the zero-terminated username of the current printing job, if one exists. If the destination is not currently printing, this will be an empty string, and the rest of the structure has no meaning.
USHORT uJobId	The job ID of the current printing job, or 0 if no job is currently printing.
USHORT fsStatus	A set of bits indicating the status of the current printing job. The status has no meaning if the destination is idle. The bitmasks are as follows:

Bitmask	Value	Meaning
PRD_STATUS_MASK	0x0003	Used to retrieve the next two values. They can be 0 (active) or 1 (not active).
PRD_ACTIVE	0x0000	The destination is currently printing.
PRD_PAUSE	0x0001	The destination has been paused in the middle of a print job or is currently idle.
PRJ_DEVSTATUS	0x1FC	A mask for retrieving the rest of the values in *fsStatus*.
PRJ_COMPLETE	0x0004	The destination has completed printing the job.
PRJ_INTERV	0x0008	The destination requires human intervention. For example, a paper tray might need to be changed.
PRJ_ERROR	0x0010	The destination is in an error state.
PRJ_DESTOFFLINE	0x0020	The destination is off line.
PRJ_DESTPAUSED	0x0040	The destination is paused.
PRJ_NOTIFY	0x0080	A printing alert should be raised.
PRJ_DESTNOPAPER	0x0100	The destination is out of paper.

Member Name	Description
PSZ pszStatus	An ASCII string providing additional information about the status.
USHORT time	The number of minutes the job has been printing. This is valid only when the destination is printing or paused while printing.

A _PRDINFO3 structure—also defined as a PRDINFO3 type—contains the following members:

Member Name	Description
PSZ pszPrinterName	The associated printer name as defined in PM_SPOOLER_PRINTER.
PSZ pszUserName	Same as in PRDINFO.
PSZ pszLogAdr	The logical address that the printer prints on.
USHORT uJobId	Same as in PRDINFO.
USHORT fStatus	Same as in PRDINFO.
PSZ pszStatus	Same as in PRDINFO.
PSZ pszComment	A further description of the printer.
PSZ pszDrivers	A comma-separated list of drivers compatible with this printer.
USHORT time	Same as in PRDINFO.
USHORT usTimeOut	The number of seconds the device driver waits before telling the spooler that the device doesn't respond. This value is not used by LAN Manager version 2.0 and should be set to 0.

NOTE: *The _PRDINFO structure exists for compatibility with older versions of LAN Manager. New applications should use the _PRDINFO3 structure.*

DosPrintDestEnum

Retrieves a list of all print destinations at a server.

```
unsigned far pascal
DosPrintDestEnum(
    char far * servername,    /* where to execute        */
    short level,              /* information level       */
    char far * buf,           /* data buffer             */
    USHORT buflen,            /* buffer length           */
    USHORT far * eread,       /* number of entries read  */
    USHORT far * etotal       /* total entries available */
    )
```

Levels:
Supports level 0, 1, 2, and 3 data structures.

Remote access:
Any user with a valid account at the server can call this API remotely.

Error returns:

If successful, *DosPrintDestEnum* returns 0. If unsuccessful, it returns one of the standard Enum return codes or the following error code:

Error Return	Meaning
NERR_SpoolerNotLoaded	The spooler service must be running.

An overview:

The *DosPrintDestEnum* API returns a list of all destinations assigned to any print queue. The information can be at four levels, with buffer contents as shown:

Level	Buffer Contents
0	An array of destination names, each a szName[PDLEN+1] value
1	An array of PRDINFO structures
2	An array of printer names, each a szPrinterName[PRINTERNAME_SIZE+1] value
3	An array of PRJINFO3 structures

DosPrintDestGetInfo

Retrieves information about a specific print destination at a server.

```
unsigned far pascal
DosPrintDestGetInfo(
    char far * servername,    /* where to execute     */
    char far * destname,      /* destination name     */
    short level,              /* information level    */
    char far * buf,           /* data buffer          */
    USHORT buflen,            /* buffer length        */
    USHORT far * btotal       /* total bytes available */
    )
```

Levels:

Supports level 0, 1, 2, and 3 data structures.

Remote access:

Any user with a valid account at the server can call this API remotely.

Error returns:

If successful, *DosPrintDestGetInfo* returns 0. If unsuccessful, it returns one of the standard GetInfo return codes or one of the following error codes:

Error Return	Meaning
NERR_SpoolerNotLoaded	The spooler service must be running.
NERR_DestNotFound	The destination is not assigned to the routing list of any of the print queues.

An overview:

The *DosPrintDestGetInfo* API returns information about a specific print destination. The information can be at four levels, with buffer contents as shown:

Level	Buffer Contents
0	A destination name, as a szName[PDLEN+1] value
1	A PRDINFO structure
2	A printer name, as a szPrinterName[PRINTERNAME_SIZE+1] value
3	A PRDINFO3 structure

DosPrintDestSetInfo

Modifies the configuration of a print destination at a server.

```
unsigned far pascal
DosPrintDestSetInfo(
    char far * servername,    /* where to execute       */
    char far * name,          /* the destination name   */
    short level,              /* must be 3              */
    char far * buf,           /* data buffer            */
    USHORT parmnum            /* parameter number       */
    )
```

Levels:

Supports level 3 structures.

Remote access:

Only an administrator or print operator can call this API remotely.

Error returns:

If successful, *DosPrintDestSetInfo* returns 0. If unsuccessful, it returns one of the standard SetInfo return codes or one of the following error codes:

Error Return	Meaning
NERR_SpoolerNotLoaded	The spooler service must be running.
NERR_DestNotFound	The logical address is not a previously configured one.
NERR_BadDev	The logical address was not a previously defined one.

An overview:

The DosPrintDestSetInfo API changes the values associated with an existing printer. If the *parmnum* argument is 0, the *buf* argument must contain a PRDINFO structure. The data items that can be set and their corresponding *parmnum* values are as follows:

Name	parmnum	Value
pszLogAddr	PRD_PORT_PARMNUM	2
pszComment	PRD_COMMENT_PARMNUM	6
pszDrivers	PRD_DRIVERS_PARMNUM	7

If the *pszLogAddr* member is NULL, it disconnects the logical address from the printer. See the *DosPrintDestAdd* API below for more details on the settable parameters.

DosPrintDestAdd

Adds a print destination to a server.

```
unsigned far pascal
DosPrintDestAdd(
    char far * servername,    /* where to execute */
    short level,              /* must be 3        */
    char far * buf,           /* data buffer      */
    USHORT buflen,            /* buffer length    */
    )
```

Levels:

Supports level 3 data structures.

Remote access:

Only an administrator or print operator can call this API remotely.

Error returns:

If successful, *DosPrintDestAdd* returns 0. If unsuccessful, it returns one of the standard Add return codes or one of the following error codes:

Error Return	Meaning
NERR_SpoolerNotLoaded	The spooler service must be running.
NERR_DestExists	The destination already exists.
NERR_BadDev	The logical address was not a previously defined one.

An overview:

The *DosPrintDestAdd* API creates a new printer definition for the spooler. The printer is set up to print to the logical address specified by the *pszLogAddr* member. If *pszLogAddr* is NULL or an empty string, the printer is created but not associated with any logical address, and no printing can occur on that printer. A logical address must be previously defined in the PM_SPOOLER_PORTS section of the OS2SYS.INI. This must be done through the Presentation Manager control panel. All device drivers and queues must already exist.

DosPrintDestDel

Deletes a print destination from a server.

```
unsigned far pascal
DosPrintDestDel(
    char far * servername,    /* where to execute */
    char far * printername    /* name to delete   */
    )
```

Remote access:

Only an administrator or print operator can call this API remotely.

Error returns:

If successful, *DosPrintDestDel* returns 0. If unsuccessful, it returns one of the standard Del return codes or one of the following error codes:

Error Return	Meaning
NERR_SpoolerNotLoaded	The spooler service must be running.
NERR_DestNotFound	The printer does not exist.
NERR_DestInvalidState	A job is currently printing.

An overview:

The *DosPrintDestDel* API deletes a printer from the spooler. If a job is currently printing on the printer, the call fails.

DosPrintDestControl

Cancels, pauses, continues, or restarts the specified print destination.

```
unsigned far pascal
DosPrintDestControl(
    char far * servername,    /* where to execute */
    char far * destname,      /* destination name */
    USHORT opcode             /* operation code   */
    )
```

Remote access:
Only an administrator or print operator can call this API remotely.

Error returns:
If successful, *DosPrintDestControl* returns 0. If unsuccessful, it returns one of the standard API return codes or one of the following error codes:

Error Return	Meaning
NERR_SpoolerNotLoaded	The spooler service must be running.
NERR_DestNotFound	The destination is not assigned to the routing list of any of the print queues.
NERR_InvalidOp	The opcode is not defined.
NERR_DestIdle	The destination is not currently printing a job and will not accept the PRDEST_DELETE or PRDEST_RESTART opcode.

An overview:
The *DosPrintDestControl* API communicates with whatever print processor is currently using the named destination. The *opcode* argument can be one of the following values:

opcode	Value	Meaning
PRDDEST_DELETE	0	Delete the current printing job. This stops printing immediately. The print processor will then clean up and exit.
PRDDEST_PAUSE	1	Stop printing, but do not exit. It is expected that at a later time another opcode will tell the print processor to continue printing.
PRDDEST_CONT	2	Continue printing. It is not an error to send this opcode if the destination is not paused.
PRD_RESTART	3	Restart printing the current job.

The values 4 through 127 are reserved for use by Microsoft. The values 128 through 255 are reserved for OEM use.

The PRDEST_PAUSE opcode can be sent to an idle destination, causing the destination to stop accepting print jobs until it is sent a PRDEST_CONT. If the PRDEST_DELETE or PRDEST_RESTART opcode is sent to an idle destination, an error occurs.

More on the Presentation Manager Spooler

LAN Manager version 1.0 and OS/2 version 1.2 have two sets of APIs (functions beginning with DosPrint and Spl) and two ways of writing programs that use the spooler. The Spl APIs are the standard Presentation Manager Spooler APIs for OS/2 1.2. The DosPrint APIs, described in this chapter, provide additional functions for dealing with print queues.

Presentation Manager applications must query the system profile (the OS2SYS.INI file) to learn about available print resources. This file is often not available for remote computers. The DosPrint APIs make this information available remotely and hide the details of the configuration file. In addition, the DosPrint APIs dynamically update the system profile when queues, jobs, or destinations are manipulated.

NetBIOS APIs

The NetBIOS device driver is the lowest level of network communications accessible through LAN Manager. (The more abstract layers of redirected file I/O—named pipes, remote administration, and so on—all use the Net-BIOS for their essential communication.) Few applications need direct access to NetBIOS, but for those that do, this chapter presents the APIs suited to the tasks.

> **NOTE:** *This chapter is not intended to teach how to use the NetBIOS, but rather how to use the LAN Manager NetBIOS APIs. This overview of Net-BIOS is a simple one to help make the concepts clear. For a more detailed account of NetBIOS programming, refer to the following resources:*

- IBM NetBIOS Application Development Guide
- C Programmer's Guide to NetBIOS, *W. David Schwaderer, Howard W. Sams & Company, 1988.*

NetBIOS Communication

The NetBIOS can be viewed functionally as a piece of software installed as a device driver. All NetBIOS functions are performed by passing a standard data structure called the *Network Control Block* (NCB) to the NetBIOS driver. The NetBIOS performs three major functions:

- **Local name management.** Names can be registered with the Net-BIOS. The NetBIOS ensures that the names are unique within the local area network. Each NetBIOS driver can have multiple unique names registered, up to a configurable limit (the default is 12). A special type of name, the *group name*, can be shared by more than one NetBIOS.

- **Virtual circuit establishment.** A reliable communication channel can be set up between two NetBIOS names. The virtual circuit provides complete end-to-end reliability, performing retries if necessary.

- **Datagram communication.** One-way communications can be made between two NetBIOS names. Delivery isn't as reliable as virtual circuits, but it is faster. Datagram communications to a NetBIOS group name provide a simple broadcast mechanism.

All NetBIOS operations have an active and a passive side. The passive side submits an NCB (LISTEN) indicating its willingness to establish a virtual circuit to one of its registered names. The active side submits an NCB (CALL) indicating its desire to establish a virtual circuit between one of its names and a known name at the passive side. After the virtual circuit is established, either side can submit an NCB (RECEIVE) indicating that it will accept data on a particular virtual circuit, or an NCB (SEND) indicating that it wants to send data on a virtual circuit. A SEND can succeed only if a RECEIVE exists at the other end.

An NCB submitted to the NetBIOS driver is marked as a synchronous (wait) or an asynchronous (no-wait) operation. In a synchronous operation, control returns only when the operation is complete. In an asynchronous operation, control returns immediately, and a signaling mechanism lets the program know when the operation is complete. Asynchronous signaling is done in two ways:

- **Polling.** The application periodically checks the command-complete field of the NCB. This field has an initial value of 0xFF, but the NetBIOS changes this value when the operation is complete or is canceled.

- **Post addressing.** Under OS/2, a post address is the address of an open semaphore cleared when the operation is complete. (The semaphore must be created as a system semaphore.) Under DOS, a post address is the address of a subroutine called when the operation is complete.

The Net Driver Interface Specification

When the NetBIOS was first specified, it was specified in the same kind of "black-box" view shown in the previous section. A network hardware manufacturer wanting to support NetBIOS had to write a NetBIOS driver that talked to the network adapter (the network hardware). But under LAN Manager, the NetBIOS is broken into two parts, as shown in Figure 12-1.

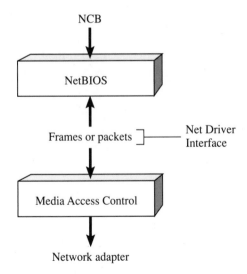

Figure 12-1.
NetBIOS under LAN Manager.

Now network hardware manufacturers have a much easier time working with NetBIOS: They need only supply software written to the *Net Driver Interface Specification* (NDIS), a specification developed jointly by Microsoft and 3Com. This "Media Access Control" driver (MAC) need only know how to get packets from the NetBIOS driver and write them to the network adapter, and how to receive packets from the adapter and pass them to the NetBIOS.

The Protocol Manager

The NDIS does more than simplify the lives of network hardware manufacturers. It also allows the construction of multiple *virtual* NetBIOS drivers, as shown in Figure 12-2.

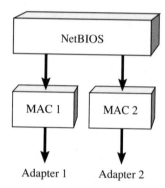

Figure 12-2.
Multiple virtual NetBIOS drivers.

As shown, one upper-level NetBIOS driver can behave like two complete NetBIOS drivers. For example, one of the adapters might be for an Ethernet and the other for a token ring. If the manufacturers have provided the MAC drivers, you can create the appearance of a complete Ethernet NetBIOS and a complete token-ring NetBIOS.

The Protocol Manager is a part of LAN Manager that binds the NetBIOS and MAC drivers together into a logical whole. The Protocol Manager was developed jointly by Microsoft and 3Com. Specifications are available from either company.

Multiple NetBIOS Drivers

You can use multiple NetBIOS drivers at one time—either completely separate device drivers or combinations of NetBIOS drivers and MAC drivers bound together with the Protocol Manager. No matter what the structure,

LAN Manager must be told about all logical NetBIOS drivers. The LAN-MAN.INI file contains a component named [networks] whose parameters describe logical NetBIOS drivers for LAN Manager. Each parameter is of the following form:

```
netname = driver,lana,type,NCBs,sessions,names
```

Table 12-1 lists the meaning of each part of the parameter.

Parameter	Meaning
netname	The logical NetBIOS name. Each logical driver must be given a name so that it can be easily opened by a program. Each name must be unique.
driver	The actual NetBIOS device-driver name. LAN Manager must know what device driver to communicate with for each logical NetBIOS.
lana	The local area network adapter. If the Protocol Manager is used to create more than one logical NetBIOS (by binding a NetBIOS driver to multiple MAC drivers), the *lana* identifies which MAC is being used. This parameter is optional and defaults to 0.
type	Two NetBIOS driver types are available: *LM10* is a Lan Manager 1.0 or higher driver; *NetBIOS NB30* is a NetBIOS 3.0 driver. This parameter is optional and defaults to LM10.
NCBs	The number of NCBs that can be outstanding at one time. This parameter is optional and defaults to a value specified by the driver.
sessions	The number of virtual circuits that can exist at one time. This parameter is optional and defaults to a value specified by the driver.
names	The number of NetBIOS names that can exist at one time. This parameter is optional and defaults to a value specified by the driver.

Table 12-1.
The NetBIOS device driver parameters supported by LANMAN.INI.

For example, consider a LANMAN.INI file with the following parameters:

```
[networks]
net1 = mynbios$,0,LM10,32,32,16
net2 = mynbios$,1,LM10,32,32,16
net3 = loopback$
```

Two logical NetBIOS drivers are bound to the *mynbios$* device-driver program. Each is a LAN Manager NetBIOS and has the prescribed limits on NCBs, virtual circuits, and names. Programs wanting to interact with these two logical drivers will know them as *net1* and *net2* respectively. The third logical driver, *net3*, uses a different device-driver program than do the other two.

The [network] component is read by the LAN Manager redirector during initialization. The redirector then passes information to each of the logical NetBIOS drivers.

Each actual NetBIOS device driver must be installed as a device driver at system boot. Installation occurs through the CONFIG.SYS file and is specific to each driver.

The workstation view

How do multiple NetBIOS drivers affect a workstation? Consider a workstation existing simultaneously on two different local area networks, as shown in Figure 12-3.

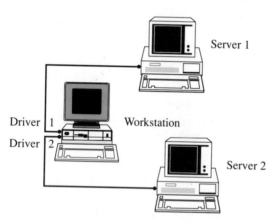

Figure 12-3.
A workstation with two NetBIOS drivers.

A program writing directly to a logical NetBIOS could use NetBIOS functions on either of the local area networks. Names added to one NetBIOS driver would not affect the other. The two networks wouldn't communicate.

At a more abstract level, however, you could have the workstation automatically duplicate its actions on each of the networks. In the LANMAN.INI file, the *wrknets=* parameter of the [workstation] component lists all of the logical NetBIOS drivers that the LAN Manager should "manage." Whenever the redirector tries to establish a session to a particular computer, it first tries to establish a virtual circuit to that computer name. The redirector tries to create the virtual circuit on each of the managed networks, stopping as soon as it finds the name. From then on, the redirector remembers which logical driver to use for that virtual circuit. Loopback drivers (defined below) are always tried first, regardless of their order in the list of managed networks.

Because the two networks in the example are independent, there's nothing to prevent a server name from appearing on both networks. Suppose that were the case (DUPSRV, for example) and that the workstation were configured as follows:

```
wrknets=net1,net2
```

The following command would look for the name DUPSRV on net1 and, after finding it, would establish the connection:

```
net use x: \\DUPSRV\PUBLIC
```

If names are duplicated, only the first would be found. If a server named DUPSRV also existed on the second network, connections could never be made to it.

For network logon, a workstation belongs to a domain. This domain is implemented in terms of the NetBios *group name*. When the workstation starts, it adds the same group name to all of its managed networks, and this becomes its *domain name*.

The workstation can also receive browser announcements from servers on all of its managed networks. If the workstation is configured to listen for other domains, it will do so on all of its managed networks.

Note that the Netlogon service replication of the user accounts database (Single System Image) cannot cross network boundaries. In the preceding example, the two servers could share a domain name with the workstation, but the UAS database could be different. An administrator will want to ensure that this never happens.

The server view

How do multiple NetBIOS drivers affect a server? Consider a server existing simultaneously on two different local area networks. The server can establish sessions with workstations on either network. The LANMAN.INI file contains a *srvnets=* parameter in the [server] component which tells the server what logical NetBIOS drivers to act as a server on. The server accepts sessions on all of its ''srvnets.'' The server also sends Alerter messages on all of its ''srvnets.''

Can one network workstation establish a session with or in any way communicate with a workstation or server on the other network? Not in the core LAN Manager. Some LAN Manager OEMs allow such interaction through *bridges* or *gateways*. A bridge is a connection between two local area networks that makes them appear logically as a single larger network. Gateways are network nodes that take information from one network, perform protocol translations or routing decisions on it, and then place the information on another network.

The loopback driver

A special NetBIOS driver—the *loopback driver*—is part of the core LAN Manager. The loopback driver is a full-featured NetBIOS driver that passes information back to itself; it doesn't talk to network hardware. Although a server can always create a session with itself, the use of the loopback driver eliminates the need for writing data to the network. When the redirector searches through the "wrknets" to establish a session, it always tries the loopback driver first.

The loopback driver is useful for debugging network programs and for plugging some security holes in the access-control system. (Local filesystem requests that are routed over a redirected drive back to the server go through the LAN Manager access-control software.)

Summary of Multiple Networks

Table 12-2 summarizes what happens when a workstation or a server is on more than one logical network at a time.

Action	*Result*
Sharing a resource	Share resource on all *srvnets*.
Using a resource (files, print queues, character devices, and named pipes	Try all managed networks until the shared resource is found.
Sending messages to a specific name	Try all managed networks until the name is found.
Sending messages to * or a domain name	Broadcast to all managed networks.
Receiving messages	Receive from all managed networks.
Adding a message alias name	Add the name to all managed networks.

Table 12-2. *(continued)*
Results associated with the actions of a computer on more than one logical network.

Table 12-2. *continued*

Action	Result
Forwarding a message name	Not supported. The *NetMessageNameFwd* API returns ERROR_NOT_SUPPORTED.
Receiving forwarded messages	No difference from single network.
Network logon validation	Initiate logon validation to all managed networks. Only one server on one network is used for validation.
Mailslots (first-class)	Make mailslot visible on all of the server's managed networks. The workstation tries all of its managed networks until the mailslot is found.
Mailslots (second-class)	Make mailslot visible on all managed networks. The message is sent (or broadcast) on all managed networks.

The NetBIOS APIs

The NetBIOS APIs let you program a logical NetBIOS driver directly. Five NetBIOS APIs are available:

- *NetBIOSEnum*
- *NetBIOSGetInfo*
- *NetBIOSOpen*
- *NetBIOSClose*
- *NetBIOSSubmit*

To use the NetBIOS APIs, you must include *netcons.h* and *netbios.h* at compile time. The *ncb.h* include file contains the definition of the NCB data structure, all of the NCB operation codes, and the error values that can be returned in the NCB. The program must be linked with the *netapi.lib* stub library.

Two basic information structures are available for the NetBIOS APIs. The *netbios_info_0* structure contains the following member:

Member Name	Description
char nb0_net_name[NETBIOS_NAME_LEN+1]	This is a zero-terminated array of characters. It is the network name, or logical name of the driver as defined in the [networks] component of LANMAN.INI.

The *netbios_info_1* structure contains the following members:

Member Name	Description
char nb1_net_name[NETBIOS_NAME_LEN+1]	A zero-terminated array of characters. It is the network name, or logical name of the driver as defined in the [networks] component of LANMAN.INI.
char nb1_driver_name[DEVLEN+1]	The actual NetBIOS device driver corresponding to this logical NetBIOS.
UCHAR nb1_lana_num	The LAN adapter number within the actual device driver. If multiple logical drivers are constructed from an actual device driver and more than one MAC driver, the *nb1_driver_name* and *nb1_lana_num* pair identify each logical driver.
USHORT nb1_driver_type	The driver can be one of two types: NB_TYPE_NCB 1 A standard LAN Manager NetBIOS driver. NB_TYPE_MCB 2 A NetBIOS 3.0 driver.
USHORT nb1_net_status	The status of the logical driver. This is a set of bitmasks and a bitfield:

Bitmask	Value	Meaning
NB_LAN_MANAGED	0x01	If TRUE, this logical driver appears in the *wrknets=* parameter and is managed. The redirector tries to look for names on this net during session establishment.
NB_LAN_LOOPBACK	0x02	If TRUE, this is a loopback driver.
NB_LAN_SENDNOACK	0x04	If TRUE, this driver supports SEND_NO-_ACK NCB.
NB_LAN_LMEXT	0x08	If TRUE, LAN Manager extended NCBs are supported.
NB_LAN_INTNCB	0x10	If TRUE, then NCBs can be submitted to the driver at interrupt time. If this is not TRUE, interrupt-time sub-mission can have unknown consequences.

In addition to these bits, a bitfield indicates the privilege mode with which the NetBIOS driver was opened (with the *NetBiosOpen* call). The possible values are as follows:

Bitmask	Value	Meaning
NB_OPEN_REGULAR	0x4000	Regular mode
NB_OPEN_PRIVILEGED	0x8000	Privileged mode
NB_OPEN_EXCLUSIVE	0xC000	Exclusive mode

Both of the following bitfields have masks defined for obtaining the whole field:

Bitmask	Value	Meaning
NB_LAN_FLAGS_MASK	0x3FFFF	The driver flags
NB_LAN_OPEN_MASK	0xCFFFF	The *NetBiosOpen* mode
ULONG nbl_net_bandwidth		The network bandwidth in bits per second
USHORT nbl_max_sess		The maximum number of virtual circuits supported by the driver
USHORT nbl_max_ncbs		The maximum number of pending NCBs supported by the driver
USHORT nbl_max_names		The maximum number of names that can be registered with the driver

The following code fragment checks to see whether the NetBIOS driver is a loopback driver supporting interrupt-time submission and determines whether the NetBIOS driver is open in privileged mode:

```
if (nbl.nbl_net_status & (NB_LAN_LOOPBACK & NB_LAN_INTNCB)
    /* yes, loopback and interrupt submission */

if ((nbl.nbl_net_status & NB_OPEN_MODE_MASK) == NB_OPEN_PRIVILEGED)
    /* yes, it is open in privileged mode */
```

> **NOTE:** *The handle value of 0 is a special-case handle that always refers to the first logical driver—that is, the first logical name encountered in the [networks] component of the LANMAN.INI file. The first driver is implicitly open.*
>
> *A logical driver is opened in a privilege mode, which prevents applications from getting in each others' way because some of the NCB operations affect the entire workstation, not just the process trying to use the NetBIOS.*

NetBiosEnum

Gets the names of all installed NetBIOS device drivers.

```
unsigned far pascal
NetBiosEnum(
    char far * servername,      /* where to execute       */
    short level,                /* information level      */
    char far * buf,             /* space for return data  */
    USHORT buflen,              /* size of buf            */
    USHORT far * entriesread,   /* number of entries read */
    USHORT far * totalentries   /* total entries available */
    )
```

Error returns:

If successful, *NetBiosEnum* returns 0. If unsuccessful, it returns one of the standard Enum return codes or the following error code:

Error Return	Meaning
NERR_NetNotStarted	The NETWKSTA.SYS device driver was not installed.

An overview:

The *NetBiosEnum* API returns a list of logical NetBIOS drivers as described in the [network] component of the LANMAN.INI file. If the *level* argument is 0, the *buf* buffer contains as many *netbios_info_0* structures as will fit. If the *level* argument is 1, the *buf* buffer contains as many *netbios_info_1* structures as will fit. This call can be made remotely but requires *admin* privilege at the server.

NetBiosGetInfo

Gets information about the NetBIOS device driver specified.

```
unsigned far pascal
NetBiosGetInfo(
    char far *server,       /* where to execute        */
    char far *netbiosname,  /* logical driver name     */
    USHORT level,           /* level of detail         */
    char far *buf,          /* where to return data    */
    USHORT buflen,          /* size of buf             */
    USHORT far *ta          /* total bytes available   */
    )
```

Error returns:

If successful, *NetBiosGetInfo* returns 0. If unsuccessful, it returns one of the standard GetInfo return codes or one of the following error codes:

Error Return	Meaning
NERR_WkstaNotStarted	The workstation must be started to use the NetBIOS APIs.
NERR_NetNotStarted	The NETWKSTA.SYS device driver was not installed.

An overview:

The *NetBiosGetInfo* API returns information about a specific logical NetBIOS driver. If the *level* argument is 1, the *buf* buffer returns with a *netbios_info_1* structure. This call can be made remotely but requires *admin* privilege at the server.

NetBiosOpen

Creates a device-driver handle for sending NCBs to the specified NetBIOS device driver.

```
unsigned far pascal
NetBiosOpen(
    char far * netbiosname,    /* logical NetBIOS name     */
    char far * reserved,       /* must be NULL             */
    USHORT options,            /* open mode options        */
    USHORT far * nethandle     /* the open NetBIOS handle  */
    )
```

Error returns:

If successful, *NetBiosOpen* returns 0. If unsuccessful, it returns one of the standard API return codes or one of the following error codes:

Error Return	Meaning
NERR_WkstaNotStarted	The workstation must be started to use the NetBIOS APIs.
NERR_NetNotStarted	The NETWKSTA.SYS device driver was not installed.
ERROR_FILE_NOT_FOUND	The logical NetBIOS name does not exist.
ERROR_ACCESS_DENIED	There is an open mode conflict.
ERROR_INVALID_PARAMETER	The open mode is an illegal value.

An overview:

The *NetBiosOpen* API obtains a handle to a logical NetBIOS driver so that NCBs can be submitted to it. If the *netbiosname* argument is a null string (" "), it implicitly refers to the first NetBIOS driver in the [networks] list.

The *options* argument can be one of the following values:

Option	Value	Meaning
NB_EXCLUSIVE	3	The process has exclusive access to the driver. Any other *NetBiosOpen* calls fail as long as this instance is open. This call fails if any other process has the driver open. The NB_EXCLUSIVE mode allows a process to issue all NCBs to the driver.
NB_PRIVILEGE	2	Only one process may have the driver open in NB_PRIVILEGE mode, although other processes can open the driver in NB_REGULAR mode. In NB_PRIVILEGE, the process can issue all NCBs except the following:
		RESET
		RECEIVE ANY TO ANY
NB_REGULAR	1	If a process opens the driver in NB_REGULAR mode, it cannot issue the following NCBs:
		RESET
		RECEIVE ANY TO ANY
		RECEIVE BROADCAST DATAGRAM (any use of the permanent node name)

The NetBIOS handles are not inherited by child processes. Subsequent Net-BIOS handle operations such as *NetBiosClose* or *NetBiosSubmit* can be executed only by the process that did the *NetBiosOpen*.

NetBiosClose

Closes a NetBIOS device driver.

```
unsigned far pascal
NetBiosClose(
    USHORT nethandle,        /* the open net handle */
    USHORT reserved          /* must be 0           */
    )
```

Error returns:

If successful, *NetBiosClose* returns 0. If unsuccessful, it returns one of the standard API return codes or one of the following error codes:

Error Return	Meaning
NERR_WkstaNotStarted	The workstation must be started to use the NetBIOS APIs.
NERR_NetNotStarted	The NETWKSTA.SYS device driver was not installed.
ERROR_INVALID_HANDLE	The handle is not a valid handle for a NetBIOS driver.
ERROR_ACCESS_DENIED	The handle does not belong to this process.

An overview:

The *NetBiosClose* API closes an open instance of a logical NetBIOS driver. If pending NCBs exist, they are canceled. If a process exits with open Net-BIOS handles, a *NetBiosClose* call is automatically executed for each handle.

NetBiosSubmit

Submits one or more NCBs to a NetBIOS device driver.

```
unsigned far pascal
NetBiosSubmit(
    USHORT nethandle,       /* the NetBIOS handle */
    unsigned options,       /* submit options     */
    struct ncb far * pncb   /* the NCB            */
    )
```

Error returns:

If successful, *NetBiosSubmit* returns 0. If unsuccessful, it returns one of the standard API return codes or one of the following error codes:

Error Return	Meaning
NERR_WkstaNotStarted	The workstation must be started to use the NetBIOS APIs.
NERR_NetNotStarted	The NETWKSTA.SYS device driver was not installed.
ERROR_INVALID_HANDLE	The handle is not a valid handle for a NetBIOS driver.
NRC_*	Any of the NRC_ error codes defined in NCB.H

An overview:

The *NetBiosSubmit* API passes an NCB to a NetBIOS driver that has been opened with *NetBiosOpen*. A *nethandle* argument of 0 refers to the first Net-BIOS driver declared in the [networks] component of LANMAN.INI and will be implicitly opened by the API.

You can use *NetBiosSubmit* to submit a single NCB or a linked chain of NCBs. Chained NCBs must be in the same memory segment. Each NCB is preceded by a 16-bit near pointer which is the offset of the next NCB in the chain. The value 0xFFFF indicates the last NCB in the chain. You can have any number of NCBs in the chain provided they fit in a single segment. Figure 12-4 shows a chain of NCBs.

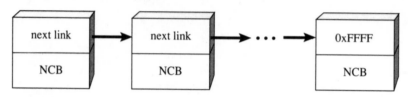

Figure 12-4.
An NCB chain with an ending NCB containing 0xFFFF.

Chained NCBs can be of any type; they go to the NetBIOS driver in the order in which they appear in the chain. Note that not all sequences are useful. For example, you can't submit a CALL followed by a SEND because the SEND requires the logical session number from the successful CALL. A chain with a SEND followed by a RECEIVE is valid and is useful for trans-action-oriented operations.

If a chain is submitted, the NetBIOS can be told to proceed down the chain in the case of an error or to stop processing and return immediately on an error. If an error is encountered during the processing of a "proceed on er-ror" chain, the *ncb_retcode* field is set appropriately. If the chain is "stop on error," all subsequent NCBs will have their *ncb_cmd_cplt* field set to NRC_CMDCAN (command canceled).

A chain can contain asynchronous NCBs (no wait), but the *ncb_retcode* value will indicate only that the NCB was submitted. If the entire chain con-sists of synchronous NCBs (wait), then each waits for the preceding NCB to complete.

If a single NCB is submitted, the *NetBiosSubmit* API can also be instructed to retry if certain errors occur. If the NetBIOS error code is any of the fol-lowing, *NetBiosSubmit* can be told to retry 20 times:

Error Code	Meaning
NRC_NORES	No resources are available.
NRC_REMTFUL	The remote session table is full.
NRC_IFBUSY	The interface is busy.

The *options* argument can be one of the following values:

Value	Meaning
0	Single NCB. Do not retry on error.
1	Single NCB. Retry on error.
2	Chain NCBs with "proceed on error."
3	Chain NCBs with "stop on error."

Unfortunately, no symbolic definitions exist for these values, so the raw numbers will have to do.

If a single NCB is submitted, the *pncb* value points to the NCB. If a chain of NCBs is submitted, the *pncb* value points to the first link word.

Any submitted NCBs do not need the *ncb_lana_num* field filled in. This will be done by the *NetBiosSubmit* API. If an NCB is an asynchronous NCB, the *ncb_post* field should be a system semaphore handle, or 0 if polling is to be done. It is important that the *DosCreateSem* call used to get the semaphore handle specify that the *fNoExclusive* argument be set to CSEM-_PUBLIC. Otherwise, the NetBIOS driver will be unable to clear the semaphore when the operation is complete. The application should set the semaphore before calling *NetBiosSubmit* so that the transition will not be missed.

DOS compatibility-mode restrictions

Under MS-DOS version 3 running the MS-NET or PC-LAN networks, only a single NetBIOS driver was available. NCBs were submitted to it using the int 5C or the int 2A interrupt vectors. In OS/2's DOS compatibility mode, you can still use this mechanism—with the restriction that NCBs be submitted to only the first NetBIOS driver defined in the [networks] component of the LANMAN.INI file.

A NetBIOS Example

The DRIVERS.C program (Figure 12-5) uses the NetBIOS APIs to enumerate all of the logical NetBIOS drivers, open each one, submit an NCB to get the adapter status, and display the information.

```
/*
 * DRIVERS.C--This program enumerates all of the NetBIOS drivers
 * and issues an Adapter Status NCB for each one.  The results
 * are sent to stdout.
 *
 * Compile with:  C> cl drivers.c netapi.lib
 *
 * Usage:  C> drivers
 *
 */

#include <stdio.h>
#include <stdlib.h>
#include <string.h>
#include <netcons.h>
#include <ncb.h>
#include <netbios.h>
#include <ctype.h>

/* ADAPTER STATUS:
 * The adapter status return information is described in
 * the source documents on NetBIOS.
 */

struct astat
    {
    unsigned char  as_uid[6];   /* unit identification number      */
    unsigned char  as_ejs;      /* external jumper status          */
    unsigned char  as_lst;      /* results of last self-test       */
    unsigned char  as_ver;      /* software version number         */
    unsigned char  as_rev;      /* software revision number        */
    unsigned short as_dur;      /* duration of reporting period    */
    unsigned short as_crc;      /* number of CRC errors            */
    unsigned short as_align;    /* number of alignment errors      */
    unsigned short as_coll;     /* number of collisions            */
    unsigned short as_abort;    /* number of aborted transmissions */
    unsigned long  as_spkt;     /* number of successful packets sent */
    unsigned long  as_rpkt;     /* no. of successful packets rec'd */
    unsigned short as_retry;    /* number of retransmissions       */
```

Figure 12-5.
The DRIVERS.C program.

(continued)

Figure 12-5. *continued*

```
        unsigned short as_exhst;    /* number of times exhausted      */
        unsigned char  as_res0[8];  /* reserved                       */
        unsigned short as_ncbfree;  /* free NCBs                      */
        unsigned short as_numncb;   /* number of NCBs configured      */
        unsigned short as_maxncb;   /* max. configurable NCBs         */
        unsigned char  as_res1[4];  /* reserved                       */
        unsigned short as_penses;   /* sessions in use                */
        unsigned short as_numses;   /* number of sessions configured  */
        unsigned short as_maxses;   /* max. configurable sessions     */
        unsigned short as_maxdat;   /* max. data packet size          */
        unsigned short as_names;    /* no. of names in local table    */
        struct as_namelist          /* name entries                   */
            {
            unsigned char as_name[16]; /* name          */
            unsigned char as_number;   /* name number   */
            unsigned char as_status;   /* name status   */
            } as_struct[16];           /* name entries  */
        };

int main()
    {
    NCB ncb;
    int err, i, j;
    struct netbios_info_1 nbuf[10]; /* handle up to 10 */
    struct netbios_info_1 *pn;
    struct astat as;
    unsigned short entriesRead;
    unsigned short totalEntries;
    unsigned short netHandle;
    struct as_namelist *pnm;

    /* Get list of NetBIOS drivers: a level 0 Enum */
    pn = nbuf;
    if ((err = NetBiosEnum(NULL,
                        1,         /* level 1 info */
                        (char far *)pn,
                        BUFSIZ,
                        &entriesRead,
                        &totalEntries)) != 0)
        {
        fprintf(stderr, "NetBiosEnum failed with err = %d\n", err);
        exit(1);
        }
```

(continued)

Figure 12-5. *continued*

```
/* for each NetBIOS name */
for ( ; entriesRead--; pn++)
    {
    printf("%s:\n", pn->nb1_net_name);

    /* open the NetBIOS */
    if ((err = NetBiosOpen(
                        pn->nb1_net_name, /* logical driver */
                        NULL,             /* reserved       */
                        NB_REGULAR,       /* privilege mode */
                        &netHandle        /* return handle  */
                        )) != 0)
        {
        printf("   NetBiosOpen failed with err = %d\n", err);
        continue;
        }

    /* format the Adapter Status NCB */
    ncb.ncb_command = NCBASTAT;               /* Adapter status */
    ncb.ncb_buffer = (char far *)&as;         /* where data goes */
    ncb.ncb_length = sizeof(struct astat);    /* abuf size      */
    ncb.ncb_callname[0] = '*';                /*  local node    */

    /* submit it to the NetBIOS */
    if ((err = NetBiosSubmit(
                        netHandle,
                        0,                    /* single NCB */
                        &ncb)) != 0)
        {
        printf("   NetBiosSubmit failed with err = %d\n", err);
        continue;
        }

    /* print the results */
    printf("\t%-50s0x%02x%02x%02x%02x%02x%02x\n",
            "Unit identification number",
            as.as_uid[0],
            as.as_uid[1],
            as.as_uid[2],
            as.as_uid[3],
            as.as_uid[4],
            as.as_uid[5]);
    printf("\t%-50s%s%s\n",
            "External jumper status",
            ((as.as_ejs & 0x80) ? "W2 is ON, ": "W2 is OFF, "),
            ((as.as_ejs & 0x40) ? "W1 is ON": "W1 is OFF"));
```

(continued)

Figure 12-5. *continued*

```
printf("\t%-50s%0x02\n",
       "Results of last self test", as.as_lst);
printf("\t%-50s%03u.%03u\n",
       "Major.Minor version number",
       as.as_ver,
       as.as_rev);
printf("\t%-50s%u minutes\n",
       "Duration of reporting period", as.as_dur);
printf("\t%-50s%u\n",
       "Number of CRC errors received", as.as_crc);
printf("\t%-50s%u\n",
       "Number of alignment errors received",
       as.as_align);
printf("\t%-50s%u\n",
       "Number of collisions encountered",
       as.as_coll);
printf("\t%-50s%u\n",
       "Number of aborted transmissions",
       as.as_abort);
printf("\t%-50s%lu\n",
       "Number of successfully transmitted packets",
       as.as_spkt);
printf("\t%-50s%lu\n",
       "Number of successfully received packets",
       as.as_rpkt);
printf("\t%-50s%u\n",
       "Number of retransmissions", as.as_retry);
printf("\t%-50s%u\n",
       "Number of times resources exhausted",
       as.as_exhst);
printf("\t%-50s%u\n",
       "Number of free NCBs", as.as_ncbfree);
printf("\t%-50s%u\n",
       "Maximum number of NCBs", as.as_maxncb);
printf("\t%-50s%u\n",
       "Number of pending sessions", as.as_penses);
printf("\t%-50s%u\n",
       "Maximum number of pending sessions",
       as.as_numses);
printf("\t%-50s%u\n",
       "Maximum number of possible sessions",
       as.as_maxses);
printf("\t%-50s%u\n",
       "Maximum data packet size", as.as_maxdat);
printf("\t%-50s%u\n",
```

(continued)

Figure 12-5. *continued*

```
                "Number of names in the name table",
            as.as_names);
    printf("\tName Table:\n\n");
    printf("Name (ASCII)        Name (HEX)");
    printf("                                    N/N G/U STATUS\n");
    for (i = 0, pnm = &as.as_struct[0]; i < as.as_names; ++i, ++pnm)
        {
        for (j = 0; j < 16; ++j)
            {
            printf("%c",
                    isprint(pnm->as_name[j]) ? pnm->as_name[j]: '.');
            }
        printf("  ");
        for (j = 0; j < 16; ++j)
            {
            printf("%02x ", pnm->as_name[j]);
            }
        printf("%2u   %c    %u\n", pnm->as_number,
                (pnm->as_status & 0x80) ? 'G' : 'U',
                pnm->as_status & 7);
        }
    printf("\n\n");

    /* close the NetBIOS */
    NetBiosClose(netHandle, 0);
    }
return(0);
}
```

PROGRAMMING TECHNIQUE

WRITING DISTRIBUTED APPLICATIONS

This chapter describes how to write *distributed applications*—applications with segments on different nodes in the network. Two models are developed here:

- The *distributed data model* allows programs at workstations to interact with programs at other workstations by sharing data at a server. The data can be in files, in spooled print queues, or can be I/O to character devices. In the distributed data model, the program intelligence resides at the workstation.

- The *distributed intelligence model* allows programs at the workstation to communicate with programs at the server. In the most extreme case, the workstation program simply formats and forwards (using a named pipe or mailslot) requests for work to a server program. In the distributed intelligence model, the program intelligence resides at the server.

Network Transparency

One of the keys to developing distributed applications is deciding whether to have programs make explicit use of the network or whether to use APIs. Whereas programming to the NetBIOS APIs requires some degree of network awareness, using named pipes is a fairly transparent use of the network: After a remote named pipe is opened, the program functions in the same way whether the pipe is local or remote.

The two distributed program models in this chapter strive for network transparency. Once a distributed resource is located, the rest of the program is treated like a local program.

Locating Remote Resources

You can use several methods to ensure that programs can locate remote resources:

- In the simplest but least flexible method, you place remote resource names right into the program, as in the following example:

```
DosOpen("\\\\MYSRVR\\PIPE\\DATAREQ", ....)
```

- Or you can ask the user where to find the resource. This method allows flexibility in resource placement, but it is only as reliable as the user's knowledge and memory.

- You can also use an environment variable to list the directories that might contain the resource. These directories can be on the local computer or on the network. In OS/2, the DPATH environment variable lists directories in which data files might be found. In Figure 13-1, the *dpfopen* subroutine searches the DPATH list and opens a file or named pipe. If DPATH were set as follows:

```
DPATH=c:\data;x:\user\data;\\myserver\public
```

then no matter what the current directory, a program could look for a data file or a named pipe in the three places specified.

```
/*
 * DPFOPEN.C -- This subroutine opens a file from along a path.
 * It behaves like the fopen function except that the "fname"
 * argument should be a filename with no path component.
 *
 * The following arguments are defined:
 *
 *      "fname" is the filename to be opened
 *      "type" is the type of file open
 *      "path" is a list of paths or an environment variable
 *      "control" is the same as the DosSearchPath argument, where
 *           1 means search local directory and
 *           2 means the path is an environment variable
 *
 * dpfopen returns a FILE pointer, or NULL if an error occurs.
 *
 */

#include <stdio.h>
#include <os2.h>
#include <netcons.h>
#include <examples.h>   /* defined in Chapter 4 */

FILE *dpfopen(fname, type, path, control)
char *fname;
char *type;
char *path;
unsigned control;
    {
```

Figure 13-1.   *(continued)*
The dpfopen *subroutine.*

Figure 13-1. *continued*

```
    char buff[PATHLEN];

    if (DosSearchPath(control, path, fname, buff, PATHLEN))
        return(NULL);
    return(fopen(buff, type));
    }
```

■ You can use a configuration file to configure a workstation. A good example of this is the LANMAN.INI file used by LAN Manager. Programs can access configuration information from this file by using the *NetConfigGet* API. CFGFOPEN.C (Figure 13-2) uses the *cfgfopen* subroutine to retrieve a pathname list from LANMAN.INI and pass it to the *dpfopen* subroutine, which then locates and opens a file.

```
/*
 * CFGFOPEN.C -- This subroutine opens a file along a path
 * from LANMAN.INI.  It returns a FILE pointer or NULL if
 * an error occurs.
 *
 */

#include <stdio.h>
#include <netcons.h>
#include <config.h>
#include <examples.h>  /* defined in Chapter 4 */

FILE * cfgfopen(fname, type, section, param)
char *fname;      /* fname is the base filename */
char *type;       /* open type: see fopen */
char *section;    /* LANMAN.INI section */
char *param;      /* LANMAN.INI parameter */
    {
    char buf[PATHLEN];
    unsigned short len;

    if (NetConfigGet(section, param, buf, PATHLEN, &len))
        return(NULL);
    return(dpfopen(fname, type, buf, 1));
    }
```

Figure 13-2.
The cfgfopen *subroutine.*

Dynamic Resource Finding

You've learned how to configure a workstation so that programs can locate resources. Using these methods still requires the user or administrator to know where the resources will be located when the program runs. Dynamic resource finding locates resources at the time they are needed.

The LAN Manager *NetServerEnum* API returns a list of servers, and *NetShareEnum* returns a list of all shared resources at a particular server. One way to find a resource is to check the availability of every shared resource on every available server. An alternative to this potentially time-consuming method is to assign a known share name to a particular set of resources.

The *srvfopen* subroutine (Figure 13-3) takes a name argument that is ex-pected to match a server share name. Then it creates a list of all matching share names and passes the list to the *dpfopen* routine. Note that instead of calling *NetServerEnum* directly, *srvfopen* calls *NetEnum*, passing the func-tion name as an argument. (*NetEnum* was developed in Chapter 4 as a gen-eral way of handling the buffer-sizing requirements of the Enum APIs.)

```
/* SRVFOPEN.C -- This subroutine opens a file along a path built
 * of matching shares from NetServerEnum.  The following arguments
 * are used:
 *
 *     "fname" is the file to be opened
 *     "type" is the open type string
 *     "shname" is the share name to be matched
 *
 */
```

Figure 13-3.
The srvfopen *subroutine.*

(continued)

Figure 13-3. *continued*

```
#include <os2.h>
#include <stdio.h>
#include <string.h>
#include <netcons.h>
#include <server.h>
#include <shares.h>
#include <string_f.h>    /* defined in Chapter 3 */
#include <examples.h>    /* defined in Chapter 4 */

typedef char far * far * PFPFC;

FILE * srvfopen(fname, type, shname)
char *fname;
char *type;
char *shname;
    {
    unsigned err;
    unsigned short nsrv, nshare;
    struct server_info_0 far *psrv0;
    struct share_info_1 far *pshr1;
    char buf[PATHLEN], sbuf[CNLEN+3];

    /* get list of available servers */
    if ((err = NetEnum(NetServerEnum, NULL, 0, (PFPFC)&psrv0, 200,
            sizeof(*psrv0), &nsrv)) != 0)
        {
        DosFreeSeg(SELECTOROF(psrv0));
        return(NULL);
        }

    /* for each server try to get list of shares */
    buf[0] = 0;
    while (nsrv--)
        {
        /* NetServerEnum requires \\ on the server name! */
        strcpy(sbuf, "\\\\");
        strcat_f(sbuf, psrv0->sv0_name);
        if (NetEnum(NetShareEnum, sbuf, 1, (PFPFC)&pshr1, 200,
                sizeof(*pshr1), &nshare) == 0)
            {
            /* look for matching share names */
            while (nshare--)
                {
                if (stricmp_f(shname, pshr1->shi1_netname) == 0)
```

(continued)

Figure 13-3. *continued*

```
            {
            /* separator needed for all but first */
            if (buf[0] != 0)
                strcat(buf, ";");
            /* format a full UNC name */
            strcat(buf, sbuf);
            strcat(buf, "\\");
            strcat_f(buf, pshr1->shi1_netname);
            }
        ++pshr1;
        }
    }
    ++psrv0;
    }
DosFreeSeg(SELECTOROF(psrv0));
DosFreeSeg(SELECTOROF(pshr1));
return(dpfopen(fname, type, buf, 1));
}
```

In the *srvfopen* subroutine, the comparison against a share name is one way that a program can recognize relevant resources. But you can use other conventions to recognize remote resources. For example, application-specific information can be encoded in the remark field of the share (*shl_remark*).

Name Service

But these methods of finding dynamic resources are not a complete solution. For example, the server list in *NetServerEnum* is restricted to servers in the same domain (langroup) and those specified in the *othdomains* component of LANMAN.INI (a maximum of four additional domains is allowed). In addition, LAN Manager provides no built-in way to describe resources. To circumvent this problem, convention dictates that share names describe the resource and that remarks contain encoded descriptive information.

The complete solution to the problem of finding resources is through a Name service (also called a Directory service). A Name service provides a centralized catalog of available network resources and routing information. Name service is not provided in LAN Manager version 1.0 but is intended for future releases. Some vendors of LAN Manager 2.0 will provide Name service as an add-on to the product. In future versions, LAN Manager will include a full set of APIs and the underlying Name service.

Shared Resources

Because distributed applications use shared resources that are available to multiple users, they are considered multiuser programs. Accordingly, they require *protection, administration,* and *auditing.*

- Protection is the practice of resource control: deciding who can have access to what. Data isn't the only resource needing protection; access to abstract resources such as named pipes and print spooler queues might also need to be restricted.

- Administration is the capability to query and control the use of system resources. An example of administration is setting permissions, which might need to be changed depending on time of day or on who is working on a particular project at a given time. An administrator might need to determine who is using a particular resource or to free an application or resource by disconnecting a user.

- Auditing is the practice of keeping a record—known as an *audit trail*—of attempts to use shared resources and keeping an *error log,* a record of error conditions that occur as applications run. Even when an application cannot conveniently report error conditions back to a user, the system or the application should record the error in the error log. An administrator can use error log information to monitor the stability of the server.

Because designing every distributed application to handle its own protection, administration, and auditing would be a tremendous burden, LAN Manager provides these three features as part of its underlying structure.

The Distributed Data Model

The distributed data model lets many workstations run a copy of an application, but it keeps only one copy of the data. (The data might be divided into several parts that are kept on more than one server, but there is never more than one copy of the data.) It also enforces security, controlling which users have access to the data. The workstation programs can access the data through an explicit connection to the server share (usually creating a redirected drive name to represent it), or through an implicit connection using a UNC name. In either case, all security is handled by LAN Manager access control at the server.

Programs developed in the distributed data model can make use of the network transparency provided by LAN Manager. When an application is developed to reside and work on the same machine as its data, distributing the data is as easy as changing the filenames that the application opens to UNC names or to names on redirected drives.

When multiple workstation programs try to access the data at the same time, the read and write requests from different processes must not interfere with each other. You can control access to three areas: to the directory (with restricted shares), to the data file (with shared modes), or to a region of the data file (with record locking). The following paragraphs outline these three methods of access control.

Controlling directory access: Restricted shares

At the server, the *NetShareSetInfo* API restricts the number of users connected at a time. If it is set to 1, only one user at a time can make the connection. *NetShareSetInfo* effectively serializes access to all files in the shared directory or its descendants.

Controlling data-file access: Share modes

When the *DosOpen* call opens a file, the applications can use an appropriate sharing mode:

- OPEN_SHARE_DENYWRITE ensures that no other process will be writing data as long as the open file is being read. (Other processes might be reading data, which is not a problem.)

- OPEN_SHARE_DENYREAD ensures that no other processes will be trying to read data while the write is taking place.

- OPEN_SHARE_DENYREADWRITE grants exclusive rights to the open file, ensuring that the process is the only process with the file open.

Controlling regional data-file access: Record locking

If a process needs to protect a portion of a data file from simultaneous access, it can use the *DosFileLocks* API to gain exclusive access to a region of the file.

Jockeying for Access

But what if the desired resource is already held by another process? If this happens, you should use a timeout loop to make the call. The TIMEOUT.C file (Figure 13-4) contains a *RetryOpen* subroutine that opens a file and retries a set number of times. (You can write similar retry routines for *NetUseAdd* or for *DosFileLocks*.)

```
/*
 * TIMEOUT.C -- This file contains the RetryOpen
 * subroutine -- a DosOpen call with retries.  If DosOpen
 * fails because of a sharing violation, the call is
 * made again after waiting "ulTimeout" milliseconds.
 * It will be retried up to "usRetry" times.  If "usRetry"
 * is 0xFFFF, an infinite number of retries will be made.
 * All other arguments are passed directly to DosOpen.
 *
 */

#include <os2.h>

int far pascal
RetryOpen(
    USHORT usRetry,      /* number of retries          */
    ULONG ulTimeout,     /* wait time between retries  */
    PSZ pszFileName,     /* filename                   */
    PHFILE phf,          /* return file handle         */
    PUSHORT pusAction,   /* action taken               */
    ULONG ulFileSize,    /* file size                  */
    USHORT usAttribute,  /* file attribute             */
    USHORT fsOpenFlags,  /* action if file exists      */
    USHORT fsOpenMode,   /* open/share modes           */
    ULONG ulReserved     /* must be zero               */
    )
    {
    int err;

    err = DosOpen(pszFileName, phf, pusAction, ulFileSize,
                usAttribute, fsOpenFlags, fsOpenMode, 0L);

    /* Keep trying until the file can be opened in the desired
     * sharing mode. */

    while (err == ERROR_SHARING_VIOLATION)
        {
        /* 0xffff means an infinite number of retries */
        if (usRetry == 0xffff || usRetry-- != 0)
            DosSleep(ulTimeout);
        err = DosOpen(pszFileName, phf, pusAction, ulFileSize,
                    usAttribute, fsOpenFlags, fsOpenMode, 0L);
        }
    return(err);
    }
```

Figure 13-4.
The RetryOpen *subroutine.*

This is not a "fair" solution: It doesn't guarantee that the process that's waited the longest will be the first to gain access to the resource. A "fair" solution would queue and service the requests on a first-come, first-served basis. In a local environment, the best way to do this is by using OS/2 semaphores to queue the requests. Unfortunately, semaphores do not exist in the distributed environment. Later in this chapter, you'll learn to create remote semaphores using a "Remote Procedure Call" mechanism. The example in that section will revisit the distributed data model and show a more complete solution to this problem.

The Distributed Intelligence Model

The distributed intelligence model uses workstation programs that communicate with server programs or with other workstation programs. It allows processing to be carried out at the server instead of at the workstation—an advantage over the distributed data model, and a particularly efficient advantage for such tasks as a database search: Whereas the distributed data model would transfer large amounts of data back to the workstation to be searched, the distributed intelligence model would transfer to the workstation only a small request and the results of the search.

One common distributed intelligence application consists of a workstation-based user-interface program that does little more than send requests to a server program where all of the work is done. Another consists of workstation programs that cooperate with each other through server programs, with some of the work being done at the workstation and some being done at the server.

By developing applications in the distributed intelligence model, you can make use of the network transparency provided by LAN Manager. If an application lets client and server communicate with each other on the same workstation, you can distribute the intelligence by moving the server pieces to a LAN Manager server and changing the names that the client communicates with.

The key to the distributed intelligence model is interprocess communications (IPC) among processes that might not be on the same computer.

What IPC Is the Right IPC?

Named pipes and mailslots are two kinds of IPC that make the distributed intelligence model easy to implement. (The NetBIOS APIs can also be used for IPC, but they require more programming overhead.) When is each of these IPC mechanisms appropriate?

Named Pipes

Named pipes are for applications that require a two-way dialog between a client process and a server process (for example, applications with a transaction processor at the server and a client end that initiates the transactions). The interplay between the two programs is shown in Table 13-1.

Server	Client
DosMakeNmPipe	
DosConnectNmPipe	*DosOpen* named pipe
while not done	while not done
DosRead	
	build a request
	DosTransactNmPipe
process request	
build reply	
DosWrite	process reply

Table 13-1.
A two-way dialog using named pipes.

Mailslots

Mailslots are for applications requiring only a one-way communication mechanism (for example, an application in which client processes write messages to the server's mailslot and in which the server side of the application reads and processes the messages). Mailslots also come in handy in data-collection applications in which many different workstation programs send information to a central collection point.

NetBIOS APIs

NetBIOS APIs can be used for IPC, but they require greater programming overhead because the program must provide all the services that LAN Manager provides for named pipes or mailslots: protection, administration, and auditing. NetBIOS applications are also "network-aware" applications, so they don't have the network transparency properties provided by named pipes or mailslots.

When is NetBIOS IPC useful? In the current version of LAN Manager, only limited support exists for workstation-to-workstation communication. Second-class mailslots and NetBIOS programming are the only available mechanisms. In future releases, it will be possible to put both client and server ends of a pipe on two different workstations. Also, the NetBIOS architecture is supported by some systems that are not running LAN Manager.

The NetBIOS architecture is a standard communication mechanism to some of these systems. However, as the UNIX LAN Manager product described in Chapter 15 evolves, named-pipe servers will be available on more and more types of systems.

From IPC to RPC

Remote procedure calls (RPCs) are a further abstraction of the distributed intelligence model. Consider the following program fragment:

```
result = sub1(arg1, arg2);
sub2(result, arg3);
```

Suppose this fragment is running on workstation A. When *sub1* is called, the arguments are sent over the network, and the subroutine is executed on server B. The result is sent back to workstation A. Then the *sub2* subroutine executes on server C. This example makes use of remote procedure calls.

An RPC comprises two parts: the *client side* and the *server side*. The client side is a stub subroutine that packages the arguments and sends them to the server side. The server side is an RPC server program that unpacks the arguments, makes the designated procedure call locally, and then packs the return data and sends it back to the client stub. The client unpacks the return data and passes it back to the calling program. When the client-side program makes the subroutine call, it never needs to be aware of whether the subroutine executes locally or remotely.

How does the client side know where to execute the subroutine? There are a lot of methods for doing this, ranging from hard-coded server names and explicit calls to pick a server all the way up to a complete name service to dynamically find a server that supports the RPC. This is the same name-finding question discussed with the distributed data model. As we strive for transparency in distributed programs, the entire issue of network awareness centers on the name-finding problem. The rest of the application does not need to be written with any special network awareness.

Back in the section on the distributed data model, we postponed the issue of how to coordinate several workstations in a "fair" way. If several programs on the same workstation wanted to fairly serialize access to a resource, they could use semaphores. Each program would do something like this:

```
DosOpenSem(&semhdl, sem_name);
DosSemRequest(&semhdl, timeout);
```

The program now has exclusive ownership of the semaphore and can go ahead and update the data files. Upon completion, the program executes the following call, which grants the semaphore to the next waiting program:

```
DosSemClear(&semhdl);
```

But what is to be done in a distributed environment, where semaphores cannot be opened, requested, or cleared on a remote computer? The RMTSEM.C file (Figure 13-5) contains an RPC package for remote semaphores. All of the OS/2 semaphore routines are built into the RPC package, with the *Dos* function names changed to *Rem*. The underlying communication to the server is accomplished with a named pipe.

First the name-finding problem is addressed. For simplicity, a subroutine named *RemSetServer* is used. An application calls this routine to set a server name for all subsequent RPCs. For this version, only one server at a time can be called. The extension to multiple RPC servers is straightforward.

```
/*
 * RMTSEM.C -- This file contains the RemSetServer function,
 * which sets the server to which RPC calls will be made.
 * All communications are accomplished with a named pipe.
 * Subsequent calls to RemSetServer will override the
 * previous ones.  Adaptation to multiple servers is straightforward.
 */

#include <os2.h>
#include <netcons.h>
#include <rmtsem.h>              /* described in Chapter 13 */

HFILE PipeHdl = 0;              /* RPC pipe-server handle */

USHORT APIENTRY RemSetServer(
    char far * servername      /* where to execute */
    )
    {
    unsigned err;
    USHORT action;
    char buf[PATHLEN];

    /* this version allows only one server at a time */
    if (PipeHdl)
        DosClose(PipeHdl);
```

Figure 13-5.
The RemSetServer *function.*

(continued)

Figure 13-5. *continued*

```
    /* open the RPC server pipe */
    if (servername == NULL)
        buf[0] = 0;
    else
        strcpy(buf, servername);
    strcat(buf, REMSEM_PIPENAME);
    err = DosOpen(
                    buf,                    /* pipe name         */
                    &PipeHdl,               /* return handle     */
                    &action,                /* ignored for pipes */
                    0L,                     /* ignored for pipes */
                    0,                      /* ignored for pipes */
                    FILE_TRUNCATE,          /* open flags        */
                    (OPEN_ACCESS_READWRITE |
                    OPEN_SHARE_DENYNONE),   /* open mode         */
                    0L                      /* must be zero      */
                    );

    /* set it to message mode */
    if (err == 0)
        err = DosSetNmpHandState(PipeHdl, NP_READMODE_MESSAGE);
    return err;
    }
```

Figure 13-6 shows the RMTSEM.H header file, which is used by both the client and server sides of the RPC. RMTSEM.H defines function prototypes for the RPC package and for the internal data structures used to send data to and from the server side. RMTSEM.H is used in this chapter by RMTSEM.C, REMSEMC.C, and REMSEMS.C.

```
/* RMTSEM.H -- A header file for remote semaphore support. */

USHORT APIENTRY RemSetServer(char far *);
USHORT APIENTRY RemCreateSem(USHORT, PHSYSSEM, PSZ);
USHORT APIENTRY RemOpenSem(PHSEM, PSZ);
USHORT APIENTRY RemSemClear(HSEM);
USHORT APIENTRY RemSemSet(HSEM);
USHORT APIENTRY RemSemWait(HSEM, LONG);
USHORT APIENTRY RemSemSetWait(HSEM, LONG);
USHORT APIENTRY RemSemRequest(HSEM, LONG);
USHORT APIENTRY RemCloseSem(HSEM);
```

Figure 13-6.
The RMTSEM.H header file.

(continued)

Figure 13-6. *continued*

```
/* The remote procedure calls are made by calling DosOpen
 * for the REMSEM_PIPENAME.  Fill in a REMSEM_S structure
 * with the opcode and appropriate arguments for the
 * call, and use DosWrite to send it to the pipe.  The return
 * values are read from the pipe in a REMSEM_R structure.
 */

#define REMSEM_PIPENAME "\\PIPE\\EXAMPLE\\REMSEM"

/* RPC opcodes */
#define REMSEM_CREATE    1
#define REMSEM_OPEN      2
#define REMSEM_CLEAR     3
#define REMSEM_SET       4
#define REMSEM_WAIT      5
#define REMSEM_SETWAIT   6
#define REMSEM_REQUEST   7
#define REMSEM_CLOSE     8

/* Semaphore RPC Send structures -- The member names
 * follow the Dos API argument names.  This structure is
 * used to send the arguments to the server.
 */

typedef union
    {
    struct
        {
        int op;
        USHORT fNoExclusive;
        char pszSemName[PATHLEN];
        } Create;
    struct
        {
        int op;
        char pszSemName[PATHLEN];
        } Open;
    struct
        {
        int op;
        HSEM hsem;
        } Clear;
    struct
        {
        int op;
        HSEM hsem;
```

(continued)

Figure 13-6. *continued*

```
                LONG lTimeOut;
                } Request;
        struct
            {
            int op;
            HSEM hsem;
            } Set;
        struct
            {
            int op;
            HSEM hsem;
            LONG lTimeOut;
            } Wait;
        struct
            {
            int op;
            HSEM hsem;
            LONG lTimeOut;
            } SetWait;
        struct
            {
            int op;
            HSEM hsem;
            } Close;
        } REMSEM_S;

/* Semaphore RPC Receive structures -- The member names
 * follow the Dos API argument names.  This structure is
 * used to send the return data back to the client.
 */


typedef union
    {
    struct
        {
        int err;
        HSEM phssm;
        } Create;
    struct
        {
        int err;
        HSEM phssm;
        } Open;
    struct
        {
        int err;
        } Clear;
```

(continued)

Figure 13-6. *continued*

```
        struct
            {
            int err;
            } Set;
        struct
            {
            int err;
            } Wait;
        struct
            {
            int err;
            } SetWait;
        struct
            {
            int err;
            } Request;
        struct
            {
            int err;
            } Close;
    } REMSEM_R;
```

The REMSEMC.C file (Figure 13-7) contains all client-side stubs. Each stub packs the arguments into a REMSEM_S structure and writes it to the server. All communication assumes that a previous call has been made to *RemSet-Server* to establish the named-pipe communications. This version allows only one RPC server to be used at a time. More than one thread or process can make Rem calls at once. This version also has no stopping mechanism. A production version of this program should be created as a LAN Manager service program so that it can be started and stopped conveniently.

```
/*
 * REMSEMC.C -- This collection of routines makes up the
 * client side of a remote semaphore package.  This
 * implementation requires that all calls be directed
 * to the same server, which is established by a call to
 * RemSetServer.
 *
 * The remote routines are as follows:
 *
 *     RemCreateSem   Create a remote semaphore
 *     RemOpenSem     Open a remote semaphore
```

Figure 13-7. *(continued)*
The REMSEMC.C file, containing client-side remote-semaphore stubs.

Figure 13-7. *continued*

```
*       RemSemClear       Clear a remote semaphore
*       RemSemRequest     Get ownership of a remote semaphore
*       RemSemSet         Set a remote semaphore
*       RemSemSetWait     Set and wait for a remote semaphore
*       RemSemWait        Wait for a remote semaphore
*       RemCloseSem       Close the remote semaphore
*/

#include <os2.h>
#include <netcons.h>
#include <rmtsem.h>     /* discussed in Chapter 13 */

static HFILE PipeHdl = 0;          /* RPC pipe-server handle   */

USHORT APIENTRY RemSetServer(
char far * servername)             /* where to execute */
    {
    unsigned err;
    USHORT action;
    char buf[PATHLEN];

    /* this version allows only one server at a time */
    if (PipeHdl)
        DosClose(PipeHdl);

    /* open the RPC server pipe */
    if (servername == NULL)
        buf[0] = 0;
    else
        strcpy(buf, servername);
    strcat(buf, REMSEM_PIPENAME);
    err = DosOpen(
                buf,
                &PipeHdl,
                &action,
                0L,
                0,
                FILE_TRUNCATE,             /* open flags */
                OPEN_ACCESS_READWRITE : OPEN_SHARE_DENYNONE,
                0L                         /* open mode */
                );

    /* set it to message mode */
    if (err == 0)
        err = DosSetNmpHandState(PipeHdl, NP_READMODE_MESSAGE);
    return err;
    }
```

(continued)

Figure 13-7. *continued*

```
USHORT APIENTRY RemCreateSem(
USHORT fNoExclusive,     /* ownership flag      */
PHSYSSEM phssm,          /* returned sem handle */
PSZ pszSemName)          /* semaphore name      */
    {
    REMSEM_S Send;  /* RPC communication structure */
    REMSEM_R Recv;  /* RPC return data             */
    USHORT num;
    int err;

    /* package the arguments and send them */
    Send.Create.op = REMSEM_CREATE;
    Send.Create.fNoExclusive = fNoExclusive;
    strcpy(Send.Create.pszSemName, pszSemName);
    err = DosTransactNmPipe(PipeHdl, (PBYTE)&Recv, sizeof(Recv),
            (PBYTE)&Send, sizeof(Send), &num);

    /* unpack return data */
    *phssm = Recv.Create.phssm;
    return(err != 0 ? err : Recv.Create.err);
    }

USHORT APIENTRY RemOpenSem(
PHSEM phssm,
PSZ pszSemName)
    {
    REMSEM_S Send;  /* RPC communication structure */
    REMSEM_R Recv;  /* RPC return data             */
    USHORT num;
    int err;

    /* package the arguments and send them */
    Send.Open.op = REMSEM_OPEN;
    strcpy(Send.Open.pszSemName, pszSemName);
    err = DosTransactNmPipe(PipeHdl, (PBYTE)&Recv, sizeof(Recv),
            (PBYTE)&Send, sizeof(Send), &num);

    /* unpack return data */
    *phssm = Recv.Open.phssm;
    return(err != 0 ? err : Recv.Open.err);
    }

USHORT APIENTRY RemSemClear(
HSEM hsem)
    {
    REMSEM_S Send;  /* RPC communication structure */
    REMSEM_R Recv;  /* RPC return data             */
```

(continued)

Figure 13-7. *continued*

```
    USHORT num;
    int err;

    /* package the arguments and send them */
    Send.Clear.op = REMSEM_CLEAR;
    Send.Clear.hsem = hsem;
    err = DosTransactNmPipe(PipeHdl, (PBYTE)&Recv, sizeof(Recv),
            (PBYTE)&Send, sizeof(Send), &num);

    /* unpack return data */
    return(err != 0 ? err : Recv.Clear.err);
    }

USHORT APIENTRY RemSemSet(
HSEM hsem)
    {
    REMSEM_S Send;  /* RPC communication structure */
    REMSEM_R Recv;  /* RPC return data            */
    USHORT num;
    int err;

    /* package the arguments and send them */
    Send.Set.op = REMSEM_SET;
    Send.Set.hsem = hsem;
    err = DosTransactNmPipe(PipeHdl, (PBYTE)&Recv, sizeof(Recv),
            (PBYTE)&Send, sizeof(Send), &num);

    /* unpack return data */
    return(err != 0 ? err : Recv.Set.err);
    }

USHORT APIENTRY RemSemWait(
HSEM hsem,
LONG ITimeOut)
    {
    REMSEM_S Send;  /* RPC communication structure */
    REMSEM_R Recv;  /* RPC return data            */
    USHORT num;
    int err;

    /* package the arguments and send them */
    Send.Wait.op = REMSEM_WAIT;
    Send.Wait.hsem = hsem;
    Send.Wait.ITimeOut = ITimeOut;
    err = DosTransactNmPipe(PipeHdl, (PBYTE)&Recv, sizeof(Recv),
            (PBYTE)&Send, sizeof(Send), &num);
```

(continued)

Figure 13-7. *continued*

```
    /* unpack return data */
    return(err != 0 ? err : Recv.Wait.err);
    }

USHORT APIENTRY RemSemSetWait(
HSEM hsem,
LONG ITimeOut)
    {
    REMSEM_S Send;   /* RPC communication structure */
    REMSEM_R Recv;   /* RPC return data             */
    USHORT num;
    int err;

    /* package the arguments and send them */
    Send.SetWait.op = REMSEM_SETWAIT;
    Send.SetWait.hsem = hsem;
    Send.SetWait.ITimeOut = ITimeOut;
    err = DosTransactNmPipe(PipeHdl, (PBYTE)&Recv, sizeof(Recv),
            (PBYTE)&Send, sizeof(Send), &num);

    /* unpack return data */
    return(err != 0 ? err : Recv.SetWait.err);
    }

USHORT APIENTRY RemSemRequest(
HSEM hsem,
LONG ITimeOut)
    {
    REMSEM_S Send;   /* RPC communication structure */
    REMSEM_R Recv;   /* RPC return data             */
    USHORT num;
    int err;

    /* package the arguments and send them */
    Send.Request.op = REMSEM_REQUEST;
    Send.Request.hsem = hsem;
    Send.Request.ITimeOut = ITimeOut;
    err = DosTransactNmPipe(PipeHdl, (PBYTE)&Recv, sizeof(Recv),
            (PBYTE)&Send, sizeof(Send), &num);

    /* unpack return data */
    return(err != 0 ? err : Recv.Request.err);
    }
```

(continued)

Figure 13-7. *continued*

```
USHORT APIENTRY RemCloseSem(
HSEM hsem)
    {
    REMSEM_S Send;   /* RPC communication structure */
    REMSEM_R Recv;   /* RPC return data              */
    USHORT num;
    int err;

    /* package the arguments and send them */
    Send.Close.op = REMSEM_CLOSE;
    Send.Close.hsem = hsem;
    err = DosTransactNmPipe(PipeHdl, (PBYTE)&Recv, sizeof(Recv),
            (PBYTE)&Send, sizeof(Send), &num);

    /* unpack return data */
    return(err != 0 ? err : Recv.Close.err);
    }
```

The server side of the RPC package is a complete program for servicing the requests. It appears below as REMSEMS.C (Figure 13-8). When REMSEMS.EXE is started, it must be told how many threads to run. It creates a thread for every simultaneous instance of a client, which is also an instance of the named pipe.

```
/*
 * REMSEMS.C -- This collection of routines makes up the
 * server side of a remote semaphore package.  The command line
 * specifies the number of serving threads (simultaneous
 * clients attached).  A thread is used for each connected
 * client to handle all of the blocking required by the
 * various semaphore calls.
 *
 * The remote routines are as follows:
 *
 *      RemCreateSem    Create a remote semaphore
 *      RemOpenSem      Open a remote semaphore
 *      RemSemClear     Clear a remote semaphore
 *      RemSemRequest   Get ownership of a remote semaphore
 *      RemSemSet       Set a remote semaphore
 *      RemSemSetWait   Set and wait for a remote semaphore
 *      RemSemWait      Wait for a remote semaphore
 *      RemCloseSem     Close the remote semaphore
 *
```

Figure 13-8.
The REMSEMS.C program.

(continued)

Figure 13-8. *continued*

```
 * Compile with:  C> cl remsems.c netapi.lib
 *
 * Usage is:  C> remsems <threads>
 *
 */

#include <os2.h>
#include <netcons.h>
#include <rmtsem.h>   /* discussed in Chapter 13 */

#define STACKSIZE 8096
RemSemProc(REMSEM_S far *, REMSEM_R far *);
int Instances = 0;

main(argc, argv)
int argc;
char **argv;
    {
    int i;
    SEL sel;          /* receives allocated selector */
    TID tid;
    char far *pstack;
    void far RemSem(void);

    if (argc != 2)
        {
        printf("syntax:  remsems <threads>\n");
        exit(1);
        }

    /* create the required additional copies of RemSem */
    Instances = atoi(argv[1]);
    for (i = 0; i < Instances - 1; ++i)
        {
        DosAllocSeg(STACKSIZE, &sel, 0);
        pstack = MAKEP(sel, 0);
        DosCreateThread(RemSem, &tid, pstack + STACKSIZE);
        }

    /* and one for this thread */
    RemSem();
    exit(0);
    }
```

(continued)

Figure 13-8. *continued*

```
/*
 * RemSem -- This routine is the actual service loop.
 * There are "instance" threads running this loop.  After
 * creating a pipe instance, this routine enters a processing
 * loop, which reads REMSEM_S requests, executes the appropriate
 * call, and returns a REMSEM_R with the return data.  There
 * might be a lengthy block in waiting for a semaphore operation.
 */

void far RemSem(void)
    {
    int err;
    unsigned hdl;
    USHORT action;
    USHORT num;
    REMSEM_S FromClient;
    REMSEM_R ToClient;

    DosMakeNmPipe(
        REMSEM_PIPENAME,
        &hdl,
        NP_ACCESS_DUPLEX,
        NP_WAIT : NP_READMODE_MESSAGE : NP_TYPE_MESSAGE : Instances,
        128,
        128,
        0L);

    /* forever */
    while (1)
        {
        DosConnectNmPipe(hdl);

        /* new client connected -- get commands */
        err = DosRead(hdl, &FromClient, sizeof(FromClient), &num);
        while (err == 0 && num != 0)
            {
            RemSemProc(&FromClient, &ToClient);
            DosWrite(hdl, &ToClient, sizeof(ToClient), &num);
            err = DosRead(hdl, &FromClient, sizeof(FromClient), &num);
            }

        /* get ready for new client */
        DosDisconnectNmPipe(hdl);
        }
    }
```

(continued)

Figure 13-8. *continued*

```
/*
 * RemSemProc -- Process the RPC for the semaphore routine.
 */

RemSemProc(
REMSEM_S far * From,      /* request for RPC      */
REMSEM_R far * To)        /* return data from RPC */
    {
    PHSYSSEM phssm;
    int err;

    switch (From->Create.op)
        {
        case REMSEM_CREATE:
            To->Create.err = DosCreateSem(
                From->Create.fNoExclusive,
                &(To->Create.phssm),
                From->Create.pszSemName);
            break;

        case REMSEM_OPEN:
            To->Create.err = DosOpenSem(
                &(To->Open.phssm),
                From->Open.pszSemName);
            break;

        case REMSEM_CLEAR:
            To->Clear.err = DosSemClear(
                From->Clear.hsem);
            break;

        case REMSEM_SET:
            To->Set.err = DosSemSet(
                From->Set.hsem);
            break;

        case REMSEM_WAIT:
            To->Wait.err = DosSemWait(
                From->Wait.hsem,
                From->Wait.lTimeOut);
            break;

        case REMSEM_SETWAIT:
            To->SetWait.err = DosSemSetWait(
                From->SetWait.hsem,
                From->SetWait.lTimeOut);
            break;
```

(continued)

Figure 13-8. *continued*

```
    case REMSEM_REQUEST:
        To->Request.err = DosSemRequest(
            From->Request.hsem,
            From->Request.lTimeOut);
        break;

    case REMSEM_CLOSE:
        To->Close.err = DosCloseSem(
            From->Close.hsem);
        break;

        break;
    }
}
```

Considerations of a Named-Pipe Server

As you build the server end of a named-pipe application, you must decide how to handle multiple instances of the pipe. The RPC example in the previous section created a thread for every instance of the pipe. For some applications this is a good method; for others it can be a waste of threads, which are a limited resource.

Rather than create *n* threads to handle *n* pipes and have the threads sitting idle when they are not needed, you can dynamically create threads as needed and kill threads when they've served their purpose. The following code fragment keeps two idle threads, adds new threads as clients connect, and removes threads as clients disconnect.

```
int Instances = MAX_INSTANCES;
int IdleThreads = 0;
int TotalThreads = 0;

Process()
    {
    ++TotalThreads;
    while (1)
        {
        DosMakeNmPipe ...
        DosConnectNmPipe ...
        if (TotalThreads != Instances)
            DosCreateThread(Process, getstack);

        /* process */
```

```
        DosDisconnectNmPipe
        if (++Idle > 2)
            {
            --IdleThreads;
            --TotalThreads;
            DosExit
            }
        }
    }
```

In practice, you should update the *IdleThreads* and *TotalThreads* variables by protecting the test and increment/decrement logic with a semaphore to keep concurrent threads from developing a race condition.

But what if the number of instances is very large or even unlimited? After all, the number of available threads *is* limited.

This is where the *DosSetNmPipeSem* API comes in handy. By associating a semaphore with many different instances of a pipe, you ensure that all pipes can be serviced by a couple of threads. Figure 13-9 is a template for building efficient pipe-server applications. It uses two threads to service MAX-_CLIENT named-pipe instances.

```
/*
 * PIPESRV.C -- This program is a prototype for an event-
 * driven pipe server.  There are two threads, one for
 * connecting and one for processing.  The Connect
 * loop (mail thread) creates pipe instances and waits for
 * a client to connect.  It reuses disconnected instances
 * where it can.  The Process loop waits for the system to
 * tell it that there is pipe I/O to be done and then
 * does it.
 *      Two semaphores are also used.  WorkSem is associated
 * with named-pipe instances through DosNmPipeSetSem and is
 * strobed whenever there is pipe I/O to be done.  MySem is
 * used by the Process loop to tell the Connect loop that a
 * pipe instance is available.
 *
 * Compile with:  C> cl pipesrv.c netapi.lib
 *
 * Usage:  C> pipesrv
 *
 */
```

Figure 13-9.   (*continued*)
The PIPESRV.C prototype program.

Figure 13-9. *continued*

```
#include <os2.h>
#include <netcons.h>

/* Change these to whatever your application needs */
#define MAX_CLIENTS 200          /* max pipe instances   */
#define PIPE_NAME "\\PIPE\\MYPIPE"  /* pipe being served    */
#define IN_SIZE  512             /* whatever size        */
#define OUT_SIZE 512             /* whatever size        */
#define WSIZE 0xffff             /* work buffer size     */
#define SSIZE 8192               /* stack size           */


#define STATE_UNUSED 0
#define STATE_CONNECTED 1
#define STATE_DISCONNECTED 2

struct ptable
    {
    int state;        /* state of the pipe instance */
    unsigned hdl;     /* pipe handle                */
    char far * base;  /* base of write-data buffer  */
    char far * wbuf;  /* pending write data         */
    unsigned num;     /* size of write              */
    } Ptable[MAX_CLIENTS] = {0};

#define WORKSEM "\\SEM\\WORKSEM"  /* WorkSem semaphore   */
#define MYSEM   "\\SEM\\MYSEM"    /* MySem semaphore     */

HSYSSEM WorkSem = 0;
HSYSSEM MySem = 0;
char ProcStack[SSIZE] = {0};     /* ProcessLoop stack   */
void far ProcessLoop();

main()
    {
    struct ptable *pt;
    unsigned hdl;
    int i;
    TID tid;

    DosCreateSem(CSEM_PUBLIC, &WorkSem, WORKSEM);
    DosCreateSem(CSEM_PUBLIC, &MySem, MYSEM);
    DosCreateThread(ProcessLoop, &tid, ProcStack + SSIZE);
```

(continued)

Figure 13-9. *continued*

```
/* connect loop -- forever */
while (1)
    {
    /* try to get a disconnected pipe instance */
    pt = Ptable;
    for (i = 0; i < MAX_CLIENTS; ++i)
        {
        /* look for disconnected instance */
        if (pt->state == STATE_DISCONNECTED)
            break;
        }
    if (i == MAX_CLIENTS)
        {
        /* none exist, so make a new instance */
        for (i = 0; i < MAX_CLIENTS; ++i)
            {
            if (pt->hdl == 0)
                {
                DosMakeNmPipe(
                    PIPE_NAME,                /* pipe name      */
                    &hdl,                     /* for handle     */
                    NP_ACCESS_DUPLEX,         /* bidirectional  */
                    (NP_NOWAIT :              /* non-blocking   */
                        NP_READMODE_BYTE :    /* read mode      */
                        NP_TYPE_BYTE :        /* pipe type      */
                        MAX_CLIENTS),         /* instance count */
                    IN_SIZE,
                    OUT_SIZE,
                    OL
                    );
                pt->hdl = hdl;
                break;
                }
            }
        }
    /* if no instances available, wait for them */
    if (i == MAX_CLIENTS)
        {
        DosSemRequest(MySem, -1L);
        continue;           /* top of forever loop */
        }

    /* block waiting for a client */
    DosConnectNmPipe(hdl);
    pt->state = STATE_CONNECTED;
```

(continued)

Figure 13-9. *continued*

```
            /* a client is attached -- set to nonblocking */
            DosSetNmpHandState(hdl, NP_NOWAIT);

            /* associate sem with the handle. The key
             * is the index in the Ptable.
             */
            DosSetNmPipeSem(hdl, WorkSem, pt - Ptable);

            /* now go wait for another client to connect */
            }
        }

void far ProcessLoop()
    {
    static char far Wbuf[WSIZE] = {0}; /* work buffer    */
    struct npss far * np;              /* work structure */
    struct ptable *pt;                 /* instance table */
    unsigned short hdl;                /* pipe handle    */
    unsigned num;

    /* These variables represent the input and output
     * buffers from your application and their sizes. */

    extern char far * InBuf;
    extern unsigned InSize;
    extern char far * OutBuf;
    extern unsigned OutSize;

    /* initialize the semaphore */
    DosSemClear(WorkSem);
    while (1)
        {
        DosSemRequest(WorkSem, -1L);

        /* find out what there is to do */
        DosQNmPipeSemState(WorkSem, (struct npss far *)Wbuf, WSIZE);
        np = (struct npss far *)Wbuf;

        /* for each record */
        while (np->npss_status != NPSS_EOI)
            {
            pt = &Ptable[np->npss_key];
```

(continued)

Figure 13-9. *continued*

```
            hdl = pt->hdl;
            switch (np->npss_status)
                {
                case NPSS_CLOSE:
                    /* disconnect and mark the state */
                    DosDisconnectNmPipe(hdl);
                    pt->state = STATE_DISCONNECTED;

                    /* notify the Connect loop */
                    DosSemClear(MySem);
                    break;

                case NPSS_RDATA:
                    DosRead(hdl, InBuf, InSize, &num);

                    /* INSERT YOUR PROCESS CODE HERE */

                    DosWrite(hdl, OutBuf, OutSize, &num);
                    if (num != OutSize)
                        {

                        /* WARNING!  Your data needs to be in
                         * a buffer that will not get reused. */

                        pt->base = OutBuf;
                        pt->wbuf = OutBuf + num;
                        pt->num = OutSize - num;
                        }
                    break;

                case NPSS_WSPACE:

                    /* The pipe write buffer is empty.  See if
                     * there is any saved stuff to write. */

                    if (pt->wbuf == NULL)
                        break;
                    DosWrite(hdl, pt->wbuf, pt->num, &num);
                    if (num != pt->num)
                        {
                        pt->wbuf = pt->wbuf + num;
                        pt->num = pt->num - num;
                        }
```

(continued)

Figure 13-9. *continued*

```
                    else
                        ; /* free up pt->base */
                    pt->wbuf = NULL;
                    break;
                }
            ++np;
            }
        }
    }
```

Efficiency: Named Pipes or NetBIOS?

The computer industry likes to paraphrase Mark Twain: "There are lies, damned lies, and benchmarks." An often-asked question is "Are named pipes more efficient than direct programming to NetBIOS?" As you'll soon see, this question can't be answered with a simple yes or no.

Because named pipes are a more abstract mechanism, it might seem that they would require more overhead and that high-performance applications should use NetBIOS. But because named pipes are built into the OS/2 kernel, and because the NetBIOS interface must travel a complex path through the operating system and the redirector, named pipes are usually more efficient than direct use of the NetBIOS. A test of bytes-per-second transaction rates of the two IPC mechanisms appears in Tables 13-2 and 13-3.

Client	*Server*
get xact size	
CALL	LISTEN
start timing	
repeat 100x	repeat until done
SEND xact	RECEIVE xact
RECEIVE xact	SEND xact (same data)
end timing	
HANGUP	
compute total bytes / total time	

Table 13-2.
Testing NetBIOS transaction rates (NetBIOS pseudocode).

Client	Server
	DosMakeNmPipe
DosOpen	
	DosConnectNmPipe
start timing	
repeat 100x	repeat until done
DosTransactNmPipe	*DosRead* (message)
	DosWrite same data
end timing	
DosClose	
compute total bytes / total time	

Table 13-3.
Testing named-pipe transaction rates (named-pipe pseudocode).

Tests using these two methods were run on an AT workstation and a 16-MHz 386 server using a broadband network and the DWB NetBIOS driver. The named pipes were created with a buffer size of 512 bytes. Table 13-4 summarizes the results, with throughput measured in bytes per second. The ratio of NetBIOS times to named-pipe times should be independent of hardware and NetBIOS driver implementation.

Transaction Size	*NetBIOS (BPS)*	*Named Pipe (BPS)*
1	63	71
64	3855	4183
128	7441	7901
512	15900	18220
1000	21505	22075
5000	30372	27091
32000	33226	27631
64000	34008	27668

Table 13-4.
Transaction throughput in bytes per second.

The named-pipe transaction rate starts to fall off at transaction sizes above 1000. Note, however, that if the named-pipe buffer size is increased, the throughput rates start increasing. Table 13-5 shows sample throughput rates for transactions of 32000 bytes.

Pipe Buffer Size	Throughput (BPS)
512	27631
1024	29183
4096	30331
8192	30563
16384	30607

Table 13-5.
Transaction throughput by pipe buffer size.

These named-pipe numbers were produced with workstation and server request buffers configured at 4096 bytes. These are set through the LANMAN.INI file by the *sizworkbuf* parameter of the [wksta] component and the *sizreqbuf* parameter of the [server] component. If the transfer buffer size is increased to 8096 bytes, the transaction rate for 32000 bytes and 16384-byte pipe buffers is 31311 BPS.

What is the point of all of these numbers? First, to show that even with the overhead of higher abstraction, named pipes are usually more efficient than direct NetBIOS programming. The second point is that many factors affect performance in a network environment. The transaction size, the pipe buffer size, and the network buffer size all affect the overall performance. When you make measurements of efficiency, be sure that you know all of the factors that you are measuring.

DEBUGGING DISTRIBUTED APPLICATIONS

This chapter contains miscellaneous programming tips that will help you develop error-free distributed applications. The first part of the chapter describes how to use the APIs to debug distributed applications. The last part of the chapter describes problems associated with distributed applications that reside in different time zones.

Minimizing Distributed GP Faults

Imagine an application that writes a far pointer to a named pipe. The server side of the application reads the pointer out of the pipe and attempts to dereference it. The pointer likely has no meaning at the server and will cause a general protection (GP) fault when it is dereferenced. This kills the server side of the application.

Or, a bit more subtly, suppose the client side of an application passes buffers of variable-length information to the server and includes a header of offsets to this information. If an offset is wrong, the server side of the application might reference nonexistent memory, resulting in a GP fault.

Because a GP fault at the server effectively shuts down an application at all workstations (not just at the workstation that encountered the fault), you must be sure to write distributed programs in such a way that potential fault damage is restricted to the client end of the application.

Probing

Whenever you call a LAN Manager API that operates at a remote location, the API first examines or *probes* the buffers to be sure that they are addressable. For example, imagine an API with the following arguments:

```
NetObjectVerb(
char far * servername,
char far * buf,
USHORT buflen
)
```

The first lines of code would be something like this:

```
tmp = strlen_f(servername) + buf[0] + buf[buflen - 1];
```

This ensures that all passed arguments are addressable and that if they are going to result in a GP fault, they will do so on the client side.

When you design distributed applications, and particularly when you design distributed procedures that will be used by other programmers, you should always probe the arguments in a similar fashion.

Debugging Strategies

Multiprocess applications are usually harder to debug than single-process applications. And distributed multiprocess applications are harder to debug than local multiprocess applications. Accordingly, it is usually easiest to develop and debug single-process applications, split them into multiple processes on one machine, and then distribute pieces to different nodes for further debugging.

RPC—The Ultimate in Distribution

Eventually you'll be able to use a remote procedure call (RPC) compiler to help you distribute the pieces of your single-process application. But until an RPC compiler is part of LAN Manager, plan your debugging strategy ahead of time.

The Error Log as a Debugging Tool

When debugging multiprocess applications (particularly those that are distributed), you might find the following approaches of use in writing debugging or error information to the screen:

- You can use the *NetErrorLogWrite* API to put arbitrary information into the error log and then use the *NetErrorLogOpen* API or command-line interface commands to display this information at a later time. LOGERR.C in Chapter 8 is an example of this method.

- You can use an *audit log* when debugging your applications. Server programs can create and use audit records to tuck away information for the developer. See the Audit API information in Chapter 8 for details on designing your own audit records.

Alert! Errors are afoot

One of the principles of defensive programming requires that you be aware of the assumptions you make and that you write assertion-checking code to ensure the assumptions are true. Assertion-checking code informs an administrator when problems occur. For example, a stand-alone program might include the following code whenever you make assumptions that a pointer can never be null:

```
ASSERT(p != NULL);
```

You can also use the Alert APIs to create a multiprocess assertion mechanism, as shown in the *AssertAlert* routine (Figure 14-1). This routine can be called with a statement similar to the following:

```
AssertAlert(p != NULL, "bad pointer");
```

```c
/*
 * ASSRT.C -- This file contains the AssertAlert subroutine
 * that raises an alert on the event "ASSERTION" and passes
 * along the specified character string when the specified
 * condition is false.
 *
 */

#include <netcons.h>
#include <alert.h>
#include <time.h>

void AssertAlert(condition, str)
int condition;
char * str;
    {
    char buf[64];
    struct std_alert *ps = (struct std_alert *)buf;

    if (condition)
        return;

    ps->alrt_timestamp = time(NULL);
    strcpy(ps->alrt_eventname, "ASSERTION");
    strcpy(ps->alrt_servicename, "MYSERVICE");
    strcpy(buf + sizeof(*ps), str);
    NetAlertRaise(
                "ASSERTION",
                buf,                     /* alert data */
                sizeof(*ps)+strlen(str), /* length    */
                ALERT_MED_WAIT           /* wait time */
                );
    }
```

Figure 14-1.
The AssertAlert *subroutine.*

Determining Error Locations

To determine the line number and source file in which an error occurred, use the power of the C preprocessor. Consider the following macros:

```
#define str(x) #x /* turn x into a string */
#define AssertAlert(cond, arg, line) \
    AssertAlert (cond, arg, " at line " str(line) " of " \
    __FILE__)
```

The statement will result in a *NetAlertRaise* call of "ASSERTION", as follows:

```
AssertAlert(p != NULL, "bad string", __LINE__);
```

If the condition is not true, the data string will look like this:

```
"bad string at line 273 of MYFILE.C"
```

By using the technique shown in the error-log alerter example in Chapter 10, you can display the assertion on the screen with the Netpopup service.

Working with Time Zones

Another potential pitfall for a distributed application is the problem of network computers running in different time zones. Times sent to workstations from a server are often relative to the server's time zone, so a workstation must be ready to convert that information to its own time zone. The *ToLocalTime* subroutine (Figure 14-2) shows how to accomplish this. Note that the routine assumes all machines have the correct time—a condition that should be verified before the time-zone conversion.

```
/*
 * TIME.C -- The ToLocalTime subroutine compensates for time
 * zone differences in a distributed application environment.
 * It takes an uncorrected time and a server name and returns
 * an adjusted time rounded off to the nearest hour.  The assumption
 * is made that both the server and the local workstation
 * have the correct synchronized time.
 *
 */
```

Figure 14-2.   *(continued)*
The ToLocalTime *subroutine.*

Figure 14-2. *continued*

```
#include <os2.h>
#include <netcons.h>
#include <remutil.h>
#define SPH 3600

unsigned ToLocalTime(timein, timeout, servername)
unsigned long timein;          /* uncorrected time */
unsigned long *timeout;        /* corrected time   */
char * servername;             /* assumes \\name   */
    {
    struct time_of_day_info ti;
    unsigned long diff, localtime;
    int err;
    unsigned short gseg, lseg;
    unsigned long far * gsptr;

    /* get the server's time */
    err = NetRemoteTOD(servername, (char far *)&ti, sizeof(ti));
    if (err)
        return(err);

    /* get the local time */
    if (err = DosGetInfoSeg(&gseg, &lseg))
        return err;
    gsptr = (unsigned long far *)MAKEP(gseg, 0);
    localtime = *gsptr;

    /* get gross time difference */
    diff = ti.tod_elapsedt - localtime;

    /* round it off to hours -- SPH is seconds per hour */
    diff = (diff + SPH/2) / SPH;
    diff *= SPH;

    /* and compensate for the time zone */
    *timeout = timein - diff;
    }
```

LAN MANAGER VARIATIONS

Up to this point, this book has described the core Microsoft LAN Manager, which was designed to run on workstations and servers running Microsoft OS/2 and workstations running MS-DOS. But LAN Manager is not limited to these environments. As pointed out in Chapter 1, LAN Manager is a technology and, as such, has been adapted to a variety of environments. This chapter describes four important LAN Manager variations:

- MS-DOS LAN Manager, which runs under MS-DOS version 3.1 or later or under Microsoft Windows, and which provides a LAN Manager workstation environment

- LAN Manager for UNIX, the portable version of LAN Manager, which runs under UNIX and provides a LAN Manager server environment

- IBM LAN Server, which runs under IBM OS/2 Extended Edition and provides a variation of the LAN Manager server environment

- The Peer Services options of LAN Manager

MS-DOS LAN Manager

One of the main design goals of LAN Manager was interoperability with MS-NET and PC-LAN workstations and servers. Even though the LAN Manager server and workstation run under OS/2, MS-NET workstations can use a LAN Manager server without being aware of the enhanced capabilities. The MS-DOS LAN Manager allows MS-DOS workstations to use the enhanced capabilities of the LAN Manager server.

Creating LAN Manager Applications for MS-DOS

The MS-DOS LAN Manager is purely a workstation environment: You cannot write the server side of a LAN Manager application and run it under MS-DOS. The creation of the client-side applications, however, is straightforward.

You can write dual-mode programs—programs that run unchanged under MS-DOS and OS/2. Under OS/2, these programs use the dynamic link libraries for all Dos and Net APIs; under MS-DOS, they call MS-DOS versions of the subroutines that have been linked into the application. To create a dual-mode program, you first build an OS/2 version of the application and then use the Bind utility (supplied with the Microsoft C Compiler) to add the MS-DOS versions of the Dos and Net APIs. The Bind utility has a command line of the following form:

```
bind infile.exe doscalls.lib [file.lib...] [file.obj...]
[-o outfile.exe] [-m mapfile] [-n name...] [-n @file]
```

where *infile* is the name of the executable file to be bound, *file.lib* and *file.obj* are additional modules to bind, *outfile.exe* is the name of the new bound executable file (default is that specified by *infile.exe*), *name*... is a list of protected-mode-only functions to map to the *BadDynLink* function, *@file* is a text file of protected-mode-only functions to map, and −m produces a linker map file named *mapfile* (*outfile.BM* by default).

The following libraries can be specified on the Bind command line:

Library Name	Contents
DOSCALLS.LIB	Dos APIs
NETAPI.LIB	Net APIs
DOSNET.LIB	MS-DOS support for the network
SYSCALL0.LIB	Network support for Dos calls
API.LIB	Additional API support
PMSPL.LIB	Support for Print APIs

Completely specified pathnames are required for each library file.

> **NOTE:** *To create an MS-DOS–only version of a network application, include the DOSNET.LIB library at link time.*

Variations from Core LAN Manager

To a programmer, the most important feature of MS-DOS LAN Manager is its API support. Table 15-1 on the following page lists those APIs that run differently under MS-DOS than they do under core LAN Manager. Keep the following points in mind:

- Some APIs are relevant only in a server environment. These APIs are generally supported under MS-DOS LAN Manager, but only as remote calls. These APIs, noted as ''Remote only'' in the comments column of Table 15-1, return NERR_RemoteOnly if they are called with a NULL server name. As with OS/2 versions of remote calls, most require that the logged-on user have *admin* privilege at the server.

- Some APIs don't work remotely. If called with a server name other than NULL, they return ERROR_NOT_SUPPORTED. These APIs are noted as ''Local only'' in Table 15-1.

- If an API is not supported under MS-DOS, it returns ERROR_NOT_SUPPORTED when called. Dual-mode programs can still be created, but the unsupported calls fail.

API Name	Comments
DosMailslot APIs	From the application's standpoint, the way mailslots work is unchanged. However, only second-class messages are received by MS-DOS mailslots.
DosMakeNmPipe	Not supported (server side only).
DosConnectNmPipe	Not supported (server side only).
DosDisconnectNmPipe	Not supported (server side only).
DosSetNmPipeSem	Not supported (server side only).
DosQNmPipeSemState	Not supported (server side only).
DosQNmPipeInfo	Not supported (server side only).
DosSetNmPipeHandState	Not supported (server side only).
DosCallNmPipe	
DosPeekNmPipe	
DosRawReadNmPipe	
DosRawWriteNmPipe	
DosTransactNmPipe	
DosWaitNmPipe	
DosBufReset	This behaves differently in different versions of MS-DOS. In versions 3.3 and later, it returns ERROR_BROKEN_PIPE if the pipe is already closed. In versions 3.2 or earlier, it returns 0.
DosPrintDest APIs	Remote calls only.
DosPrintJobGetId	Not supported.
DosPrintJob APIs	Remote calls only.
DosPrintQ APIs	Remote calls only.
NetAccessCheck	Not supported.
NetAccess APIs	Remote calls only.
NetAlert APIs	Not supported.
NetAuditWrite	Not supported.
NetAudit APIs	Remote calls only.
NetBios APIs	Not supported.
NetCharDev APIs	Remote calls only.
NetConfigGet	Local only.
NetConfigGetAll	Local only.
NetConnectionEnum	Remote calls only.
NetErrorLogWrite	Not supported.
NetErrorLog APIs	Remote calls only.
NetFile APIs	Remote calls only.

Table 15-1.   *(continued)*
API variations under MS-DOS LAN Manager.

Table 15-1. *continued*

API Name	Comments
NetGroup APIs	Remote calls only.
NetHandle APIs	Valid only for level 1 and for handles to named pipes.
NetLogonEnum	Remote calls only.
NetMessageForward	Remote calls only.
NetMessageUnForward	Remote calls only.
NetMessageAddName	The LANMAN.INI file has an *nmsg* parameter in the [messenger] component. This defaults to 2 and must be changed if alias names are to be added.
NetRemoteExec	Not supported.
NetServerAdmin	Remote calls only.
NetServerGetInfo	Remote calls only.
NetServerSetInfo	Remote calls only.
NetServiceStatus	Not supported.
NetServiceInstall	Remote calls only.
NetSession APIs	Remote calls only.
NetShare APIs	Remote calls only.
NetStatistics	Remote only.
NetUserValidate	Not supported.
NetUserValidate2	Not supported.
NetUser APIs	Remote calls only.
NetWkstaSetInfo	*wki1_oth_domains* cannot be set locally.
NetWkstaSetUID	Local only.
NetWkstaSetUID2	Local only.

LAN Manager for UNIX

LAN Manager for UNIX is a portable version of LAN Manager designed to run under non-OS/2 environments such as UNIX. It provides print, file, and distributed application support identical to that of an OS/2 LAN Manager server. LAN Manager for UNIX is a platform for writing the server side of distributed applications. It can also run the client side of distributed applications.

Named Pipes Drive the Show

Because LAN Manager is frequently used with distributed applications, it is required to provide support for named pipes. LAN Manager for UNIX 1.1 provides fairly complete support for both the server and client sides of named-pipe applications. Source-code portability between OS/2 and other environments (primarily UNIX System V) is the driving goal.

As a platform for server-side applications, LAN Manager for UNIX provides complete support for named pipes, with the following exceptions:

- *DosSetNmPipeSem* is not supported.

- *DosQNmPipeSemState* is not supported.

- *DosWaitNmPipe* is not supported.

- *DosCallNmPipe* is not supported.

- *DosConnectNmPipe* is supported only in blocking mode.

The remaining named-pipe routines—including *DosRead*, *DosWrite*, and *DosBufReset*—are available.

For the client side of applications, LAN Manager for UNIX provides complete support for named pipes.

LAN Manager for UNIX Server Administration

The first release of portable LAN Manager, LAN Manager/X 1.0, did not support the full set of LAN Manager APIs for server administration. Administration was accomplished through the *NetServerAdminCommand* API and had a few limitations. The current release, LAN Manager for UNIX 1.1, contains full remote-administration support. As LAN Manager evolves, Microsoft will continue to improve the core LAN Manager for UNIX technology and extend LAN Manager to an increasing number of environments.

IBM LAN Server

The IBM LAN Server is a version of the LAN Manager server that has been adapted by IBM. The workstation software is a standard part of the IBM OS/2 Extended Edition, but the LAN Server is ordered as a separate piece. In IBM's terminology, the workstation is called a *Requester*.

Internally, the LAN Server and Requester differ little from the core LAN Manager. They use the same redirector and server code and the same service programs for Messenger, Netpopup, Alerter, and Netrun. They use the same command-line interface, although some LAN Manager commands are not supported. They use the same SMB and NetBIOS protocols.

The LAN Server and the core LAN Manager are interoperable when it comes to file systems, character devices, and remote IPC support for distributed applications. From a programmer's point of view, applications using either the distributed data or the distributed intelligence model will work with workstations or servers of either kind.

Some external characteristics of the LAN Server and core LAN Manager are different. LAN Server implements the concept of a logical server to present resources to the administrator and the end user. This logical server is implemented on top of the basic LAN Manager technology, however, so LAN Server is 100% compatible with the Microsoft LAN Manager API.

The IBM LAN Server does not support the LAN Manager Print and Net-BIOS APIs, but it does provide a similar printing mechanism and a similar network BIOS interface for direct submission of NCBs. Note that the IBM product does not support the Profile APIs or multiple NetBIOS drivers.

> **NOTE:** *Microsoft and IBM have announced that IBM LAN Server and Microsoft LAN Manager will be completely compatible in a future version.*

Spooling Across Systems

Both LAN Manager and LAN Server use the OS/2 Presentation Manager Spooler and support the OS/2 Presentation Manager APIs. The DosPrint APIs are not supported in the current version of IBM LAN Server. Note that any kind of workstation can use the *NetUseAdd* API to use a spooled print queue on either kind of server. Copying a file to the redirected device works in all circumstances.

Peer Services

Peer Services allow a workstation to have limited server capabilities without needing to run as a full LAN Manager server. When running Peer Services, the workstation is limited to establishing one session to a client. Only one print queue and one character device can be shared, but multiple file shares, named pipes, and mailslots are available. The APIs are identical to the LAN Manager server APIs, with the following exceptions:

- Any attempt to share a second print queue or character device with *NetShareADD* will return NERR_TooManyItems.

- The *sv2_disc* value must always be −1 (no automatic disconnect).

Applications can determine whether Peer Services are running by using the *NetServerGetInfo* API:

```
if ((sv->sv2_version_major & PRODUCT_TYPE_MASK) == PEER_BASE_VER)
    /* computer is a Peer server */
```

API SUMMARY

This appendix provides cross-reference information for each Microsoft LAN Manager API described in this book. The page numbers indicated are the locations of the API syntax descriptions.

NOTE: *For information about the supporting Microsoft OS/2 APIs, consult the* Microsoft OS/2 Programmer's Reference *(Microsoft Press, 1989).*

API Name	Page	Description
DosCallNmPipe	356	A single call combining *DosOpen*, *DosSetNmpHandState*, *DosTransactNmPipe*, and *DosClose* operations
DosConnectNmPipe	347	Waits for a client to open a named pipe
DosDeleteMailslot	372	Deletes a mailslot
DosDisconnectNmPipe	349	Closes a client's connection to a named pipe
DosMailslotInfo	372	Returns information about a mailslot
DosMakeMailslot	371	Creates a mailslot
DosMakeNmPipe	342	Creates a named pipe
DosPeekMailslot	374	Reads a message in a mailslot without removing it
DosPeekNmPipe	352	Copies a named pipe's data into a buffer for preview without removing it
DosPrintDestAdd	439	Adds a print destination to a server
DosPrintDestControl	441	Cancels, pauses, continues, or restarts the specified print destination
DosPrintDestDel	440	Deletes a print destination from a server
DosPrintDestEnum	436	Retrieves a list of all print destinations at a server
DosPrintDestGetInfo	437	Retrieves information about a specific print destination at a server

(continued)

API Name	Page	Description
DosPrintDestSetInfo	438	Modifies the configuration of a print destination at a server
DosPrintJobContinue	429	Continues a paused print job
DosPrintJobDel	428	Deletes a print job from the print queue
DosPrintJobEnum	424	Retrives information about all the print jobs in a print queue
DosPrintJobGetId	430	Gets information about a print job in a print queue
DosPrintJobGetInfo	425	Returns information about a specific print job in a print queue
DosPrintJobPause	428	Pauses a print job in the print queue
DosPrintJobSetInfo	426	Changes the instructions for a job in the print queue
DosPrintQAdd	417	Creates a print queue on a server
DosPrintQContinue	420	Restarts a paused print queue
DosPrintQDel	418	Deletes a printer queue from a server
DosPrintQEnum	411	Lists all printer queues on a server
DosPrintQGetInfo	414	Retrieves information about a specific printer queue
DosPrintQPause	420	Pauses a print queue
DosPrintQPurge	419	Removes all but the current job from a print queue
DosPrintQSetInfo	415	Sets the configuration of a printer queue
DosQNmpHandState	349	Retrieves information about the state of a named-pipe handle
DosQNmPipeInfo	346	Retrieves information about a named pipe
DosQNmPipeSemState	360	Returns information about named pipes associated with semaphores that are in blocking mode ·
DosReadAsynchNmPipe	363	Performs an asychronous read of a named pipe (DOS only)
DosReadMailslot	373	Reads a message in a mailslot
DosSetNmpHandState	351	Sets the mode of a named pipe
DosSetNmPipeSem	358	Associates a semaphore with a named pipe
DosTransactNmPipe	354	Performs read and write transactions on a named pipe in one step
DosWaitNmPipe	357	Waits for a named pipe to become available
DosWriteMailslot	375	Writes a message to a mailslot

(continued)

continued

API Name	Page	Description
NetAccessAdd	282	Adds access permission information for a new resource
NetAccessCheck	285	Verifies that a user has permission to access a resource
NetAccessDel	283	Deletes access permissions for a resource
NetAccessEnum	278	Returns information about access permission records
NetAccessGetInfo	280	Gets permission information for a resource
NetAccessGetUserPerms	284	Returns an access permission bitmap
NetAccessSetInfo	281	Changes permission information for a resource
NetAlertRaise	384	Notifies registered clients that an event has occurred
NetAlertStart	383	Registers a client for an event
NetAlertStop	386	Cancels an event alert
NetAuditClear	252	Deletes the entries in an audit file
NetAuditOpen	250	Opens an audit file for reading
NetAuditRead	246	Reads one or more records from an audit file
NetAuditWrite	250	Writes a record to an audit file
NetBiosClose	456	Closes a NetBIOS device driver
NetBiosEnum	454	Gets the names of all installed NetBIOS device drivers
NetBiosGetInfo	454	Gets information about the specified NetBIOS device driver
NetBiosOpen	455	Creates a device-driver handle for sending NCBs to the specified NetBIOS device driver
NetBiosSubmit	457	Submits one or more NCBs to a NetBIOS device driver
NetCharDevControl	401	Allows administration of character devices
NetCharDevEnum	399	Returns information about all devices that are part of any device pool
NetCharDevGetInfo	400	Returns information about a specific device
NetCharDevQEnum	402	Returns information about all device queues on a server
NetCharDevQGetInfo	403	Retrieves information about a particular server device queue
NetCharDevQPurge	405	Deletes all pending requests on a device queue
NetCharDevQPurgeSelf	406	Deletes pending device queue requests from the specified workstation

(continued)

API Name	Page	Description
NetCharDevQSetInfo	404	Sets information for a particular server device queue
NetConfigGet	180	Retrieves a single entry from a local LANMAN.INI file
NetConfigGet2	180	Retrieves a single entry from a local or remote LANMAN.INI file
NetConfigGetAll	181	Retrieves an entire component section from a local LANMAN.INI file
NetConfigGetAll2	182	Retrieves an entire component section from a local or remote LANMAN.INI file
NetConnectionEnum	219	Lists all connections to a shared server resource or all connections at a specific computer
NetErrorLogClear	261	Clears an error log file
NetErrorLogOpen	259	Returns the error log file handle
NetErrorLogRead	259	Reads an error record from the error log
NetErrorLogWrite	260	Writes an error record to an error log file
NetFileClose	230	Closes a resource
NetFileClose2	231	Closes a resource; supports file handles larger than 64 KB
NetFileEnum	226	Returns a list of open server resources
NetFileEnum2	227	Returns a list of open server resources; supports file IDs larger than 64 KB
NetFileGetInfo	229	Gets information about an open server resource
NetFileGetInfo2	229	Gets information about an open server resource; supports file handles larger than 64 KB
NetGetDCName	335	Returns the primary domain controller for the specified domain
NetGroupAdd	320	Adds a new group to the UAS database
NetGroupAddUser	322	Adds a user to a group in the UAS database
NetGroupDel	321	Removes a group from the UAS database
NetGroupDelUser	323	Removes a user from a group in the UAS database
NetGroupEnum	319	Lists all groups in the UAS database
NetGroupGetInfo	325	Returns information about the specified group
NetGroupGetUsers	323	Lists the members of a group in the UAS database
NetGroupSetInfo	326	Sets information for the specified group
NetGroupSetUsers	324	Defines the entire membership of a group in the UAS database
NetHandleGetInfo	367	Returns information about network handles

(continued)

continued

API Name	Page	Description
NetHandleSetInfo	368	Sets information about network handles
NetLogonEnum	332	Returns information about all users logged on to a server
NetMessageBufferSend	133	Sends a buffer of data to a message name
NetMessageFileSend	133	Sends a file to a message name
NetMessageLogFileGet	137	Retrieves the name and status of the message log file
NetMessageLogFileSet	136	Sets a log file to receive messages
NetMessageNameAdd	126	Registers a username in the message name table
NetMessageNameDel	127	Deletes a username from the message name table
NetMessageNameEnum	124	Lists information about the message name table
NetMessageNameFwd	129	Forwards messages from one workstation username to another
NetMessageNameGetInfo	125	Retrieves information about a user's entry in the message name table
NetMessageNameUnFwd	131	Stops the forwarding of messages from one user to another
NetProfileLoad	141	Loads environment commands from a file
NetProfileSave	140	Saves the environment in a file
NetRemoteCopy	149	Copies files from one location to another on a remote server
NetRemoteExec	153	Executes a program on a remote server
NetRemoteMove	152	Moves a file from one location to another on a remote server
NetRemoteTOD	147	Returns the time of day from a remote server
NetServerAdminCommand	197	Executes a command on a server
NetServerDiskEnum	197	Retrieves a list of disk drives available on the server
NetServerEnum	200	Returns information about the visible servers and workstations on the network
NetServerEnum2	200	Returns information about the visible servers and workstations in a domain
NetServerGetInfo	195	Retrives information about a server
NetServerSetInfo	196	Sets configuration information at a server
NetServiceControl	167	Controls the operation of started (installed) services
NetServiceEnum	170	Retrieves information about all started services
NetServiceGetInfo	170	Retrieves information about a specific service

(continued)

continued

API Name	Page	Description
NetServiceInstall	171	Starts a network service
NetServiceStatus	173	Updates status information for a service
NetSessionDel	217	Deletes a session between a server and a workstation
NetSessionEnum	216	Retrieves a list of all active sessions
NetSessionGetInfo	216	Gets information about a specific server/ workstation session
NetShareAdd	210	Creates a share to a server resource
NetShareCheck	213	Checks whether a device is being shared by a server
NetShareDel	211	Deletes a shared server resource
NetShareEnum	207	Retrieves information about the shared resources on a server
NetShareGetInfo	208	Retrieves information about a specific share on the network
NetShareSetInfo	209	Changes a share's parameters
NetStatisticsClear	271	Clears a workstation or server statistics
NetStatisticsGet	265	Returns server or workstation statistics
NetStatisticsGet2	267	Returns information about a server or workstation service
NetUseAdd	109	Establishes a connection between a workstation and server
NetUseDel	112	Terminates a connection to a server resource
NetUseEnum	114	Lists current connections between workstation and servers
NetUseGetInfo	117	Retrieves information about a connection to a shared resource
NetUserAdd	296	Establishes an account on a server
NetUserDel	299	Removes an account from the UAS
NetUserEnum	295	Returns information for all accounts
NetUserGetGroups	304	Lists all the groups to which a user belongs
NetUserGetInfo	300	Returns specific information for one account
NetUserModalsGet	316	Returns information about the UAS database
NetUserModalsSet	317	Sets global modal-related information in the UAS database
NetUserPasswordSet	302	Changes a user's password
NetUserSetGroups	304	Sets the groups to which a user account belongs

(continued)

continued

API Name	Page	Description
NetUserSetInfo	300	Modifies a user's account
NetUserValidate	329	Validates a user's password
NetUserValidate2	330	Validates a user's password and returns a buffer of information
NetWkstaGetInfo	98	Returns information about the workstation
NetWkstaSetInfo	100	Configures a workstation
NetWkstaSetUID	101	Logs a user on to the network
NetWkstaSetUID2	102	Logs a user on to the network in the specified domain

ERROR CODES

Redirector error codes

Code	Value	Meaning
50	ERROR_NOT_SUPPORTED	Unsupported network request
51	ERROR_REM_NOT_LIST	Remote computer not listening
52	ERROR_DUP_NAME	Duplicate name on network
53	ERROR_BAD_NETPATH	Network name not found
54	ERROR_NETWORK_BUSY	Network busy
55	ERROR_DEV_NOT_EXIST	Device no longer on the network
56	ERROR_TOO_MANY_CMDS	NetBIOS command limit exceeded
57	ERROR_ADAP_HDW_ERR	Error in network adapter hardware
58	ERROR_BAD_NET_RESP	Incorrect network response
59	ERROR_UNEXP_NET_ERR	Unexpected network error
60	ERROR_BAD_REM_ADAP	Remote adapter incompatible
61	ERROR_PRINTQ_FULL	Print queue full
62	ERROR_NO_SPOOL_SPACE	Insufficient memory available for print file
63	ERROR_PRINT_CANCELLED	Print file canceled
64	ERROR_NETNAME_DELETED	Network name deleted
65	ERROR_NETWORK_ACCESS_DENIED	Network access denied
66	ERROR_BAD_DEV_TYPE	Incorrect network device type
67	ERROR_BAD_NET_NAME	Network name not found
68	ERROR_TOO_MANY_NAMES	Network name limit exceeded

(continued)

continued

Code	Value	Meaning
69	ERROR_TOO_MANY_SESS	NetBIOS session limit exceeded
70	ERROR_SHARING_PAUSED	File sharing temporarily paused
71	ERROR_REQ_NOT_ACCEP	Network request not accepted
72	ERROR_REDIR_PAUSED	Print or disk redirection paused
88	ERROR_NET_WRITE_FAULT	Network data fault
230	ERROR_BAD_PIPE	Nonexistent pipe or invalid operation
231	ERROR_PIPE_BUSY	Specified pipe busy
232	ERROR_NO_DATA	No data on nonblocking pipe read
233	ERROR_PIPE_NOT_CONNECTED	Pipe disconnected by server
234	ERROR_MORE_DATA	Additional data available
240	ERROR_VC_DISCONNECTED	Network session canceled

General LAN Manager error codes

Code	Value	Meaning
2102	NERR_NetNotStarted	The workstation device driver isn't installed.
2103	NERR_UnknownServer	The server cannot be located.
2104	NERR_ShareMem	An internal error occurred. The network cannot access a shared memory segment.
2105	NERR_NoNetworkResource	A network resource shortage occurred.
2106	NERR_RemoteOnly	This operation is not supported on workstations.
2107	NERR_DevNotRedirected	The device is not connected.
2114	NERR_ServerNotStarted	The Server service isn't started.
2115	NERR_ItemNotFound	The queue is empty.
2116	NERR_UnknownDevDir	The device or directory does not exist.
2117	NERR_RedirectedPath	The operation is invalid on a redirected resource.
2118	NERR_DuplicateShare	The name has already been shared.
2119	NERR_NoRoom	The server is currently out of the requested resource.

(continued)

continued

Code	Value	Meaning
2121	NERR_TooManyItems	Requested add of item exceeds maximum allowed.
2122	NERR_InvalidMaxUsers	The peer server will support only two simultaneous users.
2123	NERR_BufTooSmall	The API return buffer is too small.
2127	NERR_RemoteErr	A remote API error occurred.
2131	NERR_LanmanIniError	An error occurred when opening or reading LANMAN.INI.
2134	NERR_OS2IoctlError	An internal error occurred when calling the workstation driver.
2136	NERR_NetworkError	A general network error occurred.
2138	NERR_WkstaNotStarted	The Workstation service has not been started.
2139	NERR_BrowserNotStarted	The requested information is not available.
2140	NERR_InternalError	An internal LAN Manager error occurred.
2141	NERR_BadTransactConfig	The server is not configured for transactions.
2142	NERR_InvalidAPI	The requested API isn't supported on the remote server.
2143	NERR_BadEventName	The event name is invalid.

Config API error codes

Code	Value	Meaning
2146	NERR_CfgCompNotFound	Could not find the specified component in LANMAN.INI.
2147	NERR_CfgParamNotFound	Could not find the specified parameter in LANMAN.INI.
2149	NERR_LineTooLong	A line in LANMAN.INI is too long.

Spooler API error codes

Code	Value	Meaning
2150	NERR_QNotFound	The printer queue does not exist.
2151	NERR_JobNotFound	The print job does not exist.
2152	NERR_DestNotFound	The printer destination cannot be found.
2153	NERR_DestExists	The printer destination already exists.

(continued)

continued

Code	Value	Meaning
2154	NERR_QExists	The printer queue already exists.
2155	NERR_QNoRoom	No more printer queues can be added.
2156	NERR_JobNoRoom	No more print jobs can be added.
2157	NERR_DestNoRoom	No more printer destinations can be added.
2158	NERR_DestIdle	The printer destination is idle and cannot accept control operations.
2159	NERR_DestInvalidOp	The printer destination request contains an invalid control function.
2160	NERR_ProcNoRespond	The printer processor is not responding.
2161	NERR_SpoolerNotLoaded	The spooler is not running.
2162	NERR_DestInvalidState	This operation cannot be performed on the print destination in its current state.
2163	NERR_QInvalidState	This operation cannot be performed on the printer queue in its current state.
2164	NERR_JobInvalidState	This operation cannot be performed on the print job in its current state.
2165	NERR_SpoolNoMemory	A spooler memory allocation failure occurred.
2166	NERR_DriverNotFound	The device driver does not exist.
2167	NERR_DataTypeInvalid	The data type is not supported by the processor.
2168	NERR_ProcNotFound	The print processor is not installed.

Service API error codes

Code	Value	Meaning
2180	NERR_ServiceTableLocked	The service does not respond to control actions.
2181	NERR_ServiceTableFull	The service table is full.
2182	NERR_ServiceInstalled	The requested service has already been started.
2183	NERR_ServiceEntryLocked	The service does not respond to control actions.
2184	NERR_ServiceNotInstalled	The service has not been started.
2185	NERR_BadServiceName	The service name is invalid.
2186	NERR_ServiceCtlTimeout	The service is not responding to the control function.
2187	NERR_ServiceCtlBusy	The service control is busy.

(continued)

continued

Code	Value	Meaning
2188	NERR_BadServiceProgName	LANMAN.INI contains an invalid service program name.
2189	NERR_ServiceNotCtrl	The service cannot be controlled in its present state.
2190	NERR_ServiceKillProc	The service ended abnormally.
2191	NERR_ServiceCtlNotValid	The requested pause or stop is not valid for this service.

Wksta and Logon API error codes

Code	Value	Meaning
2200	NERR_AlreadyLoggedOn	This workstation is already logged on to the local area network.
2201	NERR_NotLoggedOn	The workstation isn't logged on to the local area network.
2202	NERR_BadUsername	The username or groupname parameter is invalid.
2203	NERR_BadPassword	The password parameter is invalid.
2204	NERR_UnableToAddName_W	The logon processor did not add the message alias.
2205	NERR_UnableToAddName_F	The logon processor did not add the message alias.
2206	NERR_UnableToDelName_W	The logoff processor did not delete the message alias.
2207	NERR_UnableToDelName_F	The logoff processor did not delete the message alias.
2209	NERR_LogonsPaused	Network logons are paused.
2210	NERR_LogonServerConflict	A centralized logon-server conflict occurred.
2211	NERR_LogonNoUserPath	The server is configured without a valid user path.
2212	NERR_LogonScriptError	An error occurred while loading or running the logon script.
2214	NERR_StandaloneLogon	The logon server was not specified. Your computer will be logged on as STANDALONE.
2215	NERR_LogonServerNotFound	The logon server cannot be found.
2216	NERR_LogonDomainExists	A logon domain already exists for this computer.
2217	NERR_NonValidatedLogon	The logon server could not validate the logon.

ACF API (access, user, group) error codes

Code	Value	Meaning
2219	NERR_ACFNotFound	The accounts file NET.ACC cannot be found.
2220	NERR_GroupNotFound	The group name cannot be found.
2221	NERR_UserNotFound	The username cannot be found.
2222	NERR_ResourceNotFound	The resource name cannot be found.
2223	NERR_GroupExists	The group already exists.
2224	NERR_UserExists	The user account already exists.
2225	NERR_ResourceExists	The resource permission list already exists.
2226	NERR_NotPrimary	The UAS database is a replica and will not allow updates.
2227	NERR_ACFNotLoaded	The user account system has not been started.
2228	NERR_ACFNoRoom	Too many names are in the user account system.
2229	NERR_ACFFileIOFail	A disk I/O failure occurred.
2230	NERR_ACFTooManyLists	The limit of 64 entries per resource was exceeded.
2231	NERR_UserLogon	Deletion of a user within a session is not allowed.
2232	NERR_ACFNoParent	The parent directory cannot be located.
2233	NERR_CannotGrowSegment	Unable to grow UAS session cache segment.
2234	NERR_SpeGroupOp	This operation is not allowed on this special group.
2235	NERR_NotInCache	This user is not cached in UAS session cache.
2236	NERR_UserInGroup	The user already belongs to this group.
2237	NERR_UserNotInGroup	The user does not belong to this group.
2238	NERR_AccountUndefined	This user account is undefined.
2239	NERR_AccountExpired	This user account has expired.
2240	NERR_InvalidWorkstation	The user is not allowed to log on from this workstation.
2241	NERR_InvalidLogonHours	The user is not allowed to log on at this time.
2242	NERR_PasswordExpired	The password of this user has expired.
2243	NERR_PasswordCantChange	The password of this user cannot change.
2244	NERR_PasswordHistConflict	This password cannot be used now.
2245	NERR_PasswordTooShort	The password is shorter than required.

(continued)

continued

Code	Value	Meaning
2246	NERR_PasswordTooRecent	The password of this user is too recent to change.
2247	NERR_InvalidDatabase	The UAS database file is corrupted.
2248	NERR_DatabaseUpToDate	No updates are necessary to this UAS database.
2249	NERR_SyncRequired	This database is outdated; synchronization is required.

Use API error codes

Code	Value	Meaning
2250	NERR_UseNotFound	The connection cannot be found.
2251	NERR_BadAsgType	This *asg_type* is invalid.
2252	NERR_DeviceIsShared	This device is currently being shared.

Messenger service error codes

Code	Value	Meaning
2270	NERR_NoComputerName	A computer name has not been configured.
2271	NERR_MsgAlreadyStarted	The Messenger service is already started.
2272	NERR_MsgInitFailed	The Messenger service failed to start.
2273	NERR_NameNotFound	The message alias cannot be found on the local-area network.
2274	NERR_AlreadyForwarded	This message alias has already been forwarded.
2275	NERR_AddForwarded	This message alias has been added but is still forwarded.
2276	NERR_AlreadyExists	This message alias already exists locally.
2277	NERR_TooManyNames	The maximum number of added message aliases has been exceeded.
2278	NERR_DelComputerName	The computer name cannot be deleted.
2279	NERR_LocalForward	Messages cannot be forwarded back to the same workstation.
2280	NERR_GrpMsgProcessor	An error exists in the domain message processor.
2281	NERR_PausedRemote	The message was sent, but the recipient has paused the Messenger service.
2282	NERR_BadReceive	The message was sent but not received.

(continued)

Code	Value	Meaning
2283	NERR_NameInUse	The message alias is currently in use. Try again later.
2284	NERR_MsgNotStarted	The Messenger service has not been started.
2285	NERR_NotLocalName	The name is not on the local computer.
2286	NERR_NoForwardName	The forwarded message alias cannot be found on the network.
2287	NERR_RemoteFull	The message alias table on the remote station is full.
2288	NERR_NameNotForwarded	Messages for this alias are not currently forwarded.
2289	NERR_TruncatedBroadcast	The broadcast message was truncated.
2294	NERR_InvalidDevice	This is an invalid device name.
2295	NERR_WriteFault	A write fault occurred.
2297	NERR_DuplicateName	A duplicate message alias exists on the local area network.
2298	NERR_DeleteLater	This message alias will be deleted later.
2299	NERR_IncompleteDel	The message alias was not successfully deleted from all networks.
2300	NERR_MultipleNets	This operation is not supported on machines with multiple networks.

Server API error codes

Code	Value	Meaning
2310	NERR_NetNameNotFound	This shared resource does not exist.
2311	NERR_DeviceNotShared	This device is not shared.
2312	NERR_ClientNameNotFound	A session with this computer name does not exist.
2314	NERR_FileIdNotFound	No open file with this ID number exists.
2315	NERR_ExecFailure	A failure occurred during execution of a remote administration command.
2316	NERR_TmpFile	A failure occurred during opening of a remote temporary file.
2317	NERR_TooMuchData	The data returned from a remote administration command has been truncated to 64 KB.
2318	NERR_DeviceShareConflict	This device cannot be shared as both a spooled and a nonspooled resource.

(continued)

continued

Code	Value	Meaning
2319	NERR_BrowserTableIncomplete	The information in the list of servers might be incorrect.
2320	NERR_NotLocalDomain	The computer is not active on this domain.

CharDev API error codes

Code	Value	Meaning
2331	NERR_DevInvalidOpCode	The operation is invalid for this device.
2332	NERR_DevNotFound	This device cannot be shared.
2333	NERR_DevNotOpen	This device was not open.
2334	NERR_BadQueueDevString	This device-name list is invalid.
2335	NERR_BadQueuePriority	The queue priority is invalid.
2337	NERR_NoCommDevs	No shared communication devices exist.
2338	NERR_QueueNotFound	The specified queue does not exist.
2340	NERR_BadDevString	This list of devices is invalid.
2341	NERR_BadDev	The requested device is invalid.
2342	NERR_InUseBySpooler	This device is already in use by the spooler.
2343	NERR_CommDevInUse	This device is already in use as a communications device.

Name validity–checking error codes

Code	Value	Meaning
2351	NERR_InvalidComputer	This computer name is invalid.
2354	NERR_MaxLenExceeded	The string and prefix specified are too long.
2356	NERR_BadComponent	This path component is invalid.
2357	NERR_CantType	Cannot determine type of input.
2362	NERR_TooManyEntries	The buffer for types is not big enough.

NetProfile error codes

Code	Value	Meaning
2370	NERR_ProfileFileTooBig	Profile files cannot exceed 64 KB.
2371	NERR_ProfileOffset	The start offset is out of range.
2372	NERR_ProfileCleanup	The system cannot delete current connections to network resources.

(continued)

continued

Code	Value	Meaning
2373	NERR_ProfileUnknownCmd	The system was unable to parse the command line in this file.
2374	NERR_ProfileLoadErr	An error occurred while loading the profile file.

NetAudit and *NetErrorLog* error codes

Code	Value	Meaning
2377	NERR_LogOverflow	This log file exceeds the maximum defined size.
2378	NERR_LogFileChanged	This log file has changed between reads.
2379	NERR_LogFileCorrupt	This log file is corrupt.

NetRemote error codes

Code	Value	Meaning
2380	NERR_SourceIsDir	The source path cannot be a directory.
2381	NERR_BadSource	The source path is illegal.
2382	NERR_BadDest	The destination path is illegal.
2383	NERR_DifferentServers	The source and destination paths are on different servers.
2385	NERR_RunSrvPaused	The Run server you requested is paused.
2389	NERR_ErrCommRunSrv	An error occurred when communicating with a Run server.
2391	NERR_ErrorExecingGhost	An error occurred when starting a background process.
2392	NERR_ShareNotFound	The shared resource you are connected to could not be found.

NETWKSTA.SYS (redir) error codes

Code	Value	Meaning
2400	NERR_InvalidLana	The LAN adapter number is invalid.
2401	NERR_OpenFiles	Open files exist on the connection.
2402	NERR_ActiveConns	Active connections still exist.
2403	NERR_BadPasswordCore	This net name or password is invalid.
2404	NERR_DevInUse	The device is being accessed by an active process.
2405	NERR_LocalDrive	The drive letter is in use locally.

Alerter error codes

Code	Value	Meaning
2430	NERR_AlertExists	The specified client is already registered for the specified event.
2431	NERR_TooManyAlerts	The Alerter service table is full.
2432	NERR_NoSuchAlert	An invalid or nonexistent alertname was raised.
2433	NERR_BadRecipient	The Alerter service recipient is invalid.
2434	NERR_AcctLimitExceeded	A user's session with this server has been deleted because his or her logon hours are no longer valid.

Additional error and audit-log error code

Code	Value	Meaning
2440	NERR_InvalidLogSeek	The log file does not contain the requested record number.

Additional UAS and NETLOGON error codes

Code	Value	Meaning
2450	NERR_BadUASConfig	The user account system database is not configured correctly.
2451	NERR_InvalidUASOp	This operation is not permitted when Netlogon service is running.
2452	NERR_LastAdmin	This operation is not allowed on last admin account.
2453	NERR_DCNotFound	Unable to find domain controller for this domain.
2454	NERR_LogonTrackingError	Unable to set logon information for this user.
2455	NERR_NetlogonNotStarted	The Netlogon service has not been started.
2456	NERR_CanNotGrowUASFile	Unable to grow the user account system database.

Server integration error codes

Code	Value	Meaning
2460	NERR_NoSuchServer	The server id does not specify a valid server.
2461	NERR_NoSuchSession	The session id does not specify a valid session.

(continued)

Code	Value	Meaning
2462	NERR_NoSuchConnection	The connection id does not specify a valid connection.
2463	NERR_TooManyServers	No space exists for another entry in the table of available servers.
2464	NERR_TooManySessions	The server has reached the maximum number of sessions it supports.
2465	NERR_TooManyConnections	The server has reached the maximum number of connections it supports.
2466	NERR_TooManyFiles	The server cannot open more files because it has reached its maximum number.
2467	NERR_NoAlternateServers	No alternate servers are registered on this server.

UPS error code

Code	Value	Meaning
2480	NERR_UPSDriverNotStarted	The UPS driver could not be accessed by the UPS service.

Remoteboot error codes

Code	Value	Meaning
2500	NERR_BadDosRetCode	The specified program returned an error code.
2501	NERR_ProgNeedsExtraMem	The specified program needs the extra memory (KB).
2502	NERR_BadDosFunction	The specified program called an unsupported 21H function.
2503	NERR_RemoteBootFailed	Remote boot is terminated.
2504	NERR_BadFileCheckSum	The file below is corrupt.
2505	NERR_NoRplBootSystem	No system loader exists in remote boot files.
2506	NERR_RplLoadrNetBiosErr	NetBIOS returned an error; the NCB and SMB are dumped above.
2507	NERR_RplLoadrDiskErr	Disk I/O error.
2508	NERR_ImageParamErr	Image parameter substitution failed.
2509	NERR_TooManyImageParams	Too many image parameters span disk sectors.
2510	NERR_NonDosFloppyUsed	The image was generated from a non-DOS-format diskette.

(continued)

continued

Code	Value	Meaning
2511	NERR_RplBootRestart	Remote boot will be restarted later.
2512	NERR_RplSrvrCallFailed	The call to the remote boot server failed.
2513	NERR_CantConnectRplSrvr	Cannot connect to image server.
2514	NERR_CantOpenImageFile	Cannot open image file on remote boot server.
2515	NERR_CallingRplSrvr	An error occurred when calling the remote boot server.
2516	NERR_StartingRplBoot	Starting remote boot of system.
2517	NERR_RplBootServiceTerm	Remote boot service was terminated; check the error log to find out why.

FTADMIN API error codes

Code	Value	Meaning
2525	NERR_FTNotInstalled	FT.SYS is not installed.
2526	NERR_FTMONITNotRunning	FTMONIT is not running.
2527	NERR_FTDiskNotLocked	FTADMIN has not locked the disk.
2528	NERR_FTDiskNotAvailable	Some other process has locked the disk.
2529	NERR_FTUnableToStart	The verifier/correcter cannot be started.
2530	NERR_FTNotInProgress	The verifier/correcter cannot be aborted because it has not been installed.
2531	NERR_FTUnableToAbort	The verifier/correcter cannot be aborted.
2532	NERR_FTUnableToChange	The disk could not be locked/unlocked.
2533	NERR_FTInvalidErrHandle	The error handle was not recognized.
2534	NERR_FTDriveNotMirrored	The drive is not mirrored.

INDEX

NOTE: *Italicized page numbers refer to figures and illustrations.*

S

SCHKDSK.C program *202–4*
Security
  addressed by client-server model 17
  local, with HPFS386, loopback driver, and
    local logon 32
  logging on and 20–21
  remote program execution and 41, 156
  shared resources and 474
  share-mode (*see* Share-mode security)
  user-mode (*see* User-mode security)
Segment, memory address 46, *47. See also*
    Code segment
Segment register 47
Semaphore(s)
  associating named pipe with 358–60, 494
  queueing requests with 477
  race conditions produced with named pipes
    when using *360–61*
  returning information about named pipes
    associated with 360–63
  RPC package for remote 480–81
Server 25–42
  architecture *26*
  basic services 26–36, 163,
    access control 27, 29–32
    administrative privilege 32–33
    auditing 34
    interprocess communication 35–36
    operators 33
    security 26, 32
    user accounts and groups 27, 28
  clearing statistics on 271
  concept of 16
  establishing connection between workstation
    and 109–12
  executing commands on 197–99
  IBM LAN 514–15
  LAN Manager/X 514
  listing available disk drives on 197
  logging on to 21
  other services 36–43
    alerter help 37
    distributed logon validation 37–39
    remote program execution 40–42
  profiles 139
  remote (*see* Remote servers)
  retrieving information about 195
  returning information about connections
    between workstations and 114–16

Server (*continued*)
  returning information about services of 267,
    270–71
  returning information about visible
    workstations and 200–204
  returning statistics on 265–67
  setting configuration information at a 196–97
  terminating connections to 112–14
Server, APIs for routine administration of
    189–231
  Connection APIs 218–24
  File APIs 225–31
  Server APIs 190–204
  Session APIs 214–18
  Share APIs 204–14
Server APIs 190–204
  data structures for *190–95*
  NetServerAdminCommand 197–98, 202
    vs. *NetRemoteExec* 199
  NetServerDiskEnum 197
  NetServerEnum 190, 199–202
  NetServerGetInfo 195
  NetServerSetInfo 196–97
SERVER.H file 190
server_info_0 data structure *190*
server_info_1 data structure *191*
server_info_2 data structure *191–93*
server_info_3 data structure *194–95*
Server privilege 33
Service(s), LAN Manager 20–42
  adding new, with a service program 183–87
  controlling operation of started 167–69
  defined 162
  logging on 20–21
  multiple NetBIOS drivers and 449–50
  nonprogrammable 164
  providing status information on, during
    pending operations 174–78
  retrieving information about specific 170–71
  retrieving information about started 170
  server 25–42
  standard 162–64
  starting 171–73
  updating status information for 173–74
  workstation 21–25
Service APIs 165–74
  data structures for *165–67*
  NetServiceControl 167–69, 186
  NetServiceEnum 170
  NetServiceGetInfo 170–71

X

Ralph Ryan

Ralph Ryan worked at Microsoft from 1982 to 1988. He led the group that produced the Microsoft C compiler and then became the project manager for LAN Manager 1.0. After leaving Microsoft, Ralph became one of the founders of Echelon Development, producing Windowcraft, a Windows-based hypermedia authoring tool.

Ralph plays guitar in a rock and roll band around the Seattle area and has released an album of original music.

The manuscript for this book was prepared and submitted to Microsoft Press in electronic form. Text files were processed and formatted using Microsoft Word.

Principal word processor: Debbie Kem
Principal proofreader: Shawn B. Peck
Principal typographer: Carolyn A. Magruder
Interior text designer: Darcie S. Furlan
Principal illustrator: Rebecca Geisler-Johnson
Cover designer: Thomas A. Draper
Cover color separator: Rainier Color

Text composition by Microsoft Press in Times Roman with display type in Eurostile Demi, using the Magna composition system and the Linotronic 300 laser imagesetter.

Printed on recycled paper stock.

*Microsoft*University'

Training That Makes Sense

At Microsoft University, we believe the proof of excellent training is in a student's ability to **apply** it. That's not a complicated philosophy. And, it's not a new idea. But it does represent an uncommon approach to training in the microcomputer industry, mainly because it requires extensive technical and educational resources, as well as leading-edge programming expertise.

When you attend Microsoft University, our courses take you to the heart of our microcomputer software architecture. Lab sessions provide practical, hands-on experience and show you how to develop and debug software more efficiently. Our qualified instructors explain the philosophy and principles that drive our systems designs.

OUR LAB-BASED DISTINCTION

Because our courses are lab-based, when you graduate from Microsoft University, you'll begin applying what you've learned immediately. Throughout our courses, you'll be designing a software application that demonstrates the principles you've just learned in class.

The power of our sheepskin pays off in the increased knowledge and time savings as soon as you begin your next development project.

PLOT YOUR OWN COURSE

Our curriculum allows you to customize your course of study from timely, fundamental courses for support personnel to highly focused, technical courses for sophisticated developers. We offer courses on Microsoft Windows,™ Microsoft OS/2, Microsoft OS/2 Presentation Manager, Microsoft LAN Manager, Microsoft SQL Server, and Microsoft C.

TIME IS OF THE ESSENCE

To find out more about Microsoft University, call our registrar at (206) 867-5507, extension 602. We'll send you our current course schedule, which describes our courses in detail and provides complete registration information for our campus facilities in Seattle, Boston, and Baltimore, as well as our growing, nationwide network of Microsoft University Authorized Training Centers.

Microsoft University also offers our courses on-site at your location, when it's convenient for you and your staff. To find out more about hosting an on-site course, contact the Microsoft University Sales Manager at (206) 867-5507, extension 602.

Our courses fill up quickly—so don't delay.

I'D LIKE TO KNOW MORE!

☐ Please send me the most current course schedule.

☐ Please send me the Microsoft University catalog.

☐ Please have a representative call me regarding an on-site course for

_____
Course / Topic

☐ Please send me more information on the Authorized Training Center program.

☐ Please send me the latest information on The Lecture Series.™*

☐ Please send me more information on the following Microsoft University courses:

☐ MS® OS/2   ☐ Microsoft SQL Server

☐ MS OS/2 Presentation Manager   ☐ Microsoft Windows™

☐ MS LAN Manager   ☐ Microsoft C

When it's available, please send me information on:

☐ Microsoft University Technical Training Video Courses

_____
Course / Topic

* Seminars and lectures on highly focused topics

X602

PLEASE PRINT

Name: _____

Job Title/Function: _____

Company (if applicable): _____

Street Address: _____

_____

City: _____ State: ____ Zip _____

Daytime Phone: _____

Please clip along dotted line and mail to:

*Microsoft*University'

One Microsoft Way, Redmond, WA 98052-6399

Other Titles from Microsoft Press

MICROSOFT® OS/2 PROGRAMMER'S REFERENCE LIBRARY
Microsoft

The Microsoft OS/2 Programmer's Reference Library is a low-cost way to explore Presentation Manager's Application Programming Interface (API) and start creating intuitive, easy-to-use software applications for its graphical environment. The library of four volumes—companions to the affordably priced Microsoft OS/2 Presentation Manager Softset development tools—is packed with detailed information on every MS OS/2 system function, related data types, macros, structures, messages, and file formats.

Each volume in the series is written by a team of OS/2 specialists—many involved in the development and ongoing enhancement of OS/2 at Microsoft. The Microsoft OS/2 Programmer's Reference Library is the cornerstone of every OS/2 developer's programming library.

MICROSOFT® OS/2 PROGRAMMER'S REFERENCE: VOL. 1
Including Presentation Manager
A thorough overview of the MS OS/2 system functions and the concepts and principles behind the functions. Sections include *Introducing MS OS/2, Window Manager, Graphics Programming Interface,* and *System Services.* This is the fundamental information needed to understand MS OS/2.
768 pages, softcover   7 ³/₈ x 9 ¹/₄ $29.95   Order Code OSPRR1

MICROSOFT® OS/2 PROGRAMMER'S REFERENCE: VOL. 2
Including Presentation Manager
A comprehensive, alphabetic reference to all the version 1.1 Presentation Manager functions that address the window management and graphics features of MS OS/2. Complete with information on syntax; descriptions of each function's action and purpose; parameters and field definitions; return values, error values, and restrictions; source code examples; and programming notes.
576 pages, softcover   7 ³/₈ x 9 ¹/₄ $29.95   Order Code OSPRR2

MICROSOFT® OS/2 PROGRAMMER'S REFERENCE: VOL. 3
Similar in format to Volume 2, this volume covers all the MS OS/2 version 1.1 base system (kernel) functions that carry out tasks such as reading from and writing to disk files; allocating memory; starting other programs; and controlling the keyboard, mouse, and video screen.
448 pages, softcover   7 ³/₈ x 9 ¹/₄ $19.95   Order Code OSPRR3

MICROSOFT® OS/2 PROGRAMMER'S REFERENCE: VOL. 4
Including Presentation Manager
Volume 4 covers the additional MS OS/2 functions and services that are new to version 1.2. As in Volumes 2 and 3, the descriptions include not only parameters and syntax, but also source code examples, programming notes, and references to related functions. System functions new to version 1.2 let you carry out tasks such as reading and writing extended attributes for disk files and creating and accessing disk files through installable file systems.
432 pages, softcover   7 ³/₈ x 9 ¹/₄ $19.95   Order Code OSPRR4

ADVANCED OS/2 PROGRAMMING
The Microsoft® Guide to the OS/2 Kernel for Assembly Language and C Programmers
Ray Duncan

From the OS/2 Programmer's Library, here is the most complete and accurate source of information on the features and structure of OS/2. With insight and economy, Duncan explains the OS/2 services for controlling the user interface, programming mass storage, and exploiting advanced features such as multitasking and interprocess communications. Advanced chapters discuss the writing of filters, device drivers, monitors, and dynamic link libraries. Program examples are provided in both assembly language and C. ADVANCED OS/2 PROGRAMMING contains a complete, example-packed reference section on the more than 250 OS/2 1.1 kernel functions, with complete information on their calling arguments, return values, and special uses.

800 pages, softcover 7³/₈ x 9¹/₄ **$24.95** **Order Code ADOSPR**

ADVANCED MS-DOS® PROGRAMMING, 2nd ed.
The Microsoft® Guide for Assembly Language and C Programmers
Ray Duncan

The preeminent source of MS-DOS information for assembly language and C programmers—now completely updated with new data and programming advice covering the ROM BIOS for the IBM PC, PC/AT, PS/2, and related peripherals (including disk drives, video adapters, and pointing devices); MS-DOS through version 4; "well-behaved" *vs.* "hardware-dependent" applications; version 4 of the LIM EMS; and compatibility considerations for OS/2. Duncan, a DOS authority and noted columnist, explores key programming topics, including character devices, mass storage, memory allocation and management, and process management. Examples included were developed using Microsoft Macro Assembler version 5.1 and Microsoft C Compiler version 5.1. And the reference section, detailing each MS-DOS function and interrupt, is virtually a book within a book.

688 pages, softcover 7³/₈ x 9¹/₄ **$24.95** **Order Code ADMSP2**

MS-DOS® FUNCTIONS: PROGRAMMER'S QUICK REFERENCE
Ray Duncan

This great quick reference is full of the kind of information programmers—professional or casual—need right at their fingertips. You'll find clearly organized data on each MS-DOS system service (accessed via Interrupts 20H through 2FH) along with a list of the parameters it requires, the results it returns, and version dependencies. Duncan includes valuable programming tips, notes on usage, and precautions. Covers MS-DOS through version 4.

128 pages, softcover 4³/₄ x 8 **$5.95** **Order Code QRMSFU**

RUNNING UNIX®
An Introduction to SCO™ UNIX System V/386 and XENIX® Operating Systems
JoAnne Woodcock, Michael Halvorson, and Robert Ackerman

Novice through advanced users will welcome the concise, practical information in this hands-on guide to UNIX. Explore each of the working environments, including the Bourne shell and the C shell. Learn how to run DOS, UNIX, and XENIX applications from within Open DeskTop—UNIX's exciting new graphical user interface. A special section provides information of particular importance to system administrators—UNIX installation, system management, disk management, and security provisions.

416 pages, softcover 7³/₈ x 9¹/₄ **$24.95** **Order Code RUUN**

Microsoft Press books are available wherever quality computer books are sold,
or credit card orders can be placed by calling 1-800-MSPRESS.
Please refer to BBK.